Theories of the Flesh

Studies in Feminist Philosophy is designed to showcase cutting-edge monographs and collections that display the full range of feminist approaches to philosophy, that push feminist thought in important new directions, and that display the outstanding quality of feminist philosophical thought.

STUDIES IN FEMINIST PHILOSOPHY

Published in the Series:

Theories of the Flesh

Latinx and Latin American Feminisms, Transformation, and Resistance

Edited by ANDREA J. PITTS,
MARIANA ORTEGA, AND JOSÉ MEDINA

OXFORD
UNIVERSITY PRESS

Oxford University Press is a department of the University of Oxford. It furthers the University's objective of excellence in research, scholarship, and education by publishing worldwide. Oxford is a registered trade mark of Oxford University Press in the UK and certain other countries.

Published in the United States of America by Oxford University Press
198 Madison Avenue, New York, NY 10016, United States of America.

Library of Congress Cataloging-in-Publication Data
Names: Pitts, Andrea J., editor.
Title: Theories of the flesh : Latinx and Latin American feminisms, transformation, and resistance / edited by Andrea J. Pitts, Mariana Ortega, and José M. Medina.
Description: New York : Oxford University Press, 2020. |
Includes bibliographical references.
Identifiers: LCCN 2019015805 | ISBN 9780190062972 (pbk.) |
ISBN 9780190062965 (hardback) | ISBN 9780190063009 (online) |
ISBN 9780190062989 (updf) | ISBN 9780190062996 (epub)
Subjects: LCSH: Feminism—Latin America. | Imperialism—Latin America.
Classification: LCC HQ1460.5 .T46 2019 | DDC 305.42098—dc23
LC record available at https://lccn.loc.gov/2019015805

CONTENTS

PREFACE

MARIANA ORTEGA

> Words are blades of grass pushing past the obstacles, sprouting
> on the page; the spirit of words moving in the body is as
> concrete as flesh and as palpable; the hunger to create is as
> substantial as fingers and hand.
>
> —GLORIA ANZALDÚA (1987, 71)

> The decolonial imaginary is intangible to many because it acts much
> like a shadow in the dark. It survives as a faint outline gliding against
> a wall or an object. The shadow is the figure between the subject
> and the object on which it is cast, moving and breathing through an
> in-between space.
>
> —EMMA PÉREZ (1999, 6)

Flesh, spirit, longing, wisdom, and desire intermix in the pages that follow. Latina/x and Latin American thinkers share their words, words that have traveled like shadows in the dark, not always seen, not recognized appropriately in various US academic circles, in the hallways of philosophy departments, in the works of those who claim to have knowledge. Like the decolonial imaginary that Emma Pérez recognizes both in its invisibility and as breathing through an in-between space of possibilities, these words indeed sprout in the page and in the flesh. These words have spirit, Anzaldúa says, spirit to move our bodies, spirit-through-and-with-flesh that leads us to create so as to survive—and to thrive.

Sometimes these words have been given space, but only as tokens. Indeed, they have been like faint outlines gliding against the walls of philosophy. But as faint as they have been, they have also been powerful. They are "theories in the flesh" informed "by the physical realities of our lives, our skin color, the land or concrete we grew up on, our sexual longings" (Moraga and Anzaldúa 1983, 23)—they reveal a strong spirit. They constitute intersectional analyses of lives that, like shadow words, occupy in-between spaces. They inform new generations of Latina, Latinx, and Latin American writers with hunger to create.

Hidden away by familiar operations of gatekeeping and the coloniality of knowledge, now these words full of spirit and lived experience are slowly entering the halls of academic philosophy. You see, in loneliness one looks for company. In meetings of the Latina/x Feminisms Roundtable (formerly the Roundtable on Latina Feminism) (2006 to present), activists, philosophers, and thinkers from other disciplines have shared their knowledge and love of Latina/x and Latin American feminisms. A new generation of Latinx philosophers have found words by philosophers such as María Lugones, Linda Martín Alcoff, and Ofelia Schutte; by foundational Chicana theorists such as Norma Alarcón, Gloria Anzaldúa, Cherríe Moraga, Emma Pérez, and Chela Sandoval; and by key Latin American feminists such as Luisa Capetillo, Rosario Castellanos, Sor Juana Inés de la Cruz, Graciela Hierro, and Julieta Kirkwood.

In the hands of the contributors to this anthology, words are transformed and transforming. They help theorists, philosophers, lovers of words, think and write the decolonial in its possibility to forge everyday forms of resistance attuned to material, historical, and cultural difference and to rethink gender and feminist methodology. They also help to construct feminist selves who tell their stories in order to heal, to share their shame, fear, and vulnerability but also to disclose new desires and aesthetic longings—and to image new philosophical worlds and futures.

References

Anzaldúa, Gloria. 1987. *Borderlands/La Frontera: The New Mestiza*. San Francisco: Aunt Lute Books.
Moraga, Cherríe, and Gloria Anzaldúa, eds. 1983. *This Bridge Called My Back: Writings by Radical Women of Color*. 2nd ed. New York: Kitchen Table, Women of Color Press.
Pérez, Emma. 1999. *The Decolonial Imaginary: Writing Chicanas into History*. Bloomington: Indiana University Press.

NOTES ON CONTRIBUTORS

Linda Martín Alcoff is Professor of Philosophy at Hunter College and the Graduate School, CUNY. She is a past president of the American Philosophical Association, Eastern Division. Recent books include *Rape and Resistance* (Polity, 2018); *The Future of Whiteness* (Polity, 2015), and *Visible Identities: Race, Gender and the Self* (Oxford University Press, 2006), which won the Frantz Fanon Award for 2009. For more information go to www.alcoff.com.

Mary K. Bloodsworth-Lugo is Professor of Comparative Ethnic Studies and Director of American Studies in the School of Languages, Cultures, and Race at Washington State University. She has coauthored several books with Carmen R. Lugo-Lugo, including *Feminism after 9/11: Women's Bodies as Cultural and Political Threat* (Palgrave Macmillan, 2017), *Projecting 9/11: Race, Gender, and Citizenship in Recent Hollywood Films* (Rowman & Littlefield, 2014), and *Containing (Un)American Bodies: Race, Sexuality, and Post-9/11 Constructions of Citizenship* (Rodopi, 2010). She coedited *Race, Philosophy, and Film* (Routledge, 2013) with Dan Flory, and coauthored *Animating Difference: Race, Gender, and Sexuality in Contemporary Films for Children* (Rowman & Littlefield, 2010) with C. Richard King and Carmen R. Lugo-Lugo. Professor Bloodsworth-Lugo is also author of *In-Between Bodies: Sexual Difference, Race, and Sexuality* (SUNY Press, 2007).

Kevin Cedeño-Pacheco is a dual-title PhD candidate in philosophy and African American studies at Pennsylvania State University. His research focuses on the overlap between aesthetics and politics in critical philosophies of race and gender advanced by African American and Latina women theorists and philosophers. In his current project, he aims to examine the ways that art and other seemingly "secondary" modes of expression are given primacy and significance in the work of African American, Latina, and Chicana feminist political theorists and commentators.

Natalie Cisneros is Assistant Professor of Philosophy at Seattle University. Her recent work appears in *Hypatia: A Journal of Feminist Philosophy, Carceral Notebooks, Radical Philosophy Review, Active Intolerance: Michel Foucault, The Prison Information Group, and the Future of Abolition* (ed. Perry Zurn and Andrew Dilts), and *Philosophy Imprisoned: The Love of Wisdom in the Age of Mass Incarceration* (ed. Sarah Tyson and Joshua M. Hall). Currently, she is completing a book manuscript that draws on the work of Michel Foucault and Gloria Anzaldúa, as well as other feminists and critical race theorists, to suggest a new approach to political and ethical questions surrounding immigration.

Theresa Delgadillo is a Professor of Comparative Studies at Ohio State University. She is the editor of *Latinx Talk*, an online forum for critical dialogues in Latinx studies and the author of *Spiritual Mestizaje: Religion, Gender, Race, and Nation in Contemporary Chicana Narrative* (Duke University Press, 2011) and *Latina Lives in Milwaukee* (University of Illinois Press, 2015) as well as numerous articles and book chapters. Her research is focused on three topics: religion and spirituality in Latinx text and contexts, Latinx in the Midwest, and Afro-Latinidad in literature and film.

Pedro J. DiPietro is Assistant Professor in the Department of Women's and Gender Studies and a member of the Democratizing Knowledge Collective at Syracuse University. They work at the intersection of decolonial feminisms, transgender studies, and women-of-color thinking. They are one of the coeditors of *Speaking Face to Face: The Visionary Philosophy of María Lugones* (SUNY Press, 2019). Prior to joining Syracuse, DiPietro was a Mellon Postdoctoral Fellow in the Humanities in the Department of Ethnic Studies at the University of California, Berkeley. They are currently at work on a manuscript under the title *Sideways Selves: The Decolonizing Politics of Trans* across the Américas*. This book project examines the ways that *we* do, think, and practice *transing* at three collective sites: networks of *travesti* sex workers from the Andean region, queer and trans* Latinx performers in the San Francisco Bay Area, and Xicana/Latina feminisms.

María Luisa Femenías, PhD, is Professor at Universidad Nacional de La Plata; former chair of the Department of Philosophy; cofounder and Chair (2006–16) of Interdisciplinary Center for Research on Genders and of the Specialization on Education, Gender and Sexualities (2013–17). As a researcher, she coordinates groups of junior and senior researchers and PhD candidates. She has been a Visiting Scholar at Toulouse University (Jean Jaurés), Universià degli Studi di Perugia, University of California, Berkeley, and Universidad Rey Juan Carlos, among others. She has published a number of articles (some translated into English and French) and books on gender and violence in Latin America. Recently, she edited six volumes on sexist violence and multiculturalism. In 2016, she received the Konex Price as Researcher on Feminist Philosophy and Gender Studies (fundacionkonex.org).

Francesca Gargallo is a Mexican writer and poet. She studied philosophy in Italy at the Università degli studi di Roma and then in the National Autonomous University of Mexico. Gargallo's published research includes *Garífuna, Garínagu, Caribe* (Siglo Veintiuno Editores, 2002), *Ideas Feministas Latinoamericanas* (UACM, 2014), and *Sarahauis: La sonrisa del sol* (Fundación Editorial El Perro y la Rana, 2006). Her published poetry books and novels include *Calla mi amor que vivo* (Ediciones Era, 1990), *Estar en el mundo* (Ediciones Era, 1994), *La decisión del capitán* (Ediciones Era, 1997), and *Marcha seca* (Ediciones Era, 1999).

Erika Grimm is a dual-title PhD candidate in philosophy and women's, gender, and sexuality studies at Pennsylvania State University. She earned her BA in philosophy with a minor in linguistics from California State University, Fullerton. Her doctoral research is situated within Latina feminist phenomenology, where she investigates language through critical and interpretive phenomenological analysis, examining the ways in which linguistic interactions serve as sites of oppression and resistance in the lived experiences of marginalized selves and communities.

Claudia De Lima Costa teaches literary theory, feminist theories, and cultural studies at the Federal University of Santa Catarina, in Florianópolis, Brazil. She is coeditor of *Translocalities/Translocalidades: Feminist Politics of Translation in the Latina/a Américas* (Duke University Press, 2014).

Carmen R. Lugo-Lugo is Professor of Comparative Ethnic Studies and Director of the School of Languages, Cultures, and Race at Washington State University. Her books, *Feminism after 9/11: Women's Bodies as*

Cultural and Political Threat (Palgrave Macmillan, 2017), *Projecting 9/ 11: Race, Gender, and Citizenship in Recent Hollywood Films* (Rowman & Littlefield, 2014), and *Containing (Un)American Bodies: Race, Sexuality, and Post-9/11 Constructions of Citizenship* (Rodopi, 2010), were coauthored with Mary K. Bloodsworth-Lugo. Her book *Animating Difference: Race, Gender, and Sexuality in Contemporary Films for Children* (Rowman & Littlefield, 2010), was coauthored with C. Richard King and Mary K. Bloodsworth-Lugo. Dr. Lugo-Lugo has also published numerous articles and book chapters on cultural productions of 9/11, and constructions of race, citizenship, immigration, and gender, as well as Latinas/os in US popular culture.

María Lugones is an Argentine feminist philosopher, social critic, and Associate Professor of Comparative Literature and Philosophy, Interpretation and Culture, and of Philosophy, and of Women's Studies at Binghamton University in New York. She is author of *Pilgrimages/ Peregrinages: Theorizing Coalition against Multiple Oppressions* (Rowman & Littlefield, 2003).

José Medina is Walter Dill Scott Professor of Philosophy at Northwestern University. He works primarily in critical race theory, feminist and queer theory, political philosophy, communication theory, and social epistemology. His books include *The Epistemology of Resistance: Gender and Racial Oppression, Epistemic Injustice, and Resistant Imaginations* (Oxford University Press; recipient of the 2013 North-American Society for Social Philosophy Book Award), and *Speaking from Elsewhere* (SUNY Press, 2006). His most recent coedited volumes are *The Handbook of Epistemic Injustice* (Routledge, 2017) and *Cosmopolitanism and Place* (Indiana University Press, 2017). His current projects focus on how social perception and the social imagination contribute to the formation of vulnerabilities to different kinds of violence and oppression. These projects also explore the social movements and kinds of activism (including what he terms "epistemic activism") that can be mobilized to resist racial and sexual violence and oppression in local and global contexts.

Xhercis Méndez is Assistant Professor of Women and Gender Studies and an affiliate faculty of African American Studies at California State University, Fullerton. She is an activist, organizer, and transdisciplinary scholar whose research focuses on decolonial feminist practices and methodologies and transformative justice. She is also a consultant for Michigan State University, where she develops transformative justice responses to gender-based violence and campus sexual assault. During her time as Assistant Professor of Philosophy and African American and African Studies at MSU, she co-organized the collaborative hurricane recovery project in Puerto Rico, #ProyectoPalabrasPR, and founded the Transformative Justice Speaker Series. Her published work includes "Notes toward a Decolonial Feminist Methodology: The Race/Gender Matrix Revisited" (2015) and her forthcoming chapter, "Not Your Papa's Wynter: Women of Color Contributions toward Decolonial Futures." She is currently working on her book project entitled *Decolonizing Feminist Methodologies from the Dark Side.*

Julie Avril Minich is Associate Professor of English and Mexican American and Latina/o Studies at the University of Texas at Austin, where she teaches courses in Latinx literary and cultural studies, gender and sexuality studies, and disability studies. She has published scholarly articles in a number of journals and anthologies, including *GLQ, Modern Fiction Studies*, and the *Journal of Literary and Cultural Disability Studies*. Minich is the author of *Accessible Citizenships: Disability, Nation, and the Cultural Politics of Greater Mexico* (Temple University Press, 2014), winner of the 2013–2014 MLA Prize in United States Latina and Latino and Chicana and Chicano Literary and Cultural Studies. Minich is currently completing a new book about compulsory able-bodiedness, Latinx literature, and racial health disparities.

Paula M. L. Moya is the Danily C. and Laura Louise Bell Professor of Humanities and the Burton J. and Deedee McMurtry University Fellow in Undergraduate Education at Stanford University. She is appointed in the Department of English and, by courtesy, Iberian and Latin American Cultures. She currently serves as Director of Graduate Studies in the English department and Director of the Research Institute of Comparative Studies in Race and Ethnicity. Moya's book publications include *The Social Imperative: Race, Close Reading, and Contemporary Literary Criticism* (Stanford University Press, 2016) and *Learning from Experience: Minority Identities, Multicultural Struggles* (University of California Press, 2002). She has also coedited three collections of original essays, *Doing Race: 21 Essays for the 21st Century* (Norton, 2010), *Identity Politics Reconsidered* (Palgrave, 2006) and *Reclaiming Identity: Realist Theory and the Predicament of Postmodernism* (University of California Press, 2000).

Mariana Ortega is Associate Professor of Philosophy, Women's Gender and Sexualities Studies and Latina/o Studies at the Pennsylvania State

University. Her main areas of research are main areas of research and interest are women of color feminisms, in particular Latina feminisms, twentieth-century Continental philosophy, phenomenology (Heidegger), philosophy of race, and aesthetics. She has published in various journals including *Journal of Speculative Philosophy, International Philosophical Quarterly, Critical Philosophy of Race, Hypatia, Radical Philosophy Review*, and *philoSOPHIA*. She is coeditor with Linda Martín-Alcoff of the anthology *Constructing the Nation: A Race and Nationalism Reader* (SUNY Press, 2009) and author of *In-Between: Latina Feminist Phenomenology, Multiplicity, and the Self* (SUNY, 2016). She is the founder and director of the Latina/x Feminisms Roundtable (formerly the Roundtable on Latina Feminism), a forum dedicated to discussions of Latina and Latin American feminisms. Her current project examines questions at the intersection of aesthetics, practices of othering, memory, the epistemology of ignorance, and Latinidad.

Laura E. Pérez is Chair of the new interdisciplinary and trans-Americas research hub, the Latinx Research Center, formerly the Center for Latino Policy Research. She is author of *Eros Ideologies: Writings on Art, Spirituality, and the Decolonial* (Duke University press, 2019), and *Chicana Art: The Politics of Spiritual and Aesthetic Altarities* (Duke University Press, 2007). She curated UC Berkeley's first and only US Latina/o Performance Art series in 2001–2; co-curated, with Delilah Montoya, the multimedia exhibition *Chicana Badgirls: Las Hociconas* at 516 ARTS gallery in Albuquerque, New Mexico, from January to March of 2009, and curated *Labor + a(r)t + orio: Bay Area Latin@ Arts Now* at the Richmond Art Center, CA (April–June 2011). She has published in numerous publications on feminism, Chicana/o, and hemispheric decolonial cultures. She is also coediting a book on the multimedia artist Consuelo Jimenez Underwood with Dr. Ann Marie Leimer.

Andrea J. Pitts is Assistant Professor of Philosophy at University of North Carolina, Charlotte. Their research interests include critical philosophy of race, feminist theory, Latin American and US Latinx philosophy, and critical prison studies. Their publications appear in *IJFAB: The International Journal of Feminist Approaches to Bioethics, Hypatia, Radical Philosophy Review*, and *Inter-American Journal of Philosophy*. Pitts is also coeditor of *Beyond Bergson: Examining Race and Colonialism through the Writings of Henri Bergson* (SUNY Press, 2019).

Stephanie Rivera Berruz is Assistant Professor at Marquette University. She received her PhD in Philosophy from SUNY Buffalo in 2014. She is the recipient of the Woodrow Wilson Career Enhancement Fellowship (2017–18) for her work on Latinx feminisms and Latin American Philosophy. Her main research interests lie in Latin American philosophy and Latina feminism as well philosophy of race, gender, and sexuality. She approaches these topics at their intersections as she is committed to the importance of diverse approaches to philosophical praxis. She recently published a coedited anthology: *Comparative Studies in Asian and Latin American Philosophies* (Bloomsbury, 2018), and her work has been published in *Hypatia, Inter-American Journal of Philosophy,* and *Essays on Philosophy.*

Elena Flores Ruíz is Assistant Professor of Philosophy and Global Studies at Michigan State University. She is from Ciudad de México. Her primary areas of research are in political philosophy and feminisms of the global South. Her work examines the philosophical dimensions of violence, structural oppression, and theories of harm (cultural, epistemic, linguistic) in the context of violence affecting women and marginalized populations in the global South. Her work has appeared in *Hypatia, Feminist Philosophy Quarterly, The Routledge International Handbook to Contemporary Social and Political Theory*, as well as in edited collections and interdisciplinary journals.

Ofelia Schutte is Professor Emerita of Philosophy at the University of South Florida. Born in Havana, Cuba, she emigrated at a young age with her parents to the United States. After receiving a PhD in philosophy from Yale in 1978, she has taught at the University of Florida, Gainesville, and University of Southern Florida in Tampa. She is the author of *Beyond Nihilism: Nietzsche without Masks* (University of Chicago Press, 1984), *Cultural Identity and Social Liberation in Latin America Thought* (SUNY Press, 1993), and numerous articles on feminist theory, Latin American thought, and continental philosophy. A former Fulbright Research Fellow to Mexico and coeditor of *A Companion to Latin American Philosophy* (Wiley-Blackwell, 2010), her work has appeared in numerous journals and edited collections. Schutte's current interests include feminism in Cuba, decolonial theory, and Latina/Latin American feminisms.

Theories of the Flesh

| Introduction

ANDREA J. PITTS AND JOSÉ MEDINA

THIS VOLUME IS A collection of writings forged out of decades and generations of work dedicated to critical engagement with the lives of Latinx and
Latin American peoples.[1] The authors we have included in this volume are
philosophers, literary theorists, cultural critics, artists, and activists. Their
contributions draw their strength from methods and innovations attuned to
lived experience.

Historically, as Laura E. Pérez outlines in her essay in this collection,
the academic field of Latinx feminism in the United States developed
alongside the work of black, indigenous, and Asian American feminisms
throughout the 1970s and 1980s. The work of a number of those early
theorists is highlighted throughout this volume, including that of Gloria
E. Anzaldúa, Cherríe Moraga, and María Lugones. Often through the development of writing groups, ethnic studies, and women's studies programs,
and publishing houses, figures like Anzaldúa, Babara Smith, Audre Lorde,
Moraga, and Hattie Gossett were among the first to forge a generation
of printed materials for women-of-color feminists in both Latinx feminism and black feminism (De Veaux 2004). Many of the writers during
this formative period foregrounded the conceptual, affective, and institutional resources within academia that continue to shape scholarly production in Latinx feminist projects today. Throughout the 1980s, 1990s,
and 2000s, numerous articles, books, and events focusing on Latinx feminism continued to circulate. For example, scholarly collectivities such

---

[1] While we honor the history and intellectual production of the many feminists who forged
the field through solidarity work under the titles of "Latina feminism" and "Chicana feminism,"
in an effort to further recognize the plurality of Latin American-descended communities in the
US, we use the terms "Latinx" and "Chicanx" to provide gender neutral framings of identity.
When referring to the gender-specific identities of women (transgender and cisgender women of
any gender expression) and/or any people who use feminine gender adjectives, we use the term
"Latina."

Andrea J. Pitts and José Medina, *Introduction* In: *Theories of the Flesh*, Edited by: Andrea J. Pitts,
Mariana Ortega, and José Medina, Oxford University Press (2020). © Oxford University Press.
DOI: 10.1093/oso/9780190062965.003.0001

as MALCS: Mujeres Activas en Letras y Cambio Social (founded in 1986) and the Roundtable on Latina Feminism (founded in 2006, now called the Latina/x Feminisms Roundtable) have provided resources and support to generations of Chicanx and Latinx scholars in the United States. Also, as noted by Francesca Gargallo and other Latin American contributors in the volume, the trajectories of feminism and academic feminist projects have developed along different genealogical trajectories across the Americas. With this critical difference in mind, we hope to highlight the historically and culturally diverse forms of feminist engagement possible through Latinx and Latin American feminist critiques. Building bridges across generations of scholars, this volume seeks to demonstrate the strength and breadth of the field of Latinx and Latin American feminist theory today.

In what follows, we provide several groupings to demonstrate some common themes and areas of research that characterize some of the work within contemporary Latinx and Latin American feminist theory. While we by no means offer a comprehensive survey of the field, we hope to invoke the spirit of the early innovators we have mentioned by showcasing a variety of interests, critiques, and political stakes in the essays we have included. Accordingly, the works collected here on Latinx and Latin American feminisms stem from complex and multifaceted genealogies of political mobilization and everyday forms of resistance. Tracing comparable paths, these works offer a lens through which we hope our readers can view the multiplicitous dimensions of Latinx and Latin American feminist engagement, including the plurality of feminist projects offered here that trace divergent, yet often overlapping historical, geopolitical, and embodied trajectories of analysis.

Section I. Decolonial *Movidas*: Gender, Community, and Liberation

The collection opens with a series of essays exploring the theoretical contours of decolonial *movidas*.[2] While many contemporary writings undertaking "decolonization" as their end have cited the work of Latin American men as foundational figures in the field,[3] in this collection our contributors draw from a number of notable US Latinx and Latin American

---

[2] We use the term *movida* here to highlight both its use by one of our contributors in this section, Xhercis Méndez, and the work of Chicana feminist theorists such as Marta Cotera and Chela Sandoval. For more on the meaning and use of *movidas* in Chicana feminism, see Espinoza, Cotera, and Blackwell 2018.

[3] Authors such as Walter Mignolo, Enrique Dussel, and Aníbal Quijano are among the commonly cited figures within decolonial studies.

women to explore the relationship between colonialism and the contemporary global situation. Notably, as Mariana Ortega (2017) describes in a recent article dedicated to decolonial theory, US Latina theorists have long offered veins of feminist decolonial scholarship from which to develop critical strands of analysis. Accordingly, the essays offered in Section I each draw from distinct sources within Latin American and US Latinx feminism to articulate novel approaches to questions involving gender as a category of analysis, coalition building, and tools for liberatory struggle that, too, seek to overturn the colonial matrices of power that have long impacted marginalized peoples.

Linda Martín Alcoff opens the section with a chapter titled "Decolonizing Feminist Theory: Latina Contributions to the Debate," which delves into the importance of everyday forms of resistance within decolonial studies. In particular, Martín Alcoff focuses on the function of feminism within the preservation of neoliberal economic policies that serve to further widen the financial and political gaps between the global North and the global South. Feminist theory, she cautions, can become another monological narrative used to justify the dominance and wealth of the Global North. Accordingly, she utilizes the work of María Lugones, Ofelia Schutte, and Ada María Isasi-Díaz to localize methods of resistance to what she calls a pattern of "imperial feminism."

The second chapter, by María Lugones, "Revisiting Gender: Toward a Decolonial Feminism," examines the work of Rita Segato, an Argentine anthropologist whose work focuses on indigenous history and women's activism within Latin America. Lugones carefully draws out political threads of Segato's work that speak to the relationship between formations of the nation-state and the use of "gender" as a category of analysis. The piece also provides a revised articulation of Lugones's conception of the "coloniality of gender," a term used to describe the desires, embodiments, and framings of binary gender roles imposed by European colonizers that continue to impact formerly colonized peoples.

The following chapter, by María Luisa Femenías, titled "From Women's Movements to Feminist Theories (and Vice Versa)," also engages Latin American women theorizing decolonization strategies. Notably, she analyzes, among others, the work of Zulma Palermo, an Argentine cultural theorist whose work has explored conceptions of polyphony and epistemic dimensions of "experience" and "voice" among Latin American women. Femenías examines carefully whether a number of feminist decolonial efforts, in effect, end up essentializing or further ontologizing notions of gender. From this analysis, she then outlines to what extent identities can be "negotiated" across sites of material, historical, and cultural difference.

In "Enrique Dussel's *Etica de la liberación*, US Women-of-Color Decolonizing Practices, and Coalitional Politics amid Difference," Laura

E. Pérez discusses a difficult but crucial topic, the necessity of critically assessing the very practices of decolonial politics. By way of an engagement with the work of Enrique Dussel's *Etica de la liberación*, Pérez reveals a painful gap between Latin American decolonial thought and US women-of-color thought insofar as the latter is not known or simply ignored or disregarded by Latin American decolonial thinkers. Her analysis shows that gender and sexuality are at the heart of decolonizing politics and calls for an embodied practice critically attuned to patriarchal and heteronormative stances within decolonial projects. By pointing to what she considers "key nodes of intellectual solidarity" with Dussel, Pérez opens the possibility for future *encuentros* between Latin American decolonial scholars and scholars of color engaged in decolonial praxis and theory in the United States.

The final chapter in this section by Xhercis Méndez, titled "Decolonial Feminist *Movidas*: A *Caribeña* (Re)thinks 'Privilege,' the Wages of Gender, and Building Complex Coalitions," takes up questions of method and practical engagement within decolonial strategizing. Drawing inspiration from Lugones's conception of the coloniality of gender, Méndez seeks to utilize gender as a politicized category of analysis. In an effort to critique contemporary racialized and gendered dimensions of identity and embodiment, the author underscores ways of knowing and being that make coalition building across difference difficult. Méndez's piece is thus a step toward a decolonial methodology that aims to develop strategies that center collective and liberatory forms of praxis.

Section II. Making Feminist Selves: Self-Authority, Affect, and Narrativity

The second section of the volume directs our attention to storytelling, self-styling, and healing as modes of US Latinx and Latin American feminist praxis. The essays gathered here highlight the importance of narrative and genealogical exercises in exploring aspects of individual and collective existence. Notably, these essays shift through differing narrative moments to show the often tense border zones between past and present, self and world, language and feeling, and divine and earthly being. Moving through these divides, each author demonstrates the transformational possibilities inherent within narrative rearticulations of racial embodiment, ancestry, and history.

The first chapter in this section by Francesca Gargallo, offers a genealogy of feminist philosophy in Latin America. Gargallo's analysis spans a broad range of themes and figures across Latin American history to develop a series of philosophical trajectories among women writers. Her chapter engages questions of multiculturalism, indigenous rights and resistance, questions of pleasure and transformation, and conceptual strategies among differing feminist contexts, writers, and traditions in Latin American philosophy. Her work here provides a broad set of themes that help frame the analyses offered throughout this volume, and her chapter aids in further situating the contributions and strategies of resistance developed from feminist thought across the Americas more broadly.

The second chapter, by Ofelia Schutte, "Crossroads and In-Between Spaces: A Meditation on Anzaldúa and Beyond," brings readers to existential dimensions of shame, fear, and the possibility of self-actualization. Schutte examines the affective and aesthetic resonances between Anzaldúa and Nietzsche to provide a description of the transformational processes of self. Namely, by looking specifically at the overcoming of shame, Schutte combines insights from the respective writings of both authors to argue for a richer understanding of identity and collective becoming.

The third chapter of this section, " 'Remaking Human Being': Loving, Kaleidoscopic Consciousness in Helena María Viramontes's *Their Dogs Came with Them*," by Paula M. L. Moya, returns the volume to a discussion of decolonial thought. However, Moya's approach, rather than exploring methodological or thematic elements of the categories of analysis within decolonial theory, takes up, instead, a work of fiction by Helena María Viramontes. Moya, draws, in particular, from Viramontes's 2000 novel *Their Dogs Came with Them* to analyze how specific methods of writing fiction can create resistant and polyphonic imaginaries that are shared among decolonial projects. Weaving conceptions of everyday resistance, love, and multiplicity found within Viramontes's writings, Moya provides another rich narrative example of the transformational potential of US Latinx and Latin American feminist theory.

The final chapter, by Theresa Delgadillo, titled "African, Latina, and Feminist: Marta Moreno Vega's Remembrance of Life in El Barrio in the 1950s," concludes the section through a study of Marta Moreno Vega's 2004 memoir, *When the Spirits Dance Mambo*. Drawing from Moreno Vega's articulation of dynamic formations of embodiment, spirituality, and temporality within the memoir, Delgadillo offers her work as "a unique form of Latina feminisms that emerges from the experiences of Afro-Latinas." Notably, the Afro-diasporic tones and shapes found throughout the memoir become the means through which Delgadillo offers a novel approach to feminist deployments of temporality, embodiment, and kinship.

Section III. Knowing Otherwise: Language, Translation, and Alternative Consciousness

The third section of the book addresses issues of (mis)communication, (mis)understanding, and the (de)articulation of subjectivity across different languages, expressive styles, gender configurations, and cultural contexts. In this section Latinx feminist scholars discuss normative problems concerning knowledge, understanding, and communication that arise from the oppression and marginalization of Latinx peoples, but also the liberating potential of alternative ways of talking, knowing, and being critically aware that can be found in the nonconforming practices and sensibilities of Latinx resistant subjectivities.

In the opening essay of this section, Claudia de Lima Costa writes on the relationship between decoloniality and translation practices in Latin America. De Lima Costa interrogates the hegemonic position of white feminism and the hermeneutical challenges that Latin American feminisms face. She proposes a "radical, decolonial notion of translation" that calls attention to equivocation and multiplicity, highlights the coloniality of power and gender, and plays a key role in forging alternative, decolonial feminist epistemologies.

In "Embodied Genealogies: Anzaldúa, Nietzsche, and Diverse Epistemic Practice," Natalie Cisneros builds on Ofelia Schutte's scholarship and develops a conception of *embodied genealogy* as a critical-historical methodology that can be put to liberatory uses in Latinx feminist theory and practice. Cisneros shows how reading Anzaldúa's thought and Nietzschean genealogy together can make critical contributions to philosophical conversations about knowledge, identity, and community, as well as provide a critical methodology grounded in embodied (gendered and racialized) experiences for the intellectual and political practices of Latinx feminisms.

In the next chapter, Elena Flores Ruíz develops a discussion of the "hermeneutical violence" inflicted upon the voices of Latina women. Ruíz elucidates how Latina feminist theorists (such as Anzaldúa and Norma Alarcón) have developed "alphabets of survival" that can be used to resist and survive practices of marginalization, distortion, and silencing. Ruíz's essay critically examines the epistemic side of "the continued resilience and systematicity of neocolonial oppression against women of color," and discusses the ways in which *resistance* has become "a structural feature of our existence" as Latina women and women of color more generally.

In the final essay, "Hallucinating Knowing: (Extra)ordinary Consciousness, More-Than-human Perception, and Other Decolonizing *Remedios* within Latina and Xicana Feminist Theories," Pedro J. DiPietro examines the performative presentations and interrogations of queer Latinidades in the work of Latinx spoken-word artists and poets from the San Francisco Bay Area. In particular, drawing from Latina and Xicana feminist theorists, DiPietro elucidates the role that *hallucinating* perceptual repertoires play in denormalizing and decolonizing experiences and memories of mobility and transit across spaces and genders. DiPietro's interrogation of queer belonging raises questions about the contradictions and resistant possibilities in embodiment, sexuality, desire, and collective memory, especially in relation to the mixed-race realities of queer Latinidades.

Section IV. Aesthetic Longings: Latina Styles, Bodily Vulnerability, and Queer Desires

The fourth section of the book focuses on practices of representing, performing, and perceiving embodied Latinx subjectivities, and on the issues of vulnerability, identity, and desire that arise in those practices and in the expressive styles within them. In this section Latinx feminist scholars discuss how a sense of identity is intimately connected to the aesthetic aspects of self-expression, (mis)representation, and (mis)perception. The authors in this section address complex normative and theoretical issues concerning expressivity, representationality, identity, and vulnerability.

In the opening essay, Stephanie Rivera Berruz develops a critical discussion of perceptual practices in which the nonwhite body is subject to the normative expectations of the white body. Following María Lugones, Rivera Berruz emphasizes that in *boomerang perception* women of color are treated as *mirrors* that often reflect things that are inconsistent with white women's self-image, creating trouble for white perceptual practices and possibilities of resistance. Rivera Berruz criticizes the way in which Latinas have become part of a commercialized homogenized identity that reproduces boomerang perception.

The critical discussion of homogenized representations of Latina femininity is continued in Carmen Lugo-Lugo and Mary Bloodsworth-Lugo's essay. Focusing on the aesthetic and political aspects of media representations, Lugo-Lugo and Bloodsworth-Lugo analyze a shift in popular culture, mass media, and marketing forces in portraying Latinas as a diverse cultural group, rather than as a one-dimensional racial group. Lugo-Lugo and Bloodsworth-Lugo analyze the shift from racial to cultural representations of Latina femininity as indicative of a characteristically twenty-first-century aesthetics of ethnicity that works by deflecting or even negating race.

The intersectional discussion of aesthetic representations of Latinas is expanded to include desire and sexuality in Mariana Ortega's essay on visuality, ambivalence, and longing. Drawing from José Esteban Muñoz's notion of "disidentification," Ortega argues that viewing photographs by artists such as Manny Serratos and Ken González-Day through the lens of disidentification allows us to see the ways in which these artists present powerful critiques of normative views of desire and sexuality, and offer articulations of melancholic longing that reconfigure the relations among memory, belonging, and desire in Latinx subjectivities.

Bringing this intersectional discussion of public representations and perceptions of Latinas to a close, in the final essay, Julie Avril Minich examines gender, race, class, disability, and environmental justice in the murals of Bay Area artist Juana Alicia. Minich's analysis shows how Juana Alicia's complex engagement with multiple social justice movements—including US woman of color feminism, environmental justice activism, and the Chicano movement—provides a paradigm through which we might imagine a future in which working-class communities of color are not systemically forced to bear the brunt of pollution, pesticide poisoning, the privatization of natural resources, and other environmental risks and disasters. In this way, Juana Alicia's murals provide an occasion for reconsidering the relationship between Latinx feminisms, bodily vulnerability, and environmental justice activism.

References

De Veaux, Alexis. 2004. *A Warrior Poet: A Biography of Audre Lorde*. New York: Norton.

Espinoza, Dionne, María Eugenia Cotera, and Maylei Blackwell. 2018. *Chicana Movidas: New Narratives of Activism and Feminism in the Movement Era*. Austin: University of Texas Press.

Ortega, Mariana. 2017. "Decolonial Woes and Practices of Un-knowing." *Journal of Speculative Philosophy* 31, no. 3: 504–16.

SECTION I | Decolonial *Movidas*
Gender, Community, and Liberation

CHAPTER 1 | Decolonizing Feminist Theory
Latina Contributions to the Debate

LINDA MARTÍN ALCOFF

THE RECENT DEVELOPMENT OF what some have called "imperial feminism" has made a decolonial turn in feminism more urgent than ever. Feminism has always been internally divided, yet we are observing today the emergence of a new era in which powerful states make use of feminism to advance neoliberal economic policies. For example, the dismantling of the welfare state has been justified on the grounds of helping women into the paid labor force, no matter their family situation, and the United Nations has celebrated forced migrations of women workers to the global North on the grounds this exposes them to ideas about gender equality (Eisenstein 2009). States from the global North have also given feminist arguments to justify unilateral military invasions, and a number of prominent feminist organizations, such as the Feminist Majority Foundation, have played along.[1] These arguments echo older colonialist strategies that justified annexations on the grounds that in this way gender practices in poorer areas of the world would be "modernized" (Ahmed 1992).

Nonstate actors have also practiced troubling forms of avowedly feminist transnational activism that should compel a thorough decolonial analysis. Alice Walker's 1993 film *Warrior Marks* treated the issue of clitoridectomy with a framing that exacerbated racist anti-African assumptions, as Kenyan feminist Kagendo Murungi and others argued (Murungi 1994; Kaplan 1997). Debates over the wearing of the hijab continue to animate feminists in the global North, often without any colonial contextualization (Abu-Lughod 2013; Al-Saji 2006). Recently, the non-Muslim Ukrainian

---

[1] For example, the Feminist Majority Foundation supported the war in Afghanistan as late as 2009. See Kolhatkar and Rawi 2009.

Linda Martín Alcoff, *Decolonizing Feminist Theory* In: *Theories of the Flesh*, Edited by: Andrea J. Pitts, Mariana Ortega, and José Medina, Oxford University Press (2020). © Oxford University Press. DOI: 10.1093/oso/9780190062965.003.0002

group Femen took it upon themselves to initiate a "Topless Jihad Day."[2] As global media systems proliferate, transnational activism will become easier to engage. But without a decolonial approach, transnational feminist activism risks colluding with colonial rhetorics about backward societies that need to be "westernized."

The problem with imperial feminism, whether performed by state or nonstate actors, is simultaneously political, theoretical, and epistemological. It is wrong to assume the right of unilateral intervention into far-flown contexts, especially as this often disenables local female agency and curtails livelihoods. It is also wrong to presume to know people in advance.

Imperial feminism assumes a fixed and stable universal meaning to the idea of feminism. It knows what liberation looks like, and is there to teach, not learn or engage in dialogue. It does not view feminism as a dialogic, irreducibly multiple and local project. Some feminists reject the category of "imperial feminism" on the grounds that this cannot be true feminism if it is not truly liberatory. Yet the reality is that feminists disagree about what is liberatory, so it is more realistic to understand feminism as a loosely amalgamated set of diverse discursive and practical activities. There is no central committee or unified genealogy or set of texts that can adjudicate disagreements (Roth 2004). Further, it may disable self-critique if we portray feminism as always anticolonial, especially if this is done by a facile definitional stipulation.

Imperial forms of feminism can be especially subtle and difficult to overcome in the realm of theory, since theory, like philosophy, usually understands itself to have a rather general and abstract charge: to theorize "gender," "identity," "sexual violence," "sexism," and so on, in a non-local way. Philosophy often tries to subsume differences between contexts within some meta-level rubric that takes itself as transcendent of context. Decolonizing feminist theory may in fact be more difficult than decolonizing feminist practice.

Achieving a completely decolonized theory is no doubt a quixotic quest. And yet the decolonial *aspiration* should become a standard part of self-reflexive knowledge practices. We must at least *attempt* to understand the effects of our material and local contexts on the formation of our knowledge.

In this paper, I will suggest an approach to decolonial feminism drawing from Latina feminist theory and practice. While the embrace of intersectional approaches that explore the co-imbrication of gender, race, class, and sexuality has produced more variegated and contextualized analyses, I agree with Chandra Talpade Mohanty and Jacqui Alexander's view that

---

[2] A recent example here is the group Femen, which initiated a "Topless Jihad Day." See Walsh 2013.

intersectionality has focused too little on *national* difference, or geopolitical locations. Latina feminism has generally been an exception to this rule, as Sonia Saldivar-Hull explains: "Our histories as Chicana-Latina feminists force us to examine geo-politics as well as gender politics. . . . [because] our subject position exists in the interstices of national borders" (2000, 55). Latinas in the United States and other parts of the diaspora often have transnational identities of one sort or another, as well as transnational familial ties and direct experiences of the power differences among international agents. As a region Latin America has experienced more than fifty US interventions since its independence from Spain, from the annexation of Mexican territory in 1846 to the 1989 invasion of my home country of Panama to an attempted coup in Venezuela in 2002 and support for the military coup in Honduras in 2009. To be Latino/a is to be aware that colonialism is a central feature of the contemporary world, not a relic of the past.

I will argue here that rejecting an imperial approach involves something else besides "going local": it requires a genuine reorientation of feminist theory toward the quotidian or the everyday, toward a democratic epistemology that takes the activist oppressed as the ultimate makers of their own liberation. Intersectional approaches will necessarily lead to pluralist feminist conclusions; since forms of oppressions and identities are varied, their solutions must be as well. Further, these varied solutions are not going to be reducible to a unified criterion of validity, or a litmus test administered across contexts. The theorist's role is to translate and connect, to support and augment understanding and collaboration, and to engage in the tradition of committed militant research in specific locations.

I will begin with a brief overview of the emergence of the decolonial question within feminism, and then turn to the thorny question of the relationship between gender identities, gender liberation, and the decolonial turn. Finally, I will turn to the work of dissident Catholic theologian Ada María Isasi-Díaz as a positive model of theory attentive to local differences and the need for a democratic epistemic practice.

Emergence of Decolonial Feminism

If second-wave feminism spawned an era of multiple feminisms and intersectionality, I would define decolonial feminism as a more recent development.

The history of second-wave feminism has begun to be recognized as a traversal of separate roads, as Benita Roth put it (2004). Many of the feminisms of this period gave serious attention to both race and class—given their genesis in the civil rights, antiwar, and anti-imperialist movements (see, e.g., Crow 2000). But the mainstream face of feminism took on such a white, middle-class presentation that this more complex reality was obscured. And certainly, in liberal political organizations such as the National Organization for Women, racial, ethnic, sexual, and religious differences were systematically downplayed. Some theorists, such as Mary Daly, developed justifications for separating out and prioritizing gender oppression over other forms of identity oppression.

Separatist organizations became a necessity for focused work on women who were not white, Christian, or straight. What became known as black feminism probably developed first; then Latina feminism, Asian American feminism, Jewish feminism, indigenous feminism, Muslim feminism, and Arab feminism emerged with their own organizations, conferences, scholarship, and activism, and there were numerous splinters along the lines of sexuality and class that further divided these. When I was a young activist, I supported but never considered joining mainstream white feminist groups: they were much too narrow. I enacted my feminism in multiracial groups engaged in class struggle, antiracism, and anti-imperialism.

Theories of intersectionality and of identity politics emerged out of this internal political ferment in which different constituencies of women articulated different priorities. Issues of spirituality, immigration, citizenship, family formation, care work, and religion were foregrounded and formulated differently. These differences called into question what was taken to be the common lot of women, the common agenda of feminism, and the common political strategy of the movement.

Although this work was latently decolonial in intent, it was not always theoretically elaborated as such (Perez 1999). More recent work has begun to articulate a decolonial project, not as an issue of shifting priorities across different groups, but as a critique of founding concepts, particularly the category "women" and the term "gender," in light of colonial histories. This is the stage I would call the decolonial. For example, María Lugones (2003, 2012), Oyèrónké Oyèwùmí (1997), and Nkiru Nzegwu (2006) have argued in various ways that colonialism inaugurated a gender system that was not in place in precolonial societies. Oyèwùmí holds that for the Yoruba societies before colonialism, gender markers of identity were inessential in establishing one's status and social role, and age was much more important. Lugones uses the term "coloniality of gender" to adapt Aníbal Quijano's idea that colonialism inaugurated new social ontologies and categories of identity. Nzegwu argues that, in the case of Igbo families, the subordination of daughters and wives was a historically specific practice that developed only after the colonial takeovers.

In general, these authors argue that many have been too quick to translate preconquest concepts into our familiar gender concepts, thus inviting a host of assumptions and connotations that may not obtain. For example,

Lugones warns that *chachawarmi* in the Aymara language signifies a set of complementary opposites not necessarily analogous to man/woman (2012, 78). Most strongly, these theorists support a deconstruction of the importance of gender, but much of their emphasis is on the role of colonialism in creating newly oppressive conditions for women and for the work of social reproduction in general. They warn us not to assume that the currently configured gender structures we see in various parts of the world have ancient cultural roots rather than a more recent genealogy (Mani 1998).

Taking a different tack, indigenous feminists have argued that gender complementarity in their societies preexisted colonialism. Many defend gender differences, arguing that these are not always linked to domination (Allen 1992; Mikaere 1994; Lawrence 2015). Indigenous groups in the Americas vary in their gender arrangements, but it is indisputable that in many groups women held significant political power. From as far back as 1540, European settlers began writing about numerous Native women chiefs they encountered, such as the Jamestown colonists in Virginia who described their encounter with the queen of Appomattoc in the early 1600s. George Washington recounted that in 1753 he was required to visit the Seneca leader Allaquippa in order to be permitted to travel through the territory she supervised (Venables 2004, 221–22).

Yet the case for gender systems existing without domination does not rest on a few exceptional leaders, but on the political and economic organization across status. Haudenosaunee tribal leaders are always male but always chosen exclusively by older women known as Clanmothers. We now know that the political and economic power of women in the Iroquois Nation in upstate New York inspired the development of feminism among white settlers in the eighteenth and nineteenth centuries (Wagner 2003). In groups such as the Kuna Indians today women are not isolated as individuals inside the home facing an unchecked male authority but play critical social roles in the productive economies and land stewardship of their tribes and communities. Matrilineal family formations that exist in numerous kinship systems around the world also give women power and status through exclusive inheritance.

The claim that some groups have nonhierarchical gender based divisions of economic labor and political roles challenges the long-standing Western feminist critique of the doctrine of separate spheres. Both of the kinds of decolonial arguments described above—that gender was not a universal status term everywhere in the precolonial world, and that significant gender divisions could coexist with equal political and economic power—suggest that the colonial difference requires more fundamental work within feminist theory than it has been given. Ahistorical and universalist assumptions about patriarchy and the oppressive effect of gender-based separate spheres need to be reconsidered.

Doing feminist *theory* and feminist *philosophy* in a decolonial way poses particular challenges. Research in the social sciences is generally focused on specific phenomena in local contexts, such as women in the Caribbean who work in the informational sector or women in South Asia who work in food production.[3] But theory and philosophy usually understand themselves to have a more generic charge with global application. Although most now recognize that femininity and masculinity are culturally mediated and that gender formations are local, it remains a common assumption that gender itself can be theorized in the abstract. Some argue, for example, that the diverse ideations of gender have a common process of subject formation in which individuals must conform to a "logic" or "script" imposed from without, even if the content of that script varies. In this way feminist theory and feminist philosophy can perform their usual abstract analytic procedures without attending to the specificity of material contexts.

The leading position of feminist theory in the global North is that gender itself needs to be overcome given that gender identity is a prison house of coercive performances, rigid boundaries, and identitarian logics, and embroiled in a *necessary* subordination. Theorists as methodologically diverse as Sally Haslanger and Judith Butler take this view (Haslanger 2012; Butler 2004). There are certainly good reasons to worry that two-term gender systems suppress *actual* physical and biological variability and tend to naturalize gender meanings. As a result, feminist political practice has taken an increasingly oppositional stance toward gender identity itself, calling for the project of undoing gender and dismantling identities. Some theorists have called for a dismantling of women's studies as a discipline given its organization around a category that needs undoing (Brown 1997). Although feminist theory is in truth a hugely complex and contested terrain, in the academic spaces of the global North it sometimes appears that the only theoretically correct position defines feminism as a deconstruction of gender.

A decolonial approach indicates the need for caution. In some cases, gender systems may not be oppressive, either because gender *is not the determining status term* that preempts all others, or because gender systems can work with a two-term scale of meanings associated with female/male *but without an exclusivity of two socially recognized identities.* Examples of the latter would be communities that operate with female and male significations and social roles, yet endorse individuals such as "female husbands," "two-spirit people," and other identity categories beyond the binary. Among Igbo communities, for example, the category of "female

---

[3] Though even here the category of analysis—"women"—cannot be taken for granted.

husbands" includes females who play the social role of a husband when a wife has been widowed (Nzegwu 2006). Interestingly, such marriages are not sexual unions but legally and socially acknowledged relationships where inheritance, succession, and patronage can be secured without the presence of a male. Anatomy is not decisive in what kind of role one can play in marriage.

These latter identity formations are sometimes read as transgender, thus supporting the ongoing effort to complicate normative binary systems (Feinberg 1996; Stryker 2008). As David Valentine's ethnography of transgender communities shows, it is not at all clear that transgender operates "outside representation itself," or, in other words, is aiming to deconstruct and dismantle all identity terms (Valentine 2007, 136). Rather, category policing and negotiations are an important feature of trans interactions, although these work sometimes to scramble the mainstream options.

Interestingly, Valentine shows that transgender self-ascriptions sometimes appear inconsistent and hence become "unrepresentable." He relates this to the fact that nineteenth-century European and US anthropologists portrayed Native groups as "primitive" for precisely this reason—because their language was inconsistent—until Franz Boas suggested that it was the anthropologists' inadequate conceptual frames that made them unable to understand the cultures they encountered. Similarly, today, theorists must consider the impact of the hermeneutic injustice of linguistic systems that have worked to maintain a naturalism about Western gender binaries.

The lesson here is that we should be cautious about assimilating trans experiences to the universalist deconstructive framework on the grounds that the "inconsistency" is "obviously" an attempt to dismantle all gender. Trans identities no less than others require an intersectional approach that considers culture and context, and we should be cautious in making transnational comparisons that oversimplify the analogies. Furthermore, the coexistence of a two-term *meaning* system in some indigenous groups alongside multiple identity possibilities for actual embodied variations counsels against taking binary concepts as necessarily exclusivist (Jacobs et al. 1997). The ideational contrasts of masculine/feminine, sun/moon, yin/yang, hard/soft, and so on that animate many ancient spiritualities do not appear to mandate exclusivist binary logics for gender identity and in fact generally emphasize the interconnections and interdependencies. A complex variety of socially acknowledged gender formations can make use of these two-term systems of meaning without being limited to a choice of two.

We need to apply a decolonial frame on the contested meanings and roles in a variety of relationships, both settler/native as well as cisgender/transgender, yet I would urge a local rather than generic theoretical approach. Trans identities and experiences themselves are mediated and local.

The universalist theories of gender and of gender resistance emerging today need some decolonial work. The intersectional nature of identities, and the need for a decolonial hermeneutics of suspicion toward reductive or abstracted approaches, challenges universally imposed agendas of all sorts. All social identities may not operate in the same way to curtail multiplicity or legitimate domination. If gender cannot stand alone because its form is always the product of diverse, mediated processes, then we should reconsider whether we can theorize a universal response to gender, or a resistance to gender, or a solution to gender, while ignoring the hybrid nature of gender.

In my view, the decolonial approach to feminist theory needs to address three projects. (1) The first is a task of critique: What of our concepts and categories carry an implicit legacy of their colonial genealogy? (2) The second task involves developing tools for cross-cultural communication. How do we engage in dialogic encounters under conditions of unequal power and against the backdrop of colonialism? How do we "speak with" under conditions of inequality and legitimate mistrust? (3) The third task involves methods for conducting local analyses within a global frame, so that we can contextualize local conditions within a relational, transnational framework that is capable of charting both local and global causality. I will return to these three tasks in the conclusion to show how the notion of gender figures in each of these tasks.

Latina Feminism and the Decolonial Turn

The project of decolonizing feminist theory has mostly been happening, unsurprisingly, from theorists coming from the global South, and Latina feminists have played a crucial role. Latina theorists in the United States generally, as Saldivar-Hull remarks, have the doubled focus on the domestic and the international. This follows necessarily from a concern with the conditions of the many Latinos who come here from elsewhere and remain connected to what they left behind by familial, affective, legal, and material bonds. Questions of citizenship, concerns over loyalty, and levels of political participation play out very differently for peoples whose home countries are across the ocean rather than right next door. Latino/a theory is, then, of necessity cognizant of the need for a transnational analysis even when seeking to understand quite local issues.

María Lugones, Ofelia Schutte, and Ada-María Isasi-Díaz are among those who have initiated the decolonial project within feminism. Schutte's (2000) work on Latin American feminism, cultural alienation, and the requirements of cross-cultural communication has broadened our conceptual repertoire and developed a way to think about the epistemic issues across differences. For Schutte the problem is more than an unfair burden of translation work across contexts, in which Latinas or other less empowered individuals are expected to do the work of decoding and deciphering. Even more importantly she shows how aspects of one's self may be undecipherable in mainstream venues, hence left behind in a process of forcible self-alienation to create truncated subjectivities. This self-alienation is often the price of intelligibility in Anglo-dominant spaces.

Lugones has been working tirelessly to theorize difference within feminism itself, and both she and Isasi-Díaz have addressed the need for an insurrection of subjugated voices and knowledges that will expand the domain of theory to the level of the quotidian, or *lo cotidiano*. This means starting theory from the difficult material reality of the daily life of the impoverished and oppressed. Isasi-Díaz argued that what one will find here is not simply an uncritical "reproduction or repetition of all that we have learned or to which we have become accustomed" but "a powerful point of reference from where to begin to imagine a different world" (2012, 48–49). Lugones has imaginatively theorized the epistemic resources available to those who exist at the street level of society, such as streetwalkers. The practice here of "hanging out" produces "a rather large sense of the terrain and its social intricacies" in which one must learn "to listen, to transmit information, to participate in creative communications, to gauge possibilities, to have a sense of the directions of intentionality, to gain social depth." And, she says, "Unlike enclosures of the social that are conceived as less permeable, hangouts are highly permeable," generating the need for quick flexibility of communicative styles (2003, 209). I was struck by the contrast in this approach from Jürgen Habermas's critique of the distorting effects of the transactional forms of intercourse on discursive interaction. Habermas's account views strategic aims, such as securing a client, as necessarily compromising communication, rendering trust and truthfulness secondary to other goals. Lugones presents a picture of a discursive context in which transactional relationships are multilayered and epistemic agents necessarily develop complex skills of judgment and communication. Streetwalkers are looking for economic opportunities and potential collaborations but also watching out for trouble and conveying their knowledge among themselves. Hence, for Lugones, the arena of the street is a rich environment full of epistemic resources.

In much of her work Lugones has argued that critical theory occurs among the popular classes, thus requiring a more democratic epistemology. Gramsci makes a similar claim when he says, "Each man, finally, outside his professional activity, carries on some form of intellectual activity, that is, he is a 'philosopher,' an artist, a man of taste, he participates in a particular conception of the world, has a conscious line of moral conduct, and therefore contributes to sustain a conception of the world or to modify it, that is, to bring into being new modes of thought" (1971, 9).

If we accept the idea that every individual is a reflective thinker in this way, we must also acknowledge that our different social locations and identities have varied epistemic and critical resources. Chilean economist Manfred Max-Neef coined the term "barefoot economics" to highlight the need for a methodological approach that works from the ground up based in the experiences of the poor (1992). His point is not simply a call for economists to *serve* the poor, but to *learn* from the poor. Max-Neef argued that the poor are our most creative thinkers, having to find new ways to survive every day, establishing innovative forms of cooperation and work-sharing, with a mobile flexibility of skills and a high-level knowledge of their local conditions. Certainly the poor are strategic thinkers by necessity in order to survive within the existing systems in which they find themselves, but they also give evidence of creativity, producing new modes of productivity and distribution, from informal insurance and communal loans to innovative bartering. The rising visibility of the new "sharing economy" is a testament to the grassroots ingenuity of those with scarce resources.

My own extended family relations, which extend pretty far from sharecroppers in the United States south to schoolteachers and homemakers in the *global* South, bears this out. The poorest live lives of dignity and community, looking out for others, managing homelessness and job losses with innovative methods, and sharing what they have with neighbors, even strangers. Their lives are not textbook examples of blinkered gender ideology; women have maintained solidarity against abusive men and found ways to pursue their own interests and dreams, to nurture beauty and friendship and their children, even the children of their husband's mistresses. The older generations were particularly fascinating to me, without much formal education and yet independent, self-reliant, and inventively creative.

Following this lead, I want to consider how we might approach gender in the context of learning from, rather than teaching, *lo cotidiano* of the impoverished. This would counter the popular accounts of identity formation that view it as necessarily involving either authoritarianism from above, or irrationality from below. In 1922 Max Weber, for example, articulated a theory of the formation of racial and ethnic identities as resulting from false origin stories manipulated by elites (Weber 1996). Sigmund Freud (1989) placed the blame more clearly on universal processes in which the inherent vulnerability of the ego latches onto compensatory but illusory ideas about stable and coherent identities. These approaches came to inform much of twentieth-century social theory, from liberal critics of ethnic movements and multiculturalism such as Nathan Glazer, Daniel

Patrick Moynihan and Arthur Schlesinger, to more left-wing critics of identity politics such as Nancy Fraser and Paul Gilroy. The contemporary skepticism among feminist theorists toward gender identities follows in this tradition of thinking that identities are the product of nefarious elites and opportunists. Everyday people who actually believe in identities are viewed as either dupes or knaves or both. There is certainly nothing for the theorist to learn from the woman on the street.

Ada María Isasi-Díaz and Democratic Epistemic Practice

The late theologian Ada-María Isasi-Díaz, one of the first Latina feminist theorists published in the United States during second-wave feminism, wrote about the different and distinct experiences and approach of US Latinas. She later developed what she called a *mujerista* theology that adapted certain aspects of liberation theology's "preference for the poor" to US Latinas. Isasi-Díaz argued that applying this dictate without condescension requires acknowledging poor women as already regularly engaging in the theological work of seeking, interpreting, and bringing forth the sacred. Echoing Anzaldúa (2000), she held that "for us the sacred is an integral part of our daily lives" (1993, 178–79). In other words, she defines the sacred as involving all of the practices that validate Latina lives and ways of being against efforts to *invisibilize* or commercialize or denigrate our traditions, including such everyday things as ways of cooking, gardening, dressing, expressing faith, and forming community. There is an intentionality in these practices, she insists, that requires a conscious epistemic self-validation. "Those who are influential in society are not our models" (180). Their reasons are not our reasons, nor are their values our values, she asserts. Validating Latina lives requires facing the challenge of finding and protecting and preserving the value in the everyday existence of the oppressed. This is what Isasi-Díaz refers to as sacred work.

Isasi-Díaz identified the obstacles to this work as including church authorities, traditional academic theology, and feminist theory. In the first pages of *Mujerista Theology* she quotes one of her young Puerto Rican students who expresses a long-standing discomfort with feminist theory since it never took into account her own understandings, or allowed her the space to contribute in her own terms and "not in the shadow cast by the Anglos" (1996, 2–3). Hence, the corrective is not simply to incorporate analysis of Latina lives within feminist theory but to empower Latinas as theorists themselves. Throughout her own writing and religious practice, Isasi-Díaz appropriates the position of the theorist and authority, revising the methodology of the theologian, reinterpreting the liturgy, even rewriting a contemporary version of Psalm 137.

Isasi-Díaz's work thus modeled an epistemic self-authorization as part of the overall project of enhancing and preserving the space for collective theological practice. As she began to elaborate what she called a *mujerista* theology, she explained that

> the moral agency of Hispanic women has to be the determining factor in our methodological considerations . . . though we understand the elaboration itself of *mujerista* theology itself to be a liberative praxis, *mujerista* theology as a discourse cannot be considered more important than Hispanic Women's development as agents in our own lives and of our own history. (1993, 63)

Isasi-Díaz's work is one place where we can observe a decolonial turn enacted in feminist theory, and it is instructive to note the focal points of her work: collective celebrations of community and identity, and transformations and relocations of the realm of the sacred. *Mujerista* liturgies are first of all orchestrations for celebrating the sacred. She explains that the sacred is brought forth through rituals that "celebrate the identity of the people gathered . . . and bring about an experience of individual and communal transformation" (1996, 194).

A consistent theme of Isasi-Díaz's account is this twoness of celebration and transformation, directives that may well seem to be at odds. We think of celebrations as recognitions and acknowledgments of what is, while transformations endeavor to make change. Is, then, the scope of the transformation limited by its call to celebrate identity? Two points she makes suggest otherwise.

First, the baseline methodology she advocates is an ethnography of lived experience, where lived experience refers "not only to what has happened—what a person has endured or made happen—but to that experience upon which she reflects in order to understand its significance and value it accordingly." This is not reportage but critical thought, or what she also calls practical rationality, required by the conditions of diaspora. Latinas in the United States live in a dominant cultural context that devalues our lives, beliefs, relations, and choices. We thus become, she says, an "invisible invisibility," the backdrop to functioning cities, institutions, and families that is so routine that it recedes from view. Lived experience in such a context cannot but be self-conscious, reflective, and critically aware of its own erasure. "By using our lived-experience as the source of theology, Hispanic women start from a place outside of those structures, outside the traditional theology which is controlled by the dominant group. This gives us an opportunity to be self-defining, to give fresh answers, and what is most important, to ask new questions" (1993, 73). To mobilize lived experience in this way is to mobilize critical, outsider consciousness.

Second, Isasi-Díaz says, the conditions of mestizaje and of our identities as Latinas attempting to survive in a dominant and hostile context are necessarily the products of intentional interpretive choices. She claims that ethnicities are the product of "biological and cultural characteristics" but also the current social and economic conditions of a community, such as poverty and marginalization (1993, 186). As an element of our identity, mestizaje is not a natural condition, or something to be idealized, she holds, but the result—one possible result—of the work of self-definition. As a self-ascription mestizaje is a way of consciously acknowledging and naming difference as central to one's historical lineage and formation. Overall, then, identity for Latinas is the product of a struggle for self-definition within a context that poses a complex set of particular challenges, from invisibility, to heterogeneity, to misrepresentations, to the need for an adaptive fluidity. It is the end point of communal and individual work.

Throughout her writings, Isasi-Díaz called out the dangers of romanticizing and idealizing mestizaje as well as the condition of the poor. She was quite aware that a valorization of *lo cotidiano*, including the claiming of theoretical resources inherent in the condition of everyday struggles of survival, could lead to romanticizing. And she constantly called herself out as a "middle class" woman, even though she described herself as being two to three paychecks away from not being able to pay her bills. But despite her awareness of the dangers, Isasi-Díaz continued to insist on a democratic epistemology, claiming that "there is no such thing as academic mujerista theology on one hand and grassroots mujerista theology on the other" (1993, 177). The praxis of theory as she envisioned it, and practiced it, was one where each person makes a contribution according to her own gifts, with none more important than another.

Mujerista theology effects a relocation of the space of the sacred in the midst of the marginalized. In the last years of her life, Isasi-Díaz's beloved parish church in East Harlem was shut down by the church authorities for financial reasons, and in response, the women of the church held regular services on the sidewalk. There they performed the liturgy themselves, reciting the rosary together, and reconsecrating the space of their barrio and their lives. This was simply a repetition of a practice Isasi-Díaz had done many times before. In 1985 for example, at the Third National Hispanic Pastoral Encuentro held in Washington, DC, five hundred women protested against the Catholic Church's refusal to allow their full participation with a demonstration on the steps of the National Shrine, "successfully relocating the sacred," she explained, outside the church (1996, 200). Where, I believe, it remains.

Isasi-Díaz's work reminds us of two important lessons critical to a decolonial project. The first is that identities, in any full and meaningful sense as aspects of lived experience, are the product of praxis at the level of *lo cotidiano*. They are not always imposed and may in fact be critical achievements. The second aligned idea is that the meaning of the sacred need not be understood as a celebration of what is, but as a claim about what has value for a community, even if that is just a sidewalk, or a life that is invisibly invisible. The everyday practices of celebrating what is sacred are thus not necessarily in conflict with the domain of critical thought, but can be a "point of reference to begin to imagine a different world" (2012, 49).

At the start of this paper I outlined three tasks necessary for the project of decolonizing feminist theory: the tasks of criticizing our concepts, of developing tools for communication across our geographical and cultural differences, and of contextualizing the local within the global. I will conclude by summarizing the contributions of Isasi-Díaz to each of these. Certainly a major concept that requires decolonial critique is the way in which we understand the nature of gender identity and what it would mean to be liberated in relation to gender.

If we accept the intersectional thesis that gender identities are always coconstituted in relation to other aspects of one's life, then we must allow that the process of forming gender identities, the strictness as well as the content of gender "scripts," and the bodily practices that emerge from the sexually specific aspects of human reproduction and physiology are all variable across contexts. As it intersects with other ways of being, gender changes not merely in degree but in kind. Isasi-Díaz's work makes particularly vivid that what changes is not simply the intensity with which gender is lived, or enforced, but its political meaning and its political value.

I suggest that to interpret Isasi-Díaz's description of *mujerista* practices as a form of strategic essentialism would be a colonizing move, framing this community by the meta-level abstractions of gender liberation I have characterized as a hegemony seeking deconstructive feminism emerging from the global North. In so doing the point of view of community members is eclipsed, on the grounds that the theorist knows better what they are really about. Isasi-Díaz's participatory and dialogic approach provides a democratic corrective to this kind of authoritarian epistemology.

The trend toward gender eliminativism, I'd suggest, has more to do with the specific context of Western philosophical and political traditions developed in the period of colonization than it offers a universal blueprint genuinely liberatory for all. To see this, it is helpful to look at Max Weber's account of the interrelationships between racial, ethnic, and gender identities. On his account, ethnic and racial groups are dependent on reproductive communities that operate not just through biological processes but through the inculcation of specific cultural practices passed down to the young. We know this is a typical task allocated to women and often a major source of the oppression of women: as the perceived bearers of culture, the protection and survival of cultures are often seen to depend on restricting our options in love, in family formation, in religious choice, and in creative cultural interpretation and transformation. There is no question that burdens are placed on women to enact traditions.

For Weber, who, we should recall, is studying down, the work of maintaining and reproducing social group identities is necessarily conservative rather than transformative, and those who perform this work only have agency insofar as they *re*create, rather than create or interpret anew. This is precisely why such cultures are defined in his terms as less than fully modern. His tools allow him to only see oppression in such communities. Notice how different his characterization of women's cultural and familial labor is from Isasi-Díaz's, who describes celebratory functions as *opportunities for creativity and participation*.

Isasi-Díaz helps us to see that there are likely to be contrasting affective ties to gender identities in the context of colonized communities, given the role of gender in community survival as well as recognitions of value in the lives of the invisibilized. This should alert us to the fact that some groups may be more ready to deconstruct gender than others, and that we should understand this impulse as sometimes the product of mediations involving their ethnic or racial identities. If my culture/race/ethnicity is something I want to escape, this can lead me toward gender deconstructionist politics. On the other hand, if gender expression is part of the way I am connected to a culture, a history, a genealogy with values that deserve continuation, then my attitude may be quite different. Here Weber is helpful in reminding us that our attachment to our gender identities cannot be disambiguated from other aspects of my social identities. If gender is the means to produce group identities such as ethnicity, then undoing gender, on such a view, will be the means to undo ethnicity, adding to its precarious condition in hostile colonial contexts.

Hence, an apparently abstract concept of "gender," and of gender liberation, may be carrying a contextual specificity. In order to communicate across the diverse contexts of gender meanings and formations, we need to be able to make these contextual variations intelligible. Dialogic processes cannot presume prior frames of analysis; rather, everything must be on the table for discussion, including the political effects of gender identities.

Relations between women of diverse identities are often the intimate front-lines of cross-racial communication. We are often closely contiguous in the labor market, even if divided by hierarchies of status, and we often coinhabit gender segregated spaces, such as in religious, educational, or carceral communities where groups are divided by gender, and yet many sorts of division—of class, generation, nationality, and sexuality—remain alive in the organization that emerges. Gender often mediates the possibilities, and challenges, that exist in these encounters, making this a fruitful arena for dialogic understanding if the implicit monolingual conceptual frames can be set aside.

Decolonizing communicative practices requires letting go of a priori frames of judgment that often block our ability to link global and local phenomena. I'd suggest that this is precisely what obscures Weber's capacity to "see" the creative agency involved in colonized communities. He sees only the perpetuation of ancient and unchanging belief-systems—whereas, if we were to link local phenomena to the long history of colonialism, we might be able to see variation, resistance, and the transformations in identity structures put in place by colonialism, as Oyěwùmí and Nzegwu show. We might also be able to see the subversive agency of religious women such as Isasi-Díaz describes.

Decolonizing feminist theory cannot succeed without an epistemic shift in methodology that recognizes the intentional *self-defining* practices that occur in the sphere of the everyday, as Isasi-Díaz recounted. We have to move in two directions at once: (1) localizing our analyses of gender formation in order to understand the specificity of its form and its effects, and to avoid portraying any given gender practice as mere symptom, but also (2) relating the local cultural, religious, or ethnic practices to a transnational, colonial history. This requires being alive to the capacity of everyday agency, and the disparate realities of colonial contexts.

Acknowledgments

Thanks go to Marilyn Friedman, Karen Ng, and the editors of this volume for their astute comments on this paper.

References

Ahmed, Leila. 1992. *Women and Gender in Islam: Historical Roots of a Modern Debate*. New Haven, CT: Yale University Press.

Allen, Paula Gunn. 1992. *The Sacred Hoop: Recovering the Feminine in American Indian Traditions*. Boston: Beacon Press.

Anzaldúa, Gloria E. 2000. *Interviews/Entrevistas*. Edited by AnaLouise Keating. New York: Routledge.

Brown, Wendy. 1997. "The Impossibility of Women's Studies." *Differences: A Journal of Feminist Cultural Studies* 9, no. 3: 79–101.

Butler, Judith. 2004. *Undoing Gender*. New York: Routledge.

Crow, Barbara. 2000. *Radical Feminism: A Documentary Reader*. New York: New York University Press.

Eisenstein, Hester. 2009. *Feminism Seduced: How Global Elites Use Women's Labor and Ideas to Exploit the World*. New York: Routledge.

Feinberg, Leslie. 1996. *Transgender Warriors: Making History from Joan of Arc to Dennis Rodman*. Boston: Beacon Press.

Freud, Sigmund. 1989. *Introductory Lectures on Psychoanalysis.* Translated by James Strachey. Standard Edition. New York: Norton.

Gramsci, Antonio. 1971. *Selections from the Prison Notebooks of Antonio Gramsci.* Edited by Quintin Hoare and Geoffrey Nowell-Smith. New York: International Publishers.

Haslanger, Sally. 2012. *Resisting Reality: Social Construction and Social Critique.* New York: Oxford University Press.

Isasi-Díaz, Ada-María. 1993. *En la lucha / In the Struggle: Elaborating a Mujerista Theology.* Minneapolis: Fortress Press.

Isasi-Díaz, Ada-María. 1996. *Mujerista Theology: A Theology for the Twenty-First Century.* Maryknoll, NY: Orbis Press.

Isasi-Díaz, Ada-María. 2012. "Mujerista Discourse: A Platform for Latinas' Subjugated Knowledge." In *Decolonizing Epistemologies: Latina/o Theology and Philosophy,* edited by Ada María Isasi-Díaz and Eduardo Mendieta, 44–67. New York: Fordham University Press.

Jacobs, Sue-Ellen, Wesley Thomas, and Sabine Long. 1997. *Two-Spirit People: Native American Gender Identity, Sexuality, and Spirituality.* Urbana: University of Illinois Press.

Kaplan, E. Ann. 1997. *Looking for the Other: Feminism, Film, and the Imperial Age.* New York: Routledge.

Kolhatkar, Sonali, and Mariam Rawi. 2009. "Why Is a Leading Feminist Organization Lending Its Name to Support Escalation in Afghanistan?" *Alternet,* July 7. http://www.alternet.org/story/141165/why_is_a_leading_feminist_organization_lending)_its_name_to_support_escalation_in_afghanistan.

Lawrence, Salmah Eva-Lina. 2015. "Witchcraft, Sorcery, Violence: Matrilineal and Decolonial Reflections." In *Talking It Through: Responses to Witchcraft and Sorcery Beliefs and Practices in Melanesia,* edited by Miranda Forsyth and Richard Eves, 55–74. Canberra: Australian National University Press.

Lugones, María. 2003. *Pilgrimages/Peregrinajes: Theorizing Coalition against Multiple Oppressions.* New York: Rowman and Littlefield.

Lugones, María. 2012. "Methodological Notes Toward a Decolonial Feminism." In *Decolonizing Epistemologies: Latina/o Theology and Philosophy,* edited by Ada María Isasi-Díaz and Eduardo Mendieta, 68–86. New York: Fordham University Press.

Max-Neef, Manfred. 1992. *From the Outside Looking In: Experiences in "Barefoot Economics."* London: Zed Books.

Mikaere, Annie. 1994. "Maori Women: Caught in the Contradictions of a Colonised Reality." *Waikato Law Review* 2.

Murungi, Kagendo. 1994. "Get Away from My Genitals: On Warrior Marks." *Interstices* 2, no. 11: 13.

Nzegwu, Nkiru Uwechia. 2006. *Family Matters: Feminist Concepts in African Philosophy of Culture.* Albany: State University of New York Press.

Oyěwùmí, Oyèrónké. 1997. *The Invention of Women: Making an African Sense of Western Gender Discourses.* Minneapolis: University of Minnesota Press.

Pérez, Emma. 1999. *The Decolonial Imaginary: Writing Chicanas into History.* Bloomington: Indiana University Press.

Roth, Benita. 2004. *Separate Roads to Feminism: Black, Chicana, and White Feminist Movements in America's Second Wave.* Cambridge: Cambridge University Press.

Saldivar-Hull, Sonia. 2000. *Feminism on the Border: From Gender Politics to Geo-Politics.* Berkeley: University of California Press.

Schutte, Ofelia. 2000. "Cultural Alterity: Cross-Cultural Communication and Feminist Theory in North-South Contexts." In *Decentering the Center: Philosophy for a*

Multicultural, Postcolonial, and Feminist World, edited by Uma Narayan and Sandra Harding, 47–66. Bloomington: Indiana University Press.

Stryker, Susan. 2008. *Transgender History*. Berkeley, CA: Seal Press.

Valentine, David. 2007. *Imagining Transgender*. Durham, NC: Duke University Press.

Venables, Robert W. 2004. *American Indian History: Five Centuries of Conflict and Coexistence. Vol. 1*. Santa Fe: Clear Light Publishers.

Wagner, Sally Roesch. 2003. *Sisters in Spirit: Haudenosaunee (Iroquois) Influence on Early Feminists*. Summertown, TN: Native Voices Book Publishing Company.

Walsh, Michael. 2013. "Amina Tyler's Femen Supporters Declare Topless Jihad Day after Death-by-Stoning Threats for Topless Pics." *New York Daily News*, March 28. http:// stream.aljazeera.com/story/201304050033-0022659.

Weber, Max. 1996. "Ethnic Groups." In *Theories of Ethnicity: A Reader*, edited by Werner Sollors, 52–56. New York: New York University Press.

CHAPTER 2 | Revisiting Gender
        | *A Decolonial Approach*

MARÍA LUGONES

I WILL BEGIN BY describing the work of Rita Segato, an influential Latin American anthropologist, theorist, and committed activist with enormous experience. I will place my project in contrast to hers because I think doing so makes clearer what is my direction and company. I will also detail the character of my philosophical/political project. I emphasize a an analysis and critique of gender as a category but also as a structural feature of the kingdom of Spain, of colonial governance, and of nascent nation states. That analysis is followed by a critique of the use of the concepts of gender and patriarchy in both the social scientific study of the peoples of Abya Yala and of coalitional attempts with them. Including women who are indigenous and women who are Afro-descendants in Abya Yala. That is the name that the Puna of Panama have given to the territory named America by the colonial powers; it has been adopted by a significant number of insurgents in the region, including intellectuals, activists, and indigenous movements. The longer version of this critique is a chapter in *Decolonial Feminism*, a book that I am writing in conversation with indigenous women intellectuals, activists, and women in communities in Bolivia and the northwest and the south of Argentina, and with intellectual activists who are Afro-descendants from the Caribbean and South America.

Segato

Segato is doing extraordinary work with indigenous pueblos and women in Brazil, deep into the Amazonia. She focuses on women's situation in

María Lugones, *Revisiting Gender* In: *Theories of the Flesh*, Edited by: Andrea J. Pitts, Mariana Ortega, and José Medina, Oxford University Press (2020). © Oxford University Press. DOI: 10.1093/oso/9780190062965.003.0003

the complexity of what she calls the *mundo aldea* within the reach and intervention of the nation state. She does this because her overall project is to think of the pueblo as a historical project rather than a present or a fixed past. That project moves from preintrusion, to the colonial intrusion, to nation states. She takes up gender in the use it has in the anthropological literature as a practical device that she does not criticize. The gender system that is a central aspect of the *mundo aldea* she characterizes as a low-intensity patriarchy that is constituted as a duality rather than a binary. The distinction is important for her and for me, as it is for many women working on decolonial feminism. Thus she understands that arrangement as one that is significantly different from the dichotomous modern gender system, which she thinks of as a binary. The difference between them she explains in terms of ontology. In the occidental binary, each being is incomplete in a supplementary relation, while in the duality each being is complete in a relation of complementarity. During the colonial intrusion, it was indigenous men who were approached and given a much more extensive power, since they were the ones chosen by Europeans/whites to engage in negotiations and are now negotiating with the nation state. This was the colonizers' move. They gave dehumanized males, people who, thus, were without gender, a position that makes sense only from their—the colonizer's—gender logic. The nation state has reinforced the hierarchy of low-intensity patriarchy very significantly, and women, enclosed in the domestic space, have the political agency that they have had in the *mundo aldea* reduced. Men are invading domestic space, and women are being subjected to significant violence. The gender system of the pueblos still survives in the margins. Men get together to discuss and make decisions, but they have to consult with women outside of the meeting place, and only after consulting with women is the decision made. Some of the time, women themselves present their opinions outside of the meeting place. This way of life is being undermined, colonized, by the nation state, as it was by the Portuguese colonizers.

Is important to notice that Segato's understanding of the mundo aldea is in gender terms, though she never analyzes the propriety of her use of gender or patriarchy. Women did have a role in decision making. Why and from what source were females thus conceived? If the form of governance laced in the structure of governance, why is that? What role does their cosmological understanding of relations in the universe and thus in the mundo aldea have in the dual relation between males and females?

The decolonial possibilities that Segato thinks need to be pursued are within a nation state that gives after having taken. The demands that indigenous women organizations articulate are demands to the nation state. To understand the complexity of what she backs up, consider the following passage:

Cómo es posible llevar el recurso de los derechos estatales sin proponer la progresiva dependencia de un Estado permanente colonizador cuyo proyecto histórico no puede coincidir con el proyecto de las autonomías y de laa restauración del tejido comunitario? Es contradictorio afirmar el derecho a la autonomía, y simultáneamente afirmar que el estado produce las leyes que defenderán a los que se ven perjudicados dentro de esas propias autonomías.

[How is it possible to bring to (the *mundo aldea*) state rights without proposing the growing dependence on a continuously colonizing state whose historical project cannot coincide with the project of autonomies and the restoration and the rebuilding of the communal fabric? It is contradictory to affirm the right to autonomy, and simultaneously affirm that the state produces the laws that will defend those who are harmed inside those very autonomies.] (Segato 2011, 22)

For her, the nation state tries to develop an antidote for the poison it has already injected. It has inherited from the administration on the other side of the sea the permanent interventionist and colonizing character that weakens autonomies, trespasses into the institutional life, renders the communitarian weave, generates dependence, and offers the discourse of egalitarianism. At the same time it dominates with instrumental liberal reason and racism; it emasculates nonwhites and stresses them.

Segato uses the word "gender" to point to something that she also describes in Western terms, in my analysis. She has a categorization that is understandable to social scientists, but why should it be one that someone seeking coalition would use in understanding the *mundo aldea*? It is important to me to express what she is doing as "pointing to something." That is what I understand her as doing as probably a useful and normal way of communicating and getting together with women from many different *mundo aldeas* to think together about the coloniality and what to do about it. I want to stop that impulse to use a word in a colonial language to point to something that one already has in mind. I want to stay in the uncertainty of not having a name for what I want to point to, to reject the sense that I know what it is that I cannot name, and to avoid singling something out by pointing, instead of seeking a larger web of meaning. I do not have something already in mind like gender, feminine, patriarch as I point to people with names like "gender," "feminine," "patriarch" in casual Anglo-European conversation. It is indisputable, I think, that "woman" has not been the name for a desirable position in the social realm, among Anglo and European people, simply because the name is entrenched in an ensemble of violence and power backed up by philosophical/ideological justifications. When I think of transformation from woman to something else, I certainly do not want to keep the meaning alive. But that is not easy, since it requires a serious disruption in that ensemble of violence. So becoming one with the violence in a friendly relation with power will not do. Why do we want to think of people who have very different relations among themselves, backed up by very different philosophies/cosmologies, in terms of "men" and "women," as if the meaning of words can be lifted out, the words emptied of it and still be something that we can use to point to something we know is men and women in some alternative sense of the word? It is crucial to dwell in the fact that the peoples we are thinking of and relating with are racialized, dehumanized, their knowledges dismissed. We are considering concepts and words that are entrenched in academic usage and have become ordinary, common-sense ones, like patriarchy, gender, men, women, female, male. Given colonial violence, the Portuguese words for "men" and "women" are used by the indigenous women she works with. The word "woman" is used together with words in indigenous languages that Segato understands as equivalent to "woman." The back and forth in indigenous women's tongues of both words needs to be considered as deliberative autonomy regarding "gender," and understood as central to the pueblos as historical projects. I want to both shake the ease and certainty in the use of these terms but also prepare us as women of color to think toward transformations of beings and relations muted by the coloniality, but as people who constantly "speak," perform in gestures, practices, beliefs, knowledges passed on, recreated, changed from person to person with a long memory defying their erasure. So I want to combine uncertainty and alertness to ways that can be gathered from our past and present that can be woven into our metamorphosis.

I am at one with Segato when she thinks of a pueblo as a project of being a history that is woven collectively.

> Cuando la historia que tejida colectivamente, como el tramado de un tapiz donde los hilos diseñan figuras, a veces acercándose y convergiendo, a veces distanciandose y en oposición, es interceptada, interrumpida por fuerza de una intervención externa, este sujeto colectivo pretenderá retomar los hilos, hacer pequeños nudos, suturar la memoria, y continuar. En ese caso, deberá ocurrir lo que podríamos llamar de una devolución de la historia, restituir la capacidad de tramar su propio camino histórico, reanudando el trazado de las figuras interrumpidas, tejiéndolas hasta el presente de la urdimbre, proyectándose hacia el futuro. (Segato 2011, 25)

When history woven collectively as the weave of a tapestry in which the threads trace figures, sometimes getting close and converging, sometimes distancing and in opposition, is intercepted, interrupted by the force of an external intrusion, that collective subject will attempt to pick up the threads again, make small knots, suture the memory, and continue. In that case, what needs to happen is what we could call a taking back of history, *una devolucion*, a restitution of the capacity to weave t their own historical path, continuing the trace of interrupted figures, weaving them up to the present of the weave, projecting it to the future" (Segato 2011, 25)

Segato thinks of this weaving as done in collective debate and deliberation. When she asks whether there is a way of inhabiting decoloniality within the matrix of that state and inducing it to a recomposition of the communities, she puts the question as one addressed to the "situation we live in," which she understands as an in-between world, because the only things that really exist are intermediary situations, interfaces, transitions, between the state reality and the *mundo aldea*, between the modern colonial order and the preintrusion order. Good and bad from both the state and the *mundo aldea* circulate and cross-influence each other.

In this passage Segato uses words that are familiar in Gloria Anzaldua's writing, "interfaceand" "in between," and her writing is inspiring, recalling Mary Louise Pratt's transculturation. But then, there is the state. It is worth spending a few words in thinking about a crucial difference between them Segato and Anzaldua. For Segato, the poles of the in between are the mundo aldea and the state, for Anzaldua, the poles are the Anglo culture and the Mexican culture, both place her in a state of intimate terror and take away her capacity for responsibility.

My Own Project

What I am doing is to continue the work of U.S. Women-of-Color feminisms which is the from where I think across to other places where racialized women resist dehumanization. I think of the possibilities of transformation away from the oppression of the different forms of coloniality, away from the logic of modernity/coloniality, its various understandings of "reality," its practices and ideologies of production, its perception and imagination. This work has paid attention to subjectivity and intersubjectivity as it has focused on women of color doing the radical work of metamorphosis. While the Western modern construction of what since the 1970s is called "gender" and "gender relations" is oppressive to proletarian and bourgeois women from what came to be Europe, it did not racialize those women as of an inferior race. The racialization of the modern Western gender system began at the end of the violent "transition" from the Middle Ages to the Renaissance; from feudalism to capitalism; from a theocentric understanding of Christian religiosity and cosmovision to a humanistic understanding of both. To think "gender" relations radically and decolonially entails thinking the formation and transformation of the self and of the self inrelation and in relation to all there is in the world in terms that do not follow the logic of coloniality. It entails thinking relationally, intersubjectively, without losing the beings in relation in their integrity. A first moment in understanding human relations decolonially is the moment of facing with clear awareness the epistemological construction of who and what the colonized are in the racialized, colonial perception and imagination as their perception of themselves. Facing the colonial imagination, perception, construction of the colonized as not human, seeing oneself being perceived, understood, imagined that way by white Europeans is to separate their perception of oneself from oneself and from one's sense of oneself, to consider the perception fictitious even if the system of thought and the construction of reality seem of a piece with that perception of oneself as not human, as inferior by nature. "Gender" cannot be the concept that can take Women of Color to that first decolonial moment precisely because colonized women were not gendered as they were understood, treated, perceived, imagined, desired, and used as nonhuman. Gender as a concept cannot lead us to see coloniality because it does not take it into account the relation of power that erases or attempts to erase what relations constitute the people that are colonized and racialized. So, away from gender, I want to think the relations among people and other beings that include the erotic, the sexual, the corporeal, the embodied spirit in the production and reproduction of life in everyday work with others, the raising of children, the production of knowledge, parturition, the relation to the spirits of ancestors (*las almitas*), the living in a world of permeable beings, a world where everything and everyone exists in connection—as someone who is herself in the midst of those relations of power seeking coalitional insurgency. There is a tendency to think that people of color, indigenous people, Afro-descendants, mestizos, and mulattoes who live against racism and have particular ways of thinking are and will do the movement on their own. The one who have that tendency place themselves outside of that moving. As I am and thinking from inside that moving, I think of the anchors, marks, threads of our historical agency as we recreate ourselves coalitionally in that moving. I think of communal agency that enables a communal "I" to be creative in taking back our possibilities.

Gender

As I embark in the task of moving across space and time in a nonlinear understanding of time and a nonabstract understanding of space, the concept of gender is problematic for me. I am moving historically and spatially with a conviction that my own constitution needs to be questioned, in particular my cognitive lenses and my being taught not to think incarnately. So in moving, I am cautious and mistrustful of what seems right to me as well as of what my feminist contemporaries have thought and written.

In order to understand the coloniality/decoloniality of gender in the concrete, I need to do more than argue the falsehood of "woman" as a universal subject, subjected to the transhistorical or ahistorical patriarchy. I need to gather the ingredients that will enable me to keep in focus actual people within social, economic, religious, political histories within structures of power in changing historical conflicting processes of formation and transformation. It will be in relation to those structures as historical and to the collective responses against oppression, injustice, abuse that there will be no univocal meaning for "woman," even when the term—in various colonial languages—is used everywhere in everyday life as well as in the law, often as in the man-woman binary. Indeed, it is not just that "woman" is not universal. Rather, the issue, in terms of universality, rests on those relations of power that attempt to control the false universal and what it hides. What it hides is not "seen" by hegemonic/white feminists, even though the control is incalculably more devastating to the life, labor, creativity, self, self-understanding, and understandings of the world of those women who are under the coloniality of gender. Those relations of power involve changing understandings of the nature of men and women in Western terms and do not include attempts to create a critique of Western gender that can redirect the direction of those changes. The critique of Western gender relations is lived by those dehumanized by power in intersubjective and collective attempts to survive relations of power without erasure.

I do not believe that indigenous and Afro-descendant populations in Abya Yala brought to the cataclysmic encounter with Spanish and Portuguese conquerors and colonizers in the sixteenth century a dichotomous understanding of their universe, their selves, or their sexual and social relationality. Understanding the contemporary meanings given to their sexual-social relationality requires a historico-philosophical investigation into the tense production of a sense of that relationality that takes seriously the philosophical underpinnings of both indigenous and European understandings of the social. The tension between them and the importance of both domination and resistance to domination in their historicity endures. This work is necessary for the sociosexual decolonial possibilities in the contemporary formation of plurinational states, since the dichotomizing of decolonization and depatriarchalization, and the ideological construction of indigenous sociosexual identities into a noncontinuous, not fluid binary where women are complete only in relation to men, lifegivers in a narrow reproductive sense, a continuity of milk flowing into the earth, takes in much that is colonial. Segato sees this clearly.

I am arguing that the Western colonial, modern, capitalist structuring of the construction of social life, the production of knowledge included, is saturated with racialized gender meanings and gives form to particular, historical systems of racialized gender formation. In introducing the coloniality of gender, I mean to unveil the tight relation between gender and race. The denial of full humanity to the colonized is central here. I am particularly interested in the modern, colonial, capitalist gender system as it constructs the meaning of gender in tense relations with very different understandings that guide the colonized in their societies. So, instead of thinking of a univocal, transhistorical understanding of patriarchy as subordinating women viewed as reproducers, I analyze dominating systems of gender as producing different beings and relations and different beings in relation. When I think of those who are resisting their positioning in the modern colonial gender system or are resisting the gender system itself, I will not understand them as advancing a different gender system, since such a system requires a structure like the one of the nation-state which is very unlike that of the mundo aldea. The inbetween then is between two very different ways of relating. Gender belongs only on one side, the state. The concept of gender itself carries conceptual, social, metaphysical, historical meaning that is inimical to the on-the-ground resistance by the inhabitants of Abya Yala, even when their habitats have been largely destroyed. I treat the term "gender" with suspicion, because it may be nothing other than a Western descriptive or analytical artifact. The descriptive use of "gender" often promotes the characteristically Western modern thinking in terms of categories, understood as homogenous, impermeable, separable, and monadic.

My point is not to look at, observe so as to manipulate, reorganize, or theorize the ways, lives, relations, metaphysics, cosmologies of the people of Abya Yala. The point is to understand their conceptual and practical living so as to accompany the struggle for its survival and flourishing in a coalitional spirit. If we are going to have decolonial possibilities, the position of outside observer has to be questioned and abandoned, not for the purpose of going native, but joining their struggle in coalition. It has to be abandoned for the purpose of learning people, of arriving at an understanding that makes living with those who have undergone the horror of dehumanization and have survived resistantly, possible. The contemporary South American and Chiapaneco movements are testimonies to that resistance. On that possibility rests decolonial coalition. So, if gender could not be used to reach an understanding of self in relation in—not about—their lives, the use of gender as a social scientific tool is a colonial intrusion that blocks coalition, even when it is used by indigenous authorities. In that spirit, as a US woman of color, ready to abandon the term "feminist" if it is antagonistic to decolonial relational possibilities, I want to think the coloniality and decoloniality of gender, the body, desire, interpersonal and political relations, the production of knowledge in a coalitional, theoretical vein that is provisional and is in constant conversation with the women of Abya Yala and the Caribbean, and US racialized women.

Conclusion

I am looking in the direction of possibility as we ask ourselves about co-alition from within. The perspective I am suggesting must be different from and antagonistic to the ones of Eurocentric modernity. The direction of possibility lies in looking for and working toward the recuperation of resistant historical tapestries that weave understandings of relations to and of the universe, of realities that are resistant to the logic of modernity and show us alternatives that enable a communal sense of the self in relation to what there is. That work includes a rethinking, a philosophizing with a long memory, a looking again at these values, practices, understanding the recuperated sense of reality critically. That critical work needs to open and maintain possibilities of deep coalition with a long memory that is not just one of promoting one's own interests. That critical work also needs to avoid fixed cultural stereotypes and cultural fundamentalisms. The re-cuperation of the communal self understood and recreated as permeable rather than closed in circles of life and meaning is central to my thinking. In thinking and recreating with a long memory social, ecological, spiritual relations in particular habitats, we take them up as concrete and incarnate and think the body as lived in those realities. This thinking is not practical in the sense of contemporary renegotiating relations with the state or with capitalism but a practical look at pueblos as historical communal agents changing in the face of colonial intrusion seeking a reconstitution, a rec-reating, an enabling of the incarnate subject in an interconnected universe. This search calls us to rethink the most fundamental terms in which we think reality. With Segato I think that people's customs "are transformed constantly since a people's permanence depends neither on the repetition of their practices nor on the immobility of their ideas" (Segato 2011, 24).

References

Segato, Rita Laura. 2003. *Las estructuras elementales de la violencia: Ensayos sobre género entre la antropología, el psicoanálisis y los derechos humanos*. Brasilia: Universidad Nacional de Quilmes Editorial.

Segato, Rita Laura. 2011. "Genero y colonialidad: En busca de claves de lectura y de un vocabulario estratégico descolonial." In *Feminismos y poscolonialidad: Descolonizando el feminismo desde y en America Latina*, edited by Karina Bidaseca y Vaneza Vazquez Laba, 17–48. Buenos Aires: Ediciones Godot.

CHAPTER 3 | From Women's Movements
to Feminist Theories
(and Vice Versa)

MARÍA LUISA FEMENÍAS

IT IS NOT AN easy task to elucidate the general trends of feminist theory,
the vitality of women's movements, and the impact of gender categories in
Latin America in recent decades. With a strong propensity toward noncon-
ventional direct action and participatory structures of a communitarian,
congregational, and multisectoral variety, women are often at the center
of liberation movements. They promote national and transnational social
networks tied to peace processes, women's rights, and human rights in general, and more recently they fight against environmental pollution. I consider a "movement" a form of collective action that appeals to solidarity
in order to promote social changes, exceeding the limits of the system
of norms and social relations within which it operates, thus having the
capacity to produce new norms and legitimations in society (de Miguel
2000, 1). The practices of women's movements prefigure reality and subvert dominant cultural codes. This view does not aim to ontologize the
notion of "movement" itself (unless we develop an ontology of dynamic
facts rather than of substances); nor does it require a discourse about the
"Latin American Woman" identity, although it is possible to recognize
some common features among the women who populate our continent
(Femenías 2006, 2009, 2013, 2015).

Since the 1980s, the agenda of various women's movements received
the noticeable impact of gender categories and identity claims (Schutte
and Femenías 2010, 397–411). In addition, it was from the 1980s on that
the central axis of women's movements began to move from "equality" to
"identity" claims, bringing to the fore problems of sexual orientation, trans
identity, and ethnoracial claims. These heavily debated identity problems
were influenced and taken up by postmodern and decolonial discourses

María Luisa Femenías, *From Women's Movements to Feminist Theories (and Vice Versa)* In: *Theories
of the Flesh*, Edited by: Andrea J. Pitts, Mariana Ortega, and José Medina, Oxford University Press
(2020). © Oxford University Press.
DOI: 10.1093/oso/9780190062965.003.0004

(Schutte 2008, 165–67; Femenías 2005, 153–57; 2015, 138–39; Bidaseca 2011, 62–68; Espinoza Miñoso 2014, 8–12). The topic of the contributions and developments of Latin American feminisms calls for many discussions that I cannot develop in this essay. I therefore concentrate on offering a view and a critical analysis of the decolonial stance. I first briefly describe the decolonial stance and examine the work of one of its representatives. Subsequently, I focus on how several concepts ontologize themselves and how they ignore or minimize women's status, and hence the importance of their movements in the public sphere. Lastly, I describe my view on the question of identity and women's movements in public space.

Decolonial Turn

Decolonial thought calls into question epistemological frameworks that define the relations of domination of modernity, appealing to conceptual tools grounded in postmodern thought, subaltern studies, liberation theory, and the critique of enlightened universalism, among other frameworks (Bidaseca 2011; Schutte 2008; Femenías 2005, 2013, 2015, 2017; Palermo 2010a, 2010b, 2009a, 2009b, 2008, 2000). As a critical approach, decolonial thought has some advantages, among which I would like to highlight the following: (1) it goes along with what happens at the level of practices in ethno-racial movements; (2) it shows the necessity of "redistributing power" between racialized groups and hegemonic powers; (3) it renders more complex ways of understanding effective power networks; and finally, (4) it gives visibility to the work of some theorists who remain mostly peripheral within academia.

To begin with, it is clear that in Latin America, as in other parts of the world, "modernity" developed hand in hand with colonization. In a well-known work Serge Gruzinski denounced the colonization and transformation of Latin American social and cultural imaginaries, collective memories, and personal self-identifications of the communities of indigenous peoples. His work encouraged further research on "indigenous reactions" to models of conduct and thought introduced by Europeans, and further analysis of ways of perceiving the "new world" and "violence, chaos, and colonial domination" (1988, 13). Some decolonial works have made progress in this direction. Aníbal Quijano—as well as other decolonial researchers—considers that neither the church nor local groups that adopted the hegemonic viewpoint as a strategy for survival or for gaining prestige are exempt from responsibility in the process of colonization (Quijano 2000, 2011). He further says that if the "colonial" phase of "modernity" ended more than a century ago, "coloniality" remains. In fact, the concept of "coloniality" is coined in order to account for the persistence of certain structures that survive colonization as such. For if "colonialism" refers to historical occupation of America (among other places) by the British, the Spanish, the Portuguese, and the French using the model of territorial domination in their disputes, "coloniality," refers to a cultural strategy, that is, to the colonial heritage that persists and reproduces itself even after colonial occupation has ended (Mignolo 2007, 18–19). According to Mignolo, colonial heritage (a notion taken from Frantz Fanon) can be identified by certain fundamental features, such as racism, epistemic Eurocentrism, and violent or consented westernization of lifestyles (Mignolo 2007, 34). Other features pointed out by Mignolo are (1) economic domination (territorial appropriation, exploitation of local manual labor); (2) political control of authority; (3) control of gender and sexuality; and (4) epistemic and subjective control (Mignolo 2007, 36).

Although many of these features intersect, I will analyze them separately for the sake of investigating and presenting specific problems. According to Quijano, the coloniality of power does not only institute hierarchies in society, but also concentrates wealth and social privileges, putting "whites" at the top and racialized groups below (Quijano 2000, 2011). This "pigmentocratic" hierarchization evades the idea of the black/white racial binary, as in the United States, in a pernicious oversimplification, and disrupts the idea that Latinos have homogeneous political effects on our shared public culture (Femenías 2013, 224). That is, ethnicity is related to the politics of demarcating limits of a collective, making it possible to divide up the world between "us" and "them," thus erasing internal disagreements, in particular women's subaltern situation. Many female thinkers who accept the decolonial stance object to this sexist bias. Critical analyses, such as those of Silvia Rivera Cusicanqui, Gloria Anzaldúa, María Lugones (Femenías 2013, 215–35), Catherine Walsh (Palermo 2010a, 79–81), and Zulma Palermo herself formulate specific criticisms against this bias. In the next section I focus on some not widely known contributions of Zulma Palermo.

Zulma Palermo: Polyphony and Essentialism

Zulma Palermo (born in 1938), emeritus professor of the Universidad Nacional de Salta (Argentina) and essayist, focuses her research on Latin American cultural criticism, in particular on the local processes of orality/writing in pursuit of the role of university studies in Latin American countries (2010a, 2010b, 2009a, 2009b, 2008). She insists on the need to create ways to disarticulate the "coloniality of knowledge" (in Mignolo's sense), and on the need to develop strategic cultural constructions

(Palermo 2010b, 79–88). She submits that one cannot ignore either "colonial heritage" or "*frontería* and otherness" as complementary issues for the examination of the imaginary built in *this place* and from women's viewpoints (Palermo 2000, 478–79). That is, like Anzaldúa, she proposes to live-write "the border" (*frontera*). The issue of borders has been broadly studied throughout Latin America, with multiple cultural and ethnoracial meanings, and almost always as a contrast between selective binary pairs: educated/barbarian; white/Indian; Christian/untamed (Viñas 2003). Palermo situates herself in a space of fragile and unstable senses in perpetual tension (Palermo 2000, 478). Born and brought up in a boundary area at the border, what concerns Palermo is the border as a continuity, "a transit area," the "undefined border" of the Inca Empire before the conquest and the "unstable line," mobile and conflictive line of the wars of independence. According to Palermo, the border is the tense web of social, historical, and cultural belonging to the Alto Perú core, Aymara and Quechua, and the Spanish colonization. Perhaps that is the reason why she is not concerned about the self-other relationship, typical of the politics of recognition—an issue that she brands as "obsessive" in the current academic field (Palermo 2008, 1). Rather, she focuses on a "double need." On the one hand, there is the need to dismantle and revert the "coloniality of knowledge" from the "center of the imperialistic fallacies," and, on the other, there is also the need to build the "assertiveness of peripheries" (Palermo 2008, 2). That is, there is the need to deconstruct the distinctive consolidated image from the gaze of the other, typical of dependent cultures, not to be seen from "the place of subordination and impotence" (Palermo 2006, 216) but from assertiveness.

Bearing that goal in mind, Palermo examines the concerns of Latin American universities in our time. She demands the "availability to think" from a place *other*; different, but not excluding the center-Western design and structure. To think from that place *other* would allow for the enunciation of some concerns of nonmetropolitan universities, their bond with emergent systems of the economic globalization crisis, their rupture with the prevailing model that "validates the only way of knowledge, the European-centered *ratio*" (Palermo 2008, 4); and allow for the "release from epistemic coloniality" (2009b, 43).

Palermo holds that a radical reflection should be promoted about "where from, what for and who for" knowledge is given and built (2009b, 44). That is, the question is how to identify the localization, aims, and addresses of knowledge production. This is so because the "output of that critical decentralization" is a dialogical and polemic relationship between theoretical discourses that would contribute to the symbolic and ideological production of a culture that generates representations and social formations of *this place* (2008, 3–5). In that relational game, in a Latin

America "immobilized by the most deceptive ways of the projects of late capitalism," Palermo proposes to understand *her* cultural field (2006, 215), diving into the "multiform and heteroclitic constitution of subjectivities" in a network of "complex discursive weaves" (216). Questioning the "*mestizo* culture" category, Palermo also rejects notions such as "transculturation," "phagocytosis," "anthropophagy," and "hybridization," all of them, she asserts, emerging from the "global academy" and the Western episteme that describes all of Latin America as devaluated cultures (216–17).

For Palermo, "polyphony" is the most fruitful notion, given its productivity and explanatory capacity (2006, 213–15). Drawing on Peruvian Antonio Cornejo Polar, she claims that polyphony includes the discursive operation of otherness and allows validating the distinctive voices of "Latin American difference," bearing always in mind its resemantizations (216). The author also warns about the risks of metaphors, the trans(de) formations of the explanatory categories in their displacements between disciplines and geopolitical localizations, the construction of subjects *in* and *for* culture, the social operation of discourses, and, lastly, the oral texts of prealphabetical cultures in conflictive "contemporaneity with learned cultures" (217–18). Similar to movements in the 1960s, Palermo detects in the category of "Woman" a moment of strength and rebellion within an emancipatory attitude. Those emancipatory feminine subjects differentiate themselves from the familiar and social structure of domesticity and "transmute the feminine role itself," acquiring "a transvestism" with an "intensely feminine" look that allows for a redefinition of oppositions such as those of the countryside/city and barbarianism/civilization, and that opens public-political space for the textualization of experience beyond the domain of the household (2000, 487). Thus, she examines what she calls "woman's voice" (484), analyzing texts of border woman writers. She articulates these authors as "thinking the feminine issue," not in "oppositional difference," but rather in "relational contrast" with the discourses of the gendered *other*, and the "practices of patriarchal structure," and "values of colonial culture" within that construction of *the other* (485–86).

Suggestive as Palermo's proposals are, I am interested in raising some critical questions. To begin with, how are we to understand "polyphony" within the scope of "woman's voice?" Does "voice," as well as "woman," constitute a theoretical essentialized and homogeneous construction? How are we to make possible a dialogue between an essentialized collective that homogenizes voices, roles, and figures of "the feminine issue," with masculine voices built in the same way? How are we to understand that interlocutors validate themselves in a "wider dialogic space, Latin Americanism," *as if* masculine and feminine voices were per se equiphonic? The problem of essentializing some key concepts permeates Palermo's work. So, how to understand "difference" in "oppositional difference?" As Deleuze or Heidegger would use them? As Irigaray or Braidotti do? Similar problems arise by appealing to a "Latin American identity" without ever defining it. In addition, is essentialization favored by reinforcing a construction similar to "orientalism," as in Edward Said's work (Said 2002; Polo Blanco 2018)? That is, without confronting the decolonial theorists, as Lugones does, there are two consequences for Palermo: on the one hand, an essentialist shift that keeps women and their collectives bound to traditional definitions; and, on the other, the re-edition of the "theory of complementarity," defended by indigenous communities as well as by Christianism (Sciortino 2016, 106–7; Laurenzi 2012, 19–21). Palermo concludes—against Spivak (1999, 175)—that, based on "complementarity," listening to "feminine culture" is favored, diverging from the "manipulations of the literary market that successfully exploits the double marginality of the feminine and Latin American issues" (2000, 486). Palermo finds that "differentiation" in women's social relations is a process of weaving and examining "the role" and "the experience" of "Woman," which, expressed in the singular, quickly shifts toward essentialism and concealment of dissident voices. Does Palermo accept the essentialism already present in Quijano and other decolonial thinkers?[1] For the time being, I leave this question open, but will come back to it later.

Revisiting Decolonial Thought

To move forward, we thus need a new starting point. Teresa de Lauretis asserts that critical questioning is only possible after the abandonment of ideological complicity with the "oppressor," which means putting into action a deep change in consciousness (de Lauretis 1993, 74–75). Is Palermo (and other decolonial female thinkers) able to disidentify herself (themselves) from the gender biases of decolonial discourse, transform her (their) "scientific canon," and generate an alternative discourse? In the majority of cases, as in Palermo's texts, the discourse is caught up in essentialist commitments and stereotypes of "the culture of the weak" (2008, 139). That is, the adoption of certain notions according to their traditional meaning hinders them from challenging the biased conceptual cores of decolonial discourses. As Mellino asserts in his analysis of postcolonial thought—applicable to this case—adopting such notions would amount to "discourses between accomplices and critics" (2008, 122). In other words,

---

[1] Categories such as Nelson Maldonado-Torres's "coloniality of being" (2011), with an undeniable tie to Heideggerian philosophy, seem highly problematic. They take us back to the problem of essences and the ontologization of Being. Some Foucauldian categories, such as "disciplinary power" or "biopower," seem to be more useful for explaining relations of domination and subordination and processes of "westernization of lifestyles."

the gender critiques offered by decolonial female thinkers like Palermo are thwarted to the extent that such thinkers are not able to dismantle the founding sexist biases of their main authors' discourses.

If de Lauretis's goal was to constitute a cognitive practice and an "unusual knowledge" aware of eccentricity and change, Palermo, to a great extent, aims at building an eccentric locus to abandon the "objective no place of the Eurocentric position" and to denounce "colonial difference" (2010a, 80). But, despite her effort, she does not penetrate the conceptual correlation implicit in the enunciation, and essentialism reappears with its homologous voices. However, women's movements' claims in the public space show dynamics that refute ontologically closed positions. As I will show below, their negotiated identities mobilize a double dimension of individual and collective civic micronegotiations (Femenías 2013, 295–98).

Women make part of Quijano's classifications of "colonized races," including "Amerindians," "blacks," and, in a more complex way, "*mestizos*" (Quijano 2011, 208; 2000, 37–39). However, he considers each "colonized race" as a homogenous whole without recognizing the subaltern position of women, *as if* men and women had the same status. Also, he does not take into account their claims or the ways they establish their own voices in the public sphere. In this sense, although Quijano proposes a "redesign of power" in the social taxonomy of "races" and the "control of historical ways of labor" at a global scale (2011, 202), in no way does he suggest that such redistribution includes women qua a differentiated collective. When Palermo calls attention to women's subordination, denouncing the "patriarchal structures of coloniality" (2000, 486), she clashes with the theory of complementarity of sexes, without solving it (Palermo 2000, 485; Laurenzi 2012, 18–27). Regarding women, Quijano does not even submit strategies to revert their condition, consolidating, by omission, traditional cultural forms identified by their racial and territorial belonging, unaware of the sex-gender variable as a subordinating structure. However, as many studies show, the same women account for their discomfort and resistance in the face of certain traditional rites and customs, rites and customs that men claim belong to their ethnic and cultural identities. Consider, as an example, sexual "initiation rapes" or intrafamiliar violence or "disciplinary" violence (Tarducci 2013, 8–10; Sciortino and Guerra 2009, 100–124; Soza Rossi 2015, 128–36). To sum up, Quijano remains insensitive to the peculiar situation of women in colonized and noncolonized "races," and his homogenizing or essentializing prevents him from perceiving dynamically both structures of power (ethnoracial and sexual). Despite her efforts, Palermo inherits some of these difficulties not solving them.

A Dual Gaze

I concur with Yuval Davis and Amorós that ethnicity is not unique to oppressed minority groups. Hegemonic groups are sexually and ethnically
marked, even though men establish themselves as "neutral" by naturalizing a set of essentialized values with their ideologies and practices.
Their own benefits are at play in racism and sexism (Yuval Davis 2010,
66–67; Amorós 1998, 40–54), delegating to women the role of "symbolic
guardians of national purity," together with their own duties (Amorós
1998, 39–41; 2005, 63; Yuval Davis 2010, 65). The narrow link between
the colonial policies and the gender biases is sustained thanks to the implicit, interclassist, interethnic, and metastable "patriarchal agreements"
(Amorós 1990, 2), which reaffirm themselves in games of power that
consolidate double or bivalent hierarchical structures (1998, 40). Briefly
stated, my position is that the mainstream decolonial stance ignores the
subaltern status of women, whereas it builds only racialized, homogenous,
equiphonic, and equipotent collectives internally ignoring the sex-gender
variable. In the remaining sections of this essay, I develop the idea that
mainstream decolonial works do not use critically sex-gender-ethnorace
categories.

In my own view, "coloniality" should be understood as having (1) a
racial meaning articulated by, among others, decolonial thought; and
(2) a sex-gendered meaning articulated and denounced by feminists who
refer to the colonization of women under the headings "patriarchal ideology," "androcentric gaze," and/or "masculinist bias" (Amorós 1990, 2–
3; Femenías 2015, 137–46). If the first sense concerns racist discourses,
the second one concerns sexist discourses, which, based on biological,
ontological, cultural, religious, linguistic, and/or territorial assumptions,
legitimize exclusion, subordination, invisibilization, and/or exploitation of
women and of the sexually differentiated collectives. The acritical ways
in which many decolonial thinkers appeal to identity, constitute a serious
problem for women.

Negotiated Identities

To address how we might construct a theory of the subject or a social identity that would allow us to look in detail at the relationship between gender
and ethnorace to undermine the Western concept of a transcendental, unified, and rational subject would bring this essay out of focus. Parting company with essentialism and avoiding turning the insights from *this place
other* (Palermo 2008, 1–2) into relativism are not easy tasks (Femenías
and Soza Rossi 2011, 9–24). In order to understand identity as a political

and strategic construction, I start with Homi Bhabha, who acknowledges that identitarian constructions are created thanks to different discourses, practices, and positions (1994, 145; 2013, 23–44). Relationships between diverse identity movements are tense and difficult. Certain narrations can break with cumulative, continuing, repetitive, and recursive temporality to allow the emergence of the new and a move away from normative origins that respond to a bivalent culture: us/others; inclusion/exclusion. When social relations are articulated as plural structures of identification, they give rise to multiple, ambivalent, and "negotiated" identifications by virtue of priorities and needs, where some features are more persistent than others. Repetition in difference and successive shifts follow an always open process that is provisory and is an undetermined continuous production of identity. Socially and individually undetermined, the constant negotiation process of partial, variable, critical, and incomplete identities, in part individual and aware, in part collective and unconscious, intersects psychosocial variables, and makes of identity an always provisional result that works as a *supervenient* property. Acknowledging the instability and the constant pursuit of equilibrium facilitates dismantling rigid, closed, substantial, and determined traditional conceptions (Femenías 2013, 241–42).

The rejection of strong ontological conceptions of identity has led to the understanding of identities as strategic psycho-socio-political constructions. In this context, I propose to talk about *negotiated identities* and to situate them in the domain of *problems of negotiation*. This domain is informed by discrete interests and general objectives as well as by people's implicit psychic structures and implicit social powers. It is also under the influence of linguistic elements relative to one's native tongue(s) (including cases of plurilingualism), which shape styles of thought and access to "reality" and its problems.

In order to open up a space of negotiation, it is imperative to recognize that indigenous communities have suffered (and continue to suffer) the impact of conquest and colonization. The investigations of Silvia Rivera Cusicanqui, Irene Silverblatt, and Marisol de la Cadena, among many others, address intersectional issues of gender and ethnicity among indigenous women through an exhaustive historical analysis that takes the chronicles of the conquest as its source. This research sheds light on the role of women in the conservation and transmission of cultural patterns and rituals, as well as on how public policies of "assimilation-inclusion" or "ghettoization-marginalization" used women as mediators in various processes that worked jointly with other forms of power, such as those of the church, unions, and other social institutions. Research of this kind can help disclose the path of constitution of contemporary group identities, which can idealize, imitate, or underestimate the ethnic and cultural charge of those identities.

In order to negotiate group identities, it is necessary to work toward the cooperative resolution of conflicts, which is not always possible. There are two different strategies that seem to offer, in interesting ways, a basis for the negotiation of ethnicity and gender: the strategy around the notion of "positional objectivity," as defended by Amartya Sen (1993); and the strategy around the notion of "reflective equilibrium," as defended by Alicia Gianella (2001). In the former, there is an implicit appeal to the ideas of equality and universality, with the notion of "equivalence" underscoring irreducible particularity and normativity. In the latter, reflective equilibrium enables us to connect normative issues with concrete experiences and situations. For Gianella, reflective equilibrium is a tool for recognizing existing disequilibrium. Nonrecognized groups that aim at social change to meliorate their situation must work on two fronts simultaneously: on the one hand, generating new norms in the political sphere; and, on the other, producing substantive changes in practice. The recognition of instability and the need for constant negotiation contribute to a conception of reflective equilibrium understood as an aspiration that needs to take into account what Miranda Fricker calls "epistemic injustice" (2007, 1–2).

Both strategies can help us conceptualize and address issues of exclusion and can contribute to the development of an *eman(anti)cipatory imagination*. This imagination can provide the resources for anticipating a universality that has not yet been reached, a universality that cannot be imposed but should not be rejected either. Creating consensus and consciousness-raising with respect to inequity are pressing challenges and tasks that appear in different stages of development in Latin America. If inequality is not the same as difference, and equality is not the same as identity, cultural recognition must be gender-sensitive (or gender-conscious) because striving toward equality should not mean neglecting differences. To erase these tensions is to cover over the challenges that arise from efforts to articulate networks of inequality and conflict, and to erase the paradoxical tensions that emerge from outlining desires for translational bridges that we cannot help but want to construct.

Working with the notion of negotiated identities can be enlightening and enriching. Undoing ossified identitarian and identifying structures is a difficult process for both groups and subjects-agents. Promoting this debate and the progressive options within it already involves a game of negotiated identities and a critical revision of components of identity. This task would undoubtedly benefit women because it would favor analysis of the nexus that informs categories of ethnicity, sex, gender, class, religion, social status, sexual orientation, and so on, in order to affirm their negotiated inclusion in an open-ended set. In a process of nonnaturalized self-affirmation, critical space is fundamental. In this context, identity functions as if it were a supervening property capable of generating alternative social policies.

Open social and political structures favor such a dynamic. Understood as an unstable equilibrium, the notion of "negotiated identities" benefits women in particular, but also any other person who is willing to establish a critical relationship with oneself and with his/her environment. From a grid that comprises categories of ethnorace, sex-gender, class, religion, culture, sexual option, wishes, and personal interests, one chooses to belong to a certain group that is not determined a priori. In this way women's movements incorporate a certain implicit conception of identity, exercise it dynamically, and offer it to energize democratic life and processes of acknowledging and deepening equity.

Women's Movements / Women on the Move

In recent decades, certain claims have been developed that link social unrest to an "unusual multiplicity" called "new social movements" (de Miguel 2004, 12). Among these movements "women's movements" stand out: they are not homogeneous and they coalesce around identities built on the basis of concrete, circumstantial claims, limited to certain and clearly identified rights. They are highly dynamic and involve the restructuring of social and political organizations and practices implicit in the liberal state. That is, civil society, in its social dynamic dependent upon rights claims, expresses itself outside the political parties and other usual political structures. In general, women's movements that claim their rights, protest against sex-gender violence and feminicide, reclaim women of indigenous peoples, demand acknowledgment of sexual diversities, and so on, are ambivalent and even contradictory (Femenías 2013, 23–24).

However, if understood as collective action and experimentation in citizenship assertion, women's movements are seen as answering to a social dynamics ruled by urgency and intensity of demands. For some women theorists, these movements show the unequal distribution of authority among people and groups; for others, they obey a structural insufficiency in the distribution of the value of acknowledgment. Be that as it may, women's movements overflow the traditional channels of representation and, indirectly, denounce the deep distortion of representative institutions in place (Ferrajoli 2011, ix). Therefore, as an antidote, they use the social guarantee of civil surveillance, which is an effective use of public space based in democratic values (Ferrajoli 2011, viii). They jointly claim the intention of boosting their counterhegemonic voices and widening the democratic political horizon non absent of tensions. From a theoretical viewpoint, they move away from the risks of essentializing and homogenizing the whole, even if they use an identitarian, aggregative motto. In addition, since groups consolidate and reinforce themselves a posteriori, they benefit women from the outside of networks of hegemonic power.

Epilogue

As a closing thought, let's consider subjects and their identities as the effects of social discourses and practices that have to be specified. There cannot be a discourse of decolonization, a theory of decolonization, apart from decolonized practices. This means to question at the same daily practices and discourses. To begin with, the very concept of "colonization" has to be closely analyzed, as, for example, it means "races and cultures colonization" but also patriarchal "colonization" of women's minds, as is well known, which covers up and actualizes new forms of subalternity and dependence. Women's movements specify those practices in the public sphere. Although hegemonic decolonial thought does not account for them, they prefigure reality and subvert dominant patriarchal cultural codes. For instance, when Quijano encourages "redistributing power" between racialized groups, he excludes sex-gender power distribution. This is the case because he has homogeneously construed women and men as members of "the races," presupposing that their situation is equivalent. Mostly he refers to "women" as remaining naturally subordinated to the traditional order. Therefore, the coloniality of power does not only institute hierarchies in society, but also concentrates wealth and social privileges, setting "white men" at the top and racialized and sexual-gendered groups below, paradigmatically with women in a subordinate status. The construction of racial, essentialized, and homogeneous groups and of "the Woman's voice" is not a solution for subsuming the expressions of desires and needs in distinctive voices in women's movements, but rather is a fundamental problem. For its intrinsic democratic value, I call for a genuinely "polyphonic" presence of the plural voices of women in positions of political representation and in national and transnational public spaces.

Acknowledgments

I would like to thank Andrea Pitts, Mariana Ortega, and José Medina, who kindly invited me to participate in this volume, for their careful reading and valuable suggestions. As well, my acknowledgment to Graciela Vidiella and Maria Spadaro for our long conversations on the matter and to Paula Soza Rossi and Luisina Bolla for reading previous versions of this article, whose accurate recommendations I tried to include. Also, I want to thank Teresa La Valle, Andrea Altare, and José Medina for helping me with the English version.

References

Amorós, Celia. 1990. "Violencia contra las mujeres y pactos patriarcales." In *Violencia y sociedad patriarcal*, edited by Virginia Maquieira and Cristina Sánchez. Madrid: Pablo Iglesias Editores: 1–15.

Amorós, Celia. 1998. "Política el reconocimiento y colectivos bi-valentes." *Lógos, Anales del seminario de Metafísica* 1: 39–56.

Amorós, Celia. 2005. "Crítica de la identidad pura." *Debats* 89: 62–72.

Bhabha, Homi. 1994. *The Location of Culture*. London: Routledge.

Bhabha, Homi. 2013. *Nuevas minorías, nuevos derechos*. Buenos Aires: Siglo XXI.

Bidaseca, Karina. 2011. "Mujeres blancas buscando salvar a mujeres color café: Desigualdad, colonialismo jurídico y feminismo postcolonial." *Andamios: Revista de Investigación Social* 8, no. 17: 61–89.

de Miguel, Ana. 2000. "Movimiento feminista y redefinición de la realidad." *Mujeres en Red*. http://www.nodo50.org/altas.htm.

de Miguel, Ana. 2004. "Nuevos conflictos sociales, nuevas identidades sociales: La lucha por el reconocimiento." *Tabanque* 18: 11–30.

de Lauretis, Teresa. 1993. "Sujetos excéntricos: La teoría feminista y la conciencia histórica." In *De mujer a género*, edited by María Cecilia Cangiano and Lindsay DuBois, 71–114. Buenos Aires: CEAL.

Espinoza Miñoso, Yuderkis. 2014. "Una crítica descolonial a la epistemología feminista crítica." *Montevideo: El Cotidiano* 184: 8–12.

Femenías, María Luisa. 2005. "El feminismo postcolonial y sus límites." In *Teoría feminista: De la ilustración a la globalización*, edited by Celia Amorós and Ana de Miguel, 153–213. Madrid: Minerva Ediciones.

Femenías, María Luisa, ed. 2006. *Feminismos de París a La Plata*. Buenos Aires: Catálogos.

Femenías, María Luisa. 2009. "Género y feminismo en América Latina." *Debate Feminista* 20, no. 40: 42–74.

Femenías, María Luisa. 2013. *El género del multiculturalismo*. Bernal: UNQui.

Femenías, María Luisa. 2015. "Una mirada desde Latinoamérica: Feminismos, movimientos de mujeres y postcolonialidad." In *Sin género de dudas*, edited by Rosa María Rodríguez Magda, 137–46. Madrid: Biblioteca Nueva.

Femenías, María Luisa. 2017. "Algunos apuntes sobre feminismos en America Latina." *VirtuaJus* (Universidade Federal de Minas Gerais, Belo Horizonte, Pontificia Universidade Catolica de Minas) 13, no. 1: 48–73.

Femenías, María Luisa, and Paula Soza Rossi. 2011. *Saberes situados / teorías trashumantes*. La Plata: Facultad de Humanidades y Ciencias de la Educación.

Ferrajoli, Luigi. 2011. *Poteri Selvaggi: La crisi della democrazia italiana*. Rome: Laterza.

Fricker, Miranda. 2007. *Epistemic Injustice: Power and the Ethics of Knowing*. New York: Oxford University Press.

Gianella, Alicia. 2001. "The Reflective Equilibrium and Women's Affairs." In *Wissen Macht Geschlecht / Knowledge Power Gender: Philosophie und die Zukunft der "condition féminine" / Philosophy and the Future of the "Condition Féminine"*, edited by Birgit Christensen et al., 191–95. Zurich: Chronos.

Gruzinski, Serge. 1988. *La colonización del imaginario*. México City: Fondo de Cultura Económica.

Laurenzi, Elena. 2012. "Desenmascarar la complementariedad de los sexos: María Zambrano y Rosa Chacel frente al debate en la 'Revista de Occidente.'" *Aurora* 13: 18–28.

Maldonado Torres, Nelson. 2011. "Thinking through the Decolonial Turn: Post-continental Interventions in Theory, Philosophy, and Critique. An Introduction." *Transmodernity: Journal of Peripheral Cultural Production of the Luso-Hispanic World* 1, no. 2: 1–15.

Mellino, Miguel. 2008. *La crítica postcolonial*. Buenos Aires: Paidós.

Mignolo, Walter. 2007. *La idea de América Latina*. Barcelona: Gedisa.

Palermo, Zulma. 2000. "Una escritura de fronteras: Salta en el NOA." *INTI* 52–53: 477–88.

Palermo, Zulma. 2006. "Discursos heterogéneos, ¿más allá de la polifonía?" *Acta Poetica* 27, no. 1: 215–44.

Palermo, Zulma. 2008. "Conocimiento 'otro' y conocimiento del otro en América Latina." *Revista Estudios Digital* 1 (Spring): 1–6.

Palermo, Zulma. 2009a. *Arte y estética en la encrucijada decolonial*. Buenos Aires: del Signo.

Palermo, Zulma. 2009b. "La Universidad Latinoamericana en la encrucijada decolonial." *Otros Logos* 1, no. 1: 43–68.

Palermo, Zulma. 2010a. *Pensamiento argentino y opción decolonial*. Buenos Aires: del Signo.

Palermo, Zulma. 2010b. "Una violencia invisible: La 'colonialidad del saber.'" *Cuadernos de la Facultad de Humanidades y Ciencias Sociales, Universidad Nacional de Jujuy* 38 (July): 79–88.

Polo Blanco, Jorge. 2018. "Colonialidad múltiple en América Latina: Estructuras de dependencia, relatos de subalternidad." *Latin American Research Review*, 53, no. 1: 111–25. https://larrlasa.org/articles/10.25222/larr.243/.

Quijano, Aníbal. 2000. "Coloniality of Power, Eurocentrism, and Latin America." *Nepantla: Views from the South* 1, no. 3: 533–80.

Quijano, Aníbal. 2011. *Colonialidad del poder, globalización y democracia*. Caracas: Instituto de Estudios Internacionales Pedro Gual.

Said, Edward. 2002. *Orientalismo*. Barcelona: Debate.

Schutte, Ofelia. 2008. "Postcolonial Feminisms: Genealogies and Recent Directions." In *The Blackwell Guide to Feminist Philosophy*, edited by Linda Martín Alcoff and Eva Feder Kittay, 165–76. Malden, MA: Blackwell.

Schutte, Ofelia, and María Luisa Femenías. 2010. "Feminist Philosophy." In *A Companion to Latin American Philosophy*, edited by Susana Nuccetelli, Ofelia Schutte, and Octávio Bueno, 397–411. Oxford: Wiley-Blackwell.

Sciortino, María Silvana. 2016. "La emergencia de la violencia de género como tema *originario* en los procesos de organización política de las mujeres indígenas (ENM, 1986–2011)." In *Violencia contra las mujeres: La subversión de los discursos*, edited by Irma Colanzi, María Luisa Femenías, and Viviana Seoane, 87–114. Rosario: Prohistoria.

Sciortino, María Silvana, and Luciana Analía Guerra. 2009. "Un abordaje del feminicidio desde la convergencia entre teoría y activismo." *Revista venezolana de Estudios de la Mujer* (Caracas) 14, no. 32: 99–124.

Sen, Amartya. 1993. "Positional Objectivity." *Philosophy & Public Affairs* 22, no. 2: 126–45.

Soza Rossi, Paula. 2015. "¿Qué hora era? Algunas reflexiones sobre un toque de queda encubierto para las mujeres." In *Violencias Cruzadas*, edited by María Luisa Femenías, 127–38. Rosario: Prohistoria.

Spivak, Gayatri. 1999. "¿Puede el sujeto subalterno hablar?" *Orbis Tertius* 6: 175–235.

Tarducci, Mónica. 2013. "Abusos, mentiras y videos: A propósito de la niña wichi." *Boletín de Antropología y Educación* 4, no. 5: 7–13.

Viñas, David. 2003. *Indios, ejército y frontera*. Buenos Aires: Santiago Arcos Editor.

Yuval Davis, Nira. 2010. "Etnicidad, relaciones de género y multiculturalismo." In *Nación, diversidad y género: Perspectivas críticas*, edited by Patricia Bastida Rodríguez, Carla Rodríguez González, and Isabel Carrera Suárez, 64–86. Barcelona: Anthropos.

CHAPTER 4 | Enrique Dussel's *Etica de la liberación*, US Women of Color Decolonizing Practices, and Coalitionary Politics amid Difference

LAURA E. PÉREZ

IN ITS PRELIMINARY VERSION this essay was written for a panel at the American Academy of Religion in honor of Enrique Dussel's important and necessary work on the occasion of his seventieth birthday in 2004. Given that I am not a philosopher, theologian, or historian, all areas in which Dussel holds degrees and to which he has contributed prominently, and that I was then a newcomer to his work, I could only imagine that I was asked to join the panel of his specialists and collaborators in order to ensure that a US feminist-of-color and queer-centered engagement with his work was represented. Various symposia and lectures by Enrique Dussel and by Aníbal Quijano, organized by the Department of Ethnic Studies' Chicana/o Latina/o Studies Program, had produced in me and another feminist colleague the impression that they knew little about the US civil rights movements, and knew mainly about the African American struggles. They apparently knew nothing about the crucial feminist and queer contributions of US women of color to the racial, gender, and sexual civil rights struggles. As these encounters were organized to explore intellectual bridge-building in decolonial thought, as a woman of color, my own concern was not only to engage their thought as potentially useful to new transnational resistance movements, but also to clarify what our movements had discovered, either in parallel fashion or differently than leftist intellectuals and popular movements from the 1960s to the present in Latin America. I was concerned that the transnational circulation of knowledges not be one-way, reproducing past disencounters between US Latinas/os (Chicanas/os and Puerto Ricans) and Latin American

Laura E. Pérez, *Enrique Dussel's* Etica de la liberación*, US Women of Color Decolonizing Practices, and Coalitionary Politics amid Difference* In: *Theories of the Flesh*, Edited by: Andrea J. Pitts, Mariana Ortega, and José Medina, Oxford University Press (2020). © Oxford University Press. DOI: 10.1093/oso/9780190062965.003.0005

intellectuals, where the latter were paternalistic, condescending, and ill-informed in adopting Eurocentric classist and racist stereotypes that assumed the poverty of US people of color's cultural, intellectual, and political work, and especially effacing women of color's and queer work.

The rest of the all-male panel honoring Dussel in fact did not integrate a Latin American, Third World, or US Third World (also known as US women of color) feminist and queer critique as a common basis for critique of Eurocentrism or as a part of any decolonial project of liberation. As I was the only panelist to engage a critique of patriarchy and heteronormativity, quite apart from centering this concern in feminist of color queer thought,[1] I have here revisited the conference presentation and the longer version of the essay from which it was excerpted, revised in order to elucidate what it might mean to engage in coalitions that take feminist queer-of-color critical thought seriously as central to the work of decolonization. How do we move from agreement that patriarchy and heteronormativity are oppressive, beyond imagining that this democratizing aim is accomplished by identifying gender and sexuality in a laundry list of oppressions? Inviting representative speakers as the exception to disproportionately heteronormative male-centered spaces exercising their privileges in this regard, by refusing to seriously engage with racialized gender and sexuality themselves, unwittingly reproduces these inequities, in assigning feminist queer critique to the negatively gendered and sexed spaces of intellectual labor.

I have come to think that that labor belongs to us all, regardless of our own gender, sexuality, racialization, and other subject positionings or identifications. And from this perspective I want to argue that gender and sexuality critique is at the heart of decolonizing politics and that it is a labor that we must undertake collectively, in solidarity, and alongside the critique of our own subject formation.

I also want to propose that a decolonizing politics must produce new understandings from culturally and politically or ideologically different frameworks of what gets to count as knowledge, how being is understood, both individual and collective. Therefore a decolonizing politics must introduce, engage, and circulate previously unseen marginalized and stigmatized notions of "spirituality," "philosophy," "gender," "sexuality," "art," or any other category of knowledge and existence. As it simultaneously advances political, economic, social, and cultural struggles for greater democracy, I would also argue that a decolonizing politics resides in an embodied practice rooted in lived and livable worldviews or philosophies and is therefore in decolonizing relationship to our own bodies and

---

[1] On a second, related panel, the late Marcella Althaus-Reid presented a similar critique, grounded in her work as a Latin American feminist queer theologian.

to each other as well as to the natural world. It is therefore evident in our thought, scholarship, and interactions with each other, and it is critical and transformative not only of the racialization, ethnocentrism, and classism of Eurocentric capitalist and imperialist cultures, but also of patriarchal heteronormativity as central, highly normalized forms of domination that historically precede these and fundamentally structure the logic of colonization and its aftermath up to the present.

It matters that we learn to walk our brave decolonizing talk by taking upon and into ourselves the lessons of the negatively racialized, the negatively gendered, the negatively sexed in this era of increasingly economic, social, cultural, and legal disciplining (in the Foucauldian sense) of multiculturality, feminism, and queer cultures, where wealthy subjects of these communities are absorbed best in current US culture, while the vast majority continue to be castigated through stigmatization, exclusion, violence, and the burden of multiple oppression. Coalitions that are productive are based on principled associations of mutual understanding and respect, not just declarations of solidarity that mean well but because of privileges of class, "race" or ethnicity, gender, and sexuality do not engage the work of transforming such subjectivity. What this means concretely is the need to take upon ourselves the challenges made by the variously subjugated of our times. In effect, decolonizing practice cannot simply consist in affirming that we do not buy negative hierarchies of this type or we refuse to coproduce reality as we know it; it is to think critically enough about racialization, feminism, queerness, and economic exploitation that we are able to disarticulate the false projections in dominant cultural notions regarding its "others," but also the companion false idealizations and naturalized supervalorizations of the positively racialized, gendered, sexed, "able"-bodied, and prosperous within the mainstreamed dominant cultural social imaginaries. And it is to not go untouched ourselves, but rather to recognize ourselves among both the negatively and the positively constructed. It is to deracialize ourselves, ungender, unsex, and socially rethink ourselves. It is to begin to discover another way to be "male" or "heterosexual," for example. It is to feel there must be another way of being human and free (*debe haber otro modo de ser*).[2]

What I want to argue for is a profound solidarity based on a politics of identification with the otherness of the other as an imbricated, interdependent part of our own selves and being even as it is a recognition of the irreducible difference of the other as such. I am not referring to difference subsumed in a unity based on dominant cultural translations that in effect represses what is too different and/or challenging, that renders

---

[2] From Rosario Castellanos's (1925–1974) poem "Meditación en el umbral" (Castellanos 1985).

difference into "Same," or "Totality," as rightly criticized by both Lévinas and Dussel and many others.[3] It is based on a view that is not only native to the Americas, Asia, and Africa but present possibly even in pre-Christian "pagan" and nondominant European versions of subjectivity. For me, this concept comes through Buddhism and the Maya concept of *In'Laketch, tú eres mi otro yo,* you are my other self, that has been recirculated in the Chicana/o movement from 1965 to the present, as part of an indigenous American intellectual-spiritual-social worldview. That is, that though we are not identical, we are nonetheless also one. What this means to me is not only that your fate is tied to my own, but most to the point here that some of your own actual and seeming differences may also perhaps be part of my own potential subjectivity that present power relations have rendered other or mute within me. In attending to your otherness in a way that refuses to reduce or translate it into the sameness that is familiar to me, the possibilities of me knowing some other part of me is opened, such that if I were male, the cultural understanding of "female" and "feminine" as difference (to the "male," "masculine") would open up the so-called femaleness in me, just as so-called maleness opens me up to a part of my "female" self, to some degree, and just as queer politics opens up the queerness within heterosexuality as well as different and earlier constructions of a femme or butch lesbian or male gay identity. For me, then, solidarity and coalition inevitably entail the degendering and de-heteronormativizing of our conscious subjectivities, alongside class consciousness and awareness of racialization as the idealization and rendering invisible and normal of "whiteness" and the negative marking of Third World difference as the site of the enactment of racial difference.

Addressing the hidden politics of privilege (evident in the refusal to see our imbrication, our direct tie to the interests of "the other") in and among ourselves is crucial to the task of understanding what decolonization itself might mean and therefore entail for a decolonizing practice, or a "praxical" or "theoretico-practical" thinking, as philosopher María Lugones (2003) has called it, because gender and sexuality, alongside class and racialized ethnic differences, are at the core, not the margin of, or epiphenomenal to, mutually constitutive geopolitical, economic, social, and cultural oppressions.

---

[3] See, for example, Emmanuel Levinas: "In this whole priority of the relationship to the other, there is a break with a great traditional idea of the excellence of unity. The relation would already be a deprivation of this unity. That is the Plotinian tradition. My idea consists in conceiving sociality as independent of the 'lost' unity." And, "This is the excellence of the multiple, which evidently can be thought of as the degradation of the one" (Levinas 2006, 112, 113). Also see Dussel's discussion of Levinas's *Totalité et infinité: Essai sur l'extériorité* (1968) on "the incomprehensibility of the presence of the Other" (2000, 363).

The feminist critiques of patriarchal, racialized imperialism and capitalism are basic observations in Chicana and African American feminist thought dating at least to the late 1960s and throughout the 1970s. The imbricated, mutually constitutive and simultaneous functions of these oppressions and their root in the colonial encounter were analyzed in essays originally published throughout the late 1960s and the 1970s by Chicanas Anna Nieto Gómez and Elizabeth "Betita" Martínez, by African American feminists Audre Lorde of the Combahee River Collective (1977) and Angela Davis, and in the landmark anthology *This Bridge Called My Back: Writings by Radical Women of Color* (1981).[4] The powerful contribution of these and other women of color feminists of the civil rights struggles to decolonizing liberation struggles, and to decolonizing thought, has been carefully reflected upon and theorized, in its common characteristic "differential consciousness" by which to survive dominant multiple cultural oppressions and to in turn wield agile movement through them, in Chela Sandoval's *Methodology of the Oppressed* (2000). Most recently, and also rooted in US women of color feminist and queer thought, the philosopher María Lugones has made an important critique of, and intervention in, the development of Peruvian sociologist Aníbal Quijano's theory of the "coloniality of power" that naturalizes heteronormative patriarchy in its use of seemingly universal categories of gender and sexuality that are in fact rooted in colonialism and are unlike precolonial and non-Western gender formations that appear more liberatory (Lugones 2007).[5]

Ghettoized as minority women's or queer reading, US women of color feminist and queer decolonial thought remains largely "unknown," uncited, or unengaged in the work of Latina/o and Latin American thinkers and dominant cultural Euro-American feminists, with the notable exception of queer and/or trans scholars, like Luis León, Pedro DiPietro, and Randy P. Conner. This itself is symptomatic of the patriarchal, heteronormative lens still dominating liberatory thought and practice in geopolitically and nationally marginalized thought, as among dominant cultural feminisms and other progressive thought. Patriarchal and heteronormative privilege has characterized the failures of the Nicaraguan and Cuban

---

[4] Some key early Chicana feminist writings of the late 1960s and 1970s, including those referred to here, can be found in Alma Garcia's anthology *Chicana Feminist Thought: The Basic Historical Writings* (1997). Some of Audre Lorde's writings of the 1970s can be found in *Sister Outsider: Essays and Speeches* (1984). The Combahee River Collective's 1977 statement and other important African American feminist writings can be found in *The Black Feminist Reader*, edited by Joy James and T. Denean Sharpley-Whiting (2000).

[5] See, for example, the work of Will Roscoe (2000) on the "berdache" or third-gender idea that was common and, in many cases, honored among the peoples of the Americas before the European invasions. For the latter phenomenon in present-day Burkina Faso, see the works of Malidoma Patrice Somé and Sobonfu Elizabeth Somé and the "gatekeeper" function of the queer in the Dagara tribe in, for example, Somé 1997. See also Sparks, Sparks, and Sparks 1998.

socialist revolutions, as it has the US Left and nationalist or ethnic/"racial" civil rights movements of the United States, as the emancipation of "mankind" has literally turned out to be most for the interests of heterosexual men rather than the universal liberation of humanity, as most women have been marginalized from equal power and burdened with double labor (at home and work), while queers have been criminalized as degenerates or closeted.

Interrupting (Neo)colonizing Inequities within Latin American and US Latina/o Studies

The panel organizer invited the panelists to discuss how we had become familiar with Dussel's work. This account allows for the elucidation of my location and my ideological formation as a means of contextualizing my approach to, and dialogue with, the work of Dussel in his *Etica de la liberación* and a disclosure of my profound investment, my stake, in his intellectual work in my local and global coalitionary concerns.

In doing so I reject the criticism that disclosure of the personal—that is, that making use of the autobiographical as so many women of color writers have in the United States—unwittingly reinforces the feminizing by dominant cultural intelligentsia of people of color's intellectual work (whether artistic or scholarly), relegating it to something beneath the philosophical "I" or "we." The historically specific embeddedness and the interests behind the pretension to transhistorical universality, reason, and truth are insights common to US women of color, as they are in poststructuralist thought. Women of color's autobiographical writing and locating of self within scholarly texts has often staked a claim to theory and philosophizing itself, but through a consciously different protocol than that imposed by academia or literary canons yet knowingly positioning these as alternative archives of knowing and being. Furthermore US women of color repeatedly speak from the heart in defense of love, of the humane, and against that which is dehumanizing.

I perhaps first heard about Dussel from Latin American scholars in the early 1990s at the University of Michigan, Ann Arbor, where I began my teaching career. There I developed and taught comparative twentieth-century Latin American and US Latina feminist and queer literatures, as a joint appointment in the Department of Romance Languages and Literatures and the Program of American Cultures. I had just written a dissertation studying the relationship between art and political thought and practice among the right-wing Nicaraguan literary avant-gardists of the late 1920s and 1930s, intending by this focus to contribute to a broadening of the Latin American canon of literary scholarship that marginalized Central

America and the Caribbean in favor of Mexico and parts of the Southern Cone. I had also just emerged from years of graduate student activism at Harvard University that included opposition to US military intervention in Central America and leadership in the student-led antiapartheid movement. My key contribution was to lead the successful nonviolent demand for divestiture through a petition drive gathering thousands of signatures at the shantytown we erected in the middle of campus.

These years, the second half of the 1980s, were years of building multicultural coalitions in both student and community activism. On campus, many worked together in a Third World student coalition, just as off-campus, multiethnic activists worked in Jesse Jackson's historic national Rainbow Coalition, which reached out to disenfranchised poor white farmers and unemployed steelworkers, as well as to the oppressed ethnic minority groups from which it sprang. I worked in both of these and other organizations as a campus and community activist.

My undergraduate and graduate training in the field of Latin American literary studies was both a choice made through my love of the arts and my desire to understand their relationship to the creation of a better world, and an affirmation against the blatantly racist marginalization of the Spanish-speaking cultures that I had experienced in Chicago growing up during the 1960s and 1970s.

And yet my study of Latin American literature, history, and economics, as well as my growing interactions with Latin Americans and travel to Latin America, led me to the painful and repulsive observation that racism and a particularly sharp form of classism operated there, too. In spite of leftist "anti-imperialist" critique of the United States and its racism, I found that Latin American discourses of mestizo and mulatto or mixed-"race" national identity were what I have since come to call theories of *Euromestizaje* and *Euromulataje*. They were theories of "racial" or ethnic and cultural hybridity that maintained European and Euro-American cultural and physical standards as measuring sticks of progress and beauty and thus remained Eurocentric.

For even in the inspired writings of the great Cuban poet and political figure José Martí, in his descriptions of the thick-blooded, slow-moving sons of the indigenous and African, or in the supporters of the Mexican Revolution, who largely rendered the indigenous peasants as mute objects, foregrounding the white-identified middle class, or in the so-called Boom writers of Latin America, with their heroes mocking the *cabecitas negras*, the black-haired popular classes as Cortázar put it in *Rayuela*, more often than not, I encountered not a liberating mirror but rather the paradox of a Latin American classist racism and sexism, alongside patriarchy and heteronormativity. Furthermore in the fields of literary and art-historical studies the assumption was, and remains, that Chicanos and Puerto Ricans, in particular, would progress beyond our unimportant or unsophisticated cultural and intellectual productions in the United States once we achieved more "culture." But we'd no doubt always be lagging behind the already anxiously lagging Latin Americans themselves.

To me the dominant culture of Latin America, from which proceeded a good portion of its leftist individuals, was two steps backward. Unlike those in Latin America who could pass as such and actually thought of themselves as white, and who evidently continued to buy into a Eurocentric model of cultural progress and experienced class or racialized privilege, the US civil rights movements taught us not to be ashamed of being mestizo, that is, partly indigenous or African-diasporic, "mulatto," or of simple or humble social or economic origins, but rather to be ashamed of trying to pass for "white" or non-Latino at the expense of those who could not. Accordingly, in the 1960s and 1970s Chicana/o, alongside African American, Asian American, and Native American, intellectuals, with the help of other progressive allies, were pioneering a decolonizing route of studies and consulting Third World sources to build their knowledge of the histories of oppressed, negatively racialized minority communities and to disarticulate racialized oppressions.

As I learned more about the interdisciplinary field of US ethnic studies in the 1980s, I gravitated toward it increasingly. I took a semester in graduate school to study with a Chicano professor, Tomás Ybarra-Frausto, at Stanford and began developing Chicana/o, US Latina/o, and comparative US Latina/o and Latin America literature and then, later, visual and performance art courses. Dussel's *Etica de la liberación en la edad de la globalización y la exclusión* (Ethics of liberation in the age of globalization and exclusion) was published the year before the Department of Ethnic Studies student-led 1998 strike, the first University of California, Berkeley, protest of the neoliberal downsizing of the public and private university system through the policy of no longer guaranteeing renewal of faculty losses. In our already small department, our losses would have decimated our hard-earned and highly successful department.

The strike, called on the thirtieth anniversary of the foundation of our department, was unanimously supported by the Ethnic Studies faculty, and I took an active part in it. Soon after, as a further act of solidarity, I switched what had been a joint appointment with the Department of Spanish and Portuguese, where Latin American literary studies were housed, to a full appointment in the Department of Ethnic Studies.

It was quite clear to me before doing so that a full-time affiliation with the Department of Ethnic Studies would constitute a loss of intellectual capital in a largely Eurocentric UC Berkeley. I also knew that the field of ethnic studies has transformed every branch of the humanities and social sciences, though it is disciplined by the routine negation, marginalization, caricaturization, and uncredited absorption of its historically crucial and transformative scholarship and theory. Perhaps the most difficult and important task of the 1950s and 1960s civil rights era ethnic, feminist, and queer studies programs in the United States has been to decolonize the epistemologies that we have been handed, embedded as these have been in sexist, homophobic, and racist cultural Darwinism. The critique of Eurocentrism has been a foundational building block of our intellectual and activist work since the 1960s and in the earlier thought of Du Bois at the beginning of the twentieth century, Américo Páredes in the Texas of the 1920s through the 1950s, and, before then, even among Mexican women writing or speaking about their cultural disencounters with uncouth, usurping Anglos shortly after the annexation of Mexico in 1848.

Ethnic studies scholarship and teaching are literally activism in the face of entrenched, sometimes subtle, hegemonic Eurocentrism. The road to ethnic studies scholarship is lined with the roadside graves of dropouts, even at the professorial level, with suicides and early deaths, with psychological and physical ailments related to frustration, stress, and bouts of defeatism. And women of color, in particular, have encountered harassment and hounding even from our own ethnic studies colleagues and have been literally driven from the university. This is the toll that working in hostile, constantly delegitimizing environments takes. Throughout the disciplines, there are still too few of us from oppressed or discriminated-against minority communities. At the University of California, Berkeley, housed in the state with the largest Mexican American population in the country, whose origins as a part of the United States date to the imperialist annexation of Mexico in 1848 and before that, for some, to indigenous ancestors native to the territory, I am the only female Chicana professor in the entire College of Letters and Sciences. The number of other oppressed minority women and queer professors and graduate students on campus is likewise indefensible. The logic that there aren't enough of us who are good enough to teach at the best universities, whether because of supposedly inadequate training or because of racialized and sexist bias against us that holds us to higher standards while simultaneously minimizing and subestimating our achievements, is a self-fulfilling, self-serving, and unworthy assumption rooted in, and propagating, the living legacy of patriarchal, racist imperialism.

Part of my practice as an activist intellectual, meaning a consciously decolonizing scholar and teacher, has been to read and honor and thus incorporate the work of fellow ethnic, gender, and sexuality minority scholars, not only because they are still the principal experts in these fields but quite pointedly because of their marginalization in mainstream academia, where their work is often appropriated or tokenized. To cite them extensively outside of their own fields has often produced a loss of cultural capital in the mainstream of a still patriarchal, heteronormative, Eurocentric academy since it won't acknowledge what it doesn't want to know. But ethnic, gender, and sexuality minority scholars have looked widely for, indeed anywhere we might find, allies, and this has produced particularly rich, intellectually coalitionary thought in these fields. For ethnic studies, for example, anti- and postcolonial studies, in particular the work of Frantz Fanon, Ngũgĩ wa Thiong'o, Stuart Hall, Edward Said, and Gayatri Spivak, which has similarly attempted to grapple with the condition of, and democratic possibilities for, the oppressed minority or the ex-colonial within the center, has been very useful.

But with respect to Latin America, Chicana/o intellectuals and artists of the 1960s and 1970s identified with the subjugated there, with Mexico's Native American and mestiza/o popular classes, rather than with its racist elites. Many tried to build bridges with Latin American fellow artists, intellectuals, and activists to be met with racist classism. Why should we bother to read more Eurocentric, Latin American, heterosexist and elitist men and women? From Paz to Canclini, seemingly-in-the-know belittling appraisals or dismissals of our work, though shockingly uninformed, continue to be churned out.[6] Even among recent Latin American feminist and queer theorists, the generalizations or aporias based on little to no knowledge remains striking about Latinas and other US women of color.

My interest in Dussel's work, the possibility of coalition with it, therefore has to begin with how he conceives of gender, sexuality, racism, and social change. I wondered what Dussel's attitude to us was, and I hoped it would not be yet another condescending lecture on what we US Latinas/os should do, without having informed itself deeply of what we have done. Would this be yet another US Latina/o–Latin American *desencuentro*, or disencounter, so familiar to Chicana intellectuals and artists in conferences and panels with condescending, upper-middle-class, and "white" Mexican feminists?

Dussel's *Etica*, and the Difference Gender and Sexuality Make in Liberatory Thought and Struggle

Etica is a major work, hailed by philosophers as his most important work, and demonstrating the constant evolution of his thought.[7] It is, however,

---

[6] Notable exceptions are the writings of performance artist Guillermo Gómez-Peña and ethnic studies-trained Mexican scholar Marisa Belausteguigoitia, and another longtime resident of the United States, Walter D. Mignolo, whose influential work on border gnoseology is heavily indebted to Chicana queer writer Gloria Anzaldúa's *Borderlands/La Frontera: The New Mestiza* (1987).

[7] See the essays of James L. Marsh and Eduardo Mendieta in Alcoff and Mendieta 2000.

ultimately a work for philosophers trained in European intellectual history, particularly in the philosophy of those with whom Dussel's work is most in dialogue, including Marx, Lévinas, Foucault, and Karl-Otto Apel, though Dussel takes care in his opening pages to note his intention that it not be for "minorías," but rather that it be an "*ética cotidiana, desde y en favor de las inmensas mayorías de la humanidad excluidas de la globalización*," a "quotidian ethic from and in favor of the immense majorities of globalization's excluded humanity" (2000, 15).[8]

Among many objectives, in *Etica* Dussel further develops his belief that philosophy is ultimately ethical, as the most basic task of humanity is living and thus the obtaining of sustenance that makes this possible. Thus, philosophy must fundamentally concern itself with both the ethical and the economic, as both are concerned with the most basic necessities that make existence possible. He therefore writes against the unethical and irrational core of capitalist ideology and the current multinational corporate globalization that in enriching the relatively few impoverishes the world's hungry masses even unto the death. Given the global hegemony of the European and Euro-American of the last five hundred years that ground the misery of the Third World and of the most exploited within the First World, he reviews his early critiques of the core myths of Eurocentrism that have justified imperialism and capitalism as parts of inevitable historical progress, and racism as natural and just.

My focus in reading *Etica* has primarily been to locate key nodes of intellectual solidarity with his project, from a US feminist-of-color and queer-centered perspective, however also identifying elements of his work that call for further reflection. I will limit myself to addressing five major tenets of his work, comparing these whenever possible to similar positions that emerge from the US racial, gender, and sexual civil rights movements and their intellectual and political achievements. I also will discuss the latter in some detail, when useful.

In *Etica* Dussel recognizes the importance of oppression beyond class or simultaneously with it by other forms of exploitation, exclusion, and marginalization that render a wide range of people victims, as he puts it (Deleuze and Guattari 1985). The US civil rights struggles were organized through coalitions that cut across differences with greater or lesser success, yielding important lessons that are relevant to my reading of *Etica*. To the degree that coalitions across differences within a negatively racialized group, such as the Chicano or African American / Black Power movements, marginalized and exploited women and were homophobic, they were criticized internally by women of color within each of the different groups, for

---

[8] All translations of Dussel's work from the Spanish into English are my own.

reproducing patriarchal heteronormativity. To the degree that the former failed to address class exploitation, they also produced a small percentage of economic and social successes against the vast majority of impoverished and marginalized populations for whom stigmatizing racialization is exacerbated rather than, as in the former's cases, ameliorated. With respect to the feminist movements that organized coalitionally across "race" and "class," to the degree that they reinscribed racism, Eurocentric privilege, or disinterest in economic democracy, "white" feminism elicited criticism from US women of color, as well as women in the Third World, for universalizing their own hegemonic interests within their critique of a similarly sanitized and depoliticized notion of patriarchal oppression.

At least as early as the late 1960s and throughout the 1970s, US women of color criticized dominant cultural feminism's notion of gender as essentialist and falsely universal, proposing more accurately that patriarchy does not oppress women in the same way or for the same reasons and that women of color in the United States therefore experienced "double," "triple," or "multiple" oppressions, in shifting or simultaneous fashion. They argued that these oppressions, differently experienced within the different negatively racialized groups, were the living legacies of US imperialism and slavery and nation-building where Native American, African, and Mexican American were incorporated into the national imaginary in difference to racially privileged Euro-American womanhood.

The gay and lesbian movements also organized across various differences, and to the degree that they operated hegemonically, were also called on their racism and/or class privilege. Since at least the 1980s in print, assumptions about the universality of European histories of sexuality have also been critiqued, with research in the last two decades indicating cultural difference in the understanding and practice of both gender and sexuality in Native American, African, and other world cultures.

Coalition as "Third World" (which includes Native American peoples though they are native to the United States) also characterizes activism from the 1960 through the present. US women of color worked in coalition under the rubric US Third World women in recognition of the similarities in the general phenomena of their racialized, gendered, sexed, and economic oppressions among themselves, between themselves, and with women in the Third World, vis-à-vis European and Euro-American (neo)colonialism. College and university students, faculty, and staff also worked throughout campuses in the United States in "Third World" activist coalitions to decolonize and desegregate education. They founded the Department of Ethnic Studies at San Francisco State University and University of California, Berkeley, in 1968 and 1969, respectively, and more specific programs, such as African, Native, Asian American, and Chicana/o studies.

US Third World campus coalitions led movements to broaden the Eurocentric canon throughout the 1980s and thereby helped create multicultural American studies programs and departments across the nation. They participated in solidarity movements against US military interventions and war in the Third World and the Middle East, in the anti-apartheid movement, and in the historic electoral campaigns of people of color. Finally, people of color in coalition characterized the rise of an organized US Third World Left, whose important history remains to be written, in terms of both its material accomplishments and its theoretical developments.

Thus, to return to Dussel, his shift in *Etica* from a language preferentially opting for the poor to that of the broader category of "victims," as well as his critique of Lenin's theory of leftist intellectuals as "the vanguard" of social change, concords with the many lessons of civil rights struggles in the United States of the last forty years. History has shown in the United States what those suffering the most multiple oppressions, queer women of color, have theorized for themselves that "in the final analysis," the reality of materially and psychically surviving, negotiating, and outsmarting lived multiple oppressions exceeds the abstract privileging of one over another, as Chela Sandoval has carefully argued in her *Methodology of the Oppressed* (2000). The concept of "victim" allows Dussel in effect to arrive at a theory of simultaneous oppressions compatible with that of US women of color, which he exemplifies in the multiple subject positionings of Rigoberta Menchú, the Guatemalan Maya Quiché activist and Nobel Prize winner, noting her oppression by gender, ethnicity, "race," deterritorialization, legal exclusion, social marginalization, poverty, class, illiteracy [*sic*], being Guatemalan (Dussell 2000, 13, 514).[9] I will address the difference, however, in the significance that the concept of simultaneity of oppressions makes in their thinking shortly.

The second key aspect of Dussel's *Etica* that I want to single out is his return of economics to the critique of power and oppression. Dussel's rereading of Marx as he begins to try to theorize beyond dogmatic leftist ideologies and the specter of authoritarian and abusive communist and socialist regimes is courageous in the current ideological climate. His close reading of Marx and ongoing reintegration of his thought into an ethics of liberation is likely to benefit from reflection on the difference that gender and sexuality make economically in light of the facts that the majority of the world's poor are women, including those of First World nations, and that women are the half of humanity from whom superprofit continues to be exploited in their formal and informal labor; in their disproportionate

---

[9] Rigoberta Menchú's life story widely circulated in various languages after its 1983 publication (Burgos-Debray 1985).

domestic and unpaid burdens that reinforce and enable their loss of social and cultural capital as well; and across education and employment differentials. To what degree is European patriarchy foundational and enabling of imperialism, capitalism, and neocolonizing discourses? (Freedman 2002, chs. 6 and 7).

Though the face of the symbolic victim that he sometimes pictures in his book is that of a poor, Native American woman, this is to be understood as only a stand-in for the more general category of all manner of present and future victims human societies can expect to continue producing: "*El Otro será la/el otra/o mujer/hombre: un ser humano, un sujeto ético, el rostro como epifanía de la corporalidad viviente humana; será un tema de significación exclusivamente racional filosófico antropológico*" (Dussel 2000, 16; The Other shall be the other woman/man: a human being, an ethical subject, the face as an epiphany of a living human corporality; it shall be an exclusively rational anthropological philosophical theme of signification). But it seems that what he best theorizes and what is the cornerstone of his philosophy of ethics is, in practice, the condition of poverty and the alienation of labor "*desde*," or from, the greatest understanding of the existence and conditions of the exploitation of poor or otherwise oppressed and excluded heterosexual men. The critiques of patriarchy and heteronormativity are not only on par with the other major forms of domination he analyzes carefully—Eurocentrism, capitalism, (neo)colonialism—but are intrinsic to these and arguably have at least as much to reveal about the logic of domination during at least the last five hundred years. Gender and sexual identities thus remain occluded as persistent sites of the reproduction of both otherness and privilege.

In 2000 Dussel had the occasion, in an epilogue he wrote to a collection of essays on his work, to address previous feminist and queer critiques of his earlier work (Alcoff and Mendieta 2000, 284–86). His response to the critique of his work in the volume by the feminist theologian Elina Vuola is useful here. In his defense he notes major transformations of his thought and correction of earlier views of women defined in terms of their sexual reproduction, and therefore of lesbianism and abortion as denials of life. He argues that it would have been "impossible" to hold other views at the time, however, and ahistorical to expect more from him in 1972, given that feminist criticism had not yet emerged in liberation philosophy. He points out that feminist liberation theology was possible to begin with because of liberation theology. To the degree that male centrism elicits the correction of its self-interest masquerading as universality, this would be true. But patriarchal conceptions of liberation theology as a universal theology cannot be credited with the discourse developed by feminist thought to critique it. Dussel also writes, "I think that liberation philosophy, in any event was the first philosophical movement that spoke at the beginning of the 1970s

of the 'liberation of women' as a critique against patriarchal ontology"
(Alcoff and Mendieta 2000, 285–86), a hypothesis that might well be true
within male philosophy, but that erases the work of feminist philosophers
Simone de Beauvoir and Rosario Castellanos. Finally, Dussel suggests
that the apparently late development of feminism in Latin America made
his theorization of the simultaneity of oppressions similarly impossible at
that time (286), a proposition that is also unpersuasive, given the important
body of work on the history and contribution of feminism in the nineteenth
and twentieth centuries in Latin America, such as that of Francesca Miller
(1991).

Dussel's response here and his treatment of gender and sexuality in
Etica is frankly disappointing from a feminist- and queer-centered point of
view, positions his philosophy wishes to represent as "victims" and to be
in solidarity with. Because of his limited engagement with the difference
in interests and desires with respect to normative patriarchy and heteronormativity, he unwittingly translates out the difference into the Same that he
wishes to avoid in any situation of power differential. His countercriticism
of feminist criticism of his work above not only fails to convince but fails
to sufficiently engage the invitation to examine the charge of his unwitting yet embedded patriarchal and heteronormative privilege. He ends his
response to Vuola by announcing that a rethinking of masculinity by him
is "a task already undertaken but will be developed further in the future."
Without wishing to be unkind, it is nonetheless worth reflecting upon the
fact that "second wave" feminist and queer movements and discourses
have been circulating throughout the world for forty years, and that "first
wave" feminist thought dates to the nineteenth century.

To continue with a related and third point of importance that also
requires further reflection, in his *Etica*, Dussel provides a defense of the
need for a constant critical consciousness that is attentive, precisely, to the
inevitable imperfections and thus social exclusions and blank spots of all
systems, suggesting that with a genuinely democratic sensitivity lies precisely in this capacity for constant self-criticism with regard to one's own
exclusions of new others.

Thus, Dussel points us to one of the most basic questions of all: What
is an ethics of coexistence and coalition amid differences whereby the empowerment of some is no longer achieved through social, economic, cultural, psychological, and physical violence toward others in minimizing
and negating them? I will add, how can the more fully empowered, precisely by virtue of their own imbricated simultaneity of racialized, gender,
sexual, and economic privileging, be made to understand that the unjustly oppressed and the unjustly overpowered are both dehumanized in
the exchange? Women of color in the United States have largely written
from below, as it were, because our communities have historically been

systematically stripped of power. Regardless of educational and professional achievement, we continue to experience racialized gender and cultural oppression, economic exploitation, and social disenfranchisement, but as a whole, our intellectuals and artists theorize as part of the oppressed. We are not the spokespeople of others or on their behalf, as I have already said. But how might we begin sharing power with the variously disempowered to speak for themselves without our mediation or translation, even as we refuse to essentialize such differences as incomprehensible? We speak for ourselves, our communities, and in coalitionary recognition of what we share with each other and what is nonetheless specific and different in our experiences of oppression in the United States. Dussel's *Etica* is supportive in addressing the inappropriateness, as history has shown, and the contradictions of elitist conceptions of a vanguard leading and directing the masses and speaking for them rather than struggling to empower them to speak on their own behalf.

Fourth, Dussel's *Etica* assumes that violence is, at times, necessary to eliminate the violence of the dominating unjust (e.g., 2000, 533). The success, precisely on the basis of their ethical coherence in limit situations, of Mahatma (Mohandas K.) Gandhi, Martin Luther King Jr., and Chicano farmworker leader César Chávez and of the achievement of the various civil rights as a whole invite a serious reckoning with the power of nonviolent activism, arguably as the most socially and long-lasting transformative or "radical" means of personal and social change. What radical thought must further explore, and redefine, are the cultural assumptions that naturalize violence as an essentially dominant or necessary part of human nature and in many situations, and not just limit situations, a legitimate form of behavior, as the new field of peace studies is showing us (see, e.g., Nagler 2001). And more broadly, what other forms of violence, such as discursive violence, sustain the thought and practice of both (neo)colonialism(s) and capitalism? Love, in material practices of care, of the materially poor or politically disenfranchised is the basis of Dussel's ethics. But how does this Christian philosopher reckon with the radical idea of loving the enemy, of refusing to dehumanize the dehumanizer and thus resisting our own dehumanization—an idea that is common to culturally varied spiritual philosophies that see all of creation as essentially one? What greater otherness can we experience than that which we feel for those we perceive as enemies, as deserving of their own destruction? What is the connection between this type of thinking and the otherization of Europe and then of Euro-America's own nonwhite others? Of heteronormative patriarchy's queer and female(d) others?

Fifth, more than anything else, and alongside his solidarity against injustice against people of color in the United States as everywhere, perhaps Dussel's greatest contribution to US ethnic minority studies as it is to the world is his Herculean, historically comprehensive critique of the contradictions and ethnocentrism of European philosophy and his account of its discursive construction as such at the dawn of its global rise through imperialism and colonialism, through its recent yet still Eurocentric self-criticisms.[10]

And while the critique of philosophical Eurocentrism is not new to ethnic studies, it has been largely piecemeal or indirect, and until recently, largely from outside the discipline of philosophy proper. He has also begun the dialogue of Western philosophy and non-Western "philosophy," in *Etica*, in which the latter is different systems of thought that have long meditated the most elemental questions of human nature and the meaning of existence and that, contrary to Enlightenment-produced Eurocentric myth, are neither "primitive" nor prephilosophical. He has also contributed to our seeing Western philosophy as one culturally specific reflection among many, neither exempt from the interests of the powerful nor absent from the necessarily collective pursuit of justice and well-being.

Queer theorist Chela Sandoval's *Methodology of the Oppressed* is in essence a project similar to Dussel's in *Etica de la liberación*. Fully centered, however, in the study of US feminist and queer women of color's literary and political activist writings from the 1960s through the 1980s, Sandoval interrogates progressive poststructuralist thought, showing its commonalities with civil rights and post-1960s Third World thought and practice, its indebtedness to them in crucial formulations, and its shortcomings as a result of the tautological effects of its unwitting Eurocentrism. She shows, for example, Roland Barthes's indebtedness to Fanon and argues that Fredric Jameson's political ennui before the enormity of global capital's capacity to appropriate resistance and critique is neither universal nor specific to late capitalism, but rather the condition of his own newly destabilized subject positioning as an increasingly disempowered member of male Euro-American culture, even if a deeply dissenting one. Because women of color, since the European colonial invasions of the Americas, have long confronted psychological, social, and economic disempowerment and alienation, indeed violence, and responded in myriad ways in order to survive physically and culturally, she suggests, they have much to teach about liberation struggles, and late capital's newest victims offer new possibilities for coalitionary opposition.

---

[10] Note, for example, that Dussel's critique of postmodern philosophers includes the lack of critical reflection in them with respect to the origins of difference in European global hegemony and their inability to proffer alternatives to Eurocentric power. Instead, therefore, Dussel speaks of the transmodernity of the Ethic of Liberation, as a commitment to the overthrow of "capitalism . . . liberalism . . . Eurocentrism . . . machismo . . . racism, etc." (2000, 62–64).

It is important to note that the archive of Sandoval, a queer Chicana, for her coalitionary theory of social change rooted in a politics of love as a social care for the other is primarily the creative and intellectual writings of African American, Asian American, Chicana, and Native American women. In their "creative" and ostensibly untheoretic works, they chronicle, analyze, and theorize their own lives and those of their ethnically, gender, sexually, economically, and culturally oppressed communities, knowing, as Audre Lorde observed in 1979, that "the master's tools will never dismantle the master's house" (1984, 112). And it cannot be any other way under the legacy of cultural imperialism and neocolonizing patriarchal, heteronormative, and classist Eurocentrism. Logic by which to argue and think, to imagine and act, must be found beyond the ways of thinking that maintain injustice in the present world. Yet this outsiderness, this living in the "borderlands," of women, of the queer, of artists, of the spiritual, as Anzaldúa put it, in *Borderlands* (1987), is what enables the critical intellectual distance, the empathy for those who also suffer injustice, and the commitment to greater democracy precisely because we cannot deny that injustice exists and that it can and must be eliminated. There is wisdom in the writings and other art forms in which US women of color render themselves and their lives objects of reflection. Through these creative but ideologically critical practices, they enter a record of the mechanisms of transformation. But the process of knowing one's self when one is multiply oppressed is, by necessity, a decolonizing one, as it is for the multiply privileged.

Historically marginalized from the intelligentsia, our creative writing and arts in general have thus been and continue to be an archive of resistance and the place where women of color most clearly and powerfully speak truth to power. Some of the most radical formulations with respect to political organization, reconceptualization of community, and the struggle for justice have come from the pens of women of color, and some of the most important of these have been queer feminists. It is telling that many have chosen to write "queer" mixtures of diary, poetry, revisionist history and mythology, and political essay from outside of academic disciplinarity, among these the pioneering Audre Lorde; the late Gloria Anzaldúa, June Jordan, and Paula Gunn Allen; Cherríe Moraga and Ana Castillo.

US ethnic studies, like feminism and queer studies, is therefore not merely an argument for inclusion into a canon whose disciplinary principles are derived from, and remain within, an elitist, Eurocentric, sexist, and homophobic colonial politics of domination. As part of a decolonial project, these studies contribute as well to the transformation of our understanding of what gets to count as knowledge and the appreciation of its value to humanity outside the prejudices of the Eurocentrism of cultural Darwinism that assumes that the products of Germany, France, England,

Renaissance Italy, and Euro-America, particularly those of its gender-privileged ruling classes, are most worthy of study.

Systematic and prolonged marginalization, such as that of women, the queer, and the ethnically or culturally different, has created a multiple consciousness—a cultural multilinguality with respect to different versions of truth and reality, those of the empowered and those less so. The question of gender and sexual difference, like the economic and racialized oppression of the "other," returns us not only to an ethics of responsibility for the other but also to receptivity to alterity that ultimately opens us up to the repressed alterity within ourselves. Thus, the problem of gender is hardly a woman's problem alone, for notions of masculinity change by feminist and transgender transformations of gender. Nor is sexuality the intellectual and political burden of the queer, for heterosexual identifications change in light of bisexual, gay, lesbian, and transgendered sexualities. To not engage dominant constructions of gender and sexuality in depth as fundamental conditions for exploitation across ideological regimes, including those of otherwise democratic liberation struggles, reproduces neocolonizing economic, social, and cultural domination with which they are imbricated and impoverishes our own humanity, and that of others.

As the huge corpus of feminist and gay/lesbian/bisexual/queer scholarship has shown, dominant notions of gender and sexuality we received as natural are negations of the human panorama of possibilities.[11] Patriarchy dehumanizes human beings, as does heteronormativity in its insistence that we must all be "straight," and that we must be so in particular ways. For myself, I wonder if these ancient, though not universal, divisions, are not as grave spiritually and materially as that of material poverty.

Gender and sexuality, like poverty and racialization, are not problems specific to the negatively marked bodies that bear their burden. If it is a step forward philosophically, as Dussel has so compelling argued throughout *Etica*, to listen to the other as other and not as the same-as-oneself, then it is perhaps also another, further liberatory step to allow the other's seeming alterity to dialogue within us, to make us its sameness, thus transgressing our own internalized and socialized identity dualisms, if only for a historical heartbeat. I believe I push Dussel fruitfully in my engagement with his work in this essay and in observing, by way of conclusion, my belief that coalition and solidarity toward lasting social justice and human well-being necessitate, as inevitable, profound personal as well as social transformation in a cycle of receptivity and deepening knowledge in which we open

---

[11] On our reproduction of gendered and sexual hierarchies through our performances of normative conceptions of these, see Marjorie Garber (1997) and Judith Butler, particularly *Bodies That Matter* (1993).

ourselves to the other as both other and self, as different yet same in our human, natural, and spiritual interconnectedness.

Acknowledgments

A shorter version of the present essay was presented November 21, 2004. In June 2007 I revised the essay. I revised it again in October 2009 and February 2010. My thanks to Randy P. Conner, Norma Alarcón, Jorge Aquino, Pedro J. DiPietro, Daphne Taylor-Garcia, and Irene Lara for attentive reading of the manuscript, to Sara Ramírez for research assistance and compilation of my notes, and to Marcelle Maese-Cohen for her invitation to submit an essay relating to decolonial feminism to *Qui Parle*.

References

Alcoff, Linda Martín, and Eduardo Mendieta. 2000. *Thinking from the Underside of History: Enrique Dussel's Philosophy of Liberation.* Lanham, MD: Rowman & Littlefield.

Anzaldúa, Gloria. 1987. *Borderlands/La Frontera: The New Mestiza.* San Francisco: Aunt Lute.

Butler, Judith. 1993. *Bodies That Matter: On the Discursive Limits of "Sex."* New York: Routledge.

Burgos-Debray, Elizabeth. 1985. *Me llamo Rigoberta Menchu, y asi me nacion la conciencia.* Mexico City: Veintiuno Editores.

Castellanos, Rosario. 1985. *Meditación en el umbral: Antología poética.* Mexico City: Fondo de Cultura Económica.

Deleuze, Gilles, and Felix Guattari. 1985. *Anti-Oedipus: Capitalism and Schizophrenia.* Minneapolis: University of Minnesota Press.

Dussel, Enrique. 2000. *Etica de la liberación en la edad de la globalización y de la exclusion.* 3rd ed. Barcelona: Editorial Trotta.

Freedman, Estelle B. 2002. *No Turning Back: The History of Feminism and the Future of Women.* New York: Ballantine Books.

Garber, Marjorie. 1997. *Vested Interests: Cross-Dressing and Cultural Anxiety.* New York: Routledge.

Garcia, Alma, ed. 1997. *Chicana Feminist Thought: The Basic Historical Writings.* New York: Routledge.

James, Joy, and T. Denean Sharpley-Whiting, eds. 2000. *The Black Feminist Reader.* Oxford: Blackwell.

Lévinas, Emmanuel. 2006. *Entre Nous: Thinking-of-the-Other.* Translated by Michael B. Smith and Barbara Harshav. London: Continuum International.

Lorde, Audre. 1984. *Sister Outsider: Essays and Speeches by Audre Lorde.* Berkeley: Crossing Press.

Lugones, María. 2003. *Pilgrimages/Peregrinajes: Theorizing Coalition against Multiple Oppressions.* Lanham, MD: Rowman & Littlefield.

Lugones, María. 2007. "Heterosexualism and the Colonial/Modern Gender System." *Hypatia* 22, no. 1: 186–209.

Miller, Francesca. 1991. *Latin American Women and the Search for Social Justice.* Hanover, NH: University Press of New England.

Nagler, Michael N. 2001. *Is There No Other Way? The Search for a Nonviolent Future.* Berkeley, CA: Berkeley Hills Books.

Roscoe, Will. 2000. *Changing Ones: Third and Fourth Genders in Native North America.* Basingstoke, Hampshire, UK: Palgrave Macmillan.

Sandoval, Chela. 2000. Methodology of the Oppressed. Minneapolis: University of Minnesota Press.

Somé, Sobonfu. 1997. *The Spirit of Intimacy: Ancient African Teachings in the Ways of Relationships.* Berkeley, CA: Berkeley Hills Books.

Sparks, Randy P., David Sparks, and Mariah Sparks. 1998. *Cassell's Encyclopedia of Queer Myth, Symbol, and Spirit: Gay, Lesbian, Bisexual and Transgender Lore.* London: Cassell.

CHAPTER 5 | Decolonial Feminist *Movidas*
A Caribeña (Re)thinks "Privilege," the Wages
of Gender, and Building Complex Coalitions

XHERCIS MÉNDEZ

A Brief Genealogy and Grounding

This essay is titled "A *Caribeña* (Re)thinks 'Privilege,' etc." because I wanted to engage what it means to be a light-skinned Latina who seeks to work against the erasure of my own Afro-descendancy without claiming a history of oppression I did not live. I also wanted to mark my particular location as a queer-identified cisgender Boricua, whose identity has been forged and grounded in Afro-Latinx/Caribbean ways of being and knowing and in relation to black folks (primarily African Americans and Afro-Caribbeans) in the United States. My intention is to work against a pan-Latinidad that bypasses and/or obscures the question of race and the pervasiveness of antiblackness in Latinx communities. Instead I want to be attentive to the assimilationist projects that offer benefits for disidentifying[1] with and from black communities. Indeed, the color-coded arrangement of the United States, where the ability to "pass" can significantly improve access to benefits, more often than not informs the degree to which Latinx communities identify with and/or even associate themselves with

---

[1] One of the differences between my usage and Jose Esteban Muñoz's conception of *disidentification* in this example is the directionality of the disidentifications we are concerned with. I am concerned with the political consequences of "white" folks as well as communities of color distancing themselves from racialized, impoverished, and marginalized communities in their moves to aspire to and mimic a white heterosexual upper-middle-class ideal. Muñoz is focused on the political possibilities of "minoritarian" communities, i.e., communities of color, finding ways to dissociate themselves from that very ideal of white heterosexual normativity. When mobilized in this direction, *away from the ideal*, Muñoz argues, and I agree, that this form of disidentification becomes a powerful resistant strategy. See Muñoz 1999.

Xhercis Méndez, *Decolonial Feminist Movidas* In: *Theories of the Flesh*, Edited by: Andrea J. Pitts, Mariana Ortega, and José Medina, Oxford University Press (2020). © Oxford University Press. DOI: 10.1093/oso/9780190062965.003.0006

black communities. Such assimilationist projects rely on the circulation of narratives that make distancing from and counteridentifying[2] with black communities particularly attractive, thus working against black and brown coalitions.

In my own community the disidentification with and counteridentification from "blackness" is deeply entangled with the efforts to distance themselves/ ourselves from narratives that pathologize black folks as "lazy," "ignorant," and "inherently criminal" and which are then (re)deployed in relation to Puerto Rican communities both on the island and on the mainland. These are not excuses for the ways in which antiblackness appears within Latinx communities, but rather an effort to consider how disidentification and counteridentification from the narratives and practices tied to antiblack co- lonial logics create obstacles to our building complex coalitions, one of the primary motivations behind this essay.

In addition to being attentive to race and antiblackness, my political/ coalitional orientation has been deeply informed by my experiences as a cultural broker for my mother, who does not speak English and needed these contributions in order to ensure our survival on the mainland. It has been informed by being an Ame/Rican "citizen" who became aware at an early age of our second-class access to the resources tied to citizenship.[3] My mother and family were often the subject and target of investigation by social service and welfare officials, while Child Protective Services oper- ated like the bogeyman, lurking in corners, always ready to tear our family apart. Police surveilled our community not in order to "protect and serve" but to criminalize. These are the experiences that have made me attentive to particular connections with and to other marginalized communities of color,[4] and that inform my particular brand of women of color[5]/decolonial feminism-in-the-making.

---

[2] Counteridentifying here refers to a process that foregrounds difference in a way that is oppositional. See Medina 2003. Such counteridentifications can include not only an impulse to dissociate from a given group but also how perceived differences can be construed as mutually exclusive, thus motivating actions that can work to undermine and devalue the group from which one is counteridentifying with and from.

[3] "Citizenship" as a "liberatory" project is undermined by, for instance, the lack of federal assistance to Puerto Rico after Hurricane Maria and by the ways in which it is grounded in the settler colonial logic and organization of space, land, etc. Efforts to access the "benefits" tied to "citizenship" is incommensurate with the claims from indigenous communities regarding the "constant state of land theft that is consistently disavowed" in the United States. See Tuck and Yang 2012 and Tuck 2016.

[4] These are some of the affinities I have with and to Latinx immigrant populations and their second-generation children and to African American, Pacific Islander, and Chicano populations in the United States that have been subjected to parallel racialized circumstances.

[5] "Women of color" does not simply refer to any and all racialized women. While in its mainstream usage it tends to refer to cisgender women who have been racialized through colonial processes, as both non-"white" and non-"European," I am using it as a reference to racialized females who also explicitly seek to build complex coalitions to and with one another. This includes

This essay is ambitious in that it seeks to articulate a decolonial feminist methodology that holds all of these complexities in the frame. It is ambitious because it seeks to mobilize gender as a political category of analysis that is inextricable from race, and which works to *identify, denounce,* and *transform* oppressive and (neo)colonial arrangements of bodies and power. Rather than reduce gender to a cross-cultural category of analysis that primarily focuses on the relationship between "Men" and "Women," this essay explores how gender works to entice a series of complicities from racialized folks to and with colonial logics as well as undermine our efforts to organize coalitionally across deep differences.

Decolonial Feminism: A Specific and Local/ized Political Project

This specific thread of decolonial feminism is invested in making more of the *contributions* made by women of color feminists,[6] in particular, the powerful work on and efforts to build complex coalitions across multiple differences (Brown 1992; Crenshaw 1991; Lorde 2007; Anzaldúa 2007). It also seeks to engage the contributions made by *indigena*/indigenous and Afro-Latinx/diasporic feminists resisting (neo)colonial "developments" projects and Eurocentric and heterosexist patriarchies within their own local and transnational contexts. Finally, it strategically builds on the politically productive concepts and orientations within the decolonial school of thought primarily coming from Latin American and Caribbean philosophers/thinkers.[7]

For example, the concept of *coloniality* is politically productive for orienting us toward the intergenerational consequences and violences resulting from a history of colonialism (Quijano 2000; Wynter 2003). For our purposes, coloniality can be broadly understood as referring to the colonial arrangements of bodies and power, the logics and practices, ways of being and knowing, and racialized capitalism that were born out of formal colonialism and continue to persist long after formal colonialism has ended. In other words, the coloniality of power, gender, being, , and so on, outlives formal colonialism and persists in the structures and institutions that organize the nation states that emerge after "decolonization" regardless

---

a commitment to learning each other's histories and contending with our differences both within and outside of the groups with whom we identify (Alexander 2005; Lorde 2007).

[6] I am creatively building with multiple genealogies of decolonial feminist thought, methods, and politics.

[7] Noting this particular genealogy does not make my usage of the terminology associated with it mutually exclusive with how others have previously used the term "decolonial" and/or how others are working to build "decolonial/ized" futures.

of which bodies actually operate those structures and institutions. To decolonize in this formulation refers to the active disrupting of coloniality in its many manifestations, including the ways in which racialized capitalism, and ongoing settler colonialism in the United States, continues to violently impact even the most intimate parts of our lives and relations.

In addition to the concept of coloniality, other orientations from this decolonial school of thought that are productive are the commitment to substantively engaging "non-Western" ways of being and knowing, and an attentiveness to the Eurocentric and universalizing assumptions that travel with many of the mainstream categories researchers and academics use to understand power, oppression, and by extension "liberation and decolonization" in local and transnational contexts. It is with this (re)orientation in mind that the brand of decolonial feminism I am proposing is a self-consciously *local/ized* political project. I am thinking from and with a US context and about women of color in that context, with an eye to the *transnational*.

My resistance to claiming a universal and/or universalizable approach comes from a recognition that the deployment of "gender" as a cross-cultural category of analysis has more often than not distorted and obscured alternative conceptions of being and local modalities of empowerment in transnational contexts (Allen 1986, Oyěwùmí 1997; Mohanty 2003; Wekker 1999, 2006; Méndez 2014a, 2014b). This historical and contemporary tendency has led me to ask, in what ways do racialized folks have to shift how they understand gender in order to identify and activate a communally oriented liberatory politic that does not mimic Western (neo) colonial and settler colonial arrangements of bodies and power?

In response to these questions, I first engage what is useful, suggestive, and politically productive about María Lugones's framing of the "coloniality of gender" and the "modern/colonial gender system" (2007). Second, I expand and further flesh out what I refer to as the *wages of gender*, a concept I developed in an effort to make explicit "gender's" grounding in colonial relations of power and the impact that has on the racialized communities produced as the constitutive outside of gender. Finally, I conclude with five preliminary methodological ingredients[8] and

---

[8] I use the word "ingredients" here purposefully. Different from "component," "ingredient" carries with it other layers of meaning that are important for this work. Ingredient conjures up the idea of cooking, an activity that is often correlated to female bodies and includes creatively bringing very different things together in order to create something new (a meal) that both contributes to life and is life-sustaining. The correlation to female bodies is historically produced, and my bringing it to bear here is about refusing to ignore the labor and contributions that females make to social reproduction. Moreover, the ingredients of any recipe are open and creatively tweaked to suit different needs, e.g., allergies, food restrictions, etc. I propose these steps as ingredients because they will be adjusted depending on the specificity of local and historical contexts. Finally, different from the word component, "in-gredi-ent" also carries with it the idea of "walking into" or

orientations[9] that work to identify and disrupt the coloniality of gender and move us toward complex coalitions. The methodological approach I am proposing proceeds as follows: (1) historicize gender, (2) map out relational power dynamics, (3) track the conditions produced by racialized capitalism that undergird and bolster complicities with the coloniality of gender, (4) produce new social and decolonial visions and imaginaries, and (5) develop and ritualize new lived and embodied practices.

Why We Need to Historicize Gender

In her 2007 article entitled "Heterosexualism and the Modern/Colonial Gender System," Lugones makes the claim that "gender" as we know it was and continues to be a colonial imposition. More intriguing than this particular claim is the relational system of gender she describes. As I have argued elsewhere, Lugones's relational approach to gender remains suggestive precisely because it draws our attention to the ways in which gender and "Women" were (re)defined in relation to enslaved physiognomically distinct laboring bodies, at least within the Americas and the Caribbean (Méndez 2015). As a result, Lugones's effort to begin from a historicized sense of "gender" functions to emphasize the relational process through which gender becomes racialized and a marker of humanity for colonizers. In other words, what you get from Lugones's effort to historicize gender is an attentiveness to the sets of colonial institutions and practices that produce a constitutive outside to gender. Without an understanding of how gender comes to be racialized through such colonial relationships of power we end up with a category of analysis that obscures as much as it claims to reveal.

In order to identify this relational process of racializing gender, Lugones introduces what she refers to as the "modern/colonial gender system," which is organized into "light" and "dark" sides. Within this framework the only bodies with gender are those on the light side. As a result, the gender categories of "Man" and "Woman" not only refer to specific body types, males versus females, but also to the hierarchical, incommensurate, and mutually exclusive arrangement of bodies and power that white

---

"entering" something, perhaps a journey, together. The term functions as an invitation to create a new path and world together.

[9] I am also using the word "orientation" here to explicitly conjure up another set of intentions. This methodology seeks to foreground relation, including how we position ourselves in relation to each other, the work, our communities and/or the folks with whom we want to think with. Orientation marks a position and location. It can also refer to the process of getting familiar with something new, for instance, as in an introduction into a different way of approaching and deploying gender as a category of analysis.

bourgeois heterosexual males and females idealized for themselves, as the self-selected representatives of "humanity" (Wynter 2003). We can think of the cult of domesticity as a nineteenth-century American manifestation of this logic at work (Welter 1966; Santiago Valles 2003). Within this version of a light-side gender arrangement, the category "Woman" exists as "Man's" negation. Thus, if he is of the "mind," she is of the "body"; if he is of the "public," she is relegated to the "private"; if he represents authority, she is banned from having authority, and so on and so forth.

On the "dark side" are the laboring bodies of those enslaved, whose bodies are sexed but not gendered. The reason their bodies are not gendered is because they are legally produced as chattel and because the "sex" of their bodies only matters to the extent to which they serve breeding practices and the purposes of capital accumulation. These are the colonial designs on their bodies, which is what the modern/colonial gender system framework is attempting to track. This framework then highlights how gender is intimately tied to those who are *structurally produced* and recognized as human over and against those structurally produced as a degeneration of humanity, a subhumanity with various degrees of nonhumanness. As a result, the characterizations of those on the dark side as "hypersexual" and "perverse" "animals" whose natures need to be transformed from the inside out should be understood as a racialized vision of the world that serves the purposes and practices of colonialism, settler colonialism, and (neo)colonialism.

In other words, Lugones's modern/colonial gender system delineates a *colonial cosmovision*, in that it centers how colonial actors perceived those they enslaved and colonized. Her description of the modern/colonial gender system does not center what those enslaved and colonized thought of themselves because she is attempting to track the colonial logics being produced. It is with this in mind that I would argue her description of this gender system as organized around a light and dark side should be understood as part of the critique. In my mind it is an indictment, and not a reifying, of a Western (provincial) cosmovision organized around an either/or, binary, and mutually exclusive logic that violently sought to reorganize other cosmosenses and cosmologies along these same lines.

My usage of her framework is with an eye toward tracking some of the intergenerational consequences of gender being racialized through specific colonial institutions and practices and in relation to specific geopolitics. It is not my aim to name and describe a single unified modern/colonial gender system but rather to provide a method for tracking the racialized gender arrangements produced under colonial conditions in a given context.[10] It is for this reason that I also do not understand Lugones

---

[10] For example, the Spanish modern/colonial gender system, in terms of who counts as "Man,"

as describing a system of gender that we want to identify with and/or be incorporated into. My goal is not to become or transform myself into someone that is recognized as a light-side "Woman" but rather to underscore the violence of that imposition.

In order to get a sense of why this matters for coalitional possibilities, it becomes necessary to highlight some of the colonial trappings of light-side gender and gender arrangements. Within the settler colonies that occupy the geographical space now known as the United States, for instance, there was a relational reduction of white women's worth, in that she mattered to the extent to which she participated in the imperial/colonial project through the contribution of her reproductive capacities. Depending on the location of the colony, anxieties about being outnumbered by racialized others was part of the heightened policing of sexuality and surveilling of white women's wombs. Indeed, the imperial/colonial project demanded that white women's bodies be transformed into instrumental vehicles for the reproduction of "pure" white babies that would later serve to inherit the capital that was violently being accumulated through the extracted land and labor of physiognomically distinct others.

I am aware that her participation in the imperial/colonial project was not always a question of willingness. At times her contributions to the settler colonial project were partially extracted through, for example, the ever-looming threat of impoverishment and/or being indefinitely confined to a lunatic asylum. And yet her profound reduction was also simultaneously ameliorated by the sets of "privileges/benefits"[11] (enticements) that came with being construed as desirable, feminine, passive, and delicate by white bourgeois heterosexual men and relative to racialized females. These forces were simultaneously operative and resulted in these "women" having contradictory desires, at times instrumentally motivated, but significantly acting as both oppressed and oppressor.

As I will illustrate below, the sets of privileges/benefits bestowed upon these white, heterosexual, bourgeois "women" are primarily considered privileges/benefits in relation to those on the dark side, who by comparison are subjected to exponential degrees of violence and abuse. For instance, being considered "too delicate" to work in the field was a privilege, in that it constituted *a special right* and/or *advantage* afforded light-side women in relation to racialized females since it kept them "safe" and their

---

"Woman," and ultimately "Human," may have differed from that of the Portuguese. Understanding that this is not a unified system makes evident that different colonial practices produce different types of relations. However, I would argue that whatever the modern/colonial gender system is in a given context, there are colonial arrangements of bodies and power that continue to negatively impact racialized males and females.

[11] Because I am troubling how we think privilege, for the remainder of the text the term "privilege" is to be considered bracketed.

bodies protected and intact from the hard labor of the fields. However, this skewed system functions in a way that makes accessing the benefits tied to light-side gender desirable, such as the protections only available to those deemed recognizably "delicate." It is this exchange rate that I would like to attend to when discussing privilege among differently racialized "women." Indeed, it is this exchange rate, or rather the privileges/benefits that have as part of them colonial designs on our bodies, that I refer to as the *wages of gender* (Méndez 2015). As I will argue, identifying the colonial logics and concomitant practices of relation and arrangements of bodies and power contained in these "privileges" becomes necessary for opening our imaginations to more communally oriented arrangements of bodies and power for women and communities of color.

Identifying the Wages of Gender

The wages of gender track how gender is shaped by colonial relations of power and how it continues to operate as a (neo)colonizing force. Lugones's conception of light-side gender and gender arrangements is useful here because it draws our attention to the relation of power specifically between white bourgeois heterosexual males and females. In other words, gender in her formulation does not claim to be about the relationship of power between all males and all females. Tracking how the wages of gender operate allows us to see how light-side gender and gender arrangements become the model of relation to which we are all expected to aspire, regardless of what we desire and whether or not we have the material conditions to "successfully" inhabit such gender and gender arrangements.

The *wages of gender* can be understood as the *economic, social, political, legal, psychological and affective privileges/benefits one gets for being systematically recognized as an individual who fits into light-side gender and gender arrangements.* It is important to reiterate here that light-side gender does not include all people, but rather emphasizes those who are structurally recognized as "Men" and/or "Women," and for whom this acknowledgment includes a recognition of humanity and a systemically supported freedom. It is not just the privileges we need to track but also *the processes through which one is given benefits for identifying with, aspiring to, and successfully manifesting light-side gender and gender arrangements, regardless of where you fall in the modern/colonial gender system.* For example, contemporary versions of light-side gender and gender arrangements encourage racialized folks to aspire to patriarchal arrangements of power in order to be recognized as proper "Men" and "Women," which include a presumption of heterosexuality and heteronormativity, a nuclear family structure, and a policing of sexuality grounded in an antimiscegenist logic. And yet what constitutes the actual material wages of gender shifts dramatically according to one's location in the modern/colonial gender system.

Indeed, there are differential exchange rates for complicity with light-side gender and gender arrangements. This becomes critical for identifying what is at stake for differently situated women. For instance, the wages of gender for women on the light side have included, but are not limited to, privileges such as patriarchal "protection" from work in the fields, and patriarchal "protection" from the wild dangers of the public sphere as well as a partial empowerment, an often violent exercise of power, over those enslaved/colonized both male and female (Glymph 2008). The wages of light-side gender have also been produced through antimiscegenation laws. Antimiscegenation laws are part of the structural conditions that made bourgeois heterosexual white "Women" become the "most" sought after and desirable females (sexually as well as for marriage partnerships) within the system, because they were the only females whose wombs were capable of reproducing legally recognized "humans." However, in order to access these privileges white bourgeois heterosexual "Women" had to become passive, submissive, and participate in / be complicit with the colonial/imperial project as well as the conceptions of beauty and the feminine that kept their bodies hostage to white bourgeois heterosexual "Men." Notably, many of these arrangements continue to be produced as desirable.

By contrast the wages of gender for females on the dark side have included an altogether different exchange rate. For example, enslaved black "women's" insistence on being identified as "woman" (think: Sojourner Truth's infamous speech) encompasses the hope of being recognized as human and of being freed from the violence of slavery (White 1985). Tied to being identified as "woman" is the possibility of keeping and raising her own children and of being entitled to partial protection under the law, particularly as it relates to systematic sexual assault. These are fundamentally different stakes and wages tied to a colonial process of racializing gender.

Juxtaposing the wages of gender in this way makes explicit what is materially at stake when black "women" have named and called out their exclusion from the category "Women" in the effort to access some of the privileges that white, middle-class, heterosexual females have been conditionally afforded. What also becomes clear is how the wages of gender have been racialized through colonial processes, in that white bourgeois heterosexual females have not had to worry about their children being sold or forcibly removed to boarding schools, as has been the case for indigenous communities. It is not just that the stakes for racialized women are materially different but that their claims to "womanhood," even when on light-side terms, are also bound up with their efforts to end profound degrees of violence and its intergenerational impact. However, I want to suggest that the critique that racialized females have been excluded from being recognized as "Women" is not necessarily an expression of a desire to enter into what it is yet another violent system of relations, namely light-side gender arrangements.

The Problem with Deploying Gender "As Is"

We are now in a position to identify some of the conceptual problems with applying "gender" retroactively to racialized bodies in "postcolonial" spaces. The "gender" categories of "Men" and "Women," as are most often deployed, tend to center a descriptive biology (the sexual difference) grounded in a Western, scientific, dual-sexed notion of the body (Laqueur 1990; Butler 1993, 2004; Fausto-Sterling 2000). This matters because within a Western, scientific, dual-sexed model of the human it is possible to conflate sex and gender as synonymous and/or interchangeable categories. However, as illustrated by the preceding historical examples, sex and gender were not structurally synonymous. Gender was a category reserved for those on the light side and the "gender" categories of "Men" and "Women" carried with them an acknowledgment of one's humanity and a systemically supported freedom that was not historically available to those on the dark side—and which continues to be in many ways inaccessible to racialized communities contemporarily.[12] The problem with this approach to gender as a category of cross-cultural analysis is that it has a difficult time accounting for the intergenerational impact of this history (Spelman 1988; Wynter 1990; Scott 1986, 2010). At least within "postcolonial" contexts, gender has to contend with the colonial history that produced alternatively sexed and racialized conceptions of the body.

Another way in which gender as the sexual difference becomes problematic is that it does the work of obscuring non-Western conceptions of the body, such as sacred (re)arrangements of the social (Voeks 1997; Strongman 2002; Wekker 1999, 2006). For instance, a secularized conception of gender built upon a dual-sexed notion of the body makes it difficult to contemplate *the sacred part* of two-spirit folks without unwittingly (mis)translating them into and subsuming them under a *secularized*

---

[12] See Alexander's (2011) *The New Jim Crow: Mass Incarceration in the Age of Colorblindness*. Her book illustrates in detail how racial discrimination in the American legal system is allowed to operate openly and freely as long as race-neutral language is used to bypass accountability. The Black Lives Matter movement (Garza 2014) and projects like Say Her Name (Crenshaw et al. 2015) are also organized efforts to illustrate the extent to which black communities in the United States continue to be targeted for demise with impunity. Other examples include the pattern of criminalizing Latinx communities through immigration and gang policies and Muslim communities through the war on terror.

queer and/or trans categorization (Driskill 2010). This is not to dismiss the power of identifying same-sex loving people across different spaces and times and/or the political significance of forging identities that resist mainstream and normative gender arrangements. However, these categories carry with them a history and sets of assumptions about bodies that politically matter. The problem for racialized folks is that mainstream approaches to gender obscure coeval logics with potentially greater or different liberatory possibilities.[13]

I do not want to do away with the category of gender altogether, but instead want to use it differently. Rather than using it as a way to primarily read sexual difference (think men versus women; queer versus heterosexual), the goal here is to use it as a category that works to *identify, denounce, and transform* light-side gender and gender arrangements that have been violently universalized through colonial institutions and practices, such as slavery, forced migration, and the "re-education"/cultural assaults through boarding schools (Lomawaima 1993; McClintock 1995; Stoler 1995, 2002). Retroactive inclusions into gender only obscure the violence of these histories and their intergenerational consequences. Here the *decolonial feminist movida*[14] would be to instead recognize how the gender terms "Men" and "Women" have been used to primarily refer to those males and females structurally recognized as of value to the settler state, those whose bodies and lives are protected by laws and whole armies are mobilized in their defense. The decolonial feminist *movida* I am suggesting is to use gender, particularly in "postcolonial" contexts, to track the multiplicity of oppressive relations that light-side gender and gender arrangements have produced and to attend to the sets of bodies (the enslaved, or unfree, the globally impoverished) that continue to be sacrificed on its behalf.

For communities of color this means (re)considering how we talk about the light-side gender and the gender arrangements that have been violently universalized so that we do not unwittingly make access

---

[13] For other accounts of non-western arrangements of the social see also Wekker 1999, 2006 and Allen 1986.

[14] The term *movida* has multiple valences in Spanish that I want to bring to bear. It can refer to movement, not just in terms of a specified action (moves) but also in terms of a movement that can be organized (a protest, series of protests) that has larger social cultural implications. Thinking ahead, we can ask, what would a decolonial feminist movement look like? What constitutes its politics? *Movida* can also carry with it the idea of *un revolu*, a Puerto Rican term used to refer to a situation that can be confusing and difficult to resolve, in the sense that there is a messy situation that we must deal with. The coalitions I am interested in are messy in that sense. On a more creative and productive note, it can also refer to spaces where things are "happening," and where potentially intimate shifts can happen, as in the space of nightlife. I am specifically thinking about the kinds of happenings that take place in queer nightlife, in that it is both happening (as in "this is the place to be") and happening as in there are cultural/political shifts and openings that take place through participation in and with these spaces.

and inclusion—particularly to the skewed modern/colonial system of "benefits" (wages of gender) it produces—desirable or even aspirational (Rowley 2010). It also means exploring the extent to which ahistorical incorporations into light-side gender and gender arrangements have moved us toward oppositional sexual politics (versus coalitional) and other oppressive manifestations of light-side gender (think: politics of respectability). These are political concerns because of the ways in which light-side gender and gender arrangements get framed as the only legitimate and legible way of relating and communities of color get pressured *to desire, aspire to, and mimic* those arrangements in order to actualize or give meaning to our struggles, sense of selves, bodies, sexualities, and freedom. This is the coloniality of gender in action.

For example, consider the modern/colonial narratives that claim black males have been denied their rightful place as heads and patriarchs of families by slavery and "emasculating" and/or "castrating" black women. These narratives often result in racialized males calling for a "manning up" over and against their racialized female counterparts as part of a "liberatory," "anticolonial," and "decolonial" agenda. Or consider the modern/colonial narratives framing racialized communities as "hypersexual" and as manifesting deviant sexualities.[15] These have often had the effect of producing a politics of respectability that seeks to prove the untruthfulness of the narratives. What I am suggesting is that the counteridentification and strategic distancing from these narratives then forecloses the more liberatory possibility of decentering the colonial gaze and celebrating the sexual diversity that exists in all of our communities and strengthens our collective potential.

The question for me is, how can women of color and decolonial feminists begin to develop narratives and methods that actively denounce, disrupt, and transform the coloniality of gender in its many manifestations? In what ways have we constrained our liberatory possibilities by disidentifying with and counteridentifying from the survival-rich capacities of those relegated to the dark side because they have been framed as pathological in relation to the light side?

Developing a Decolonial Feminist Critique of Gender

To respond to these political concerns, I consider the following ingredients/orientations to be productive for denouncing and transforming the coloniality of gender and for our efforts to *decolonize* our social relationships and coalitional possibilities. Given my account, identifying

---

[15] See Terry and Urla 1995; Findlay 1999; Briggs 2003; and Hill Collins 2004.

the coloniality of gender in action demands that we first historicize "gender" from within multiple local histories and bodies. This theoretical shift can keep us from reducing gender to a descriptive biology (i.e., the sexual difference) that obscures the violence of the colonial project and the ways in which those legacies continue to bind us.

Historicizing gender can also open us up to identifying and recognizing coeval and coexisting arrangements of bodies and power that are simultaneously operative in "postcolonial" spaces. For example, in her book entitled *The Invention of Women: Making and African Sense of Western Gender Discourse* (1997), Oyèrónké Oyěwùmí argues that seniority played a significant role in the (re)arranging of bodies and power from within a Yoruban cosmosense in Nigeria. Seniority as a coexisting and simultaneously operative arrangement of the social becomes difficult to contemplate, let alone recognize, under a conception of gender that foregrounds sexual difference. However, historicizing gender can help us identify and mobilize to greater effect some of the more egalitarian social arrangements that have historically existed and that continue to exist within the cosmosenses and cosmologies of those relegated to the dark side.

Second, as demonstrated through the wages of gender, I propose a practice of mapping out relational power dynamics. Mapping out relational power dynamics can trouble facile accounts of power organized around reductive understandings of sexual difference. In so doing, we are able to acknowledge and denounce the oppressive relationship white bourgeois heterosexual "Men" had and continue to have in relation to white bourgeois heterosexual "Women," while also exploring how those oppressive modes of relating were undergirded by the material conditions of those enslaved and colonized. This methodological shift nuances how we approach the feminist goal of undoing "Patriarchy," by calling us to attend to all of the bodies that were sacrificed in order to make the oppressive set of relations on the light side seem relatively more attractive and even "liberatory" by comparison.

One critical result of this decolonial feminist *movida* is that we can use these relational power mappings to get beyond the Oppression Olympics[16] that continue to undermine our efforts to build complex coalitions across our differences. By mapping out the relational power dynamics we are able to see that white bourgeois heterosexual women's complicity and participation in oppressing those on the dark side is what partially sustains the oppressive relationship between those on the light side. What I am

---

[16] Oppression Olympics refers to the practice of determining who is the "most oppressed" by creating hierarchies of disadvantages between and among differently marginalized communities, thus making it difficult to collectively organize. My approach explores some of the complicated ways in which we are simultaneously oppressed and oppressing. See Martinez 1993.

suggesting here is that *"Women" who disidentify with, counteridentify with, and/or distance themselves from those on the dark side in exchange for the wages of gender are paradoxically in some sense collaborating in maintaining their own oppression.* Thus, a myopic focus on individual access to the wages of gender afforded white heterosexual bourgeois "Men" can indeed work to undermine larger goals such as undoing institutionally supported heterosexist racialized patriarchy and decolonizing all of our relationships, including those to the sacred world and to the land.

Third, particularly for communities of color, it becomes necessary to track the conditions produced by racialized capitalism that undergird and bolster complicities with the coloniality of gender. A useful example of this is the 1965 Moynihan Report, which encouraged black males to be complicit in the oppression of black females in exchange for the promise of employment and integration into the mainstream economy. Concerned with the social movements of the time demanding civil rights and racial equality and the anticolonial movements taking place globally, Daniel P. Moynihan, the political scientist and senator, argued that the solution to racial unrest lay in providing black men with the material conditions to return to their "rightful place" as breadwinners, patriarchs, and heads of nuclear families. Moynihan's "assessment" of the black family argued that racial unrest could only be mitigated by providing black men with much-needed employment, in this case by enlisting them in the army, in order to help them correct the "dysfunctional matriarchy" (Spillers 1987) that had taken hold of the black community and had constrained the community's successful assimilation into American society. Moynihan claimed that as long as black women were "doing better" than their male counterparts, racial equality would never be achieved.

Moynihan's pathological framing of the black community was grounded in light-side gender and gender arrangements. His reading of the black community foregrounded an oppositional sexual politics (the "women" are "doing better" than the "men") by arguing that the key to racial equality was mimicking light-side gender and familial arrangements. Moynihan in many ways derailed the conversation on substantive racial equality by sparking debates around black women's "pathological tendency" to undermine black men by refusing to succumb to a patriarchal order and outperforming them in school and employment. In so doing, Moynihan framed black women, and not racialized capitalism, as both the "perpetrator" of harm and the subsequent target.

Rather than move toward an oppositional sexual politics, the decolonial feminist *movida* here would be to seek out economic solutions that foreground the well-being of all those impacted by the conditions of racialized capitalism. How does this oppositional sexual politic actually bolster capitalist exploitation at the expense of the black community? It does so by getting racialized males to focus on *outdoing* women of color (earning more money, getting more jobs, and even actively working to undermine their economic well-being) rather than identifying economic solutions and/or alternatives in which all community members' material needs are met. Ensuring that community members have what they need, and not doubling down on the recuperation of masculinity through a wage battle with and against your racialized female counterpart, is key for any version of collective racial justice. A decolonial feminist approach to "gender" provides a space for us to examine how such economic enticements and complicities both serve capitalist exploitation and undermine collective liberation.

(Re)imagining Decolonial Feminist Futures

Fourth, decolonial feminist futures are not possible for communities of color unless we seek out alternative systems and practices for (re)evaluating our worth. This decolonial feminist turn toward the "future" includes developing new social imaginaries and visions (Paredes 2008). Aspiring to and mimicking light-side gender and gender arrangements will not get us there. This is not a decolonial move, even when it is framed as such. Instead a decolonial feminist asks, what other liberatory possibilities and alternative modes of being and relating are available to us from within the communities relegated to the dark side? And perhaps these too will require creative transformations (Paredes 2008). Rather than primarily critiquing the world we don't want to live in, the (re)orientation I am suggesting includes allocating more time and energy toward imagining and activating the world we do want to live in.

In my own research on Afro-Cuban Santería, this has meant exploring how ritual enactments introduce explicitly non-Western formulations of the body that include *nongendered/nonracialized* logics, culturally specific modalities of empowerment, and an alternative system of valuation for what it means to be human (Méndez 2014b).[17] Afro-Cuban Santería *in practice* introduces its own formation and brand of power through alternative categories, such as spiritual seniority. Spiritual seniority demands that those who have invested more time in the religion have accumulated greater

---

[17] This is not the only site from which decolonial possibilities can be imagined. Science fiction and Afro-futurism are other sites where decolonial imaginaries have been and continue to be made possible. *Octavia's Brood: Science Fiction Stories from Social Justice Movements* (2015) is an example of how activists are using Octavia Butler's work to think about social movements and developing liberatory imaginations. Others who have been productively inspired by the move to take up a feminist Afrofuturism can be found at https://nolawildseeds.org/manifesta/ and http://octaviabutlerlegacy.com/

degrees of spiritual knowledge, and have been recognized as knowledgeable spiritual advisors be given deference as sacred elders. These elders are to be given deference *regardless of body type, sexual preferences, and/or actual age*. Notably, spiritual seniority as a coexisting organizing logic has provided significant avenues for Afro-Cuban women and "queer"-identified folks in the Caribbean to become well-respected and valued leaders both within and beyond spiritual and communal networks.

Methodologically, the sustained engagement with Afro-Cuban Santería has provided me with powerful examples of why we need to be attentive to the assumptions that travel with the categories of analysis we deploy in our feminist research. It has also provided me with tools to decenter the colonial representations and narratives repeatedly mapped onto racialized communities and identify an alternative ground from which to produce possibly decolonial readings of the past in ways that move us toward transformative visions for the future.

Practices such as these can be powerfully suggestive in terms of reimagining systemically devalued beings and bodies, beyond the coloniality of gender. For instance, if we were to reimagine Sojourner Truth through a ritual practice like Santería, a practice that presupposes the full humanity of all its practitioners, what we are empowered to see is that her being included or incorporated into the category "Woman" requires that we (mis)translate her body and experience into the terms of the light side. This incorporation not only distorts the historical violence of gender but can function in ways that are (neo)colonizing. An Afro-diasporic/Latinx conception of the human is suggestive in that Truth's liberatory possibilities are more likely to be found in understandings of humanity and gender that do not depart from or require her relative dehumanization in order to exist.

Finally, transforming the coloniality of gender and decolonizing gender and feminism requires more than critique. Rather, it calls us to create and "ritualize" new everyday lived practices. The engagement with Santería is my effort to engage the very practices that have sustained those who have been systematically targeted for demise. Even though I do not believe that Santería is decolonial or resistant unto itself, it does have something to tell us about alternative systems of valuation that are not reducible to merely surviving in the face of extreme violence. Beyond survival, there are lessons within these practices that remind us that being the target of violence is not synonymous with successfully being transformed into a lesser human being. These ritual practices often include a process of "rebirth," and tend to focus on making bodies sacred and cultivating a sense of one's value, even in the face of systemic violence and violent histories. As a result, Afro-Cuban Santería can habituate the body to refuse a dehumanized conception of self.

If we agree that *El camino se hace al andar*,[18] then decolonizing gender calls us to develop practices that habituate and reorient us toward "moving differently" in the world and in so doing transform what we even think is possible. For those of us who find ourselves suffocated by light-side gender and gender arrangements, producing more critical analysis is not enough. We must also seek to develop practices that actively engage our bodies in the decolonizing process. The call to develop and "ritualize" new everyday lived practices that can rehearse, embody, and habituate us to new forms of socializing, being, and relating acknowledges the extent to which we can be transformed by our embodied experiences of freedom (Abod 2016). Indeed, how can we take back our bodies, and what can and do embodied experiences of freedom look like?

Conclusion: A Call for Theory/Practice That Centers Collective Well-Beings

This approach to gender is about doing theory that is attached to practice and about rethinking gender toward transformative ends. I have argued that colonialism and processes of racialization tied to capitalist accumulation are inextricably linked to how we contemporarily understand gender, sexed bodies, and sexuality. Given how I understand the gender categories to be tied to colonial relations of power and logics, this particular brand and localized version of decolonial feminism-in-the-making is not invested in women of color being retroactively included in the category "Woman" nor being assessed through light-gender or gender arrangements. If we understand gender in this way, then accessing light-side wages of gender means simultaneously being integrated into an arrangement of bodies and power that is equally oppressive and which has little to no decolonial liberatory potential for women of color. Indeed, how we understand gender makes a difference not only for how we frame our contemporary relations, but also for what we will consider to be the necessary ingredients for reimagining our various socials in liberatory ways.

In order to address these political concerns, I have proposed these ingredients (a decolonial feminist research practice/approach) as a way to

---

[18] This saying, commonly heard in hispanophone contexts, literally translates into "The path is made by walking." The refrain serves as a reminder that the path toward something different will not be "ready-made" or even clear. It instead suggests that the path becomes a path because we choose to move in a direction. Moreover, it is a reminder that there will be emergent conditions and concerns that arise as we "walk," conditions and concerns that we cannot know at the outset. It useful for thinking about how a decolonial feminist politics will have to be open to creatively adjusting and responding to emergent conditions and concerns as they arise and as we move toward something new.

perform different gender analyses and make it more difficult to bypass the concerns of women of color and/or produce these concerns as something additive. At stake in the troubling of privilege is the impact the battle to access the wages of (light-side) gender has on foreclosing our liberatory imaginations, visions, and coalitional goals. It is for these reasons that it becomes important to historicize gender and map out the relational power dynamics; to identify the colonial value system that undergirds capitalist expansion, extraction, imperialism, and exploitation and naturalizes a multiplicity of oppressive relations; to produce new decolonial social imaginaries and visions while also creating and ritualizing new everyday lived practices. I offer these methodological ingredients as a way to disrupt the weight and space Eurocentric frames of reference have occupied in shaping how we come to understand ourselves, our bodies, and the worlds around us. My hope is to carve out a space from which to radically (re)imagine and embody decolonial modes of being, knowing, and relating that center our collective and communal well-beings.

Acknowledgments

I would like to extend my sincerest gratitude to the following people whose critical
questions and engaged dialogue made these reflections possible: Ganessa James, Mia Mingus, Kristie Dotson, Nikolay Karkov, Mariana Ortega, José Medina, and Andrea Pitts.

References

Abod, Jennifer. 2016. *The Passionate Pursuits of Angela Bowen*. Documentary film, Women Make Movies.

Alexander, M. Jacqui. 2005. *Pedagogies of Crossing: Meditations on Feminism, Sexual Politics, Memory, and the Sacred*. Durham, NC: Duke University Press.

Alexander, Michelle. 2011. *The New Jim Crow: Mass Incarceration in the Age of Colorblindness*. New York: New Press.

Allen, Paula Gunn. 1986. *The Sacred Hoop: Recovering the Feminine in American Indian Traditions*. Boston: Beacon Press.

Anzaldúa, Gloria. 2007. *Borderlands/La Frontera: The New Mestiza*. 3rd Edition. San Francisco: Aunt Lute Books.

Briggs, Laura. 2003. *Reproducing Empire: Race, Sex, Science, and US Imperialism in Puerto Rico*. Berkeley: University of California Press.

Brown, Elsa Barkley. 1992. "'What Has Happened Here': The Politics of Difference in Women's History and Feminist Politics." *Feminist Studies* 18, no. 2: 295–312.

Butler, Judith. 1993. *Bodies That Matter: On the Discursive Limits of "Sex."* New York: Routledge.

Butler, Judith. 2004. *Undoing Gender*. New York: Routledge.

Collins, Patricia Hill. 2004. *Black Sexual Politics: African Americans, Gender, and the New Racism*. New York: Routledge.

Crenshaw, Kimberlé. 1991. "Mapping the Margins: Intersectionality, Identity Politics, and Violence against Women of Color." *Stanford Law Review* 43, no. 6: 1241–99.

Crenshaw, Kimberlé Williams. 2014. "The Girls Obama Forgot: My Brother's Keeper Ignores Young Black Women." *New York Times*, July 29.

Crenshaw, Kimberlé, Andrea J. Ritchie, Rachel Anspach, Rachel Gilmer, and Luke Harris. 2015. *Say Her Name: Resisting Police Brutality against Black Women*. New York: African American Policy Forum.

Driskill, Qwo-Li. 2010. "Doubleweaving Two-Spirit Critiques: Building Alliances between Native and Queer Studies." *GLQ: A Journal of Lesbian and Gay Studies* 16, nos. 1–2: 69–92.

Fausto-Sterling, Anne. 2000. *Sexing the Body: Gender Politics and the Construction of Sexuality*. 1st edition. New York: Basic Books.

Findlay, Eileen. 1999. *Imposing Decency: The Politics of Sexuality and Race in Puerto Rico, 1870–1920*. Durham, NC: Duke University Press.

Garza, Alicia. 2014. "A Herstory of the #blacklivesmatter Movement." *Feminist Wire*, October 7. http://www.thefeministwire.com/2014/10/blacklivesmatter-2/.

Glymph, Thavolia. 2008. *Out of the House of Bondage: The Transformation of the Plantation Household*. New York: Cambridge University Press.

Imarisha, Walidah and Adrienne Maree Brown. 2015. *Octavia's Brood: Science Fiction Stories from Social Justice Movements*. Oakland: AK Press.

Laqueur, Thomas Walter. 1990. *Making Sex: Body and Gender from the Greeks to Freud*. Cambridge, MA: Harvard University Press.

Lomawaima, K. Tsianina. 1993. "Domesticity in the Federal Indian Schools: The Power of Authority over Mind and Body." *American Ethnologist* 20, no. 2: 227–40.

Lorde, Audre. 2007. *Sister Outsider: Essays and Speeches*. Berkeley, CA: Crossing Press.

Lugones, María. 2007. "Heterosexualism and the Colonial/Modern Gender System." *Hypatia* 22, no. 1: 186–209.

Martinez, Elizabeth. 1993. Beyond Black/White: The Racisms of Our Time. *Social Justice* 20, no. 1–2: 22–34.

McClintock, Anne. 1995. *Imperial Leather: Race, Gender and Sexuality in the Colonial Contest*. New York: Routledge.

Medina, José. 2003. "Identity Trouble: Disidentification and the Problem of difference." *Philosophy & Social Criticism* 29, no. 6: 655–80.

Méndez, Xhercis. 2014a. "An Other Humanity: (Re)constituting Gender, Bodies, and the Social from within Afro-Cuban Santería." PhD diss., Binghamton University.

Méndez, Xhercis. 2014b. "Transcending Dimorphism: Afro-Cuban Ritual Praxis and the Rematerialization of the Body." *Journal for Cultural and Religious Theory* 13, no. 1: 101–21.

Méndez, Xhercis. 2015. "Notes toward a Decolonial Feminist Methodology: The Race/ Gender Matrix Revisited." *Trans-Scripts* 5: 41–59.

Mohanty, Chandra Talpade. 2003. *Feminism without Borders: Decolonizing Theory, Practicing Solidarity*. Durham, NC: Duke University Press.

Moynihan, Daniel P. 1965. "The Negro Family: The Case for National Action." United States Department of Labor, March. http://www.dol.gov/oasam/programs/history/webid-meynihan.htm.

Muñoz, José Esteban. 1999. *Disidentifications: Queers of Color and the Performance of Politics*. Minneapolis: University of Minnesota Press.

Oyěwùmí, Oyèrónkẹ́. 1997. *The Invention of Women: Making an African Sense of Western Gender Discourses*. Minneapolis: University of Minnesota Press.

Paredes, Julieta. 2008. *Hilando fino: Desde el feminismo comunitario*. La Paz, Bolivia: Comunidad Mujeres Creando Comunidad.

Quijano, Anibal. 2000. "Coloniality of Power, Eurocentrism, and Latin America." *Nepantla: Views from South* 1, no. 3: 533–80.

Rowley, Michelle V. 2010. "Whose Time Is It? Gender and Humanism in Contemporary Caribbean Feminist Advocacy." *Small Axe* 14, no. 1: 1–15.

Santiago-Valles, Kelvin A. 2003. "'Race,' Labor, 'Women's Proper Place,' and the Birth of Nations: Notes on Historicizing the Coloniality of Power." *CR: The New Centennial Review* 3, no. 3: 47–69.

Scott, Joan Wallach. 1986. "Gender: A Useful Category of Historical Analysis." *American Historical Review* 91, no. 5: 1053–75.

Scott, Joan Wallach. 2010. "Gender: Still a Useful Category of Analysis?" *Diogenes* 57, no. 1: 7–14.

Spelman, Elizabeth V. 1988. *Inessential Woman: Problems of Exclusion in Feminist Thought*. Boston: Beacon Press.

Spillers, Hortense J. 1987. "Mama's Baby, Papa's Maybe: An American Grammar Book." *Diacritics* 17: 64–81.

Stoler, Ann Laura. 1995. *Race and the Education of Desire: Foucault's History of Sexuality and the Colonial Order of Things*. Durham, NC: Duke University Press, 1995.

Stoler, Ann Laura. 2002. *Carnal Knowledge and Imperial Power: Race and the Intimate in Colonial Rule*. Berkeley: University of California Press.

Strongman, Roberto. 2002. "Syncretic Religion and Dissident Sexualities." In *Queer Globalizations: Citizenship and the Afterlife of Colonialism*, edited by Arnaldo Cruz-Malav and Martin F. Manalansan IV, 176–195. New York: New York University Press.

Terry, Jennifer, and Jacqueline L. Urla, eds. 1995. *Deviant Bodies: Critical Perspectives on Difference in Science and Popular Culture*. Bloomington: Indiana University Press.

Tuck, Eve. 2016. "Urban Education and Indigenous Social Thought." Presentation, Michigan State University.

Tuck, Eve, and K. Wayne Yang. 2012. "Decolonization Is Not a Metaphor." *Decolonization: Indigeneity, Education & Society* 1, no. 1, 1–40.

Voeks, Robert A. 1997. *Sacred Leaves of Candomblé: African Magic, Medicine, and Religion in Brazil*. 1st ed. Austin: University of Texas Press.

Wekker, Gloria. 1999. "'What's Identity Got to Do with It?': Rethinking Identity in Light of the Mati Work in Suriname." In *Female Desires: Same-Sex Relations and Transgender Practices across Cultures*, edited by Evelyn Blackwood and Saskia E. Wieringa, 119–38. New York: Columbia University Press.

Wekker, Gloria. 2006. *The Politics of Passion: Women's Sexual Culture in the Afro-Surinamese Diaspora*. New York: Columbia University Press.

Welter, Barbara. 1966. "The Cult of True Womanhood: 1820–1860." *American Quarterly* 18, no. 2: 151–74.

White, Deborah Grey. 1985. *Ar'n't I a Woman? Female Slaves in the Plantation South*. New York: Norton.

Wynter, Sylvia. 1990. "Afterword: Beyond Miranda's Meanings: Un/silencing the 'Demonic Ground' of Caliban's 'Woman.'" In *Out of the Kumbla: Caribbean Women and Literature*, edited by Carol Boyce Davies and Elaine Savory Fido, 355–73. Trenton, NJ: Africa World Press.

Wynter, Sylvia. 2003. "Unsettling the Coloniality of Being/Power/Truth/Freedom: Towards the Human, after Man, Its Overrepresentation—an Argument." *CR: New Centennial Review* 3, no. 3: 257–337.

SECTION II | **Making Feminist Selves**
Self-Authority, Affect, and Narrativity

CHAPTER 6 | Philosophical Feminism
in Latin America

FRANCESCA GARGALLO

Translated by Erika Grimm and Kevin Cedeño-Pacheco

THE MAJORITY OF THE cultural experiences of Latin America women, whose thought has expressed, since the colonial period, their difficulty in accepting and being accepted by the hegemonic system of knowledge transmission and creation of ideas and art, lies in the boundaries between philosophy and literature, between activist practice and theory.

Poets like Juana Inés de la Cruz (1651–1695) of Mexico, storytellers like Teresa Margarida da Silva e Orta (1711–1793) of Brazil, and socialist activists like Flora Tristán (1803–1844) of Peru declared their right to be women of study and struggle in poems, letters, novels, essays, and manifestos in a world that rejected them for it. However, it was not until the nineteenth century, when the Argentine antislavery writer Juana Manso (1819–1875) argued for the necessity of public education and philosophical instruction free from Catholic dogma for women's moral and intellectual emancipation—along with the reunion of those thusly educated in order to restructure the country and right its moral wrongs—that a feminist political position was openly expressed. This endeavor was taken up by teachers and writers at the end of the century. Rita Cetina Gutiérrez (1846–1908) of Mexico, originator of the movement La Siempreviva, Visitación Padilla (1882–1960) of Honduras, founder of the *Boletín de la Defensa Nacional*, as well as others from countries across the region demanded women's right to education, to freedom from the male gaze over their lives, and, later, to vote. With this, they initiated a feminist movement— that is, a movement of women and concerning women's condition—in Latin America.

The intersection of various modes of expression for conveying women's thought is particularly clear in the work of Juana Inés María del Carmen

Francesca Gargallo, *Philosophical Feminism in Latin America* In: *Theories of the Flesh*, Edited by: Andrea J. Pitts, Mariana Ortega, and José Medina, Oxford University Press (2020). © Oxford University Press.
DOI: 10.1093/oso/9780190062965.003.0007

Martínez de Zaragoza Gaxiola de Asbaje y Ramírez de Santillana Odonoju, known as Sor Juana or Juana Inés de la Cruz, of whom María del Carmen Rovira writes: "The poetess is the first author who, in the Mexican philosophical tradition following the conquest, makes use of poetic form for the expression of philosophical themes" (Rovira 1995a, 109). Her own teacher, José Gaos, wrote in 1960: *"Primer sueño*, poem of Sor Juana Inés de la Cruz, has its place in the history of ideas of Mexico" (Gaos 1960, 54).

The unique protofeminism of the Hieronymite monk has been studied and recovered in the last fifty years by women literati and writers, as well by male critics and essayists, who have seen in the "Tenth Muse" not only the best baroque poet of the Castilian language, but a woman who faced suppression, censure, and threat due to her double condition as female and American (Lorenzano 2005).

The illegitimate daughter of a Creole and a Canary Islander, she was born in the town of San Miguel Nepantla, in an area inhabited by a majority population of speakers of the Nahuatl language, which she learned and in which she wrote from the age of seven, implicitly supporting the idea that the Spanish and the indigenous, women and men, are endowed with equal capacity for argumentation regarding themes such as religion, right, love, and obedience.

Although she made no reference in her letters, sonnets, or theatrical works to the legend of La Malinche—that is, the mythical figure of Doña Marina Malintzin, Totonac princess who was gifted by the chief of Tabasco to Hernán Cortés to serve as his interpreter-slave, and who was transformed in colonial Mexican culture into the woman that symbolizes the race traitor; the woman who loses her people for the sexual passion that turns her into the first mother of a mestizo—Sor Juana represented the earthly figure of the New Spanish woman who rebels and debunks the lovable weakness of all women. In fact, if the history of Malinche served to eroticize the sexual violence of the conquest—a motif repeated in the colonial mythology of many countries of the Americas—giving the semen of the white man a primary place in the symbolism that awards supremacy to the colonizers within dominant continental sectors, the image of Sor Juana, who preferred the monastic life to marriage and the friendship of literati and vicereines to erotic life, was many times associated with lesbianism—precisely for the reason that she could not be dominated by masculine power, not even by the power sacralized in priests and inquisitors.

The work of Juana Inés de la Cruz enjoyed immense fame during the life of the poet. Her works were twice published and reprinted several times in Spain between 1689 and 1725. But beginning in the second half of the eighteenth century, her fame declined, along with all of baroque poetry, considered by new tastes to be pedantic and convoluted. Her brilliance was recovered only around 1951, when Alfonso Méndez Plancarte began publication of her *Complete Works*, urging others, too, to involve themselves in the search for her lost writings. *Carta al padre Núñez* was only found by Aureliano Tapia Méndez in 1960; *Enigmas a la Casa de Placer* discovered around the same time by Enrique Martínez López; and *La carta de Serafina de Cristo* was found and published by Elías Traulse as recently as 1995.

The protofeminist position of Juana Inés de la Cruz derives from the experiences of suppression she suffered for having been a woman of deep, precocious intelligence who studied and wrote—a woman who, in speaking about theology, defied the sentence of silence that San Pablo had imposed upon all women, and whom the Inquisition made a point of punishing for the act of daring (Glantz 1997).

There exist three philosophical-theological writings of the poet that demonstrate a strength of conviction and poetic, philosophical quality unparalleled by any other New Spanish author, which are of extreme interest: *Primer Sueño, Carte Atenagórica o crisis sobre un sermón*, and *Respuesta a la muy ilustre Sor Filotea de la Cruz*.

The poem *Primer Sueño*, or *Primero Sueño*, written between the ages of thirty-five and forty, is considered by Sor Juana herself to be of singular importance—in her *Respuesta a Sor Filotea de la Cruz*, she writes that it is the only piece for which she owed credit to nothing but her own inspiration. In this piece, according to María del Carmen Rovira, she undertakes a "harrowing philosophical game" with the concepts, contrasting the epistemological and methodological character of two traditions: the Neoplatonism of the Augustinians and Franciscans, and the traditional scholasticism of Thomist thought. In *Primer Sueño*, moreover, she completely does away with argument from authority, applying to the arguments a doubt Cartesian in origin: "The soul of the poet finds itself before the confusion of the chaos that it wishes to subject to an eminently explanatory logical order" (Rovira 1995a, 104–5).

The other two texts are in prose and are either of a polemic character, as in *Carta Atenagórica o crisis sobre un sermón* from 1690, or express a defense of individual thought and the right to research and intelligence, as in *Respuesta a la muy ilustre Sor Filotea de la Cruz* from March 1, 1691—"Sor Filotea" having been a pseudonym used by the bishop of Puebla, Manuel Fernández de Santa Cruz, in attacking Sor Juana for having been a successful writer, and therefore criminal, heretic, and barbaric.

In *Carta Atenagórica*, Juana Inés de la Cruz criticizes the sermons of the Portuguese Jesuit preacher Antonio de Vieryra, performing an exceedingly audacious and dangerous act and one unheard-of for a woman. "One discovers in her lines a certain personal pleasure, an intimate satisfaction in the criticism she levels. She was conscious of just how much her words could wound the preacher's pride, and she took pleasure in it, even more so for being a woman who dared to level a critical analysis of the Sermón del Mandato" (Rovira 1995b, 65–66).

A further protofeminist position is related with certain verses that, as an official writer of the viceroyalty, Juana Inés de la Cruz composed for the women who consulted her. In these poems "on commission," one glimpses not only the ability of the poet to identify herself with the lives of the other women—those in love, married, and widowed—but moreover an ethical position, tied to an idea of an essential equality among human beings, which led her to argue against masculine censure or condemnation of those acts carried out by women that were required of them. Although they are verses of erotic-moral character, they seem to deal with matters of any ethical nature, given that in them she asserted the necessity of the triumph of reason over pleasure, understood as fancy.

This protofeminism went unmentioned by all of her male commentators, among them men of the literary status of Octavio Paz, or by anyone before the point in the middle of the twentieth century that saw the development of a political hermeneutic of daily life, sexuality, art, and the economy carried out by women and known as feminist consciousness-raising, neofeminism, or the women's liberation movement in order to differentiate it from the "suffragism"—in reality, feminism—of the nineteenth century. It is in fact feminism that is the first philosophy that pays any attention to the politics of legitimacy—that is, of the ways in which a society grants the cultural privilege of legitimating knowledges and values to one group (men, whites, aristocrats, the rich) with the aim of excluding the contributions, wisdom, values, and knowledges of other groups (women, slaves, the poor, indigenous, blacks).

The work of the Mexican poet, like the work of other extraordinary women persecuted for their deviation from cultural molds, was subjected to a revision that went further than the recovery of the presence of some women in the culture of the Americas, like that of the denunciation of their concealment by the official history. Feminists, beginning in the 1960s and 1970s, proposed a reading of the same conditions of submission and resistance, which brought about their own breakthrough into the world of aesthetic, ethical, and political definitions, centering economic criticism of the masculine expropriation of their bodies and criticism of the sciences for the interpretations given of those same bodies and of their intelligence.

In the twentieth century, the spread of the ideals of equality between women and men and the growing awareness of the systematic exclusion of the achievements of women—as well as of visibility of their condition and needs—in collective knowledge gave rise to the collection of feminist theories that comprise the philosophical feminism of Latin America and the Caribbean. This feminism has had limited reach and has been little analyzed, even in surveys of the thought of the most important political and social movement of the twentieth century. One serious problem is that the academy prioritizes the teaching of feminist texts of developed countries and does not consider Latin American women thinkers to be theorists. Feminism in the academy takes part in the intellectual subordination produced by the neocolonization that prevails across many areas of the continent. The majority of texts written about feminism in Latin America take 90 percent of their references from abroad. I would like to recall here the words of Margarita Pisano of Chile, when she declared that citation is political!

Mexican philosopher Eli Bartra (b. 1947) proposes a rethinking of the history of Latin American feminism in three, possibly four, large periods of struggle.

First, it is necessary to analyze the feminism that preceded the 1970s. It deliberately points out the problem of naming. For a long period of time, the movement for the vote was not called feminist but simply suffragist; even today there are people who refer to it as such, distinguishing it from feminism. However, this first feminism involved the struggle for rights such as education, legal parental authority over sons and daughters, and equal pay for women alongside the mobilization to obtain the vote. This feminism then directed its efforts toward the modification of legislature, making possible women's participation in the public sphere, in keeping with the standards of formal policy. It called for equality with men in the enjoyment of political, social, and economic rights that had been denied to women. In the face of the dominant inequality, it defended equality as a way of ending discrimination and subordination.

Second, Bartra proposes an analysis of the neofeminism that arose in the 1970s. This was a true movement for women's liberation; centered in the body, in sexuality, in the private sphere, it stated that the "personal is political." It was a movement directed toward the physical and psychological interior of every woman and toward the formation of small groups concentrated around the practice of consciousness-raising, understood as in-depth dialogue between women. Its public intervention was directed at the securing of spaces (as well as laws) that guaranteed a free life to women: free from the male gaze, from his word, from his violence.

Neofeminism was, at the same time, both a continuity and a rupture, and thereby uncovered the value of difference. Women are not the same as men financially, historically, nor ideologically; consequently, more radical feminists took up respect for difference as a political value.

At the dawn of the twenty-first century, Eli Bartra sees feminism once again spreading outward. She finds struggle in the public arena, in the field of institutions (governmental and otherwise), and formal policy. However, this concerns much more sophisticated, perhaps richer, struggles than those of a century and a half earlier. At the same time, she tracks the dawning of a new independent feminism in the traces of the need for feminism's revival.

In reality, Latin American feminism has neglected to refer to the differences of women as a social group opposite men, highlighting instead the existing differences among women themselves. At the same time, it has demanded equalities between the "genders," understood as social groups—products of a powerful cultural technology of molding people according to economico-cultural attributes imposed upon owners of feminine and masculine genitals—in the social sphere as well as in the private one (Bartra 2007).

Bartra is an activist philosopher. At a young age, at the start of the 1970s, she was already a radical feminist activist, and came to propose an aesthetics and politics incarnated in the feminine body and interrelated with one another. In 1979, during the Tercer Coloquio Nacional de Filosofía, she asserted that feminism is a theoretical and practical current applied to the uncovering of what it means to be a woman in the world (the concrete world, the Mexican or Latin American world). Her strategy took place on two levels: the destruction of the false, socially imposed feminine nature, and the construction of women's identity on the basis of their own needs, interests, and experiences. At the same event, she defined her sexed political role as a conscious and organized struggle against the patriarchal system that is "sexist, racist, [and] that exploits and oppresses, in multiple ways, all groups outside of spheres of power" (Hierro 1985, 129).

Being heterosexual and white, Bartra never posited a sexual or ethnic specificity in her feminist analysis; nonetheless, she was a radical critic of double militancy or of the reference (which she considered a mode of legitimation) to party politics, social movements, masculine cultural groups. Today, philosophically, the feminist movement is a political movement that concerns a subversive movement against the established order, an involved presence of women with one other, a space of autonomy that goes back to the history of women's resistance in proposing a different future, a possibility of change.

Furthermore, for Bartra, feminism is a political philosophy. She expresses it with the vehemence of an activist and the clarity of a philosopher, in terms that could not be reclaimed by any theorist of continental European feminism—too autonomous in the definition of politics for the egalitarians and too related to the existence of patriarchy for the independents—nor by the Anglo-Saxon feminists who are anchored in the analysis of gender.

At the start of the 1970s, she went through consciousness-raising, a small-group feminist practice that consisted in listening among women naming individual feelings and experiences in order to uncover the experience of the other; it was named thus by Carla Lonzi of Italy, but was of

US origin. In 1975, together with Lucero González, Dominque Guillemet, María Brumm, Berta Hiriart, and Ángeles Necoechea, she formed the collective La Revuelta, a "small group" in which one could reflect on maternity, the double shift of work, sexuality, friendship, and politics among women.

The series of military putsches that devastated South America from 1971, relegating thousands of women to torture, detention, and exile, as well as the wars of national liberation in Central America, with their 30 percent of women combatants, prevented the continuation of the practice of consciousness-raising in small groups as an expression of Latin American women's politics. The feminist response of Eli Bartra was expressed in her participation in the Encuentro Feminista Latinoamericano y del Caribe de Lima (1983), in the organization Taxco (1987), and in the academy. In 1982 she was among the founders of the research center Mujer, Identidad, y Poder in the Department of Politics and Culture of the Metropolitan Autonomous University, Xochimilco.

Since the 1980s, her philosophy has been linked with the theories of historians, anthropologists, psychologists, sociologists, and writers. She is one of the few feminist academics who, in 1990s Mexico, challenged the abuse of the category of gender when used for invisibilizing women, as well as indiscriminate usage of the now-hollow phrase "gender perspective" for analyzing the feminine condition—even when the gender relations thoroughly utilized in the analysis of reality seem fundamental. At the same time, she refuses to speak of Latin America as a postfeminst society, believing that "we live immersed in a neocolonialism in which feminism has yet to fully come about" (Bartra 1998, 141).

To conceptually reinforce the minimum commonalities that feminists share—that is, oppression and the multiple struggles that have been carried out against that oppression—she challenges seemingly vanguardist thought, like multiculturalism, as it allows "tolerance" of cultures different from the hegemonic, but does not respect them. The origin of the theory of multiculturalism can be geopolitically located in the North, producer of neoliberal economic standards. It strongly pushes a deepening of differences that would otherwise be diluted, designating groups of membership from outside and from above that in fact prevent any egalitarian contact between cultures.

For Bartra, there is not respect for difference in multiculturalism, nor even pluralism, but the construction of racist "cultural diversities" that end up being ghettos in which the hegemonic power of the white men of the North does not question its supposed universalism. At the same time, it permits the dismissal of feminist internationalism, preventing women from claiming their human rights, since the particular aggressions they suffer are considered in multiculturalism to be immutable (or perhaps ahistorical and essential) parts of specific cultures. Within the dangers of multiculturalism, Bartra distinguishes the immediate—for example, its justification of the clitoridectomy of an eight-year-old girl out of respect for the animist culture of Madagascar—from the more profound, which come together in the denunciation of a hegemonic culture that is defined by its right to produce, with its gaze, the otherness of other cultures, claiming, in the name of difference, access to benefits that it reserves for itself.

The feminist methodology that Bartra utilizes to analyze the common reality of sexism, as well as different masculine and feminine ideologies, and the artistic process of women, expresses in an explicit manner the relationship between politics and philosophy. This methodology is "the rational path traveled by a woman with political consciousness of feminine subalternity and in the struggle against it in bringing her closer to knowledge of any given aspect of reality" (Bartra 1994, 77).

For exactly this reason, she questions the history of art as a structure of androcentric and classist study from the perspective of women's popular art, a theme that has been practically ignored by feminism. In analyzing the phenomena of the hybridization of certain expressions of popular art, she uncovers a juncture between the traditional indigenous and mestizo cultures and the modern occidental culture for intra- and extra-aesthetic reasons: the economic crises, the feminization of "the popular" [*lo popular*], and the diverse creativities. Even in altars of commercialization, artistic creativity involves constant renovation and inserts the use of needle and thread, of clay, of illustration, and of religious sentiment into the world of the new—a world that has almost always denied the creative expressions of women (Bartra 2005, 8–12).

The aesthetic cannot be approached without feminist studies, since "There exist universal values neither in popular nor in elitist art. Aesthetic values must be seen with the cultural context in which they are produced, with the social classes and the genders that produce the works. All of it plays a part in aesthetic evaluation" (Bartra 2005, 178).

This detailed description of the thought of Eli Bartra serves to demonstrate that, for the set of women philosophers of Latin America, it is not easy to gather the thought elaborated in literature and political debates into one doctrine. Essays, lessons, conferences, poems, and novels do not constitute a corpus, but a route by which they configure a collective consciousness with its own language.

Equally difficult is finding a theory or feminist method before the feminist movement burst onto the academic scene around 1975, driving the production of professorships, research centers, and programs for theorizing that which had already broken out at the political level. Nonetheless, distinguished philosophers like Vera Yamuni (1917–2003) and María del Carmen Rovira (b. 1923)—who, as students of José Gaos, recognized the value of doing philosophy in Latin America and incorporated it into their particular humanism and historicism—had already been tackling in interviews and conferences the importance of being recognized as women, understanding with this the specifically historical condition of their lives, in doing philosophy. The rest, for the most part, in speaking about their experiences, based their philosophical work on that of their male colleagues.

It is worthwhile to remember the importance of Rosario Castellanos (1925–1974), teacher of philosophy and successful writer, in her 1950 presentation of a thesis entitled *Sobre cultura femenina* (Mexico, 2005), in which she maintains that the production of ideas and of art by women is in contradiction to the education that compulsively forces them into compliance with the maternal work they accept as inherent to their condition.

In the twenty-four years to follow, Castellanos published, along with the most intense proindigenous narrative of Mexico, five volumes of essays and one theatrical work, *El eterno femenino*, where she expresses a clear awareness of the problem meant by recognition of an identity in construction due to the double condition of being a woman and being Mexican.

The question of women as *philosophical subjects* was only just in the 1970s and 1980s connected to the work of liberating philosophy from its vision and structure biased in favor of masculine actions, reflections, and leadership. The new sights of feminist philosophy of Latin America were set on the history of philosophy and the relationship between gender and power, and its individual and political manifestations, in its curriculum and research. Though progress was slow, it meant a certain opening of academic circles to a feminist understanding of philosophy.

The majority of Latin American women philosophers who have taken up the existence of the women's liberation movement in the second half of the twentieth century do not hesitate to define Latin American feminist theory as a political theory of the body, culture, and expression of women, or as a hermeneutic of masculine power.

For Ofelia Schutte (b. 1945), Cuban inhabitant of the United States, feminist theory is a part of a greater theory of Latin American cultural identity: her analysis involves the contextualization of the concept of liberation in Latin America (Schutte 1993, 207). She recognizes that the struggles for women's social and political identity originated in the suffragist movement at the start of the twentieth century; moreover, she asserts that the historical roots of all feminist thought are "deeply entangled in modernity and, hence, in the conception of self emerging from the occidental humanist tradition" (Schutte 1995). She locates the motives of women's action in the Cuban Revolution and in international feminism, as well as in the impact that the UN Decade for Women conference in Mexico City had in the region. However, Schutte disregards, or does not place any value on, the movements in favor of equal rights between the sexes that occurred in Mexico and Latin America during the nineteenth century and in the first four decades of the twentieth, nor on the feminist critics of the control exercised over women by the Cuban government.

Latin American feminism may be studied as a political action of "gender." Schutte utilizes a conception of gender produced in the 1970s in English-language feminism and rounded out by Judith Butler in 1986, taken from the central idea of Simone de Beauvoir's *The Second Sex* that being is to come to be: "One is not born, but rather becomes, a woman." In this way, for Schutte, gender is a social construction with a basis in biologically given sex, to which we conform as women and men in Latin America—even though, by this construction, in countries of masculine dominance, privilege is always given to men, who are assigned roles corresponding to socially privileged gender constructions marked at the social, cultural, and linguistic (symbolic) levels. This concerns a definition of the relations of gender that is not essentialist, but geographically and historically situated.

Schutte maintains that gender consciousness is the fruit of experience and socialization. For this reason, she analyzes alternatively the concepts of gender and subjectivity, so as not to fall into the antiquated binary distinction between man and woman, and their complementary antithetical groups, like self and other, mind and body, right and wrong (Schutte 1995).

According to the presentation of the Cuban philosopher, awareness that the feminine body has been socialized as a site of normative constructions of femininity has been "acquired" by Latin American women, thanks to the numerous meetings that have taken place in Latin America since 1981 and to the diverse publications that have put them in contact with writers, intellectuals, and political activists, contributing to the expansion of feminism in the region. This idea is unclear: on the one hand, from where were they acquired? On the other, if they generated the means to meet as well as the published reflections, why would a philosopher so interested in modes, symbols, ideologies, and practices that legitimate political and philosophical activities neither describe nor analyze the thought that they produce and critique?

Schutte maintained academic relations of interlocution with the Argentine Association of Women in Philosophy and, in Mexico, with the feminist and philosopher of education Graciela Hierro. However, she never cites Latin American feminist theorists in her writings and describes the performances of these social actors for a US audience of readers from "external" political sidelines. It would seem as though she writes about and for them, but she does not inform her thought or reflection with anything they produce.

In contrast, beginning in the 1970s, Dr. Graciela Hierro Perezcastro (1930–2003) applied herself to the fundamental labor of something that could be called "academic feminist activism" in Latin American universities. Many women philosophers that today are at other institutions were once her students at Universidad Nacional Autónoma de México (UNAM), when the university was a radiant center of Latin American culture in the 1980s. In addition, she challenged tenets of international convention in order to insert herself and to put herself in contact with the philosophers of host countries. Conversations, debates, and oral lectures given by Hierro on the lawns of various universities have made it possible for students and teachers to allow themselves to express their reflections on political action in the street or in women's collectives.

At the end of the 1970s, she located in Simone de Beauvoir's idea the beginning, not just of a political theory, but of a utilitarian ethic that proposed, as a criterion of moral judgment, the social utility of equality of opportunity for women and men. The relationship between ethics and politics, according to her, is present on two levels: (1) in the moral laws that serve to orient the actions of individuals in society, and (2) in historical practice (Hierro 1985).

Hierro understands moral norms as agreements that can be revoked if the consequences of their fulfillment do not adhere to the principle of justice, which is centered around the idea that different individuals should not be treated differently. This results in an extreme suitable for proposing a reform of the idea of the feminine condition: "The ethical decision about the actual feminine condition is supported in the evaluation that is made of its tendencies and its consequences, insofar as these are beneficial for the majority" (Hierro 1985, 93–94).

For Graciela Hierro the central category applicable to the feminine condition is that of "being-for-others," which, according to de Beauvoir, situates her on an inferior level with respect to the other sex, negating for her the possibility of transcendence. "The being-for-others that de Beauvoir speaks of is concretely expressed in woman through her situation of internalization, control, and use. These are the attributes derived from her condition of oppression, as a human being to whom the possibility of realizing the transcendental project is not awarded" (Hierro 1985, 13–14). This interpretation of the masculine as the human norm that confines the feminine to the structural position of "other," that which establishes difference, implies for the Mexican philosopher a duty to be ethico-political, which coincides with the denunciation of the system of inequality between the sexes. It coincides, likewise, with the formulation of the existence of a system of gender, that is, a system of sexual and economic division of labor between the sexes and their symbolic representation.

For Hierro, politics among women is and should be a politics of demands, and so questions the situation of women according to society (of their inclusion in a society of masculine decisions and symbolisms), and not according to themselves. Having already begun to utilize the category of gender, in 1990, she wrote that the "human phenomenon" can study itself in all of its aspects in order to understand ethical behavior. These aspects that are all of equal value in the knowledge of people's lives include their socioeconomic characteristics, their geographical location, their personal and social history, their sex-gender, and their age (Hierro 1990, 35). Being-woman in itself represented for Graciela Hierro a variant and not a fundamental truth of the human condition.

However, in 2001, Hierro radicalized her feminist position and considered an ethics of pleasure for the feminine subject in the process of construction, now less identified with her gender and more willing to be associated with her sexual difference: a subject in need of a symbolic order, self-definition, and moral autonomy, which writes herself in the feminine plural: *las mujeres* (Hierro 2001, 14). In this way, one cannot avoid the recognition of the centrality of sexuality and pleasure in analyzing the relationship between power and knowledge, and reflection on the possibility of an ethics of pleasure that is not a sexualized ethics. Implicitly, Hierro critiques gender as a conceptual instrument for the moral autonomy of women, as gender is only what is thought about women and men and not a medium for uncovering and expressing the ways of life of women subjects.

The ethics of pleasure in this way transforms into an ethics for the practice of sexual difference, envisioned from various disciplines, which allows *las mujeres* to be independent of sexual conditioning. "Feminist ethics has been 'sexualized' because women, as gender, have created ourselves through the interpretation that patriarchy is constructed from our sexual whims. Undoubtedly, our oppression is sexual; gender is the sexualization of power" (Hierro 2001, 9–10). She adds that philosophy is recreated under the vigilant feminist gaze, which method leads to the awakening of consciousness, continues with the deconstruction of patriarchal language, and culminates in the creation of a feminist grammar, the ultimate foundation of which is maternal thought.

In the same manner, gender serves to identify the sexual imaginary constructed from the masculine body, that which, once identified, allows women to separate sexuality, procreation, pleasure, and eroticism. Meanwhile, the wisdom and ethics of *las mujeres* transcend this first step, through a process of liberation that involves the moral exercise of a subject that freely recognizes itself and that analyzes its actions for its good life. The twofold sexual principle is generic; the ethics of pleasure is a knowledge of *las mujeres*.

Feminist radicalism in philosophy is not an easily recognized feature. Academic discrediting and marginalization are prices not all women philosophers dare pay, because it is quite difficult in the academy to justify the relation between feminist theory and practice and philosophy. In general, the acceptance of epistemological contributions stemming from political movements is slow, and the weight of universalism is still overwhelming. Nonetheless, recognizing herself as the symbolic daughter of Sor Juana and Rosario Castellanos, two writers who philosophized, Graciela Hierro has not only appraised all feminine knowledge, granting it the value of knowledge, but has offered herself as a "symbolic mother" to numerous students who needed to bridge their activism and research, as well as various women philosophers who dared to look further than logical analysis in order to think themselves.

Just before her death, in October 2003, she wrote: "Everything that I know I owe to women, witches [brujas] who dared to think. I only read women, I've already read so many men. . . . I learned what I needed from them and I only consult with some whose ideas serve my purposes. To be feminist, for me, means to personalize everything" (Hierro 2004, 11).

Like Hierro and Schutte, Diana Maffía (b. 1953) is a feminist who has established herself in academia, but, like Bartra, is a woman who also constructs knowledge outside of the classroom by means of her connection to and interlocution with the women's liberation movement. On occasion, like the Panamanian philosopher Urania Ungo, she takes up work in state institutions to carry out a politics of demands of justice—that is, a legal struggle in favor of women—as in the Defensoría del Pueblo en la Legislatura de la Ciudad de Buenos Aires. In actuality, she was working on the questioning of gender normativity in defense of transgender and transsexual individuals (Maffía 2003).

According to Diana Maffía, feminist philosophy in the Argentine academy begins to develop in the mid-1980s—with the conclusion of the last bloody military dictatorship—thanks to the influence of three foreign women philosophers and the pivot they initiated in ethics and practice: the exiled María Cristina Lugones (b. 1951) (who has returned after twenty years in the United States), the Spanish Celia Amorós (b. 1944), and the Mexican Graciela Hierro.

Among the expressions of democratization was the return of the university to its normal mode of participatory governance to remedy—through competitive selection of faculty—the hollowing out of the academy imposed by the military from 1976 to 1986. An important contest was initiated to fill the Chair of Ethics in the School of Philosophy and Literature of the University of Buenos Aires.

Almost all of the chair-holders were men, so the contest had been preceded by a strongman dispute for the territory of moral legitimacy. The competition was, in itself, contentious for this reason—despite the fact that there were two positions. The difference was that there was a woman: on top of that, young; on top of that, almost foreign; on top of that, feminist; on top of that, anarchist; on top of that, lesbian activist. And on top of all of that, María Cristina Lugones turned each of these inscriptions into an opportunity for ethical discussion of wholly practical and political connotations, instead of proposing a scholasticism on the basis of Aristotle and Kant. At the margins of the competition, which Lugones obviously lost, a group of ten or twelve philosophy professors got together with her to have her inform them of the fact of feminist philosophy that would allow them, semantically, to unite the two tracks of life that, like Euclidean parallels, they had been given. With typical activist generosity, Lugones provided them with a bibliography, organized a seminar, and promoted the formation of an association of women in philosophy.

Maffía, one of them, recognizes appreciatively those who paved the way. Today, when talking about philosophy, she always refers to something that could be called a theoretical praxis. Indeed, for her, philosophical theory is a form of feminist praxis. She defines feminism by stating that it is the conjunction of three statements: one, descriptive—that in every society, women are worse off than men; a second, prescriptive, that affirms that it should not be this way; and one, practical, that involves the commitment to do what is in one's power to stop that inequality.

This conception of feminist philosophy is deeply tied to the dismantling of oppressive systems of power—even within the academic system. From this approach, it is not a philosophy made by women about women, but rather a type of thought that begins in the self-awareness of one's situation with respect to all subordination and that is committed to take gender relations into account as significant. It also considers theory in relation to a practice committed to the emancipation of arbitrarily imposed hierarchies.

For the professor of epistemology at the University of Buenos Aires, the practical side of her feminist theory concerns conceptually dismantling the hegemonic constructions that could contribute to the oppression of distinct subjects, women in particular, but not only women. She does not define philosophy by the answers it offers to problems that arise from reality, but by the questions, interrogations, and issues that have to do with that which extends beyond everyday life and transcends the answers given by the sciences or the constructions of common sense; that is, by a concern for the foundations of practically everything.

From the moment that philosophizing privileges the question and not the answer, the approach that the question has is no longer restricted to one discipline, but, further, must break out of the limits of discipline. Feminist theory questions disciplinary limits, because they have helped to systematically hide problems, experiences, questions, and needs that have been fundamental to women's subjectivity. To constitute a proper subjectivity and not be "hetero-designed"—that is, designed by outside existent disciplines—is one consequence of having privileged the problem in terms of answers. Meanwhile, science, philosophy, and politics maintain themselves as patriarchal institutions, always intending to bring women into "masculine territory" as a condition for their acceptance (Maffía 2000).

The epistemological tools used to critique disciplinary limits break with some academic limitations, since they make reference to the experiences, systematizations, and concepts that serve to organize knowledge with respect to the problem in which the question is the priority. The motives for those who ban certain constructions and subjects of knowledge from institutions have to do with the limitations of accepted epistemological tools. To exclude those who think in different terms is to maintain accepted forms of thought absolutely—to maintain them without discussion, with closed borders. If the questioning (or simply different) subjects were integrated into the discussion, they would advance points of view that would motivate the radical rearticulation of the concept in question.

Women have been systematically excluded from the construction of knowledge because they base their affirmations about reality in justifications that are too devalued by traditional epistemology. When a woman affirms that she is absolutely certain of something because she has a strong intuition concerning it—or that she is emotionally inclined in favor of or repelled by a response—by no means is it accepted in science. In fact, this has been quite devalued, though these are very important heuristic tools. This urges us to discuss precisely which tools are legitimate in accessing knowledge, because, as feminists, we legitimate tools and empower subjects to participate in the construction of knowledge. And when we empower subjects, new tools replenish our possibilities for knowledge.

The dialectic—in which subjects participate in the construction and legitimation of tools and what fits within and outside of the system of knowledge—is a dialectic that feminist philosophy should dismantle and rearrange. If women participated in the collective construction of knowledge, they would legitimate their own cognitive tools without transforming themselves into the only subjects who are justified to know. History is full of examples of women who have entered the sciences for their use of traditional scientific standards. Nonetheless, the presence of those women is not a big deal, because they enter into history only to have proven that they are like the master (Maffía 2001).

That said, doing feminist philosophy does not mean that one must offer something anarchic, but rather something unprejudiced: freedom in the choice of issues to address, exchange with other disciplines that are still considered contaminants in philosophy, the privileging of the complex issues over and above a specific focus, and the revealing of the motives that philosophy has discounted as insignificant and that can be recuperated as new senses. Diana Maffía thus places much attention on the endeavors of her colleagues. In actuality, Argentine women philosophers are working on a great variety of issues: the relation between gender and the construction of citizenship, feminist epistemology, the relations between gender and sexual difference, the ethics of bioethical investigation, like those between feminism and subjectivity, and the implications of multiculturalism on the body as a social construction.

The nucleus of the most reactionary ideas against which feminism collides is one that establishes a naturalization of social positions due to, among other things, a sex that is also naturalized. Something that one does not choose, biological genitalia, determines in an immutable way the sex and gender that correspond to the person and thus the immutable place one occupies in society, whose cultural goods, their obligations and rights, belong to and are alien to them.

The conceptual corset endures, for its first step established a dichotomy—two exhaustive and exclusive concepts. It is exhaustive because it is supposed that the pair of concepts, male-female, for instance, exhausts the universe of the discourse; there is no third or fourth possibility. All the possibility of the sexed self fits within the dichotomous pair. The Aristotelian principle of the excluded middle is applied. It is exclusive because if the individual can be cataloged within one of the two concepts, it is automatically excluded from the other. If it meets the conditions that define the male, I not only know that it is male, but that it is not female. The logical principle of noncontradiction is applied here.

The second step of the conceptual corset is the hierarchization of the pair that is invariably united with this difference; all difference is made, in this way, hierarchy. The conceptual pair always entails that one is superior and the other is inferior. Aristotelian logic has a strong metaphysical affirmation of the self: at once a condition of thought, language, and reality. It is a strong determination of the necessary and essential character of the dichotomies presented, not only in their differences, but also in their hierarchies. It is difficult for thought to escape this imperative, above all for subjects who, like women, have been systematically in the margins of cultural legitimation.

The exclusion of women from places of knowledge-production is not alien to this dichotomy. The power of this system of thought consists in that, in superimposing the masculine-feminine pair on the already hierarchized traditional pairs (mind-body, universal-particular, abstract-concrete, rational-emotional, identity-alterity, production-reproduction), they become sexualized; with them, they reinforce the existing hierarchy between men and women. By discounting all cognitive value associated with the feminine, it is assured that women will not have the means to revert the dichotomous logic. The corset is knitted in four simultaneous steps: first, the elaboration of the dichotomies; second, hierarchization; third, sexualization; and fourth, the exclusion of the cognitive value on the feminine side of the pair.

Why can't women think? Because they are defined by the body and not by the mind. This ideological commitment, which direct consequence is the exclusion of women from all spaces of knowledge, was precisely what prevented the body from being seen as a key epistemological condition, and it is what makes the treatment of the issue so rich and promising. Feminists saw it from the start of their reflection and, according to Maffía, thus began to discuss the same bond between sex and gender—the possibility of detaching gender from corporality.

The body is an enclave of many determinations—not just sex, but also of ethnic roots, of color, of age, of physical incapacity—that feminist revisionism considers in a nonessentialist mode. The body should not be understood as a biological no sociological category; it is rather a point of overlap between the physical, the symbolic, and the sociological.

The feminist emphasis on embodiment in philosophy comes with the radical repudiation of essentialism. In feminist theory, one speaks as a woman, although the subject women is not a monolithic essence defined once and for all. Rather, she is the site of the conjunction of multiple and potentially contradicting experiences, defined by variables that are superimposed—such as those of class, race, age, lifestyle, sexual preference, and others.

Rupturing is a common practice within Argentine political groups and academic thinking. A division arose in the Argentine Association for Women Philosophers, where several divergent strategies were presented. The first envisioned that philosophical studies of gender would be added to the traditional curriculum of the degree, inserting them within the methods recognized by philosophy—its usual thematic divisions—in a dialogue that would incorporate them without disqualifying nor threatening what had historically been constructed. One assimilationist strategy that was rejected by the radical wing of the feminist movement, though it had success in the university, was expressed in the traditional academic sense: publication in recognized philosophy journals, appointments in choice places, funding for fellowships and research projects, and recognition of one's "peers."

The second philosophical strategy was subversive: it intended to denaturalize what was instituted, question the hierarchies, not recognize the enshrined investments, ignore traditional forms of academic recognition, and privilege action and the commitment with the women's movement to dismantle the barrier lodged between the academy and the lifeworld. This strategy, adopted by Maffía, was neither well received nor rewarded. It was not even granted space in the same community of women philosophers from which she had emerged.

Despite having opted for one of these models, Maffía is opposed to considering them dichotomous, pointing in this way to the sanitization of the deepest crack into which the thought-action of the feminism of the 1990s has fallen.

The first strategy was approached by María Luisa Femenías (b. 1955), who was of the generation of women philosophers to which the Spanish Amorós opened the doors to the critical study of women as the product of discourses in philosophy. Femenías links feminism with politics, but nevertheless does not study it as a women's movement that challenges an assumed reality; rather she justifies it because the origin of feminine discrimination originates in politics. What's more, it is the axis around which Aristotle articulates the dependence relation of women due to their inferiority. Although it may appear contradictory, the strengthening of politics is erected on top of the metaphysical base that, in turn, finds its ultimate justification in biology.

Philosophy officiates as a discourse of legitimation for science; but ontology, where the "material" appears as a category for the conceptualization of the feminine, requires a grand biological narrative to demonstrate that women are amorphous and passive by nature and, therefore, not apt for public life. "The Aristotelian system is a legitimizing narrative of the inferiority of women and of a patriarchy of paternalistic and protective character. This is the case of some rhetorical passages in the works on biology, some analogies, and the presence or absence of certain terms that are uncritically picked up in his metaphysics and that definitely contribute to the final justification of the Aristotelian patriarchal system" (Femenías 1996, 22). In this way, Aristotle established what would be converted over time into a "patriarchal paradigm" in which the biology, character, historical-political position, and activities of women were studied.

This paradigm is the patriarchal system of thought. It constitutes and regenerates the same androcentrism (that is, the way of perceiving the world from the exclusive view of men) that, in some extreme cases, can be aggressively misogynist, or, as in the majority of the cases, accord to the paternalistic and protectionist Aristotelian model. When he attributes rationality per se to men, Femenías tells us, Aristotle overspecifies men to the detriment of the political activity of women and establishes a double standard, according to which rationality is considered positive in men and seen as negative in women, because women and men are valid for investigation and observations based only on the actions and thoughts of the masculine sex. "There is not, then, a single standard, but two; or, in other words, a single one, but gender-biased" (Femenías 1996, 23).

Meanwhile, the patriarchal paradigm continues to act because (recalling Femenías) the philosophy of Aristotle has permeated the occidental culture that has, over the course of centuries, left women captive to an ahistorical continuum. In this paradigm, the concepts of being human and being man are treated as synonymous, producing an overlap that excludes half of the human gender. "The form of the universal overlaps with half of the species (the males)—that which obviously excludes the other half (the women) on the basis of circumstances of birth" (Femenías 2001, 18).

Femenías does not locate her reflections in a historically determined context. She studies "occidental culture," not the occidentalized culture of Latin America, and she links this to the necessity of interpreting herself from the point of view of a universality that, nevertheless, has come apart with respect to philosophical androcentrism—that is, to the need to be recognized by an external and superior power as an "equal." Contradictorily, Femenías locates herself in the political thought of women. She does not alienate her sexed body to think about herself; she does not long for herself in the masculine other, but leaves her cultural reality that (if we follow this to the foundation of Anglo-Saxon feminist anthropological discourse) constructs the systems of sex/gender.

In *Sobre sujeto y género: Lecturas feministas desde Beauvoir a Butler*, Femenías surveys Euro-American feminist philosophical thought to demonstrate the incongruities of the Franco-Italian positions on difference—according to a lineage marked by the ideas of Celia Amorós, of which feminism of difference, like any other postmodern thought, dismisses the relevance of reason—and condemns postcolonial studies from Anglo-Saxon India and cultural studies of the Mexico-US border in terms of their approach to reality: "The incommensurability of the relations between women and men of each ethnicity does not stop having undesirable edges that impede agreement, critique, persuasion, and mutual enrichment of concepts" (Femenías 2000, 256). Therefore, Latin America is the only place today from which to analyze the history of feminist thought as, once again, an indeterminate space where the rights of women to difference should find itself with the duty to constitute democracy.

On the other hand, the Panamanian Urania Ungo Montenegro (b. 1955) and the Brazilian Sueli Carneiro (b. 1951) study the path of feminist political conscience to analyze Latin American women's desire to design different options from subordinate identity and to create alternative projects to current forms of domination. The antiracism of the Brazilian and the political study of the Panamanian constitute proposals for theoretical-practical activism.

Ungo traces a historical route of political situations in Latin America, examines the difficulty of constructing the feminist movement (and its conceptions), and, finally, synthesizes real debates between Latin American feminists (Ungo 2000). Her idea of feminist theory is that it concerns a type of thinking that is constructed on the basis of political phenomena. This is in keeping with the idea postulated two decades before by the most important theorist of feminist political resistance to the dictatorships and patriarchies in Latin America: the Chilean Julieta Kirkwood (1944–1985).

At the end of the 1980ss, Urania Ungo, activist politician influenced by Latin American socialist thought, wrote a history of Central American women, *Subordinación genérica y alienación: El discurso de las organizaciones de mujeres de la región centroamericana*. During its drafting, she approached Solange Oullet (Quebec), Sara Elba Nuño (Mexico) and Elizabeth Álvarez (Guatemala), with whom she established the Comité Feminista de Solidaridad con las Mujeres Centroamericanas (COFESMUCA) and with whom, in a second phase, she would rearrange the political analysis to "put interpersonal relation at the center of the intellectual and political discussion—rejecting all the mystique that shrouded them as natural relations without power" (Ungo 1997).

Even though she was director of the Dirección Nacional de la Mujer and technical secretary for the Consejo Nacional de la Mujer, del Ministerio de la Juventud, la Mujer, la Niñez y la Familia from 1996 to 1999, she never stopped recognizing that feminism is not a matter of the state; it is, rather, a politics of women. According to Ungo, "Feminism is the social movement that has carried out the most foundational challenges to occidental cultural order, evidencing the forms in which patriarchal domination, violence, and war are generated—and how these cross and articulate social inequalities and oppressions of every kind." (Ungo 2000, 15). Therefore, she defines feminist theory as the political theory of women and affirms that the thought of Latin American feminists regarding the relations between women and politics, as well as the debates that the political practices of women generate within feminism, are the central elements of thought and action in Latin America.

For Ungo the history of feminist philosophical ideas in Latin America is the history of the political thought of women as well as the analysis of its historicity. Comprehending the significance that feminism in Latin America has today involves "thinking that the active and passionate presence of women at the core of distinct social and political movements does not correspond with their absence from places of power and choice" (Ungo 2000, 17). For this reason, she reworks the historiographical theories of Asunción Lavrín and the practice of "the history of the present" of Edda Gabiola. Ungo intuits that the two historians do not approach the same form of the history of women, for the first does not sustain a feminist theory, nor does she look at the political body of feminism. In *Para cambiar la vida: Política y pensamiento del feminismo en América Latina* (2000), she maintains that the actual political vagueness of feminism—with its chaos of superstitions of diverse theoretico-political horizons—can find an exit if the history of the Latin American feminist movement is reread and reinterpreted, remembering that which should not be forgotten: that feminism is a political utopia that joins thought and action, and is at the same time a life practice.

Beginning a radical lesbian-feminist vision, Sueli Carneiro addresses the problem of racism in the ideological construction of Latin American feminism. For the Brazilian philosopher and educator, all situations of conquest and domination create conditions for the sexual ownership of disenfranchised women, with the goal of affirming the superiority of the victor. These conditions perpetuate violence against women in general, and, in particular, against indigenous, black, and poor women.

According to Sueli Carneiro, what can be considered legacies or remnants of the colonial period stay alive in the social imaginary and acquire new garbs and functions in a supposedly democratic social order that maintains the gender relations—according to color, race, language, and religion—instituted in the period of the couriers and slavers. During her participation in the International Seminar on Racism, Xenophobia, and Gender organized in Durban, South Africa, she argued:

The colonial violation perpetrated by white men on the indigenous, the black, and the resultant mixture is the origin of today's constructions regarding our national identity, structuring the decanted myth of Latin American racial democracy, that arrived at its final consequences in Brazil. This sexual colonial violence is also the cement of the gender and race hierarchies present in our societies that are configured with what Ángela Gilliam defines as 'the great theory of the sperm in national formation,' according to which:

1. The role of the black women is rejected in the formation of the national culture;
2. the inequality between men and women is eroticized; and
3. sexual violence against the black women has been converted into a romance (Carneiro 2005, 21–22).

A fourth phase of Latin American feminism appears to be unfolding with this antiracist and political redemption of the need for feminist transformation of reality. Opposed to the institutionalization of the demands of hegemonic feminism and the aging of many of its representatives, black women from Santo Domingo, like Ochy Curiel (b. 1962), who wrote about the political struggles of women and their strategies against racism (Curiel 2002), and indigenous activists, like the Zapatistas that redacted the Revolutionary Law of Women (Rojas 1994), reclaim specific rights to be respected in a body that they define and defend as different from the hegemonic body—not just from the masculine, but also from white women and heterosexuals.

Despite the fact that Brazilian feminists have not advanced a critique of the institutionalization of spaces for the political thought and action of women in Latin America since the beginning of the 1990s, with the fragmentation of the movement into diverse nongovernmental organizations (NGOs), it is black women philosophers of Brazil like Sueli Carneiro and Jurema Wernerk who have contributed greatly to the visibility of the subtle academic and intellectual racism of hegemonic feminism. Hegemonic feminism would never explicitly take up a discriminatory position based on ethnicity, color, or sexual orientation of a woman but, in fact, does not value cultural contributions equally in institutions (NGOs and the academy). Nor does hegemonic feminism consider them with the same level of "universality" with which they were framing new important hierarchies between the postulates of Latin American feminism, preferring the ones wielded by white, urban, and heterosexual women.

Feminist knowledge today is constituted from a hermeneutic of power and from more deeply entrenched beliefs, offering (from subjective and collective experiences) an intimately political gaze, directed toward the interior of women—not so that they will throw themselves toward the female colonization of public space, but so that they will recuperate, from their own movement, the autonomy of their thought and action.

In this sense, the intersecting of experiences and analyses that come from anthropology, literature, activism, and politics turns out to be fundamental for feminist philosophy. The study of the territoriality over the female body as a space that should submit to economic globalization and face its sovereignty against murderous violence is carried out by Rita Laura Segato (b. 1953) of the Department of Anthropology of the University of Brazil. She necessarily situates herself in political philosophy and feminist aesthetics, so the murdered body is a body upon which the system inscribes its violence (Segato 2003).

The woman's body is also the body of dominant masculine impunity against the impoverished body, of mestizaje, and of resistance. In this sense, the Mexican philosopher María del Rayo Ramírez Fierro (b. 1962) had already mentioned the need to reflect upon the violence that is visited against the female body when it acquires voice and political vindication. For her, it is necessary to think about the persistence of indigenous women's resistance in the Andes—resistance to the terror that colonial power inscribed on the body of Bartolina Ciza when she was quartered at the end of the eighteenth century for having demanded, with her husband Tupac Catari, the right to a government led by the indigenous; and of

Micaela Bastida, who was similarly tortured and killed for having organized the finances of the rebellion of her husband Tupac Amaru (Ramírez Fierro 2006, 50–51).

Although there is not an expression of protofeminism in her political approach, with the presence of her sexed and murdered body in the history of the Andean rebellion she established a tradition of women's struggle that, in the same zone, produces in actuality voices and ways of doing politics that have defied occidental feminism. Not only does Silvia Rivera Cusicanqui (b. 1948) study the role of collective memory among women of the farmer-Indian movement of Bolivia (Rivera Cusicanqui 2003), but Domitila Barrios de Chungara (of the Annual International Tribunal of Women), wife of a mineworker and mother of seven children, has also said that women's liberation is linked with the socioeconomic, political, and cultural liberation of the specific people [*pueblo*] to which she belongs (Viezzer 1982).

That said, there is no place in America where racist violence and femicide, misogyny and political repression show more evidently their nexus than in Central America, in particular, in Guatemala—a country where an indefinite number of indigenous women (close to two hundred thousand) were killed at the hands of the army in ways that combined genocidal intent and misogynistic hate. There, from the signing of the peace accords of 1996, the killing of women has multiplied without obvious cause.

It was in Guatemala, too, that the voice of a white, upper-class poet, Alaide Foppa (1914–?), raised one of the first critical reflections on the conditions of liberation for Latin American women and was suppressed by military violence that led to her disappearance on April 22, 1980. Today we hear from voices who reclaim ideas from Mayan conditions and from mestiza conditions of the self, Guatemalan women exposed to femicidal fury. These voices should be incorporated into the study of Continental and Caribbean feminist philosophy, as they demonstrate thought on the place of indigenous women in the expression of antiracist feminism.

Undoubtedly, the thinking on racism that has been carried out by black and indigenous women has its principal point of overlap in the denunciation of economic, social, and cultural aspects—and in access to functions of discrimination in the hegemonic culture. Kidnapped from their culture of provenance and enslaved, African women were violently incorporated into the modernity that, since the sixteenth century in America, "racialized" slavery—which is to say that it constructed an identification between ethnic belonging and type of work inside the colonial economy. In this way, their principal claim is to receive the equal treatment proclaimed by liberal and socialist theories of the nineteenth century, and—with respect to the historical conditions and group expressions—dissent from the hegemony reclaimed by the Left at the end of the twentieth century and beginning of the twenty-first. Antiracist Afro-Latin American feminism has often also been feminism in a lesbian voice that is dissident to reproductive heterosexuality.

The women who speak one of the two thousand American languages, identify, on the other hand, with the history of communities that have resisted modernity, opening membership to forms of life, economy, and interpersonal relation that have indeed suffered the onslaught of Christianity and capitalism; they have also known how to oppose it with an integrated vision of human, animal, and inanimate life.

Indigenous women belong to very different cultures between them, but they claim a place with respect to the interior of their community and respect for their community in the context of occidentalized America. This double exigency takes them to apparent contradictions with respect to the use of legal, cultural, and educational instruments for expressing feminist exigencies. This is without acknowledging that many feel that the use of colonial languages (Spanish, Portuguese, French, and English) "de-indianizes" them. Teachers, writers, and activists express their needs as women who freely love each other in the realm of a community that they feel is theirs and that they desire to transform. They reject the construction of an individual feminine subject; they support occidental feminist egalitarianism, but they demand that their needs and interests not be subordinate to collective will determine by the masculine collective. The Tojolabales, for example, express that "there is no plurality without difference" along with the demand that no communal decision be taken by an assembly of men with no women present.

Likewise, mestizas and the mixed begin to question their roles in the construction of indigenous identity. The poet Maya Cu (b. 1970) writes verses and literary criticism in which the condition of the indigenous woman, torn in her wish-to-be-like-herself-among-others in the achievement of an individual-collective liberation, faces censorship that comes not only from her community but also from the anthropologists and researchers who intend to reduce her necessarily to an identity determined from outside.

"When one is born in the middle of an indigenous family that migrated from the rural zone to the margins of the urban region, one grows up 'not-being.' Or at least feeling that one never stops being a part of. This is to say that you are not totally indigenous, because your family has been obligated to break with proper cultural customs in order to be accepted in the urban context. In the same manner, the urbanity does not let you be totally a part of it, because you come from an indigenous family. To this we add contextual discriminatory practices: fun made of one's name, size, color, accent" (Cu 2007, 36). In the same way, women who abandon their rural communitarian condition end up working in mixed organizations with a strong indigenous presence; they face the phenomenon of not being totally accepted, as color, stature, and name indicate one thing, but clothes and the absence of mother tongue indicate another.

Through the anthropological thought of Ana Silvia Monzón and of the Kaqchikel teacher Aura Estela Cumes, we get the conflictual construction of a feminine identity that wants to dissociate from the location that oligarchic and oppressive power imposes on women according to the ethnicity to which they belong. For many, the ethnic is a source of tension in the women's movement that should be confronted, as it is only from the assurance of antiracism that, for women—women in their bodies—the right to not suffer violence may be constructed (Cumens y Monzón 2005).

References

Bartra, Eli. 1994. *Frida Kahlo: Mujer, ideología, arte*. Barcelona: Icaria.

Bartra, Eli. 1998. "Reflexiones metodológicas." In *Debates en torno a una metodología feminista*, ed. Eli Bartra, 141–158. Mexico City: UAM-Xochimilco.

Bartra, Eli. 2000. "Tres décadas de neofeminismo en México." In Eli Bartra, Anna M. Fernández Poncela, Ana Lau, *Feminismo en México, ayer y hoy*. Mexico City: Universidad Autónoma Metropolitana.

Bartra, Eli. 2005. *Mujeres en el arte popular: De promesas, traiciones, monstruos y celebridades*. Mexico City: CONACULTA-UAM.

Bartra, Eli. 2007. "¿Y siguen las brujas conspirando? En torno a las luchas feministas en México." In *El sujeto latinoamericano*, ed. Francesca Gargallo and Rosario Galo Moya. Mexico City: Universidad Autónoma de la Ciudad de México.

Carneiro, Sueli. 2005. "Ennegrecer el feminismo: La situación de la mujer negra en América Latina desde una perspectiva de género." *Nouvelles Questions Féministes: Revue Internationale Francophone* 24, no. 2: 21–26. Edición especial en castellano, "Feminismos disidentes en América Latina y el Caribe."

Castellanos, Rosario. 2005. *Sobre cultura femenina*. Mexico City: Fondo de Cultura Económica.

Cu, Maya. 2007. "Respuesta de Maya Cu, escritora guatemalteca." *Manovuelta: Revista de la UACM para las Comunidades 3*, no. 6.

Cumes, Aura Estela, and Ana Silvia Monzón. 2005. *La encrucijada de las identidades*. Lima: Publicaciones Consejería en Proyectos.

Curiel, Ochy. 2002. "La lutte politique des femmes face aux nouvelles formes de racisme: Ver une analyse de nos stratégies." *Nouvelles Questions Féministes: Revue Internationale Francophone* 21, no. 3: 84–103.

Femenías, María Luisa. 1996. *Inferioridad y exclusión: Un modelo para desarmar*. Buenos Aires: Grupo Editor Latinoamericano.

Femenías, María Luisa. 2000. *Sobre sujeto y género: Lecturas feministas desde Beauvoir a Butler*. Buenos Aires: Catálogos.

Femenías, María Luisa. 2001. "Sobre la definición de lo humano: Cuerpo femenino negado y sacralizado." In *Lola Press* (Montevideo), no. 15, May–October.

Gaos, José. 1960. "El sueño de un sueño." *Historia Mexicana: Revista Trimestral* (El Colegio de México) 10, no. 1.

Glantz, Margo. 1997. "Ruidos con la Inquisición." *Fractal* 6 (July–September): 121–43.

Hierro, Graciela. 1990. *Ética de la libertad*. Mexico City: Editorial Fuego Nuevo.

Hierro, Graciela. 1985a. *Ética y feminismo*. Mexico City: UNAM.

Hierro, Graciela, comp. 1985b. *La naturaleza femenina: Tercer Coloquio Nacional de Filosofía*. Mexico City: UNAM.

Hierro, Graciela. 2001. *La ética del placer*. Mexico City: UNAM.

Hierro Perezcastro, Graciela. 2004. *Me confieso mujer*. Mexico City: Demac.

Juana Inés de la Cruz. 1992. *Obras completas*. Edited by Francisco Monteverde. Mexico City: Ediciones Porrúa.

Lorenzano, Sandra, ed. 2005. *Aproximaciones a Sor Juana*. Mexico City: Fondo de Cultura Económica–Universidad del Claustro de Sor Juana.

Maffía, Diana. 1993. "La filosofía sexista, la epistemología feminista y otras vicisitudes de la Razón." In *Temas Actuales de Filosofía*. Salta, Argentina: Facultad de Humanidades, Universidad Nacional de Salta.

Maffía, Diana. 2000. "Género, ciencia y ciudadanía." Paper presented to III Congreso Internacional Multidisciplinario Mujer, Ciencia y Tecnología "Visión Mundial de la Mujer en Ciencia y Tecnología desde un país plenamente soberano." Panama City, July 27–29.

Maffía, Diana. 2001. "Ciudadanía, exclusión y género." In *Contrato Social y radicalismo democrático: El pensamiento de J.J. Rousseau*. Buenos Aires: UBA/CLACSO.

Maffía, Diana, comp. 2003. *Sexualidades migrantes: Género y transgénero*, Buenos Aires: Seminaria Editora.

Manso, Juana. 1854. *La familia del Comendador*. Buenos Aires: Imprenta Benheiem.

Ramírez Fierro, María del Rayo. 2006. "Los movimientos indígenas en el siglo XXI." In *Intersticios: Filosofía/Arte/Religión. Publicación semestral de la Escuela de Filosofía de la Universidad Intercontinental* 11, no. 24.

Rivera Cusicanqui, Silvia. 2003. *Oprimidos, pero no vencidos: Luchas del campesinado aymara y qhechwa 1900–1980*. La Paz: Editorial del Thoa.

Rojas, Rosa, comp. 1994. *Chiapas: ¿Y las mujeres qué?* Mexico City: Ediciones de La Correa Feminista.

Rovira, María del Carmen. 1995a. "Lo filosófico y lo teológico en Sor Juana." In *Cuadernos de Sor Juana: Sor Juana Inés de la Cruz y el siglo XVII*, edited by Margarita Peña, 97–118. Mexico City: UNAM.

Rovira, María del Carmen. 1995b. "La recepción de la filosofía moderna y el problema del conocimiento en sor Juana Inés de la Cruz." *La Colmena: Revista de la Universidad Autónoma del Estado de México*, special issue no. 5, Winter, 65–70.

Schutte, Ofelia. 1993. *Cultural Identity and Social Liberation in Latin American Thought*. Albany: State University of New York Press.

Schutte, Ofelia. 1995. "Crítica de la normatividad del género." In *Diálogos sobre filosofía y género*, edited by Graciela Hierro, 61–74. Mexico City: UNAM–Asociación Filosófica de México.

Segato, Rita Laura. 2003. *Las estructuras elementales de la violencia: Ensayos sobre género entre la Antropología, el Psicoanálisis y los Derechos Humanos*. Buenos Aires: Universidad Nacional de Quilmas-Prometeo 3010.

Ungo Montenegro, Urania Atenea. 1997. *El feminismo ante el fin de siglo: Notas para un balance crítico*. Panama City: Editorial Portobelo.

Ungo Montenegro, Urania Atenea. 2000. *Para cambiar la vida: Política y pensamiento del feminismo en América Latina*. Panama City: Instituto de la Mujer, Universidad de Panamá.

Viezzer, Moema. 1982. *Si me permiten hablar . . . Testimonio de Domitila una mujer de las minas de Bolivia*. Mexico City: Siglo XXI.

| Crossroads and In-Between Spaces

A Meditation on Anzaldúa and Beyond

OFELIA SCHUTTE

THE QUESTION OF IDENTITY, its social construction along a range of socioeconomic and gender indicators, and its motivating role as a factor for agency continue to challenge our thinking about Latina issues and values. In this essay I address a small part of this discussion, in particular, the existential question of coming to terms with the finite conditions under which the search for self-knowledge and self-realization can take place in the midst of circumstances where multiple oppressions obstruct the creative operation of radical subjectivities. I realize that some of the terms I use here are contestable for numerous reasons (methodological, metaphysical, political, and so on).[1] My aim is simply to offer a few reflections that will provoke further thinking and discussion, or let's just say they will hopefully provide an open space for further conversation and dialogue.

In this essay I focus on some difficult passages in Anzaldúa's *Borderlands/La Frontera*, with particular interest in her narrative regarding the overcoming of shame. I examine the problem of shame in the context of existential thought (including some points of affinity between Anzaldúa and Nietzsche) since the work lends itself to this type of analysis. Of particular interest is the question of identity in the sense of "becoming who you are." When issued in the imperative form, "Become who you are," this type of maxim appears to send our heads spinning in circles in search of an origin or a foundation on which to base the meaning of being and becoming. It may happen, however, that the disoriented subject may find no ultimate believable foundation or guide. Due to the social construction of identities, foundations of this kind tend to mimic the

---

[1] It is not my intention to define each term and defend every claim I make; if I did, I would not be able to get to the matters I want to address.

Ofelia Schutte, *Crossroads and In-Between Spaces* In: *Theories of the Flesh*, Edited by: Andrea J. Pitts, Mariana Ortega, and José Medina, Oxford University Press (2020). © Oxford University Press. DOI: 10.1093/oso/9780190062965.003.0008

power structures and hierarchies into which the subject is socialized. As Sartre famously observed in his treatise "Existentialism," a young person faced with a major ethical dilemma who seeks orientation and advice will inevitably receive a different kind of answer depending on whose counsel is sought (1993, 42–45).[2] In a mostly masculine-dominant society where class, racial, and heterosexual privileges and power structures still abound, radical subjectivities departing from socially expected protocols are likely to suffer setbacks and, in the worst cases, significant trauma due to the lack of a supportive social environment, among other factors. One of the reasons Anzaldúa's narrative is so inspiring is that she addresses the topic directly even at the cost of exposing her intimate personal trauma. In taking this step she also overcomes the burden of secrecy that further dehumanizes the subject of shame. Her account shows her strength in overcoming her pain and disorientation through the awakened voice of the character in whose name she speaks, alongside offering us a window into her universe: the new mestiza.

Become Who You Are

"Becoming who you are" is not only a paradox motivating us to question our assumed identities; it is an abiding existential challenge even if one decides affirmatively to engage this paradoxical conundrum.[3] I take its meaning to be something like "Be true to yourself (or to your most deeply felt convictions and beliefs), and act accordingly." Yet this remains an unreliable oversimplification and possibly even a misleading maxim, since our deepest convictions might be held in error, and what many take to be a self might well be a metaphysical illusion. Well, then, how does one ascribe self-knowledge to oneself (or others), and how does one decide what course to take when we come face-to-face with life's important crossroads? Is one driven to a choice by powerful instincts and desires? Or, perhaps, does one look outward and survey the many social factors and forces that have come to place us at this particular point of intersection in our lives, and, with the greatest effort at understanding such a play of forces and their impact on one's life, does one deliberate and take action,

---

[2] Sartre's essay *L'Éxistentialisme est un humanisme* (Paris 1946) has appeared in English under several titles: "Existentialism," "Existentialism Is a Humanism," and "The Humanism of Existentialism."

[3] Apart from the matter of conscience to be discussed later in the essay, defining who one is gets complicated by epistemological, metaphysical, psychological, and sociopolitical assumptions about identities and by the constant manipulations of identities found in everyday life, employment and leisure, media, and marketing. I have discussed various aspects of this problem in Schutte 1993, 12–16; 2004.

ranging from trying something out experimentally to committing to long-term projects?

Under conditions of oppression and discrimination, all that a person might be able to do is fight for survival. It is a much harder step to fight for survival *and* to achieve a creative state of affairs for ourselves and our intellectual/literary projects. This last situation is one that I find instantiated in Gloria Anzaldúa's major work, *Borderlands/La Frontera* ([1987] 2007). Let's consider that, in her case, which in some ways is analogous to that of many US Latina philosophers, what is at stake is the correlation between the personal identity she longs to claim and her identity as a writer. These two aspects also mean the degree of acceptance Anzaldúa will find in the communities of interlocutors she seeks in order to retain her creative drive to write as well as her personal sanity. "I cannot separate my writing from any part of my life," she says. "It is all one" ([1987] 2007, 95).

Anzaldúa tells us that she was born and raised at the crossroads of several cultures (US, Mexican, Indian), some of which (in the order named) had oppressed and exploited the others. At least in the Mexican and US contexts, she was cast out from social acceptance because of sexist and homophobic attitudes that dehumanized her.

> In my culture . . . women are at the bottom of the ladder one rung above the deviants. The Chicano, *mexicano,* and some Indian cultures[4] have no tolerance for deviance. . . . The queer are the mirror reflecting the heterosexual tribe's fear: being different, being other and therefore lesser, therefore sub-human, in-human, non-human. ([1987] 2007, 40)

This means that her sexuality places her at odds with what she has been taught is her cultural heritage: "For the lesbian of color, the ultimate rebellion she can make against her native culture is through her sexual behavior" (41). The displacement and oppression she experiences on account of her sexuality, however, strengthens her sense of community with all others throughout the world facing a similar situation:

> As a *mestiza* I have no country, my homeland cast me out; yet all countries are mine because I am every woman's sister or potential lover. (As a lesbian I have no race, my own people disclaim me; but I am all races because there is the queer of me in all races.) (102)

In other words, despite the homophobic attempts within her community to isolate and shame her, her transgression empowers her to redefine and

---

[4] It should be noted, however, that some other indigenous cultures accept same-sex or bisexual arrangements. For example, see Lugones 2007, 195, 198–200.

recreate her cultural location as a queer Chicana and "new mestiza" as well as to forge deep alliances in solidarity with others facing comparable experiences across a multiplicity of cultural locations. She continually affirms her humanity in view of the many faces of dehumanization.

Anzaldúa is observant about the plural sources of cultural prejudice, noting that she feels trampled upon not only by demeaning Anglo prejudices against Chicanas/os and Latinas/os, but by internal prejudices held by her own people. She denounces the sexist and homophobic "elements in the Mexican-Indian culture" and upholds Chicanas' demands for equality "with the men of our race" ([1987] 2007, 106). With regard to some Latina and Chicana women, she notes some areas of discomfort. For example, she observes the prejudiced workings of internal cultural and class hierarchies among Latinas in the context of social expectations on the proper and correct ways to speak and write the Spanish language. "Often it is only with another Chicana *tejana* that I can talk freely" (78), she comments, after mentioning that she apparently embarrassed some Chicanas from the San Francisco area because her Spanish vocabulary and usage were deemed inferior. In the preface to the first edition she refers to the Chicano Spanish she uses as an "infant . . . bastard language . . . not approved by any society" for which there is no longer a need to apologize ([1987] 2007, [18]).

These forms of discrimination hurt her because the failure to display both a socially acceptable linguistic competence and a socially acceptable gender identification risks forsaking the very matrix of socially recognized personhood. These features mark the basis on which many superficial interpretations of human dignity as well as of entitlement to social recognition and respect are formed. Failure to comply with linguistic and sexual/gender norms thus constitutes a double jeopardy, the psychological and emotional effects of which can be paralyzing even to talented adults. This is especially the case when their effects are imprinted in the psyche in early childhood, when children are most vulnerable to others' power, judgment, and control, as Anzaldúa reminds her readers. She speaks of young girls being subjected to emotions of fear and shame if their gendered behavior does not comport with the traditional normative expectations of their families and community. "By the worried look on my parents' faces I learned early that something was fundamentally wrong with me. When I was older I would look into the mirror, afraid of *mi secreto terrible*, the secret sin I tried to conceal—*la seña,* the mark of the beast. . . . I tried to conceal that I was not normal, that I was not like the others" ([1987] 2007, 64–65). As an adult reflecting on all this much later (after having learned to manage this socially inflicted sense of shame), she observes that making sense of our most painful experiences "can lead us toward becoming more of who we are" (68) if one takes the hard path to self-knowledge. Just how hard this path is, I would venture to say, will depend on the intensity of oppressions suffered and the resources available to fight them. Anzaldúa describes her own path to self-overcoming as both terrifying and redemptive. She identifies with the headless goddess Coatlicue as "a rupture in our everyday world . . . plunging us into the underworld" (68) but also as a mental state through which to find the inner strength to overcome those potentially paralyzing moments of pain that haunt her psyche. I will comment on her metaphors shortly.

Decapitation, which Anzaldúa symbolically enacts when she embraces Coatlicue, implies a break with conceptually governed approaches to the world. Since in its predominant Western constructs philosophy is the science of concepts par excellence, Anzaldúa appears to plunge her readers across the shore from philosophy (metaphorically speaking). Receding into the distance are Western philosophy's mind-body dualisms and all other logocentric approaches that generally serve to guide our way in the world, whether through the creation of meaning or the practical matter of choosing the means to attain various ends. Another way to say this is that she abandons and deauthorizes the West's sense of reason as the faculty not only capable of ordering, but entitled to order, our cognitive and ethical lives. Her wisdom is anchored in an embodied sense of presence in the world sustained by a dynamic interplay of curiosity, problem-solving, and practical intuition strung together artfully by a web of indigenous and earth-nurturing cosmic beliefs.

Her testimony reveals that although psychologically dangerous perhaps it was not altogether irrational for Anzaldúa to embrace the headless goddess in her transition to a deeper type of self-knowledge. The socialization process into which she was thrust had left her multifaceted psyche in great disarray. The various norms she had internalized from her disparate Anglo, Mexican, and indigenous cultures clashed among themselves: "alma entre dos mundos, tres, cuatro, / me zumba la cabeza con lo contradictorio" ([1987] 2007, 99).[5] The resulting internalized oppressions led to yet greater intensities of guilt and shame in a spiral of "internal strife" and "psychic restlessness" (100). A radical break with such an oppressive condition was needed.

The West offers two principal culturally sanctioned alternatives to temper reason: art and religion. Anzaldúa makes use of both although, again, her journey through these domains takes shape by way of ancient Nahua myths as well as a queering of Christian/indigenous syncretic iconography, so the aesthetic and spiritual connotations of her journey and its aftermath confront normative Western culture with significant differences.

---

[5] Here she describes herself (I translate loosely) as a soul existing between two, three, four worlds, her head whirling with contradictions.

"Ethnocentrism is the tyranny of Western aesthetics," she asserts ([1987] 2007, 90). Coatlicue's severed head may also be read as a total rupture with the phallic signifier—its castration and demise—insofar as reason, as the symbolic power of the masculine to name and legitimate the lifeworld, is figuratively depicted by the head. And, again, contrasting with the cerebral abstract Western practice of deconstructing *phallogocentrism*, which we academic philosophers might be tempted to appeal to when analyzing her semiotic transaxiological operation, Anzaldúa shows us that while she can survive through this crisis, at least temporarily, without a head, what she cannot sever from herself, not even for an instant through this painful journey, is her multidimensional mestizaje and the lived, concrete body that incarnates and sustains it: the sense of self that she will eventually call *la nueva mestiza*.[6]

One philosophical genre with the potential to help her address her crisis of consciousness, provided she abides by the Chicana roots of her human condition, is existentialism. We know from her interviews that she acknowledges a debt to Nietzsche, Kafka, and Sartre, among others (Ikas 2007, 238). In fact, Anzaldúa's anguish resonates strongly with existential concepts of freedom, where it is precisely in and through these moments of anxiety, moments that disrupt our everyday complacency with the world, that we give birth to the selves we wish to become. Her approach takes it several steps further, of course, insofar as it incorporates not only her personal narrative but a kind of epic narrative about a multigenerational and pluricultural Chicana experience. It is far from my intention to essentialize Chicana experience or Latina experience. As Jacqueline Martínez has observed, Anzaldúa does not offer her approach to overcoming oppression as a general rule, prescription, or mandate for all to follow (2000, 84–85). Moreover, Anzaldúa's narrative, metaphorical, and poetic method of writing makes clear that the sensitivities she displays and her strategies for survival as a person and a writer are only one of many possible paths to take. The very notion of complacency that she fights demonstrates that the mythical universe she invents in order to preserve her sanity allows for multiple approaches to identity, as well as multiple Latina identities. Her message, then, is one of dispelling and disempowering the emotional exploitation of fear and shame, and one of rebelling against all forms of authoritarian thinking.

---

[6] In her later work Anzaldúa (2015) reflects further on healing divisions, grief, and other existential issues. She writes of *nepantleras* who, in experiencing "the web of connections" with and among others, find ways of creating "alternative forms of consciousness"; see "Geographies of Selves—Reimagining Identity: Nos/Otras (Us/Other), las Nepantleras, and the New Tribalism" (83). See Ortega 2016, 17–46, for a recent powerful reading of Anzaldúa's work through the images of the new mestiza and *la nepantlera*.

Anzaldúa's Affinities with Nietzsche

In terms of achieving a creative approach to our intellectual projects, I mentioned earlier the important correlation at stake for Anzaldúa between establishing the identity she longs to claim as a person and her identity as a writer. One might call this simply a matter of style (both personal and literary), but a more careful examination signals a greater complexity. In this context, some of Anzaldúa's affinities with Nietzsche as a writer, as well as some of their differences, may be of interest. For example, as already mentioned Anzaldúa states that she cannot sever her writing from "any part" of her life ([1987] 2007, 95). This recalls the intense bodily and spiritual passion evoked by Nietzsche when he states, in the words of Zarathustra: "Of all that is written I love only what a man has written with his blood. Write with blood, and you will experience that blood is spirit" (1966, 40). Despite the marked differences in gender positions and political outlooks contextualizing these statements, both are vivid testimonies of the deeply held link between the author's writing and that person's lived experience. This way of thinking, in both authors, allows for a multiplicity of perspectives to come into play vis-à-vis one another without getting stuck in rigid binaries such as body/mind, passion/reason, poetry/prose, or conventional dichotomies of good versus evil. While Nietzsche sheds monotheism and allegedly impartial epistemologies in favor of a plurality of perspectives, Anzaldúa sheds gender strictures and cultural monologisms in favor of what she calls the *new* (already pluralized and dialogical) *mestiza consciousness*. (In Spanish the word *conciencia* means both "conscience" and "consciousness.") Both authors reject stylistic and conceptual homogeneity in favor of aesthetic and epistemic diversification. And yet, there is a sense in which precisely in view of acknowledging the intellectual and moral relevance of plural phenomena in life experience, the question of the sociocultural construction of a mestiza identity takes on new significance.

New Mestiza Identities and Their Significance

For Anzaldúa the Borderlands are a place where multiple types of cultural experiences are compressed. The clash of cultures is so intense that the likely fragmentation, condensation, and superposition of meanings result in some of the turbulent and confusing mental states she has described. As we have seen, the path to self-knowledge she embraces—despite its discomfort—is one that is willing to confront the fragmentation and internally felt contradictions found when multiple gender, sexual, and ethnic norms and expectations come clashing against one another, and either reason cannot be trusted to settle the differences between the clashing parties or it is impotent to do so. Nor is she satisfied with taking the easy way out, adapting to whatever behavior is most expedient. Instead, she pays attention not only to external differences—the differences between her Chicana roots, for example, and the aspects of Anglo culture that oppress them, out there in society, let's say in the so-called public sector. Just as much, if not more, Anzaldúa attends to the internal differences within her, how they are conditioned by these external factors, and how the social factors touch, move, and shape her body in such a way that her body, conscience, and consciousness are inscripted by the values and expectations they convey. The paradigm of the new mestiza that emerges from this process is born out of an affirmation of her embodied radical subjectivity, one that works by awakening "dormant areas of consciousness" rather than by following society's comforting cheers to "rejoin the flock, to go with the herd" ([1987] 2007, 19).

This means that an understanding of her work remains incomplete without attending to the spiritual and existential resolutions she seeks in a synthesis of healing.[7] Specifically, there is a yearning to heal from a state of fragmentation caused by multiple forms of oppression and grades of sedimented emotional abuse—yes, much of it including epistemic violence, but not limited to this alone. It is the type of abuse that penetrates deeply into a person's moral identity, distorting and incapacitating the heart of a person's psyche through deviously entangled elements of fear, guilt, and shame. These are learned cultural constructions acquired in dysfunctional and oppressive conditions and settings, not excluding some family and community settings, and they can only be reversed by a conscious countercultural effort with regard to the specific constraints that the oppressive patterns have generated. One of the principal patterns to be overcome is the abusive inculcation of shame.

Nietzsche and Anzaldúa, in their respective ways, address the liberation from shame. In section 270 of *The Gay Science* Nietzsche writes: *"What does your conscience say?—*'You shall become the person you are'" (1974, 219). This is followed by five brief aphorisms, of which I cite the last three:

Whom do you call bad?—Those who always want to put to shame. (§ 273)

---

[7] Anzaldúa notes that by "synthesis" she does not mean a collection of separate parts or a balancing of opposites. Rather, she means a "third element," one "greater than the sum of its severed parts." This is a mestiza pluralist consciousness whose creative energy is constantly breaking down "unitary" conceptions as well as the subject-object divide and other dualities that bind the psyche ([1987] 2007, 101–2).

> *What do you consider most humane?*—To spare someone shame.
> (§ 274)
> *What is the seal of liberation?*—No longer being ashamed in front of
> oneself. (§ 275, 220)

When referring to this text in his autobiography Nietzsche celebrates *la gaya scienza* as the "highest hope" for his future readers, referring to how "a destiny finds for the first time a formula for itself, for *all* time" in "the granite words" found in these specific aphorisms (1967, 295).

For Nietzsche, in other words, the key to self-awareness is a liberated conscience (that is, a conscience no longer confused by or trapped in shame). Notice that this key provides a unique link between the person one is (just now, not any longer ashamed) and the person one shall become, thereby solving the paradox implied in the maxim "Become who you are." There is a sense that this conscience was already there, somehow, although unable to operate freely. From the phrase "no longer" one may infer that there is some sense of progression (from past to present and future), as indeed one finds in Nietzsche's remarks in *Ecce Homo* and in the general project that he called "the transvaluation of all values."[8] But there is another way to read this as well if we take the side of Nietzsche that does not wish to see the course of our lives interpreted exclusively or primarily in terms of linear time. In this latter case, the "no longer" may be conceptualized alternatively as a type of transformation or release (out from under a disabling blockage, arrest, or entrapment). This sense of release from entrapment is something Nietzsche celebrates in his notion of the free spirit.[9]

There is a deep affinity in these thoughts with the process of overcoming shame in Anzaldúa. For Anzaldúa, a personal sense of liberation also occurs. In her case, the person who is now liberated from shame and who, without shame, is free to become who she is, is none other than *la nueva mestiza*. "*La mestiza* has gone from being the sacrificial goat to becoming the officiating priestess at the crossroads" ([1987] 2007, 102).

Unlike Nietzsche's Zarathustra high in the Alps, whose major encounter with a crossroads is set at an imaginary point in-between time and eternity, Anzaldúa's new mestiza resides in late twentieth-century

---

[8] "Nietzsche's joyful wisdom or gay science . . . begins with the psychological premise that one will remain open to theoretical adventures, to different and multiple ways of interpreting reality. The richness of life cannot be exhausted by the mind. This is something that should make the lover of knowledge joyful rather than somber. It is Nietzsche's hope to be able to effect this reversal of attitudes through the transvaluation of values" (Schutte 1984, 53).

[9] The theme of the free spirit is pervasive in Nietzsche, from *Human, All Too Human* (1878), subtitled "A Book for Free Spirits," through *The Gay Science* (1882, 1887) and *Beyond Good and Evil* (1886) to his autobiography *Ecce Homo* (published posthumously in 1908). In a writer as complex as Nietzsche this theme has many variations and multiple agonistic features on which it is not possible to elaborate here.

North America at the crossroads of many cultures, where a variety of oppressive and liberating traditions intermingle and mix (hence our Latina experiences of mestizaje). If I may be allowed another reference to Zarathustra, we might reflect on an image from part of a speech on what Nietzsche calls the three metamorphoses of the spirit. In this narrative the good and dutiful spirit starts out as a camel willing to be well loaded with duties and tasks, and heads into the desert. There it meets a dragon on whose golden-like scales hang many Thou Shalts. Nietzsche indirectly lets the reader understand that just because (and precisely because) those values glitter like gold they are not *really* gold; they are simply scintillating (*funkelnd*).[10] And what might be some of the golden-like Thou Shalts that confuse us Latinas? Well, don't we always hear the voices: be quiet, keep your opinions to yourself. Or else: this is what you must do for your family; this is what you must do for your people! Countless imperatives, orthodoxies, and Thou Shalts speak to us from inside (not just outside) our own cultures as well as from our own consciences. In the background, there linger fear and shame, if one dissents. In the course of time it is possible to retain one's sanity by resignifying the meanings of "family," "friendship," "community," and the like. These constitute some of the spaces where we negotiate our identities on an on-going basis and where what we take for granted in terms of the legitimacy of these concepts may well need to be reexamined, changed, or transformed.

When as a writer Nietzsche felt that Western reason cut him off from the world of art, he invoked a reconceptualization of reason in the guise of what he called *la gaya scienza*. Nietzsche's *gaya scienza* corresponded to the free spirit's desire for knowledge; it was not to be weighed down by a ponderous spirit of gravity; it could include humor, experimentation, and irony; above all it was to be an affirmation of life. When as a queer Chicana writer Anzaldúa felt constrained by the paradigms of identity available in her time, she created the concept of the new mestiza. Hers was a full-fledged affirmation of life as well but one that allows her readers to reorient themselves within communities that choose to overcome ethnic, racial, and sexual prejudices and that support the flourishing of radical subjectivities so as to embrace a creative, inclusive approach to cultural difference and feminist values. The new mestizaje that she articulates eschews the homogenizing ideologies of assimilation and provides open

---

[10] There are different translations of this passage, but because Nietzsche uses the term *goldfunkelnd* and because it fits the context of the larger passage much better, I choose Kaufmann's translation, "sparkling like gold," over alternatives such as "sparkling with gold" (1966, 26–27).

spaces for constructive dialogue regarding sexuality, gender, ethnicity, nationality, and race.[11]

Today some thirty years after the first publication of *Borderlands/La Frontera* the proliferation of Latina identities and opportunities is undeniable. The attainment of well-deserved victories also means that we must continue to strive for social justice until everyone's needs are met. At the same time over these decades Anzaldúa's stature has resonated not only among feminists of all colors, Chicanas/os, and US Latinas/os but throughout the Americas and beyond. As we pay tribute to our diverse backgrounds, it is important not to stereotype members of any particular group and to avoid falling into unsustainable generalizations. Let's not forget that US Latinas (of all ages) comprise a wide-ranging population with respect to ethnoracial, national, and economic backgrounds. South America, the Caribbean, Mexico, and Central America—all contribute to this diversification. Every one of us has a story of what it has meant to grow up in or migrate to the United States and the degrees to which we have been shaped by or have helped to shape the course of feminism and women's rights and aspirations in this country. By reflecting on Anzaldúa's portrayal of the new mestiza we create bridges of understanding and creativity for ourselves, our extended networks of friends and supporters, and the future communities that await us.

References

Anzaldúa, Gloria. [1987] 2007. *Borderlands/La Frontera: The New Mestiza*. 3rd ed. San Francisco: Aunt Lute.

Anzaldúa, Gloria. 2015. *Light in the Dark/Luz en lo Oscuro*. Edited by AnaLouise Keating. Durham, NC: Duke University Press.

Ikas, Karen. 2007. "Interview with Gloria Anzaldúa." In *Borderlands/La Frontera: The New Mestiza*. 3rd ed, 227–246. San Francisco: Aunt Lute.

Lugones, María. 2007. "Heterosexualism and the Colonial/Modern Gender System." *Hypatia* 22, no. 1: 186–209.

Martínez, Jacqueline M. 2000. *Phenomenology of Chicana Experience and Identity*. Lanham, MD: Rowman & Littlefield.

Nietzsche, Friedrich. 1966. *Thus Spoke Zarathustra*. Translated by Walter Kaufmann. New York: Viking Penguin.

Nietzsche, Friedrich. 1967. "Ecce Homo." In *Genealogy of Morals and Ecce Homo*, translated and edited by Walter Kaufmann, 215–335. New York: Random House.

Nietzsche, Friedrich. 1974. *The Gay Science*. Translated by Walter Kaufmann. New York: Vintage.

---

[11] I argued on behalf of an ethics of cultural alterity that resists a discourse of assimilation in "Cultural Alterity: Cross-Cultural Communication and Feminist Thought in North-South Dialogue" (Schutte 1998).

Ortega, Mariana. 2016. *In-Between: Latina Phenomenology, Multiplicity, and the Self*. Albany: SUNY Press.

Sartre, Jean-Paul. 1993. "The Humanism of Existentialism." In *Jean-Paul Sartre: Essays in Existentialism*, edited by Wade Baskin, 31–62. New York: Citadel Press & Philosophical Library.

Schutte, Ofelia. 1984. *Beyond Nihilism: Nietzsche without Masks*. Chicago: University of Chicago Press.

Schutte, Ofelia. 1993. *Cultural Identity and Social Liberation in Latin American Thought*. Albany: SUNY Press.

Schutte, Ofelia. 1998. "Cultural Alterity: Cross-Cultural Communication and Feminist Thought in North-South Dialogue." *Hypatia* 13, no. 2: 53–72.

Schutte, Ofelia. 2004. "Negotiating Latina Identities." In *Latin American Philosophy for the 21st Century*, edited by Jorge J. E. Gracia and Elizabeth Millán-Zaibert, 337–51. Amherst, NY: Prometheus.

CHAPTER 8 | "Remaking Human Being"

Loving, Kaleidoscopic Consciousness in Helena
María Viramontes's Their Dogs Came with Them

PAULA M. L. MOYA

The process of true decolonization involves above all
a willingness to participate in the process of remaking human being.

—DARIECK SCOTT (2010, 45)

IN HER 1987 BOOK *Borderlands/La Frontera*, Gloria Anzaldúa warns against the dangers of remaining locked in "the counterstance." Calling for the development of a "new consciousness," a *mestiza consciousness*, she reminds her *camaradas* that while an initial reaction to the violence of domination might involve directly challenging those who subjugate us, an adherence to a logic of resistance will reduce all subsequent interactions to a "common denominator of violence" (100). She continues:

> At some point, on our way to a new consciousness, we will have to leave the opposite bank, the split between the two mortal combatants somehow healed so that we are on both shores at once and, at once, see through serpent and eagle eyes. Or perhaps we will decide to disengage from the dominant culture, write it off altogether as a lost cause, and cross the border into a wholly new and separate territory. Or we might go another route. The possibilities are numerous once we decide to act and not react. (100–101)

Anzaldúa is clear about the need to act, and definite about the necessity of moving out of the counterstance. She is, however, less clear about exactly what to do next. Refusing to offer *one* way forward, Anzaldúa instead considers an array of options characterized by a radical decentering of the terms within which people of Mexican descent in the United States have been constituted as naturally inferior persons.

Paula M. L. Moya, *"Remaking Human Being"* In: *Theories of the Flesh*, Edited by: Andrea J. Pitts, Mariana Ortega, and José Medina, Oxford University Press (2020). © Oxford University Press. DOI: 10.1093/oso/9780190062965.003.0009

An analogous dilemma is presented in an earlier foundational text by the Martinican writer Frantz Fanon. Fanon's 1952 *Black Skin, White Masks* is an instructive examination of the psychopathology of French colonialism as it affected persons (especially men) of African descent in the early twentieth century (Fanon [1952] 2008). Structured as an extended engagement with other thinkers who wrote about the psychology and biological nature of Man (so-called universal man) as well as specifically about persons of African descent, Fanon struggles to ground his humanity in something other than either the logic of European superiority or the idealization of a mythical African past.[1] Despite being deeply concerned about colonized people's experience of colonization, Fanon refuses to accept the idea that his future is determined by the historical past.[2] Specifically, he refuses the notion that his possible future is fixed by the fact of his blackness in relation to a devastated past. Like Anzaldúa, Fanon proposes an intentional—even existential—move away from the dehumanizing binary logic that has so far structured his experience, insisting, "The black man is not. No more than the white man. / Both have to move away from the inhuman voices of their respective ancestors so that a genuine communication can be born" (Fanon [1952] 2008, 206). Instead of prescribing a reactive solution to the dilemmas he describes, Fanon gestures toward the generativity of a knowledge-gathering process that is radically open-ended and always embodied. He ends his book with this "final prayer": "O my body, always make me a man who questions!" Urging us, his readers, to open ourselves up to the touch, feel, and consciousness of others as we collectively discover and "create the ideal conditions for a human world" (206), Fanon turns to prayer rather than rationality, to body rather than mind, and to questions rather than answers as he seeks to create his possible futures. In this, Fanon anticipates the work of feminist theorists of the late twentieth century and early twenty-first centuries. Consider Audre Lorde's conception of the erotic as a "resource within each of us that lies in a deeply female and spiritual plane, firmly rooted in the power of our unexpressed or unrecognized feeling" (1984, 53); Cherríe Moraga's turn to the bodies of women of color as a source of knowledge in the development of her "theory in the flesh" (Moraga 1983; Moraga and Anzaldúa 1983);[3] María Lugones's

---

[1] Over eight thematically related but conceptually distinct chapters, Fanon ([1952] 2008) draws on the work of G. W. F. Hegel, Jacques Lacan, Maurice Merleau-Ponty, Sigmund and Anna Freud, Jean-Paul Sartre, Michael Leiris, and Alfred Adler, while taking aim at O. Mannoni, Mayotte Capécia, René Maran, and Bernard Wolfe. Throughout, he is in serious dialogue with writers associated with the negritude movement, including Aime Cesaire, Leopold Senghor, and David Diop.

[2] "The density of History determines none of my acts. / I am my own foundation. / And it is by going beyond the historical and instrumental given that I initiate my cycle of freedom" (Fanon [1952] 2008, 205). But on the importance for Fanon of retaining a race consciousness, see Gines 2003.

[3] For an account by Moraga of her framework, see her interview with Norma Alarcón (Moraga 1986, 129). For an analysis, see Moya 2002, 49.

insistence that we theorize from "within the concreteness of body-to-body engagement" (2003, 207); and Karen Barad's observation that "we do not obtain knowledge by standing outside the world; we know because 'we' are of the world" (2008, 829). All these women manifest, using slightly different framings, Fanon's refusal of the divide between knowing and being.

I choose these discrete moments in the writings of Anzaldúa and Fanon because they vividly illustrate several key features of decoloniality that I highlight in this essay. Apart from illustrating the difficulties and uncertainties involved in thinking and feeling one's way out of a rationalist Western episteme under which people of color have historically been constituted as non-, not-quite-, or at least nonnormal humans, Anzaldúa and Fanon both gesture toward what decolonization might entail.[4] Decoloniality, as I understand it, refers to a capacious and evolving mode of being that is devoted to dismantling the pernicious legacies of European colonialism—particularly those related to the systemic objectification of "types" of human beings. Scholars, thinkers, and artists who have taken the "decolonial turn" hail from several disciplines (religious studies, philosophy, political theory, literary studies, psychology, and ethnic studies) and a number of geographical spaces whose indigenous peoples have suffered the experience of colonization (the Caribbean, the Americas, and Africa, among others). Although the varied projects of decolonial artists and scholars differ according to the contexts within which they work, they are united in their response to European colonialism. Their shared goal is not merely to overturn the colonial structures that resulted in the loss of political autonomy for native inhabitants of a colonized region, but more fundamentally to overturn the matrix of being, power, and knowledge that is constitutive of Western modernity and its corresponding project of civilization.[5] In choosing to describe my project as decolonial, I mean to invoke the growing body of scholarship emerging from a group of Latin American and Latina/o scholars who self-identify as such and who distinguish their approaches from postmodernist and postcolonialist approaches.[6] But in choosing Anzaldúa and Fanon together with Lorde, Moraga, Lugones, and Barad to illustrate what I mean by the term, I also make the point that the

---

[4] Wynter (2003) offers a discussion of the representation of the human, "Man," that is hegemonic in our Western bourgeois society.

[5] Both Quijano (2000) and Mignolo (1995, 2000, 2002, 2014) have argued that coloniality is the "invisible" or the "darker" side of modernity. From their decolonial perspective, the logic of "modernity/coloniality" bolsters the claim for European centrality, superiority, rationality, and universality, and promotes the false belief that some groups of people (especially nonwhites of all races) are natural slaves and/or inherently (that is, culturally or biologically) inferior to the European (or European-American) heterosexual, property-owning, and able-bodied white male.

[6] The list of scholars who affiliate in some way with decoloniality is long, and includes most of the contributors to this volume.

decolonial project has a long history and is not restricted to any one named cohort of scholars.

What makes a project decolonial? Building on the examples suggested above, I identify here several key features of decolonial thought.[7] Scholars who have taken the decolonial turn develop what Nelson Maldonado-Torres calls an "insurgent subjectivity"; they agree on the imperative to take intentional and inventive action.[8] Neither accepting nor refusing the given, decolonial thinkers turn aside and focus elsewhere to perceive anew. Because their starting point is the referential inaccuracy and genocidal logic of the European colonial racial imaginary, decolonial thinkers observe and critique key aspects of that imaginary—including its commitment to autonomous individualism, abstract and binary thinking, and Eurocentrism.[9] Championing the necessity of relationality, quotidian witnessing, and rigorous self-assessment, decolonial thinkers move away from dehumanizing binary logics toward onto-epistem-ological multiplicity and the development of complex solidarities.[10] Colonized peoples are figured not as problems to be dealt with (e.g., "The Negro Problem," the "Mexican Problem," the "Indian Problem"), but rather as potential resources whose ancestral forms of knowledge and current cultural self-ways can chart a path away from the master morality and penchant for war that undergirds unreconstructed Western modernity (Isasi-Díaz and Mendieta 2012; Maldonado-Torres 2011; Pérez 2007). Categorically rejecting the subordination or exploitation of others as either a primary goal or an unintended consequence of caring for the self, they instead put their energy and imagination into the service of remaking themselves and the world(s) they inhabit. The goal of decoloniality is thus the creation of a new world—a different kind of world "in which many worlds fit," to borrow the words of the Zapatista Liberation Army (Mignolo 2001). This "new" world entails a total renovation of the current one—a reworking of subjectivity, community, institutional arrangements, and the logics by which humans live

---

[7] My description of what is common to decolonial projects stems from my own attentive reading and teaching over the past decade of work by scholars such as María Lugones, Nelson Maldonado-Torres, Walter Mignolo, Anibal Quijano, José David Saldívar, Catherine Walsh, and Sylvia Wynter, as well as other scholars who are not identified with decoloniality but whose aims are closely aligned.

[8] On the importance of "insurgent subjectivity," see Maldonado-Torres 2011, 111; Maldonado-Torres 2018. See also Lugones 2003, 208.

[9] In addition to previously referenced works by Quijano, Mignolo, and Maldonado-Torres, see Maldonado-Torres 2008, 2011, 2012; Mignolo 2001, 2007; Saldívar 2012; Walsh 2012; Wynter 1987.

[10] Barad (2008) offers the neologism "onto-epistem-ology" to signal a refusal of the divide between knowing and being (829). In her theorizing about streetwalker theorizing, Lugones (2003) disrupts the binary logic of the strategy/tactic and mind/body divides in order to "embrace tactical strategies" as "crucial to an epistemology of resistance/liberation" (208). See also Ortega 2015 and Hames-García 2011.

together.[11] Rather than merely challenging current relations of power and the logics that structure them, decolonial thinkers seek to subvert a colonial way of being by setting aside inherited assumptions to envision new social, political, and ontological possibilities. By attending to occluded and denigrated perspectives on the social world, they open themselves up to previously disregarded as well as newly imagined possibilities—the exploration of which requires the kind of imagination and inventiveness found in the fiction of decolonial writers like Helena Maria Viramontes.

In making a claim for the importance of literature and literary criticism to the larger project of decolonization, I show how the decolonial features described above manifest in a work of literature, taking as my example Viramontes's (2007c) novel *Their Dogs Came with Them*. Viramontes incorporates into her fiction specific features that ally her with a diverse group of decolonial artists and scholars across several disciplines. Similar to the scholars with whom I compare her, she explores the dynamics of subordination while also imagining alternative and more egalitarian ways of being in the world. Differently from such scholars, however, she conducts her decolonial intervention through fiction. Neither argumentative nor analytical, Viramontes's writings nevertheless reveal the socioeconomic and ideological forces that keep Latina/os and other people of color in conditions of subordination. As aesthetic artifact that works at the level of emotion and the imagination, decolonial literature has the potential to reach a much larger audience in a more profound way than can be expected of most scholarship.

Their Dogs Came with Them is an omnibus novel set in East Los Angeles during the decades of the 1960s and 1970s. It portrays the contiguous, and occasionally intersecting, daily lives of a diverse range of characters who populate the neighborhood around the Long Beach and Pomona Freeways interchange during a time of intense social, political, and geographic upheaval. Taken as a whole, the novel explores what happens to relatively powerless people who live in a community that, because of how its residents are situated within the prevailing racial and socioeconomic order, is subject to a range of externally produced and pernicious structural forces. It shows how those most adversely affected by the building of the LA freeway system—those who are either displaced by the freeways or else condemned to live in their shadows—first encounter the coming upheaval. It then jumps forward in time by ten years to show how the neighborhood's dismemberment has negatively impacted its residents' already limited transportation and employment options. The effect is to show how the freeways enact what literary critic Rob Nixon (2011) calls *slow*

---

[11] For a decolonial intervention outlining the thought behind the importance of reforming the institution of prison, see Hames-García 2004.

violence on the East LA Mexican American community. Slow violence, according to Nixon, designates those "incremental and accretive" environmental harms that occur "gradually and out of sight" and are generally not considered to be violence at all. The harms that characterize slow violence are "delayed" and "disbursed across time and space." Their "calamitous repercussions" play out "across a range of temporal scales" in ways that make them difficult to perceive and respond to (2011, 2). Over the course of *Their Dogs*, the freeways destroy homes, disappear neighbors, displace businesses, cut off important neighborhood travel routes, introduce traffic gridlock, bring pollution, and trap the neighborhood residents into an area that had been envisioned by city planners not as a place to live but rather as a space to travel through on the way to somewhere else.[12] With an interest in emphasizing "the fragmentations of self and society" that beset East LA communities in the wake of their destruction by the construction of the freeways, Viramontes effectively uses the freeway metaphor to represent the structural forces that constrain her characters' lives.[13] This metaphorical rendering allows her to explore how and why community members might "internalize that isolation and begin to kill each other."[14]

Key to the success of Viramontes's decolonial intervention is the way she structures her narrative and personifies her characters. Although *Their Dogs* lacks a clear protagonist, its extensive and quite unusual character-system incorporates a dizzyingly large array of major and minor characters.[15] By crafting the novel so that every character can be a potential center of narrative interest, Viramontes highlights the inequitable distribution of character-space typical of most American novels; such a structuration makes a point about the full and rich subjectivity of the types of people who are frequently consigned to the margins of a society, a story, or a page. She thus demonstrates the truth of the contention, forwarded by literary critic Alex Woloch, that even the most minor character has a "case"—"an orientating consciousness that . . . could potentially organize an entire fictional universe" (2003, 22). Before continuing with my argument about the significance of *Their Dogs'* narrative structure, I pause to introduce the novel's major and minor characters.

---

[12] For excellent analyses of the environmental impacts on the East LA neighborhoods of the building of the freeways as depicted in *Their Dogs*, see Hsuan Hsu 2011; Wald 2013; Yamashita 2013. For insightful spatial analyses of the novel, see Brady 2013; Muñoz 2013; Pattison 2014. For a queer reading of the novel, see Cuevas 2014.

[13] Viramontes describes the novel as being about a "lost community divided by freeways" and the "fragmentations of the self and society" (Kevane and Heredia 2000, 154).

[14] Noting that the marginalization and isolation produced by the construction of the freeways was "not our fault," Viramontes admits being "also intrigued by how we internalize that isolation and begin to kill each other" (Dulfano 2001, 653).

[15] For an analysis of the distribution of character-space in narrative form that renders meaningful the linkages between structure and reference, see Woloch 2003.

The four characters who receive the most character-space and who focalize the narrative most frequently are Ermila Zumaya, Antonia "Turtle" Gamboa, Tranquilina, and Ben Brady.[16] The novel also distributes narrative attention and character-space across a diverse range of minor characters. Ermila is an orphan who lives with her elderly grandparents after her activist parents have mysteriously disappeared. She opens the novel as a young child of about five after she is moved from Child Protective Services to her grandparents' home.[17] We meet up with her again ten years later as a young woman who is going to school; working at a Neighborhood Youth Corp job; navigating her ambivalent relationships with her grandparents; dating a gang member named Alfonso; fending off the unwanted sexual advances of her cousin Nacho; and hanging out with her three girlfriends, Lollie, Mousie, and Rini.

Turtle is a transgender teen whose catch-as-catch-can upbringing has been shaped by her warring parents (an abusive father and an uncomprehending mother), as well as the fierce love and loyalty of her brother, Luis Lil Lizard; his unfocused anger at the poverty and dysfunction of their upbringing has turned him mean. We are first introduced to Turtle as "the bald-headed Gamboa brother, the other one who was really a girl, but didn't want to be and got beaten up for it" (Viramontes 2007c, 11). When we catch up with her ten years later, she has been abandoned by her mother (who objects to her unconventional gender presentation) and left alone to starve on the streets of East LA. Having been assigned female at birth, Turtle is prevented from being drafted alongside Luis Lil Lizard to fight in Vietnam. Without Luis Lil Lizard by her side, Turtle no longer feels part of the McBride Boys gang they joined together. Having gone AWOL from the gang, she does her best to avoid both her own and a rival gang and the several state authorities whose only interest in her is as an outlaw.

Tranquilina is the young adult daughter of two formerly indentured servants from northern Mexico who flee across the US-Mexico border to keep the owner of the ranch where they were born from transferring the peonage they had inherited from their own parents to their unborn child (Tranquilina). After a harrowing trek across the desert, during which Tranquilina's pregnant mother promises her own, her husband's, and her unborn child's lives to God in exchange for preserving them, the three begin a life of service as itinerant evangelical preachers. In the course of

---

[16] Focalization is a term that was introduced by the French literary critic Gérard Genette (1980) to make clearer the distinction in a narrative between the "question *who sees?* and the question *who speaks?*" (186). It refers to the mediation (the prism, perspective, or angle of vision) through which a story is presented by a narrator in the text.

[17] As if to emphasize Ermila's relationality rather than her individuality, the narrative identifies her as "the Zumaya child" for the whole of the chapter except for a brief proleptic passage when she is identified as "a young woman." We do not learn Ermila's first name until chapter 4.

their travels, they are traumatized by an assault in Cuero, Texas, in the course of which Tranquilina is raped and her mother and father are badly injured. Their story in the novel picks up at the point at which they decide to return to Los Angeles to open a storefront church and mission for the poor.[18]

Finally, Ben enters the novel as a young man of about twenty-one who frequents Tranquilina's mission and whose severe mental illness interferes with his ability to contend with the routines of daily life. He reappears later in the novel (in a scene set ten years earlier) as a child of eleven who is grieving the disappearance of his Mexican mother with no help from his unsympathetic and bigoted white father. Ben's story turns tragic when, as a young boy, he runs out in front of a cement truck while holding the hand of an even younger boy who is killed in the accident. Ben's incomplete recuperation, his secret guilt over the death of the younger boy, and his ongoing grief at the loss both of his mother and a classmate named Renata Valenzuela (who disappeared around the same time as his mother and whose remains are later found in the city landfill), continue to haunt him into his young adulthood.

Importantly, none of what I have shared above is conveyed in a straightforward way. Instead, information about the four major characters is distributed across the narrative so that they emerge gradually as implied people through their interactions with a vast assortment of other major and minor characters—all of whom live with, love, flirt with, offend, contend with, compliment, learn from, teach, buy from, steal from, pass by, and minister to them. The novel thus brilliantly enacts the kind of relationality championed by feminist philosopher Sarah Hoagland; it exhibits an interdependence that "involves our forming and being formed, both individually and culturally, in relation through our engagements and practices" (Hoagland 2007, 99–100).[19] Such a character-system effectively fleshes out and gives personality to the kind of subject designated by feminist philosopher María Lugones as the I ↔ we. This subject is one whose "pedestrian" perspective is "formed from inside the midst of people, from inside the layers of relationships, institutions and practices" (2003, 5).

Another important feature of Viramontes's narrative structure in *Their Dogs*, and one of the novel's signal achievements, is the way it registers the *active subjectivity* of its numerous minor characters. Active subjectivity, according to Lugones, is a highly attenuated form of agency, or "sense of intentionality" (2003, 216). Lugones introduces the notion as a

---

[18] Unlike Turtle, Ermila, and Ben, Tranquilina exists solely in the novel's present except for one flashback depicting her recent rape.

[19] She continues: "Who we are is in part a function of our relationships—in logic, an internal relation" (Hoagland 2007, 100).

conceptual alternative to late modern agency—which, she reminds us, is "a mirage of individual autonomous action" in which the social, political, and economic institutions that provide backing to the successful "agent" are effectively obscured (210–11). Noting that people without economic or social power often lack institutional backup, Lugones suggests that active subjects' ability to create social and political change will take different forms and may be unintelligible to dominant ways of understanding resistance to oppression. This is because active subjects, in contrast to agents, must move tentatively, with care; they must be aware of their lack of institutional backup, and attentive to possibilities for creating the "alternative socialities" that will be necessary for bringing their resistant intentions to fruition (211, 216–20). Key to the process of creating alternative socialities, Lugones argues, is registering the active subjectivity of low-power people. Only by recognizing others' resistant intentionality can one create alternative socialities in which oppressed peoples can live "in transgression of reduction of life to the monosense of domination" (217). Through the deft rendering of her many characters, Viramontes not only registers the active subjectivity of the types of people Fanon calls *les damnés de la terre*, but also captures the ways they register the active subjectivity of others around them. She accomplishes the first goal by reflecting upon the reality that every character (major and minor) is a potential center of interest—the hero of another, alternative, narrative (Woloch, 2003). As noted previously, virtually all the characters in *Their Dogs* stake a claim for narrative centrality, either by being a lovingly focalized object or by focalizing the narrative themselves; such focalization registers the existence of their multiple worlds of sense in a shared social world. Viramontes accomplishes the second goal by incorporating scenes that illustrate each character's subject formation in relation to those around them—in the manner theorized by Hoagland and Lugones (as discussed above).

My point here is that by embodying, in her different characters, a "collectivist (not isolated) model of the self" that is attentive to both multiplicity and difference, Viramontes creates the conditions of possibility for the development in her reader of the *complex solidarity* among oppressed social groups advanced by ethnic studies scholar Michael Hames-García.[20] Examples of minor characters who stake a claim for narrative centrality while remaining attentive to the active subjectivity of the others around them abound in the novel. They include an African American teacher named Miss Eastman who nourishes her hungry students with both kindness and food; a Japanese American store owner named Ray whose experience in Manzanar makes him sympathetic to Turtle's hunger and sense of

---

[20] For more on complex solidarity, see Hames-García 2004, 208–19, and for his theorization of the relationship between multiplicity and social identity see Hames-García 2011, 1–37.

otherness; a gay Chicano gang member named Lucho who both expresses and represses his sexual desire for his homophobic lover Alfonso; a lonely Mexican butcher named Obdulio who is traumatized by witnessing Ben's accident; an elderly homeless woman who has trouble remembering her own name; and an overworked Chicana office worker named Ana who, as Ben's older sister, cleans his apartment and drives all over the city looking for him when he loses touch with reality. Grandmother and Grandfather Zumaya each also have their "case" when the narrative dips into their heads to examine, from within their own worlds of sense, the disappointments, desires, bigotry, and shame with which they each live.

Their Dogs' sustained focus on the daily embodied lives of the kind of people who are marginalized within American society is one of its most important decolonial features.[21] Such a focus registers the significance of what the religious studies scholar Ada Maria Isasi-Díaz calls *lo cotidiano*, or "the immediate space-time and place of daily life" (2012, 48). It also helps rectify the absence of such characters from most American fiction. The novel opens with the Zumaya child walking barefoot across the newly paved street to the home of her elderly neighbor, Chavela. During the first half of the first chapter, the narrative pays meticulous attention to the unaccustomed disorder of Chavela's home. Through an accumulation of details, and with the help of Chavela's running commentary, the reader comes to understand that Chavela is packing to move in advance of the demolition of her home by the freeway construction crews. Alongside signs of the disturbance created by the activity of moving, the narrative juxtaposes evidence of Chavela's everyday life: her "linoleum floor [that] was scuffed with so many years of standing to scrub metal pots or pour a glass of tap water" and the "cigarette-stained windowsill" upon which she rests her cigarette (Viramontes 2007c, 7). The point of notating the misspelled Spanglish of the many handwritten notes Scotch-taped to Chavela's walls as she moves among the cardboard boxes and bulk-filled pillowcases that litter her floor, chairs, and table is not merely to create a Barthesian "reality effect" (Barthes 2006). Even less is it designed to further the novel's plot. Although the book has a plot, *Their Dogs* is not a plot-driven book; to imagine that it is would be to see a great deal of the narrative—even the majority of it—as extraneous and excessive and fundamentally flawed in its construction.[22] Instead, the detailed descriptions serve to document the

---

[21] Brady (2013) characterizes Viramontes's extended description of Ermila's meditation on the women who take the bus to work as a "praise song for laboring Chicanas/os" (181). See also Wyse 2013.

[22] The novel's several subplots are organized by the frequent appearances in the narrative of Ermila, Turtle, Tranquilina, and Ben. However, the four are not all acquainted with each other, and they never all occupy the same space at the same time. Their only connections are their shared Mexican ancestry and the fact that they are all living in East LA at the time that the events at the end of the novel take place.

daily routines, concerns, and cares of the sort of person who remains largely unrepresented in the American literary canon. By contrasting the present disorder of Chavela's environment with the quotidian routines of her long existence in her home, the novel effectively emphasizes the disruption that the coming of the freeways will have on her and on all the neighborhood's residents. The fact that Chavela and her belongings disappear to somewhere unknown halfway through the first chapter makes a point about the sense of loss—figured in the novel as "phantom limbs"—that is left behind when the social, institutional, and spatial bonds that constitute a community are severed (Viramontes 2007c, 33). By connecting the coming of the freeways to the traumas associated with the death and destruction that accompany natural and man-made disasters (e.g., devastating earthquakes and the European colonization of the Americas) and that break the social bonds of a community by destroying its institutions, the novel stakes an existential claim for people like Chavela who remain imperceptible to, and wholly disregarded by, the city planners who targeted her carefully tended blue stucco home for destruction.

Another characteristic of Viramontes's fiction generally is the way she bears faithful witness to her community in a demonstrative act of *decolonial love*.[23] By decolonial love I mean an empowering love of both self and others that emerges in the wake of a self-critical but radical acceptance of the formerly racially and sexually denigrated non-European self.[24] The most important way Viramontes demonstrates decolonial love is by humanizing, without sentimentalizing, the people about whom she writes. As a realist writer who creates characters who have a recognizably referential relationship to people living in our social world, Viramontes invests time and space in representing her true-to-life characters in all their fullness and complexity.[25] Consider the case of Grandmother Zumaya. Viramontes focalizes several key scenes through Grandmother's perspective, thus allowing the reader to perceive, from Grandmother's own perspective, her pain at having lost her daughter. As readers, we are privy to a variety of Grandmother's feelings and decisions: we see her stubbornness in deciding to raise her granddaughter in defiance of her husband's wishes; her shame about having been born with one arm slightly longer than the other; her embarrassment at being publicly humiliated by her husband;

---

[23] For an argument in favor of faithful witnessing, see Lugones 2003, 7. For a demonstration of faithful witnessing as a method, see Martínez 2014.

[24] For a discussion of decolonial love as it emerges in an analysis of work of Junot Díaz, see Moya 2016a. See also Díaz's (2016) take on the relationship between decolonial love and the formation of a decolonial self.

[25] Viramontes refers to herself as a realist for whom hope comes not from magic or religious faith but from a belief in the transformative power of the written word. See Viramontes 2007a. For an analysis of Viramontes's first novel, *Under the Feet of Jesus*, as a realist text, see Moya 2002.

her panic about the change that the freeways are bringing to her neighbor-hood; and her despair and fear related to her inability to prevent Ermila from becoming a sexual being. By making us witness to Grandmother Zumaya's innermost thoughts and feelings, the narrative solicits our em-pathy and allows us to better appreciate the reasons for her impatience, nagging, and curfews. But this same technique also allows us to behold Grandmother's racial bigotry. When she visits Ermila's kindergarten class-room, Grandmother perceives Ermila's African American teacher through a thick cloud of distrust and dislike. According to Grandmother, Miss Eastman cannot be a "real teacher," and her judgment of the teacher's physical and behavioral attributes is unflattering. She takes exception to what she perceives as Miss Eastman's "meaty, discolored cheeks," her "very visible mole," her "plum lips," and her "rat-a-tat-tat fast English" (Viramontes 2007c, 130). Later, when Grandmother picks up Ermila from school, she perceives Miss Eastman as the looming, dark embodiment "of the roaming packs of Negroes" who threatened to "claw out of the television's own green guts, riot-rush to lift and overturn cars and set fire to all the neighborhood had worked for" (150). What this demonstrates is that, as the product of a social world that is organized according to race, Grandmother does not question the accuracy of the negative representations of African Americans she sees on television every night. She does not consider the historical and contemporary injustices in re-sponse to which African Americans are marching in protest, nor has she developed the antiracist ability to distinguish Miss Eastman as a particular African American person from the wide range of other people who share the teacher's socially produced racial identity. By focalizing Grandmother Zumaya's biases, *Their Dogs* represents the truth of the racism toward African Americans that exists within Mexican American communities. Viramontes's narrative choices illustrate that while Grandmother may herself be victimized by a system of race that positions Mexican-origin people as disposable laborers and African American as natural slaves, she is also an active contributor to the maintenance of that same system.[26] Viramontes's willingness to examine Grandmother Zumaya's biases reminds us that individuals are not simple; people are never all good nor all bad. But it also exhibits a decolonial awareness that unflinching self-assessment of the sort demanded by faithful witnessing is a necessary step on the way to understanding how colonized individuals can inadvertently contribute to the forging of the ideological bonds that keep them in situ-ations of subordination (Díaz 2016, 392–94).

---

[26] For more on race as a world-system of social distinction, see Quijano 2000; Markus and Moya 2010.

What prevents Viramontes's representation of Miss Eastman in *Their Dogs* from being racist is that the novel also focalizes the teacher through Ermila's perspective as well as through the racially literate schema of a third-person external focalizer.[27] As I have explained elsewhere, *schemas* are sensory-motor and cognitive-affective learned structures that have been built up through past behavior and experiences in specific domains; they are central to persons' perception and cognition and serve as patterns for behavior (Moya 2016b, 1–37). The effect of reframing Miss Eastman through the additional schemas provided by Ermila and the third-person external focalizer is that Viramontes is able to provide enough information about the teacher to call Grandmother's biases into question. Whereas Grandmother Zumaya condemns Miss Eastman for "the screeching pitch of the parrots," "the jumpy jitter of the children" (Viramontes 2007c, 130), and the incongruity of the fact that Miss Eastman is serving her students cornflakes and milk, the external focalizer allows the reader to perceive how lovingly the teacher instructs her "thirty-one students plus one" in a temporary classroom with inadequate air conditioning (131). The reader understands that Miss Eastman feeds all the students in the morning because some of them are hungry; that she breaks them up into "rotating groups of math and art" (133) to manage resources; that she sees them as individuals with varying needs; that she provides for them milk and freshly baked cookies at her own expense after recess every day; and that she creates opportunities to make each one of them feel special. Viramontes's multiperspectival decolonial witnessing thus illustrates the power of schemas to create multiple worlds of sense in a shared social world.[28]

Importantly, Miss Eastman plays a crucial role in helping Ermila emerge from the trauma of her early life, which manifests as a refusal or an inability to talk. The precipitating event occurs when Ermila witnesses a tender encounter between Miss Eastman and her boyfriend, the man who bakes the children's cookies. What stands out about Ermila's perception of this moment is not only that she associates Miss Eastman's boyfriend with Chavela (whom she loved) and with her classmate Stella (who is described as "having a heart as big as a wide-open door"), but also that Miss Eastman's sweetness (symbolized by the sweetness of the baked goods she brings to the children, the "syrup" color of her boyfriend's skin, and the "sugared" sound of the word "K-I-S-S-I-N-G") precipitates Ermila's transition from the traumatized and silent "Zumaya child" to the thoughtful young woman whose burgeoning political consciousness is grounded in a desire for social justice (Viramontes 2007c, 152–53).

---

[27] For a concise account of racial literacy, see Moya and Hamedani 2017, 11.

[28] For an example of how literature represents the way schemas create multiple worlds of sense in a shared social world, see Moya 2016b, 133–62.

Although Grandmother Zumaya's bigotry remains unchanged at the end of the novel, Ermila begins to develop what I theorized in *Learning from Experience* as an *expanded literacy*—an embodied, intersubjective, and egalitarian approach to reading the social world that is so beautifully exemplified by the character of Estrella in Viramontes's (1995) first novel *Under the Feet of Jesus*.[29] Central to Ermila's ability to develop expanded literacy—and to the reader's ability to read through the several competing perceptions of Miss Eastman to pass a negative judgment on Grandmother Zumaya's racism while empathizing with Grandmother Zumaya herself—is the novel's generally postpositivist approach to truth, or objectivity. As theorized by the group of scholars who developed this understanding in the late 1990s and early aughts, a postpositivist realist approach to a fallibilistic or deflationary conception of objectivity accounts for the role of perceptual bias in the practice of interpretation (Moya 2016b, 27–29).[30] It acknowledges the existence of onto-epistem-ological multiplicity while also recognizing that one person's perception or representation of a given phenomenon might have a weaker or more ideologically mediated relationship to our shared social world than some other competing perception or representation to which one might compare it. Indeed, all decolonial projects rely (at least implicitly) on some conception of objectivity to ground their ethical claims regarding the injustice of racism.[31]

Viramontes's innovative narrative structure in *Their Dogs* thus accomplishes several decolonial goals, even as its pluralized and digressive narrative structure runs the risk of frustrating a reader who is looking for simple solutions and forward narrative progress.[32] First, by denying the status of sole protagonist to any one character, it emphasizes that no one person ever makes up the totality of the social world. Second, by giving sustained narrative attention to multiple individual characters living in the same community, it documents how painfully individual the relationally produced experience of living in such a community can feel. Third, by delving deeply into the thoughts and actions of a proliferating assortment of major and minor characters, it demonstrates the existence of multiple and widely diverse perspectives that might be used to interpret the same event. Lastly, it illustrates the power of schemas to create multiple

---

[29] For an illustration of Viramontes's signature use of focalization in that novel, see Moya 2002, 175–214.

[30] See also Alcoff 2006; Alcoff et al. 2006; Hames-García 2004, 2011; Markus and Moya 2010; Martínez 2013; Mohanty 1997; Moya and Hames-García 2000; Moya 2002; Sánchez-Casal and Macdonald 2009; Siebers 2006, 10–30, 2010; Teuton 2008.

[31] I contend that this is so, even as I acknowledge that some scholars who identify themselves as decolonial thinkers are uncomfortable with the idea or language of objectivity, or else eschew altogether the realism-antirealism debate that subtends thinking about objectivity.

[32] For an account of how *Their Dogs* enacts a critique of linear temporality, see Brady 2013, 186.

worlds of sense in a shared social world. It is worth emphasizing that providing unambiguous and unidirectional solutions is not what Viramontes has designed *Their Dogs* to do; her narrative choices recall Fanon's and Anzaldúa's refusal to provide definitive answers to the difficult questions and complex problems they confront as colonized/decolonizing beings. Indeed, Viramontes's signature use of focalization is central to a narrative structure that can create in the reader the "complex cognitive and affective achievement" that the philosopher José Medina calls a *kaleidoscopic consciousness*. According to Medina (2013), a kaleidoscopic consciousness recognizes not only that the "social fabric can generate forever more standpoints," but also that what is needed for ethical action is not an infinitely pluralized consciousness but one that "has built into it a flexible and dynamic structure so that it can always adapt to the possibility . . . of there being more ways of experiencing the world than those considered" (200). The juxtaposition in *Their Dogs* of multiple worlds of sense implicitly encourages its readers to perceive and question the different schemas used by the various characters as they severally interpret their shared social world.

At the end of *Their Dogs,* Viramontes ties up many, but not all, of the subplots that run through the novel. In a confluence of events that occur during a torrential early morning rainstorm, the storylines of the novel's four major characters converge—even though the characters themselves never do. Ermila is on her way to the bus station to warn Nacho that he has been targeted for killing by the McBride Boys gang. Turtle, high on drugs, is directed by the gang to murder Nacho, and is murdered in turn by the Quarantine Authority, a city police force that, under the pretext of eliminating rabies, turns the neighborhood into a virtual police state every night.[33] Tranquilina, who has been searching for Ben with his sister Anna, is an unwitting witness to both murders. Ben, meanwhile, remains missing. The novel ends when Tranquilina, in a final paroxysm of anger and despair, refuses the Quarantine Authority's orders to put her hands on her head and instead moves forward into the storm with her fists clenched. What happens to Tranquilina after she moves forward is crucially unclear. Does she walk into gunfire and to her death? Or does she levitate into the "limitless space" of faith and infinite possibility in a reenactment of her father's mythical flight in the desert before she was born? (Viramontes 2007c, 325). Although there are elements of Tranquilina's story that might tempt a reader to believe that she achieves transcendence within the space of the novel, there are other clues that suggest that she might be sacrificed at the hands of the Quarantine Authority. Tranquilina herself had harbored

---

[33] For more on how Viramontes built on a real historical event to make a point about police surveillance of her community, see Kevane 2008, 11–41.

doubts about the reality of Papa Tomás's mythical flight, and the novel mentions that her name begins with a letter hated by her father because its cruciform shape "reinforced the cross they had to bear" (44, 88). The novel finally refuses to answer the question of what happens to Tranquilina, just as it leaves open many other questions of plot and interpretation that its readers might have: What happened to Ermila's parents? Where did Chavela go after she moved away? Did Ben's mother run away? Has Luis Lil Lizard been killed in Vietnam? Did Ermila arrive in time to witness Nacho's death? Where, for that matter, is Ben?

On one level, Viramontes's refusal to provide answers mimics the workings of our real social world—one in which we often do not know what has happened, or will happen, to ourselves or to others. But on another level, her refusal is more pointed. By not tying up the loose threads at the end of the novel, Viramontes sends her readers searching back through its multiple plot lines to look for answers, while also denying them the catharsis that either a miracle or a tragedy might provide. The only thing the reader knows is that Ermila is the one major character who remains available to absorb the enormity of the slow violence that has been done to her community. Having intuited the unfairness of the situation, Ermila begins to stand up for herself and others in a way consistent with the mode of resistance Lugones calls *streetwalker theorizing*, one that involves "theorizing resistance from the subaltern position, and from within the concreteness of body-to-body engagement" (Lugones 2003, 207–10). Ermila's streetwalker theorizing first shows up in the novel when she thinks to herself, "I gotta do something soon" while listening to the "earth-rattling explosive motors" and watching the invasive searchlights of the Quarantine Authority helicopters that "burst out of the midnight sky to shoot dogs not chained up by curfew" (Viramontes 2007c, 12). It occurs again when she joins her friends in the carefully choreographed vandalism of the treasured car of Rini's mother's boyfriend, whose sexual advances have rendered Rini unsafe in her own home (197–99). Although at the end of the novel Ermila lacks a fully fleshed-out analysis of her own and her friends' situations, and has not yet elaborated a vocabulary to convey her insights, Ermila's positioning within the narrative suggests that she might yet develop into an streetwalker theorizer capable of leading her community toward social change.

Viramontes's choice to open up narrative possibilities at the end of the novel offers a decolonial option that extends outward to her readers by making us responsible, via our interpretive choices, for what might come next.[34] She replicates Fanon's ([1952] 2008) gesture of openness at the

---

[34] For an astute analysis of the novel that focuses on the importance to interpretation of a reader's receptivity to the text's metaphors, see Franco 2015.

end of *White Skin, Black Masks*, even as she emphasizes the importance of the imagination to the project of making sense of the racialized *locura* that has, ever since the Spanish conquest of the Americas, been undergirded by a racist and capitalist world-system. Lastly, the novel's indeterminate ending serves to locate it within a larger ongoing decolonial struggle. To look for a solution within the novel itself would be to think of it as a discrete entity—an artwork unto itself—instead of as an intervention in an epic struggle that began much earlier and will continue long after we are gone. Consider, in this context, three of the novel's most important intertextual allusions. Viramontes takes her title and epigraph from *The Broken Spears: The Aztec Account of the Conquest of Mexico* (León Portilla 1992). Originally published in Spanish in 1959 by Miguel Leon Portillo as an introduction to and compilation of accounts by the conquered peoples of Mexico to their experience of conquest, the book has since been expanded and translated into several European languages as well as the indigenous language Otomi. Viramontes's title, taken from one of the translated Nahuatl accounts, refers to the attack dogs that were used to terrify and kill the indigenous people during the Spanish conquest. Via this reference, the dogs in the novel serve to connect the damage caused by the freeways and the fictional rabies quarantine to a longer history of militarized violence and conquest.[35] Similarly, Tranquilina is linked, through her possible levitation as well as through the name her father had wanted to give her, to the character of Remedios in Gabriel García Márquez's ([1970] 2003) anticolonial masterpiece *One Hundred Years of Solitude*.[36] And finally, Viramontes's choice of the term "sharpshooters" to describe the Quarantine Authority gunmen who kill Turtle evokes the "sharp-shooting goose-steppers" whose racist bullets are "designed to kill slowly" in the Chicana poet Lorna Dee Cervantes's plaintive "Poem for the Young White Man Who Asked Me How I, an Intelligent, Well-Read Person, Could Believe in the War between Races" (Cervantes 1981, 35–37). Cervantes writes not only about the pernicious psychological and social damage caused by race, but also about the damage caused by the construction of Highway 280 through the middle of her own Mexican American neighborhood in San Jose, California.

By representing the lives of the ignored, the marginalized, the *damnés de la terre* in a way that humanizes but does not sentimentalize them; by concretizing in readily perceptible forms (freeways, rabid dogs, gendered dynamics, the Quarantine Authority) the socioeconomic and ideological forces that subordinate a community while also registering the efforts

---

[35] For an insightful explication of this point, see Wald 2013, 73–74.

[36] Hsu (2011, 167 n. 52) notes that in an earlier version of the novel, Tranquilina was named Remedios after one of García Marquez's characters.

of its residents to resist; by creating a narrative structure and character-system that radically redistributes narrative space and makes available multiple perspectives on the same event in a way that enables its readers to develop a kaleidoscopic consciousness and complex solidarities; and by opening up narrative possibilities so as to involve its readers in the creation of possible futures, Helena Maria Viramontes's "breakthrough book" enacts a turning aside and a focusing elsewhere for the purpose of perceiving anew (Viramontes 2007b).[37] In all these ways, Viramontes joins Fanon and Anzaldúa in rejecting the counterstance as she moves forward into the both/and logic of onto-epistem-ological multiplicity. With a clear understanding that changing the world will involve changing who we are in relation to that world, she enacts what Walter Mignolo has called *thinking otherwise*.[38] Grounded, directional, intentional, and relational, as well as kaleidoscopic, flexible, expansive, literate, and loving, *Their Dogs Came with Them* shows Viramontes to be a decolonial thinker par excellence. Her ability to make us understand and care about the people about whom she writes makes her a true visionary in the difficult "process of remaking human being" (Scott 2010, 45).

References

Alcoff, Linda Martín. 2006. *Visible Identities: Race, Gender, and the Self*. New York: Oxford University Press.

Alcoff, Linda Martín, Michael Hames-García, Satya P. Mohanty, and Paula M. L. Moya, eds. 2006. *Identity Politics Reconsidered*. New York: Palgrave Macmillan.

Anzaldúa, Gloria. 1987. *Borderlands/La Frontera: The New Mestiza*. San Francisco: Aunt Lute Books.

Barad, Karen. 2008. "Posthumanist Performativity: Toward an Understanding of How Matter Comes to Matter." In *Material Feminisms*, edited by Stacy Alaimo and Susan J. Hekman, 120–54. Bloomington: Indiana University Press.

Barthes, Roland. 2006. "The Reality Effect." In *The Novel: An Anthology of Criticism and Theory, 1900–2000*, edited by Dorothy J. Hale, 229–34. Malden, MA: Blackwell.

Brady, Mary Pat. 2013. "Metaphors to Love by: Toward a Chicana Aesthetics in *Their Dogs Came with Them*." In *Rebozos de Palabras: An Helena María Viramontes Critical Reader*, edited by Gabriella Gutiérrez y Muhs, 167–91. Tucson: University of Arizona Press, 2013.

Cervantes, Lorna Dee. 1981. *Emplumada*. Pittsburgh: University of Pittsburgh Press.

Cuevas, T. Jackie. 2014. "Engendering a Queer Latin@ Time and Place in Helena Maria Viramontes' *Their Dogs Came with Them*." *Latino Studies* 12, no. 1 (Spring): 27–43.

---

[37] Silverblatt refers to *Their Dogs* as Viramontes's "breakthrough book" (Viramontes 2007b).

[38] "Thinking otherwise" is a practice theorized by Mignolo across his most recent work. It refers to theorizing from locations and identities that are non-Western or not fully capitalist, the use of "in-between" or "border" epistemologies, the incorporation of coloniality as constitutive of modernity, and the imagining of noncapitalist economic structures.

Díaz, Junot. 2016. "The Search for Decolonial Love: A Conversation between Junot Díaz and Paula M. L. Moya." Interview by Paula M. L. Moya. In *Junot Díaz and the Decolonial Imagination*, edited by Monica Hanna, Jennifer Harford Vargas, and José David Saldívar, 391–401. Durham, NC: Duke University Press.

Dulfano, Isabel. 2001. "Some Thoughts Shared with Helena María Viramontes." *Women's Studies* 30, no. 5: 647–62.

Fanon, Frantz. [1952] 2008. *Black Skin, White Masks*. Translated by Richard Philcox. New York: Grove Press.

Franco, Dean. 2015. "Metaphors Happen: Miracle and Metaphor in Helena María Viramontes's *Their Dogs Came with Them*." *Novel: A Forum on Fiction* 48, no. 3: 344–62.

García Márquez, Gabriel. [1970] 2003. *One Hundred Years of Solitude*. Translated by Gregory Rabassa. New York: HarperCollins.

Genette, Gérard. 1980. *Narrative Discourse: An Essay in Method*. Translated by Jane E. Lewin. Ithaca, NY: Cornell University Press.

Gines, Kathryn T. 2003. "Fanon and Sartre 50 Years Later: To Retain or Reject the Concept of Race." *Sartre Studies International* 9, no. 2: 55–67.

Hames-García, Michael R. 2004. *Fugitive Thought: Prison Movements, Race, and the Meaning of Justice*. Minneapolis: University of Minnesota Press, 2004.

Hames-García, Michael R. 2011. *Identity Complex: Making the Case for Multiplicity*. Minneapolis: University of Minnesota Press.

Hoagland, Sarah Lucia. 2007. "Denying Relationality: Epistemology and Race and Ignorance." In *Race and Epistemologies of Ignorance*, edited by Shannon Sullivan and Nancy Tuana, 95–118. Albany: State University of New York Press.

Hsu, Hsuan L. 2011. "Fatal Contiguities: Metonymy and Environmental Justice." *New Literary History* 42, no. 1 (Winter): 147–68.

Isasi-Díaz, Ada María. 2012. "Mujerista Discourse: A Platform for Latina's Subjugated Knowledge." In *Decolonizing Epistemologies: Latina/o Theology and Philosophy*, edited by Ada María Isasi-Díaz and Eduardo Mendieta, 44–67. New York: Fordham University Press.

Isasi-Díaz, Ada María, and Eduardo Mendieta. 2012. *Decolonizing Epistemologies: Latina/o Theology and Philosophy*. New York: Fordham University Press.

Kevane, Bridget A. 2008. "Violence, Faith, and Active Miracles in East Los Angeles: *Their Dogs Came with Them* and *The Miraculous Day of Amalia Gómez*." In *Profane and Sacred: Latino/a American Writers Reveal the Interplay of the Secular and the Religious*, 11–41. Lanham, MD: Rowman & Littlefield.

Kevane, Bridget A., and Juanita Heredia, eds. 2000. "Praying for Knowledge: An Interview with Helena Maria Viramontes." In *Latina Self-Portraits: Interviews with Contemporary Women Writers*, 141–54. Albuquerque: University of New Mexico Press.

León Portilla, Miguel. 1992. *The Broken Spears: The Aztec Account of the Conquest of Mexico*. 2nd ed. Boston: Beacon Press.

Lorde, Audre. *Sister Outsider*. 1984. Freedom, CA: Crossing Press.

Lugones, Mara. 2003. *Pilgrimages/Peregrinajes: Theorizing Coalition against Multiple Oppressions*. Lanham, MD: Rowman & Littlefield.

Maldonado-Torres, Nelson. 2008. *Against War: Views from the Underside of Modernity*. Durham, NC: Duke University Press.

Maldonado-Torres, Nelson. 2011. "Thinking through the Decolonial Turn: Postcontinental Interventions in Theory, Philosophy, and Critique—an Introduction." *Transmodernity: Journal of Peripheral Cultural Production of the Luso-Hispanic World* 1, no. 2: 3–15.

Maldonado-Torres, Nelson. 2012. "Decoloniality at Large: Towards a Trans-Americas and Global Transmodern Paradigm (Introduction to Second Special Issue of 'Thinking through the Decolonial Turn')." *Transmodernity: Journal of Peripheral Cultural Production of the Luso-Hispanic World* 1, no. 3: 3–10.

Maldonado-Torres, Nelson. 2018. "The Decolonial Turn." In *New Approaches to Latin American Studies: Culture and Power*, edited by Juan Poblete, 111–27. New York: Routledge.

Markus, Hazel Rose, and Paula M. L. Moya, eds. 2010. *Doing Race: 21 Essays for the 21st Century*. New York: Norton.

Martínez, Ernesto Javier. 2013. *On Making Sense: Queer Race Narratives of Intelligibility*. Stanford, CA: Stanford University Press.

Martínez, Ernesto Javier. 2014. "¿Con quién, dónde, y por qué te dejas?" *Aztlán: A Journal of Chicano Studies* 39, no. 1: 237–46.

Medina, José. 2013. *The Epistemology of Resistance: Gender and Racial Oppression, Epistemic Injustice, and Resistant Imaginations*. New York: Oxford University Press.

Mignolo, Walter D. 1995. *The Darker Side of the Renaissance: Literacy, Territoriality, and Colonization*. Ann Arbor: University of Michigan Press.

Mignolo, Walter D. 2000. *Local Histories / Global Designs: Coloniality, Subaltern Knowledges, and Border Thinking*. Princeton, NJ: Princeton University Press.

Mignolo, Walter D. 2001. "The Zapatistas Theoretical Revolution: Its Historical, Ethical, and Political Consequences." In *The Collective Imagination: Limits and Beyond*, edited by Enrique Rodriguez Larreta, 105–42. Rio de Janeiro: Institute for Cultural Pluralism, Universidad Candido Mendes.

Mignolo, Walter D. 2002. "The Geopolitics of Knowledge and the Colonial Difference." *South Atlantic Quarterly* 10, no. 1 (Winter): 57–96.

Mignolo, Walter D. 2007. "Delinking: The Rhetoric of Modernity, the Logic of Coloniality, and the Grammar of De-coloniality." *Cultural Studies* 21, no. 2: 449–514.

Mignolo, Walter D. 2014. "From 'Human Rights' to 'Life Rights.'" In *The Meanings of Rights: The Philosophy and Social Theory of Human Rights*, edited by Costas Douzinas and Conor Gearty, 161–80. Cambridge: Cambridge University Press.

Mohanty, Satya. 1997. *Literary Theory and the Claims of History: Postmodernism, Objectivity, Multicultural Politics*. Ithaca, NY: Cornell University Press.

Moraga, Cherríe. 1983. *Loving in the War Years: Lo que nunca pasó por sus labios*. Boston: South End Press.

Moraga, Cherríe. 1986. Interview by Norma Alarcón, Norma. *Third Woman* 3, nos. 1–2: 127–34.

Moraga, Cherríe, and Gloria Anzaldúa, eds. 1983. *This Bridge Called My Back: Writings by Radical Women of Color*. 2nd ed. New York: Kitchen Table, Women of Color Press.

Moya, Paula M. L. 2002. *Learning from Experience: Minority Identities, Multicultural Struggles*. Berkeley: University of California Press.

Moya, Paula M. L. 2016a. "Dismantling the Master's House: The Search for Decolonial Love in Junot Diaz's 'How to Date a Browngirl, Blackgirl, Whitegirl, or Halfie.'" In *The Social Imperative: Race, Close Reading, and Contemporary Literary Criticism*, 109–32. Stanford, CA: Stanford University Press.

Moya, Paula M. L. 2016b. *The Social Imperative: Race, Close Reading, and Contemporary Literary Criticism*. Stanford, CA: Stanford University Press.

Moya, Paula M. L., and MarYam G. Hamedani. 2017. "Learning to Read Race: Multicultural Literature Can Foster Racial Literacy and Empower Students." *California English* 22, no. 4: 10–13.

Moya, Paula M. L., and Michael R. Hames-García, eds. 2000. *Reclaiming Identity: Realist Theory and the Predicament of Postmodernism*. Berkeley: University of California Press.

Muñoz, Alicia. 2013. "Articulating a Geography of Pain: Metaphor, Memory, and Movement in Helena María Viramontes's *Their Dogs Came with Them*." *MELUS* 38, no. 2 (Summer): 24–38, 157.

Nixon, Rob. 2011. *Slow Violence and the Environmentalism of the Poor*. Cambridge, MA: Harvard University Press.

Ortega, Mariana. 2015. *Between Worlds: Latina Feminist Phenomenology, Multiplicity, and the Self*. Albany: State University of New York Press.

Pattison, Dale. 2014. "Trauma and the 710: The New Metropolis in Helena María Viramontes's *Their Dogs Came with Them*." *Arizona Quarterly* 70, no. 2: 115–42.

Pérez, Laura Elisa. 2007. *Chicana Art: The Politics of Spiritual and Aesthetic Altarities*. Durham, NC: Duke University Press.

Quijano, Anibal. 2000. "Coloniality of Power, Eurocentrism, and Latin America." *Nepantla: Views from the South* 1, no. 3: 533–80.

Saldívar, Jose Davíd. 2012. *Trans-Americanity: Subaltern Modernities, Global Coloniality, and the Cultures of Greater Mexico*. Durham, NC: Duke University Press.

Sánchez-Casal, Susan, and Amie A. Macdonald. 2009. *Identity in Education*. New York: Palgrave Macmillan.

Scott, Darieck. 2010. *Extravagant Abjection: Blackness, Power, and Sexuality in the African American Literary Imagination*. New York: New York University Press.

Siebers, Tobin. 2006. "Disability Studies and the Future of Identity Politics." In *Identity Politics Reconsidered*, edited by Linda Martín Alcoff, Michael R. Hames-García, Satya P. Mohanty, and Paula M. L. Moya, 10–30. New York: Palgrave Macmillan.

Siebers, Tobin. 2010. *Disability Aesthetics*. Ann Arbor: University of Michigan Press, 2010.

Teuton, Sean Kicummah. 2008. *Red Land, Red Power: Grounding Knowledge in the American Indian Novel*. Durham, NC: Duke University Press.

Viramontes, Helena María. 1995. *Under the Feet of Jesus*. New York: Penguin.

Viramontes, Helena Maria. 2007a. Interview by Daniel Olivas. *La Bloga,* April 2. https://labloga.blogspot.com/2007/04/interview-with-helena-mara-viramontes.html.

Viramontes, Helena Maria. 2007b. Interview by Michael Silverblatt. *Bookworm: Book Review and Author Interviews on KCRW*, August 16. Audio, 30:00. https://www.kcrw.com/news-culture/shows/bookworm/helena-maria-viramontes.

Viramontes, Helena Maria. 2007c. *Their Dogs Came with Them*. New York: Atria Books.

Wald, Sarah D. 2013. "'Refusing to Halt': Mobility and the Quest for Spatial Justice in Helena María Viramontes's *Their Dogs Came with Them* and Karen Tei Yamashita's *Tropic of Orange*." *Western American Literature* 48, nos. 1–2: 70–89.

Walsh, Catherine. 2012. "'Other' Knowledges, 'Other' Critiques: Reflections on the Politics and Practices of Philosophy and Decoloniality in the 'Other' America." *Transmodernity: Journal of Peripheral Cultural Production of the Luso-Hispanic World* 1, no. 3: 11–27.

Woloch, Alex. 2003. *The One vs. the Many: Minor Characters and the Space of the Protagonist in the Novel*. Princeton, NJ: Princeton University Press.

Wynter, Sylvia. 1987. "On Disenchanting Discourse: 'Minority' Literary Criticism and Beyond." *Cultural Critique* 7 (August): 207–44.

Wynter, Sylvia. 2003. "Unsettling the Coloniality of Being/Power/Truth/Freedom: Towards the Human, after Man, Its Overrepresentation—an Argument." *New Centennial Review* 3, no. 3: 257–337.

Wyse, Raelene. 2013. "Constructing Community through Fiction in Helena María Viramontes's *Their Dogs Came with Them* and Susana Sánchez Bravo's *Espacios Condenados.*" In *Rebozos de Palabras: An Helena María Viramontes Critical Reader*, edited by Gabriella Gutiérrez y Muhs, 48–63. Tucson: University of Arizona Press.

Yamashita, Karen Tei. 2013. "Tropic of Orange." *Western American Literature* 48, nos. 1–2: 70–89.

CHAPTER 9 | African, Latina, Feminist,
and Decolonial

*Marta Moreno Vega's Remembrance of Life in
El Barrio in the 1950s*

THERESA DELGADILLO

MARTA MORENO VEGA'S (2004) memoir of her childhood and young adulthood, *When the Spirits Dance Mambo*, offers readers an account of Puerto
Rican life in New York's El Barrio in the 1950s that signifies on both past
and present for contemporary readers.[1] In contrast to an autobiography,
autohistoria, or *testimonio*, memoirs offer us not the whole picture but
just a tiny slice of it, a focused examination of a particular moment or
period in the life of the narrator. By their very nature, memoirs convey
the uniqueness or significance of a compressed time period, yet because
they are composed after the events themselves they may also represent
a belated consciousness of that significance, or perhaps an opportunity
to share with a wider contemporary audience, retrospectively, the significance of events understood by only a few in their original time frame.
Moreno Vega's memoir conveys the latter—a sense of the enduring im-
port of her experience as a child and young woman at her grandmother's
knee and altar. The significance of this experience, as Moreno Vega tells it,
lies in the strong bond forged between the two as Abuela teaches Moreno
Vega, known by her childhood name of "Cotito" in the narrative, about
Espiritismo and its value and power in everyday life. A Puerto Rican black
woman, Moreno Vega remembers this early spiritual training as integrally
interconnected with her family's negotiations with racialization in the
United States, her growing questions about normative gender and sexual

---

[1] "To rename is to revise, and to revise is to Signify" (Moreno Vega 2004, xvii). This essay
draws from the theory of the centrality of orality/speech in African American literary traditions to
consider both speech and the sonic in Moreno Vega (Gates 1988).

Theresa Delgadillo, *African, Latina, Feminist, and Decolonial* In: *Theories of the Flesh*, Edited
by: Andrea J. Pitts, Mariana Ortega, and José Medina, Oxford University Press (2020). © Oxford
University Press.
DOI: 10.1093/oso/9780190062965.003.0010

roles, and Latina/o popular culture of the period. Moreno Vega thereby offers readers a feminist memoir, written by an Afro-Latina, that couples an embrace of a new Americas religiosity born of African diaspora with challenges to sexist and misogynist values and practices. Hers is a narrative grounded in intersectionality that recognizes her "multiplicitous selves."[2] Though the narrative centers on an era that predates the emergence of "intersectionality" as a theory of how women of color might craft political and juridical answers to the multiple oppressions they face, I suggest that Moreno Vega's narrative resonates with observations about the roots of women-of-color feminist theory in the social movements of earlier decades.[3] Her memoir reveals a unique form of Latina feminisms that emerges from the experiences of Afro-Latinas.

When Vega discusses the work of composing this memoir, she explains in the epilogue, that it was necessary to research her own story, by interviewing family and friends she knew in the 1950s and by visiting her abuela's hometown in Puerto Rico, Lóiza Aldea, known for its strong African diaspora heritage (Moreno Vega 2004, 268). Moreno Vega doesn't mention here, perhaps taking it for granted among her readers, the decades of research, teaching, and community arts organizing in the cultures, arts, and worldviews of African diaspora peoples for which she is very well known. Founder of the Caribbean Cultural Institute in 1976 and faculty member in African diaspora studies at Hunter College and in Puerto Rico, Moreno Vega's numerous projects, initiatives, exhibits, and publications over the past forty years have been a significant contribution to creating our present-day consciousness of the African diaspora in Puerto Rico, and of Puerto Rican subjects as Afro-Latinas/os.

Having worked for decades to expand the knowledge and understanding of African diaspora in Puerto Rico through her research and institution-building within arts and ethnic communities, Moreno Vega can finally narrate her story of a childhood and youth immersed in forms of spirit and ancestor worship unique to African diaspora peoples that, in the 1950s, were not widely accepted or discussed nor known outside of insider circles. She describes this in another work: "In 1955, there were approximately twenty-five people in New York City who were believers in the Orisha tradition" (Moreno Vega 2010, 245). It is not hard to imagine the lack of acceptance or understanding that these worldviews may have encountered in the United States of the 1950s, especially given the scholarship on Puerto

---

[2] For further on intersectionality, see Crenshaw 1995; Cooper 2016. For further on "multiplicitous selves" see Ortega 2016.

[3] Blackwell focuses on the 1960s and 1970s, but Morena Vega presents the unlikely 1950s with its fusion of sacred and secular music and emerging civil rights movements as another origin point for Afro-Latinas (Blackwell 2011).

Ricans in the United States in the post–World War II era that has made plain the considerable obstacles to economic, educational, social, and political opportunity faced by this heterogeneous population—eloquently and beautifully addressed in Pedro Pietri's ([1973] 2002) poem "Puerto Rican Obituary."

When the Spirits Dance Mambo, set in the mid-twentieth century, explores the contours of Puerto Rican difference as it emerges and is reformed in encounter with mainstream white society and African Americans in the United States. It's a narrative whose time lag, following Homi Bhabha, makes visible earlier narrative attempts to fix Puerto Ricans and Puerto Rican culture in the national imaginary as homogeneous outsiders,[4] while it also disrupts the logic of horizontal national space (whether US or Puerto Rican) with the tension between the pedagogical and the performative that Bhabha notes is central to nonhomogenizing minority discourses and emergent cultural identities.[5] By remaining attentive to the multiple temporalities invoked in the narrative, this essay explores the representation of the dynamic nature of cultural change among Puerto Rican diaspora subjects in several spheres: the religious/spiritual, the sonic/musical, and the gendered/domestic. This essay also examines the inter-relation between these spheres in Moreno Vega's text, especially as this heralds a vision of feminist decolonization.

Dynamic and Feminist African-Derived Worldviews

In the opening lines of her book, Moreno Vega lists the multiple influences that informed her upbringing, emphasizing her African heritage:

---

[4] "A recent survey conducted by this paper revealed that Negroes living in close proximity to Puerto Ricans have little or no knowledge of them. Just as most American born citizens, they are guilty of viewing the habits and customs of the newly arrived people as being 'strange' and 'foreign'" (White 1950).

[5] "Minority discourse sets the act of emergence in the antagonistic in-between of image and sign, the accumulative and the adjunct, presence and proxy. It contests genealogies of 'origin' that lead to claims for cultural supremacy and historical priority. Minority discourse acknowledges the status of national culture—and the people—as a contentious, performative space of the perplexity of the living in the midst of the pedagogical representations of the fullness of life. Now there is no reason to believe that such marks of difference cannot inscribe a 'history' of the people or become the gathering points of political solidarity. They will not, however, celebrate the monumentality of the historicist memory, the sociological totality of society, or the homogeneity of cultural experience. The discourse of the minority reveals the insurmountable ambivalence that structures the equivocal movement of historical time. How does one encounter the past as an anteriority that continually introduces an otherness or alterity into the present? How does one then narrate the present as a form of contemporaneity that is neither punctual nor synchronous? In what historical time do such configurations of cultural difference assume forms of cultural and political authority?" (Bhabha 1994, 157).

I grew up surrounded by the pulsating rhythms of Tito Puente and Machito and the teasing, sensual songs of Graciela. The deep, robust voice of Celia Cruz brought Africa to our home. In our cramped living room on 102nd Street, my brother taught me to mambo. There, too, my father took my mother in his dark, powerful arms and they swayed to the tune of a *jíbaro* ballad. In the bed we shared, my older sister cried herself to sleep while the radio crooned a brokenhearted lament. And my grandmother, cleaning her altar to the spirits of our ancestors, played songs to the gods and goddesses. Imitating the motions of the sea, she let her body be carried by an imaginary wave, then, taking my hand, encouraged me to follow in her steps. In Abuela's world, our hearts beat to the drum song of the thunder god, Changó. (2004, 2)

While this opening passage suggests a rather idyllic scene of family togetherness and sharing, Moreno Vega's narrative actually offers a more complex family portrait, one in which our dark-skinned young narrator, Cotito, gradually becomes painfully aware of the gender and racial inequalities that impinge on her life and that of her family, creating fissures in the family relationships. The above passage highlights language, movement, even tears, but also the pleasure of dance and prayer as it weaves together the popular music of the era with Orisha worship characterized as inheritance, song, imagination, and bodily motion.

The narrative conveys a muted collective awareness among Cotito and her siblings of their participation in dynamic cultural practices rooted in diaspora. In this case, diaspora worldviews have a continued force at home, but are also described, at a pivotal moment in musical cultural history, as fusing with secular music movements to create new cultural phenomena in/from/about the diaspora—Puerto Rican and Cuban musicians of the era invented and performed music infused with the languages, beats, and concerns of African diaspora Orisha practices with which they were familiar. One of a few key moments in the narrative when Cotito recognizes the groundbreaking fusion of sacred Orisha sonic traditions with secular musical forms occurs at a Celia Cruz concert she attends with her brother Chachito at the Apollo Theater (Moreno Vega 2004, 242–243). Orisha and African diaspora practices here represent not a static past but a dynamic, ongoing, transformative cultural experience that comes to inhabit new sonic spaces in New York of the 1950s.[6] In this memoir, the younger generation is more willing to embrace diaspora knowledge, especially as they morph into new cultural spaces, in contrast to their parents, who do not actively pass these on to their children.

---

[6] Embodying Stuart Hall's emphasis on "routes" rather than "roots" in the study of diaspora (Hall 5).

Recognizing this entry of traditionally sacred musics and themes into new spheres is an exhilarating moment for Moreno Vega, who describes hearing

> the music of Machito. It filled the room, and my limbs. *"Zarabanda Changó ta veni, Zarabanda Changó ta veni . . ."* [sic] My body melded with the music as I practiced the steps my brother had taught me. An image came to me of Abuela dancing; it combined with the intricate mambo steps I was practicing, inspiring my movements. I played the record again and again and kept dancing until I felt the movement of my body become one with the music. (2004, 128)

Moreno Vega recognizes the song's Orisha references and rhythms, underscoring how sacred forms of dance and music influenced the new "mambo" sound and movement by connecting it to the sight of her abuela engaged in sacred dance. While a number of cultural and music critics have also written about the important sonic fusions of this period, providing invaluable insight into African American and Latina/o musical networks, innovations in form, transnational musical movements, and the emergence of Latina/o musical genres,[7] Morena Vega's memoir provides an insider narrative of what it felt to be among those hearing and experiencing this new music for the first time, and her narrative innovatively emphasizes the fusion of sacred and secular in the sonic realm by highlighting the interrelationship between worldview, body in motion, and sound—or Orisha worship, dance, and music, as it also examines how these figure in the generational and gendered differences within her own family.

Moreno Vega's narrative negatively portrays the silencing of Orisha traditions in her family (Heredia 2009, 68), but the contrast that the text creates between Orisha practices and Catholicism is primarily a contrast between distinct gender and racial norms, offering readers a woman-of-color feminist take on Orisha worship. The alternative gender norms of practices forged in diaspora become evident in this text through Cotito's observation of Abuela's healing practice, her engagement with Abuela's power and leadership as a medium and spiritual healer, and her assessment of Abuela's response to the "crisis" of her sister.

The text suggests, then, that there is a different and more feminist perspective on the female body and gender roles in operation in Orisha practices, one that unfolds for Cotito through her engagement with distinctive spiritual approaches to the body / physical self that have broader cultural influence in the realms of the social, sonic, and performative. This

---

[7] See, for example, Fernandez 2006; Glasser 1997; and the PBS documentary series *Latin Music USA.*

is not a text, in other words, that asserts a black Puerto Rican identity and a critique of gender roles but one that embraces an African and Puerto Rican identity that itself represents a challenge to Western/Christian dominant gender roles normalized through prevailing religiosities. *When the Spirits Dance Mambo*, therefore, hails both the ongoing dynamic cultural change among Puerto Rican African diaspora subjects and a feminist awareness embodied in its depiction of Orisha worship.

In his discussion of the ways that the question of gender has influenced scholarship on another diaspora religion, Candomblé, and by extension multiple forms of Yoruba-inspired rituals and worldviews in our hemisphere, J. Lorand Matory (2005) critically questions scholarly claims of traditional matriarchy or gender equity in Yoruba cultures and practices and their diasporan counterparts. Matory's analysis reveals how transnational and national ideologies, and international dialogues, influenced not only the production of scholarship but also the practice of Orisha worship in the diaspora. While Matory makes a compelling case that we cannot assume that all Orisha worship, and the traditions from which these derive, are inherently more gender equitable, his research illuminates the open acceptance of particular forms of what we might term gender fluidity (though he refers to this as metaphor or loophole) among priests of the West African Òyó-Yorùbá and among priests and priestesses of Bahian Candomblé (Matory 2005, 24–28). His research also demonstrates that at mid-twentieth century, a particular discourse about the matriarchy of Candomblé emerged that contributed to the marginalization of "a cultural persona who is as normal in the Candomblé priesthood as he is anathema to the normative vision of the nation state—the *adé*, or 'passive homosexual'" (15). While that earlier discourse gave way to what Matory views as scholarship influenced by nostalgia for a genderless pre-Western tradition, the impact these scholarly debates have had on actual Candomblé communities has not been benign. Matory believes that *adés* have been marginalized as a result, but another result is that "women have, in fact, now become the majority of the chief priests in this religion" (21).[8] Since the key work that Matory takes up as initiating the discourse on gender in relation to Candomblé appears at mid-twentieth century—the temporal setting of Moreno Vega's narrative—and, as he notes, has enduring influence in multiple ways going forward, it might even be accurate to view Moreno Vega's narrative as evidence of that influence—of the ways that discourses about gender in Orisha traditions circulated among practitioners of Orisha worship themselves, perhaps empowering some otherwise socially subordinated to exert leadership and to create more feminist communities of

---

[8] Matory credits Jocélio Teles dos Santos (1995) for information on current demographic information on priests and priestesses in Candomblé.

Orisha worship. It might also be a motivation for the adult Moreno Vega, a participant in Santeria community, to retrospectively appraise Abuela's influence in shaping her life work.

Sensory Experience and Sacred Bodies

As a medium and spiritual healer, Abuela conveys to Cotito an apprecia-tion for the sensory and aesthetic realms and how these take form in human expression and manifest the sacred. Late in the narrative, Cotito names, only once, Abuela's worldview and practice as Espiritismo, or Spiritism (Moreno Vega 2004, 259), though she more commonly names individual deities throughout the narrative—recognizing the specific Puerto Rico practice of Espiritismo while emphasizing its origins in diaspora Orisha worship. Many Puerto Ricans practice Espiritismo, also known as Mesa Blanca, which fuses Christian and African worldviews and centers wor-ship of a multicultural pantheon of spirits, including El Negro José, a male African spirit (Flores-Peña 2004). In one encounter with the African male spirit named El Negro Juango in this narrative, the spirit speaks through Abuela to Cotito: "Play music in the mornings before you leave the house. You will see tremendous changes. . . . Place a cup of fresh, cool water daily by your headboard for this spirit" (Moreno Vega 2004, 194). El Negro Juango asks her, "Don't you feel much better after you dance?" (193). And tells her that she has "una gitana dressed in yellow and blue dancing around you" (193). This exchange stresses the aesthetic dimensions of Orisha worship that represents the involvement of the entire self/body in communing with the divine, but it also suggests that spiritual health and sensory/physical pleasure are interrelated. The memoir further underscores a view of spiritual health that centers human expressions of beauty and pleasure in its descriptions of the young Cotito assisting Abuela in the cre-ation and maintenance of her home altar. Just as important is how carefully Moreno Vega describes the act of listening in this memoir, and returns to it repeatedly—Abuela listening to those in spiritual need, Abuela listening to the spirits, her parents not listening to their daughter, Cotito listening to the new rhythms of mambo and salsa with her siblings, and Cotito's high school friend Donna Stokes listening to her—as a manifestation of a full sensory awareness to be respected.[9]

---

[9] The more holistic spirituality of African-descended religious views, as Luis Barrio suggests, may be the reason why many Afro Latinas/os who maintain these practices may also be involved in Pentecostalism (2010, 252–53). He asserts that "divine possession or the trances state (montarse), where there is a combination of emotional and bodily experience and expression, is among the strongest pillars of both Pentecostal and African-based religious practices" (258). Furthermore, he argues that possession/*montarse* counteracts racism: "This body full of joy and sadness, of

Cotito describes Abuela's spiritual practice in her home, and her involvement in it, as one that demands both song and the body in motion. This description contrasts sharply with the rigidity, lifelessness, and emptiness she ascribes to Chachita and Joe's wedding at St. Lucy's. The latter is a sad rather than happy occasion—Chachita is being forced by her parents to marry Joe when her sexual relationship with him is discovered—and that sadness permeates the scene, expressed in the language of dead bodies: participants look like they are at a funeral, solemn, solitude, stone-faced, and they trudge—all terms conveying antimotion.

Moreno Vega's text, therefore, juxtaposes Orisha practices and a dominant practice of Christianity at mid-twentieth century in ways that constitute a critical assessment of their varied impact on women's opportunities for equality and women's spiritual health. In this way, Moreno Vega echoes Gloria Anzaldúa's discussion of the process of "differentiating between *lo heredado, la adquirido, lo impuesto*" as a critical and decolonial one that opens the possibility of a "conscious rupture with all oppressive traditions of all cultures and religions" (Anzaldúa 1987, 82).

The critical assessment of religiosity at mid-twentieth century in *When the Spirits Dance Mambo* and the revaluation of forms of social and cultural practices as they particularly impact African Puerto Rican women might be productively examined through the lens of Gloria Anzaldúa's *spiritual mestizaje,* which, as I suggest elsewhere, does not designate a particular practice or belief, but instead represents a critical mobility through which religious change occurs and one acquires a new consciousness. In the Anzaldúan framework, the body, as the site of experience, also holds knowledge, and this knowledge can be deciphered through combined attention to reading the body, research, and contemplation. In this way, spiritual mestizaje is a bodily process of decolonization and an examination of the imprint of ideologies and religions on the physical self. In Anzaldúa's work the spirit is an aspect of body rather than a phenomenon separate from the body, suggesting that body + mind + psyche + spirit denotes the fullness of being in the body and communicating and relating socially to others (Anzaldúa 1987; Delgadillo 2011).

Splits or imbalances in body + mind + psyche + spirit represent gender inequalities in Moreno Vega's text, and the memoir strongly suggests that worldviews that emerged from the African diaspora provide a stronger counterbalance to such splits than mid-twentieth-century Christianity by contrasting an instance in which the Orisha practices are enacted with one in which they are not. In the first instance, Cotito and her mother witness Abuela's spiritual intervention to aid a troubled neighbor, Alma, in the

---

acceptance and rejection, this body colored black that society rejects because of racism, is accepted by a divinity that enters into the body and reaffirms it as its son or daughter" (258).

botánica. Alma is visiting the botánica in hopes of getting some medicine to change her husband, Gregorio, who is cheating on her.

Her predicament sparks laughter and derision from other customers in the store. The store owner, Caridad, recognizing that Gregorio can't be changed, counsels Alma to change herself and prescribes a treatment for lessening Alma's love for Gregorio while also telling her, in what appears to be a somewhat derisive tone, that Alma should teach Gregorio a lesson by also stepping out on him. As she turns to leave the store, Alma runs into our narrator, Cotito, and her abuela and mother. Transfixed by Abuela's powerful spirit, Alma falls to the floor, and silence spreads among all present in the botánica. Abuela calmly calls forth the spirit that has taken possession of Alma's body. Alma's guardian spirit, Ochún, speaking through Alma, says, "She loves that good-for-nothing more than she loves her children, more than she loves her spirit, and more than herself. . . . She must not allow herself to be disrespected. I will not tolerate it any longer. . . . I do not allow the abuse of children or women" (Moreno Vega 2004, 54). When Alma wakes from the trance, Abuela conveys to her what Ochún has said, and Alma leaves the store with some anxiety. Shortly thereafter, Cotito hears the neighborhood news that Alma threw Gregorio out of their home after finding him there with another woman. In this episode, Ochún speaks through Alma, and this knowledge, drawn from her own body, is related back to her by Abuela, who functions as a kind of translator to Alma of her own body, returning her to a fullness of being that makes her subsequent action possible. This reading resonates with the philosophical work of Merleau-Ponty via Elizabeth Grosz, who suggests that Merleau-Ponty's

> understanding of the constructed, synthetic nature of experience, its simultaneously active and passive functioning, its role in both the inscription and subversion of sociopolitical values, provides a crucial confirmation of many feminists' unspoken assumptions regarding women's experiences. . . . He renders experience of immediate and direct relevance to philosophy and the production of knowledge . . . [and] locates experience midway between mind and body. (Grosz 1994, 94–95)

We see what Grosz describes as the active and passive functions of experience in this passage, the ways that Alma struggles with dominant expectations for women and is healed by a kind of drawing out of her own experience through communication with her guardian spirit. Grosz's discussion of experience here, and the suggestion of a mind + body continuum rather than binary, would support a reading of embodied spirituality as a form that allows for women's experience and knowledge to emerge and become authorized. Read in this way, Orisha worship enables gender critique to emerge as it also heals gender disparity. It's not insignificant that this occurs in a botánica—rather than a church—and that the healing encounter with the powerful spirit of Abuela effects real change rather than the lesser power of a commodified solution to the problem and somewhat insincere advice offered by Caridad.

Another layer of my reading of this scene of embodied spirituality involves a turn to André Lepecki (2006) and what he terms the "still act." Lepecki, drawing from anthropologist Nadia Serematakis (1994), suggests that "deployment[s] of different ways of slowing down movement and time . . . are particularly powerful propositions for other modes of rethinking action and mobility" (Lepecki 2006, 15). The still act "describes moments when a subject interrupts historical flow and practices historical interrogation . . . a performance of suspension, a corporeally based interruption of modes of imposing flow. The still *acts* because it interrogates economies of time, because it reveals the possibility of one's agency within controlling regimes of capital, subjectivity, labor, and mobility" (15). As Serematakis notes, "Stillness is the moment when the buried, the discarded, and the forgotten escape to the social surface of awareness like life-supporting oxygen. It is the moment of exit from historical dust" (1994, 12). I want to suggest that we read the scene in the botánica as just such a still act, just such a "corporeally based interruption of modes of imposing flow," in which the corporeal, Alma's body + spirit + mind + psyche and Abuela's body + spirit + mind + psyche, speaks from experience, and that gendered and racialized experience is also a "historical interrogation" of the conditions that would render both women invisible and meaningless. That moment in the botánica where an African guardian spirit appears in a small shop in mid-twentieth-century Manhattan represents not an invocation of a lost origin, but, a moment in diaspora when "identities become multiple," (Hall 2) and the narrative refuses the rigidity of neat layers of progress to insist, in a uniquely Americas way, on sustaining peoples dispersed into diaspora by force.

The contrast between Orisha traditions and Western religious institutions again appears in another episode where Abuela's channeling of the spirits yields a gender critique, but does not succeed in altering gendered relations or gender norms. The second episode involves Cotito's older sister Chachita, who surreptitiously spends several weeks living with her African American boyfriend Joe while claiming to be away working at a summer camp. When Mami finds out about Chachita's ruse, she calls her daughter "una atrevida" (Moreno Vega 2004, 153), "a disgrace," "lowlife," and "una puta" (154)—all labels that Abuela calmly asks her to reconsider, reminding Mami that Chachita isn't the first woman to have run off with a boy and won't be the last. In fact, Abuela repeats this phrase twice to Mami, and again when Papi learns the news. Cotito describes her parents as more worried about "el que dirán" than their daughter, and overly concerned with their daughter's virginity (154). When Chachita returns home, unaware that her parents have already learned of her deception, she is severely punished. Papi angrily confronts her asking, "How could you this? We did not raise you to be *una cualquiera*" (158). After physically lashing out at her, he orders Mami to "find out who he is. Arrange the wedding immediately" (159). Cotita dejectedly describes this outcome: "My sister's fate would be sealed with a handshake between our father and a man with whom she had just hoped to find a little bit of freedom" (162).

In the days following this confrontation, Cotito visits Abuela and assists her in cleaning her altar when she witnesses the spirit of the "*el negro Juango*" manifest in her Abuela. Juango, a liberated slave, speaks to Cotito through Abuela and says, "I was not consulted on the situation of Chachita. The decision your parents made is wrong. But they're so blinded by their false pride that they won't change their minds. They will lament their decision in the future" (Moreno Vega 2004, 191). Juango adds that Cotito should convey his message to her parents so that they will remember his words and regret their decision (154). When Cotito does tell her mother about what Juango said, Mami drops the plate she is washing and it shatters (197), swearing her to secrecy about the spirit's message.

We don't know if Mami's insistence on never repeating Juango's message is because she doesn't want to give others in the neighborhood ammunition with which to attack her family or if she feels the spirit's message would be powerful enough to interrupt their plans for forcing Chachita into marriage. Chachita herself becomes listless and despondent as she realizes that there is no way to exit the planned marriage. The preparations for the ceremony are described as "chores" and poorly carried off, and the ceremony itself is sad and disappointing event, despite Mami's and Papi's attempts to make it appear as though everyone involved wanted the marriage.

In this second episode, Abuela and Juango attempt to intervene to prevent an unwanted marriage and lifetime of sorrow. Abuela, in particular, recognizes that Chachita's actions are those of a young woman seeking to find and define herself in contrast to the perspective of Mami and Papi, who embrace the discourses of virginity, chastity, and honor of family embodied in the supervision of female bodies and linked to a Western and Christian religiosity—a wedding in a Catholic church. Once again, Abuela advocates a stance of listening—to Chachita's body + mind + spirit + psyche—though she is not accepting of whatever Chachita does; that is, she believes Chachita needs guidance. Attention to the Orishas allows a gender critique to emerge, though in this instance that critique is not allowed to take shape as an alternative to gender norms or to inform a different gender behavior. Instead, Chachita's body becomes an object or text upon which the beliefs of her parents and prevalent discourses will be made physically manifest.[10] In contrast to Abuela's willingness to dialogue with Chachita and to respect her whole person and experience, the parents' enforcement of marriage reveals a competing conception of the African Puerto Rican woman's body as object or text to be inscribed upon or disciplined. Law and constraint, following Grosz, replace desire and lack in the parents' model, yet "the body is not simply a sign to be read, a symptom to be deciphered, but also a force to be reckoned with" (Grosz 1994, 119–20). The narrator makes that force evident in in the epilogue as she acknowledges the force of her sister's downward physical spiral.

In both of these key episodes of Vega's text, Espiritismo represents one of the forms of African-derived Orisha worship that have emerged in the Americas as powerful counterpoints to Western ideologies and religiosities. In this memoir, Abuela is a powerful woman healer and spiritual leader, and her religion embodies and enacts progressive gender norms in the emphasis that the spirits place on the unity of African Puerto Rican women's body + mind + spirit + psyche over and above social norms that dictate either that they stay with abusive husbands "until death do us part" or that respectable women are prohibited from enjoying a sexual life outside of marriage. As Michelle A. Gonzalez suggests, literature created by women of color, and black women in particular, is essential in giving voice to and delineating womanist theology: "Autobiographical narratives, including slave narratives, as well as various related and independent literary forms are a rich resource for accessing African-American women's lives, culture, and worldviews" (Gonzalez 2006, 124). In *When the Spirits Dance Mambo*, Vega thereby reimagines corporeality in relation to spirituality from an Afro-Latina perspective, presenting her abuela as an early protofeminist figure whose feminism derives from her Espiritismo as a practice and community forged in diaspora.

References

Anzaldúa, Gloria. 1987. *Borderlands/La Frontera: The New Mestiza*. San Francisco: Aunt Lute Press.

---

[10] "The subject is marked as a series of (potential) messages or inscriptions from or of the social (Other). Its flesh is transformed into a body organized, and hierarchized according to the requirements of a particular social and familial nexus. The body becomes a 'text' and is fictionalized and positioned within myths and belief systems that form a culture's social narratives and self-representations . . . the consequences of this are twofold: the 'intextuation of bodies,' which transforms the discursive apparatus of regimes of social fiction or knowledge, 'correcting' or updating them, rendering them more 'truthful' and ensuring their increasingly microscopic focus on the details of psychical and corporeal life; and the incarnation of social laws in the movements, actions, behaviors, and desires of bodies—a movement of the text into the body and the body outside of itself and into sociocultural life" (Grosz 1994, 119).

Barrio, Luis. 2010. "Reflections and Lived Experiences of Afro-Latin@ Religiosity." In *The Afro-Latin@ Reader: History and Culture in the United States*, edited by Miriam Jiménez Román and Juan Flores, 252–61. Durham, NC: Duke University Press.

Bhabha, Homi K. 1994. *The Location of Culture*. London: Routledge.

Blackwell, Maylei. 2011. ¡*Chicana Power! Contested Histories of Gender and Feminism in the Chicano Movement*. Austin: University of Texas Press.

Cooper, Brittney. 2016. "Intersectionality." In *The Oxford Handbook of Feminist Theory*, edited by Lisa Disch and Mary Hawkesworth, 385–406. Cambridge: Oxford University Press.

Crenshaw, Kimberlé. 1995. "Mapping the Margins: Intersectionality, Identity Politics, and Violence against Women of Color." In *Critical Race Theory: The Key Writings That Formed the Movement*, edited by Kimberlé Crenshaw et al., 357–383. New York: Norton.

Delgadillo, Theresa. 2011. *Spiritual Mestizaje: Religion, Gender, Race, and Nation in Contemporary Chicana Narrative*. Durham, NC: Duke University Press.

Dos Santos, Jocélio Teles. 1995. *O dono da terra*. Salvador, Brazil: Sarah Letras.

Fernandez, Raul A. 2006. *From Afro-Cuban Rhythms to Latin Jazz*. Berkeley: University of California Press.

Flores-Peña, Ysamur. 2004. "Candles, Flower, and Perfume: Puerto Rican Spiritism on the Move." In *Botánica Los Angeles: Latino Popular Religious Art in the City of Angels*, edited by Patrick Arthur Polk, 88–97. Los Angeles: UCLA Fowler Museum of Cultural History.

Gates, Henry Louis, Jr. 1988. *The Signifying Monkey: A Theory of African-American Literary Criticism*. Oxford: Oxford University Press.

Glasser, Ruth. 1997. *My Music Is My Flag: Puerto Rican Musicians and Their New York Communities, 1917–1940*. Berkeley: University of California Press.

Gonzalez, Michelle A. 2006. *Afro-Cuban Theology: Religion, Race, Culture, and Identity*. Gainesville: University Press of Florida.

Grosz, Elizabeth. 1994. *Volatile Bodies: Toward a Corporeal Feminism*. Bloomington: Indiana University Press.

Hall, Stuart. 1999. "Thinking the Diaspora: Home-Thoughts From Abroad." *Small Axe*. Number 6 (September): 1–18.

Heredia, Juanita. 2009. *Transnational Latina Narratives in the Twenty-First Century*. New York: Palgrave Macmillan.

Lepecki, André. 2006. *Exhausting Dance: Performance and the Politics of Movement*. New York: Routledge.

Matory, J. Lorand. 2005. *Black Atlantic Religion: Tradition, Transnationalism, and Matriarchy in the Afro-Brazilian Candomblé*. Princeton, NJ: Princeton University Press.

Moreno Vega, Marta. 2004. *When the Spirits Dance Mambo*. New York: Three Rivers Press.

Moreno Vega, Marta. 2010. "The Yoruba Orisha Tradition Comes to New York City." In *The Afro- Latin@ Reader: History and Culture in the United States*, edited by Miriam Jiménez Román and Juan Flores, 245–51. Durham, NC: Duke University Press.

Moreno Vega, Marta. 2012. "Afro-Boricua: Nuyorican de Pura Cepa." In *Women Warriors of the Afro-Latina Diaspora,* edited by Marta Moreno Vega, Marinieves Alba, and Yvette Modestin, 77–95. Houston: Arte Público Press.

Ortega, Mariana. 2016. *In-Between: Latina Feminist Phenomenology, Multiplicity, and the Self.* Albany: State University of New York Press.

Pietri, Pedro. [1973] 2002. "Puerto Rican Obituary." In *The Prentice Hall Anthology of Latino Literature*, edited by Eduardo R. del Rio, 444–51. Upper Saddle River, NJ: Prentice Hall.

Seremetakis, C. Nadia. 1994. "The Memory of the Senses, Part I: Marks of the Transitory."
    In *The Senses Still: Perception and Memory as Material Culture in Modernity*, edited
    by C. Nadia Serematakis, 1–18. Chicago: University of Chicago Press.
White, Randolph. 1950. "Here Is Why Puerto Ricans Crowd Harlem! The Inside Story
    of Harlem's Puero Ricans." *New York Amsterdam News (1943–1961)*, June 3. http://
    proxy.lib/ohiostate.edu/login?url=http://search.proquest.com.proxy.lib.ohiostate.
    edu/docview/225881684?accountid=9783.

SECTION III | **Knowing Otherwise**
Language, Translation, and
Alternative Consciousness

CHAPTER 10 | Latin America, Decoloniality, and Translation

Feminists Building Connectant Epistemologies

CLAUDIA DE LIMA COSTA

Olympia and Cultural Translation

Olympia, a translation of Titian's *Venus of Urbino* (which was, in turn, a translation of Giorgione's *Venus of Dresden*), is a portrait in oil on canvas signed by Édouard Manet in 1863. The painting, exhibited at the prestigious Paris Salon in 1867, was received with shock by the public. According to many art critics, the cause of scandal was not the nakedness of Olympia, but the gaze that her nudity embodies. Olympia's defying stare confronts heartlessly those who look at her; she returns the (male) gaze with a fixed, disturbing look. Her hand draws attention to her sex while covering it. This movement of revealing and hiding leads the viewer to feel the need to stare at her sex, but not without blame, as she hides it from public view. As noted by the painting's critical reception, Olympia, rising above her gender and class, refuses to be addressed as the peaceful courtesan of French modernity, subverting forever the genre of nude painting.[1]

Why am I using *Olympia*'s image to begin my reflections on feminist decolonial turn in Latin America? I see the painting—which I appropriate here—as a metaphor for the debates on the coloniality of power. On the one hand, if we observe Titian's *Venus of Urbino*, we can see that Manet's translation of it brings to the forefront several elements constitutive of modernity/coloniality. On the other, from a feminist perspective, although

---

[1] There is already an extensive discussion about Manet's *Olympia* and its visual rhetoric. My intention here is not to engage with this criticism, but to use the painting for other purposes.

Claudia de Lima Costa, *Latin America, Decoloniality, and Translation* In: *Theories of the Flesh*, Edited by: Andrea J. Pitts, Mariana Ortega, and José Medina, Oxford University Press (2020).
© Oxford University Press.
DOI: 10.1093/oso/9780190062965.003.0011

Olympia refuses to be positioned as the object of the voyeuristic male gaze, in constituting herself as the subject of the gaze, she subalternizes (as well as Manet) the other woman in the picture (the black servant) by not even acknowledging her presence. The whiteness of Olympia's skin contrasts with the blackness of the maid in the faded pink dress, who, in turn, shares the space of the painting with the cat, also black, sitting sensuously at Olympia's feet. In quite a provocative way, bodies marked by gender, class, race, and animality, carefully arranged in a colonial narrative, intersect in the constitution of Western dualism between the human (white woman) and the nonhuman (the maid and the black cat), which is considered a hallmark of coloniality.

The painting very clearly highlights European discourses about gendered otherness, as Lugones (2010) further illustrates: white women, notwithstanding their inferiority to white men, are usually positioned on the human (gendered and civilized) side of the equation, while black and indigenous women were viewed by the colonizer as existing closer to nature, as sexualized nonhuman beings "fit for breeding, brutal labor, exploitation, and/or massacre (206). Such dehumanization of the other, as many decolonial feminists point out, "survives colonization [and] helps make sense of the contemporary issues such as feminicide, trafficking, and increased violence against non-European women" (Mendoza 2016, 117).

My translation of Manet's *Olympia* becomes a trope to explore the challenges that Latin American feminisms face in analyzing the multifaceted impact of colonization on women, and in problematizing white hegemonic feminism. The questions I want to pose are these: How do decolonial feminisms in the Latin American context translate and undermine hegemonic feminism? How can we develop critical knowledges that speak back to hegemonic epistemologies in which racialized and feminized peoples have always been marginalized and oppressed? These are some of the conundrums about contemporary theoretical trends within decolonial feminisms that I will explore in trying to map out, in a necessarily abbreviated manner, possible alternative routes for making partial connections among the several feminist formations in the Americas. More specifically, I will argue that translation—based not only on a linguistic paradigm, but more importantly, on an ontological one—becomes a key element for forging alternative, decolonial feminist epistemologies.

Considering the recent discussions on the ontological turn—briefly defined as the view that humans and nonhumans inhabit different and incommensurable realities/ontologies (as opposed to cultures, according to the cultural relativist argument)—translation both as cultural and ontological endeavors becomes a sine qua non practice for bringing these worlds into conversation.

The notion of cultural translation (drawing on debates on ethnographic theory and practice) is premised upon the view that any process of description, interpretation, and dissemination of ideas and worldviews is always already caught up in relations of power and asymmetries between languages, regions, and peoples. In the context of an endless transnational transit of theories and concepts, exacerbated by a continuous remapping of borders, the issue of translation has become a pressing concern, constituting, on one side, a single space for the analysis of the intersection (or transculturation) between the local and the global, and, on the other, a privileged perspective for the examination of representation, power, and the asymmetries between languages. In postcolonial critique, the logic of cultural translation refers to the process of shifting the notion of difference from its common understanding (as in "difference from") to the Derridean concept of *différance* that, according to Hall (1996) points to "a process that is never complete, but remains in its undecidability" (247). Viewed as *différance,* translation is always deployed whenever the self encounters the radical, unassimilable difference of the other. In the words of Venn (2006),

> Translations across heterolingual and culturally heterogeneous and polyglot borders allow for the feints, the camouflages, the displacements, ambivalences, mimicries, the appropriations, that is to say, the complex stratagems of disidentification that leave the subaltern and the subjugated with the space for resistance. (115)

To translate means to be always in transit (*"world"*-traveling (Lugones 1987), to live in the contact zone (Pratt 1992) or in the border (Anzaldúa 1987), which constitute geopolitical spaces from which the subaltern engages with and against colonial/hegemonic translations. In what follows I will advance a more radical, decolonial notion of translation based on the ontological turn, and which, in suspending the Western cogito, highlights the coloniality of power (and of gender) undergirding any encounter with difference. Instead of searching for a common ground, ontological translation emphasizes equivocations that stem from our multiple realities.

Deploying both the trope of translation and the notion of equivocation—the latter borrowed from Amerindian perspectivism (to be elaborated below)—I will reflect on the feminist decolonial turn in Latin America, taking as a starting point the debates on the coloniality of power (Quijano 2000) and the coloniality of gender (Lugones 2007). Decolonial feminisms, articulated by subaltern/racialized subjects, usually operate within an epistemological referent that is distinct from hegemonic analytical models that have historically structured the relations between center and periphery. An effect of transculturation and diasporic movements, these feminisms tend to be located at the interstices of dominant representations, and their practice is anchored in cultural translation in the constitution of other forms of knowledge (*saberes própios*) and different ways of being in the world, that is, other ontologies.

Coloniality of Power / Coloniality of Gender

For Quijano (2000), the conquest of America was the founding moment of a new pattern of power that is still dominant today—the coloniality of power—and that was based on the idea of race/racial classification. As he argues,

> This idea, together with the (racist) social classification on which it was based, originated five hundred years ago along with America, Europe, and capitalism. They are the deepest and most enduring expression of colonial domination and were imposed on the entire population of the planet in the course of the expansion of European colonialism. Since then, in the current pattern of global power, these two elements pervade each and every one of the areas of social existence and constitute the most profound and effective form of social, material, and intersubjective domination, therefore constituting the universal basis of political domination within the current model of power. (204, my translation)

The productivity of the concept of coloniality of power rests in its articulation of the notion of race as the sine qua non element of colonialism and its neocolonial manifestations. Moreover, gender domination—that is, the control of sex, its resources and products—is subordinated to a superior-inferior hierarchy of racial classification as a form of social domination.

Lugones (2007) criticizes Quijano's narrow understanding of gender in the formulation of the concept of coloniality of power because it is

> still trapped in biological determinism; . . . presupposes sexual dimorphism where none existed; . . . naturalizes heteronormativity in cultures that did not deem homosexuality either a sexual or a social transgression; and . . . presumes a patriarchal distribution of power in societies where more egalitarian social relations between men and women were prevalent. (Mendoza 2016, 116)

Lugones argues that in colonialism and in Eurocentric global capitalism, "the naturalizing of sexual differences is another product of the modern use of science that Quijano points out in the case of 'race'" (2007, 195). Moreover, the imposition of a binary gender system was as integral to the coloniality of power as the latter was constitutive of the modern gender system. Thus, both race and gender are powerful and interdependent fictions. When we bring the gender category to the center of the colonial project, then we can trace a genealogy of its formation and use as a key mechanism by which colonial global capitalism structured asymmetries of power in the contemporary world.

Anchored in the writings of both the Nigerian feminist Oyèrónké Oyěwùmí, and the indigenous feminist Paula Gunn Allen, Lugones argues that gender, along with race, were colonial constructs racializing and genderizing subaltern societies. In other words, gender had never been an organizing principle or hierarchical category in tribal communities before "contact." The sexual division of labor did not exist then, and economic relations were based on reciprocity and complementarity. However, contesting Lugones, Rita Segato (2003), in her ethnography of the Yoruba people, finds ample evidence of gender nomenclature in that culture, thereby arguing that these Afro-American tribal societies reveal the existence of a clear patriarchal order (gender functioning as an oppressive status differentiation system) that is, however, distinct from Western patriarchy. Segato calls it a "lower intensity patriarchy" or, in the words of the Aymara lesbian communitarian feminist Julieta Paredes (2010), an *entroncamiento de patriarcados* (an imbrication of patriarchal systems).

I would like to intervene in the discussion on the presence or absence of gender classification systems in precontact societies by bringing to the debate the category of equivocation. To this end, I will introduce Marisol de La Cadena's (2010) discussion of indigenous cosmopolitics as a way of reassessing Lugones's coloniality of gender through the notion of translation as controlled equivocation.

Translation as Controlled Equivocation

In her influential essay on indigenous cosmopolitics, and attempting to go beyond the neoliberal view of cosmopolitics as intercultural alliances, de la Cadena (2010) examines how Andean indigenous communities' summoning of sentient entities (such as mountains, water, animals) in antimining protests are resignifying the very meaning of culture. That is, in bringing nature and its materiality into the realm of politics, indigenous activist groups are denying the Cartesian separation between culture and nature, making the latter a question of politics as well. Conjuring other than human creatures into the antimining protests, they negate the ontological distinction between humans and nonhumans that has been a hallmark of Western modernity. These earth practices, such as considering the political needs and desires of nonhuman entities as well as inorganic matter, enact the respect and affect necessary for maintaining webs of relationality between the human and its nonhuman others in such communities. To introduce earth practices into social protest invites us, in the words of Stengers (2005), "to slow down reasoning,"[2] since it brings about a very significant epistemic rupture. As de la Cadena argues, the political sphere has always been configured as ontologically distinct from the sphere of nature, and this difference was a key element conspiring to the disappearance of pluriversal worlds,[3] understood as partially connected heterogeneous social worlds, politically negotiating their ontological disagreements. With the reintroduction of earth beings into politics, we witness the emergence of indigenous cosmopolitanism;[4] we can open up spaces for a type of thinking that allows us to unlearn/undo the ontological violence represented by the nature/culture dualism (hence allowing us to "slow down reasoning"), together with its corollaries (e.g., the imposition of linear temporality, colonial rationality, and universal truth).

It is at this point in the argument—and to make connections with the idea of pluriversality—that I want to invoke the notion of translation as equivocation, derived from Amerindian perspectivism and theoretically articulated by the Brazilian anthropologist Eduardo Viveiros de Castro (2004). In indigenous perspectivism, translation is a process of controlled equivocation, understood as "the mode of communication par excellence between different perspectival positions" (3). Amerindian cosmology posits that humans and nonhumans possess the same souls and cognitive capacities; hence they share the same conceptual views, that is, they see the same things. However, what changes from one species to the other is the conceptual referent. What jaguars see as "manioc beer," for humans it is blood, that is, the same concept (a brew), different referents (manioc beer, blood). This difference of perspective, Viveiros de Castro (2004) argues, derives not from their souls, but from the bodily differences between species/entities, constituting "their ontological differentiation and referential disjunction" (4)—one soul (perspective) and multiple natures. Moreover,

> The problem for indigenous perspectivism is not therefore one of discovering the common referent (say, the planet Venus) to two different

---

[2] According to Stengers (2005), "to slow down reasoning" refers to the generation (might we say, engendering?) of a new space for reflection by decelerating thinking, thus creating the possibility of a new awareness of the problems and situations that mobilize us.

[3] A pluriverse, as opposed to a universe, refers to worlds constituted by the entanglement of several cosmologies. The universe is made up of only one cosmology—Western cosmology. As Mignolo explains, "The universalization of universality in the West was part of its imperial project. . . . [T]he universal can only be pluriversal, which also matched the Zapatista's idea of a world in which many worlds coexist" (2013).

[4] Earth beings, in the political discourses of Western science, refer to beings or "natural resources" (matter) that exist separately from the human sphere. In indigenous cosmology, the term refers to those other beings living in nature and who have always interacted with humans, for they are a constitutive part of the latter. For de la Cadena (2015), an earth being is any entity (such as the mountain Augansate) that demands respect from both human and nonhuman others.

representations (say, "Morning Star" and "Evening Star"). On the contrary, it is one of making explicit the equivocation implied in imagining that when the jaguar says "manioc beer" he is referring to the same thing as us (i.e., a tasty, nutritious and heady brew). In other words, perspectivism supposes a constant epistemology and variable ontologies, the same representations and other objects, a single meaning and multiple referents. (2004, 4)

In what follows I will apply the notion of translation as equivocation to Lugones's discussion of the coloniality of gender to explore the insights of some Latin American feminists that were enacting a decolonial politics *avant la lettre*.

In an article entitled "Toward a Decolonial Feminism," Lugones states that the hierarchical dichotomy between human and nonhuman is a central mark of colonial modernity:

Beginning with the colonization of the Americas and the Caribbean, a hierarchical, dichotomous distinction between human and non-human was imposed on the colonized in the service of Western man. It was accompanied by other dichotomous hierarchical distinctions, among them that between men and women. This distinction became a mark of the human and a mark of civilization. Only the civilized are men or women. Indigenous peoples of the Americas and enslaved Africans were classified as not human in species—as animals, uncontrollably sexual and wild. (2010, 734)

The civilizing mission of Christianity focused on the transformation of noncolonized humans in man and woman. The colonized nonhuman female was not only racialized, but also reinvented as a woman through Western gender codes. Therefore, Lugones sees gender as imposition of modernity/coloniality: "The suggestion is not to search for a non-colonized construction of gender in indigenous organizations of the social. There is no such thing; 'gender' does not travel away from colonial modernity" (2010, 746).

However, why not think about gender, as well as other categories of difference, as equivocations, that is, as classifications possessing a single meaning and different representations from pluriversal perspectives? If we decide to take this route, then we have to engage in the difficult process of cultural translation, avoiding the pitfalls of the coloniality of language and colonial translation. According to Mignolo (2003), resistance to the coloniality of gender, as Lugones observes, implies linguistic resistance. It involves opposition to Eurocentric representational paradigms and celebration of "poly/plurilanguaging"—"an act of mapping, producing, and distributing a local, subaltern knowledge system" (Mignolo 2000, 247) to change linguistic cartographies.[5] I interpret these contestatory practices

---

[5] A classic example of plurilanguaging explored in the literature is Anzaldúa's (1987) deliberate practice of speaking in tongues / multiple registers to defy the reader's colonial attempt to (textually) master subaltern subjects.

as preconditions for the project of decolonizing gender, earth beings, and feminists' epistemologies.

Without throwing the equivocal gender category away with the bathwater, but articulating it in ways that challenge the modernity/coloniality binaries, we are able to take perhaps a more productive path, one that has already been partially trodden by many feminists—Latin American indigenous feminists and Western feminists of science—who are rethinking the boundaries between human and nonhuman, matter and discourse, bringing other earth beings into the conversation.

To allow for the existence of heterogeneous worlds and equivocal categories, while holding onto the possibility of making partial connections among them, the work of translation becomes necessary. In other words, equivocation (in the sense of misinterpretation, error) calls for translation: it is from politically motivated and unfaithful translations that the pluralities of worlds are interconnected without becoming commensurate. De la Cadena (2015) forcefully exemplifies in her ethnographic conversations with a Quechua monolingual Andean father (Nazario) and son how translation functions as a way of establishing partial connections between her worldview and that of the indigenous Andeans with whom she had prolonged interaction (I quote her at some length):

> Nazario's refusal "to explain again" highlights the inevitable, thick, and active mediation of translation in our relationship—and it worked both ways, of course. I could not but translate, move his ideas to my analytic semantics, and whatever I ended up with would not, isomorphically, be identical to what he had said or mean what he meant. . . . Our worlds were not necessarily commensurable, but this did not mean we could not communicate. Indeed, we could, insofar as I accepted that I was going to leave something behind, as with any translation—or even better, that our mutual understanding was also going to be full of gaps that would be different for each of us, and would constantly show up, interrupting but not preventing our communication. Borrowing a notion from Marilyn Strathern, ours was a "partially connected" conversation. . . . [W]hile our interactions formed an effective circuit, our communication did not depend on sharing single, cleanly identical notions—theirs, mine, or a third new one. We shared conversations across different onto-epistemic formations; my friends' explanations extended my understanding, and mine extended theirs, but there was a lot that exceeded our grasp—mutually so. And thus, while inflecting the conversation, the Turpos' terms did not become mine, nor mine theirs. I translated them into what I could understand, and this understanding was full of the gaps of what I did not get. (2015, xxv–xxvi)

Through the notion of equivocation, the engagement with translation, and the practice of "slowing down reasoning," it becomes possible to undo the perverse dualism between nature and culture, inculcated by Western epistemology and the cause of the disappearance of pluriversal worlds. By introducing earth beings in Western epistemology—and subverting the colonial nature/culture dichotomy—indigenous cosmopolitics produces a "slowing down [of] thinking" that, in turn, in decolonizing perception, provides an opening to other worlds and other knowledges. According to Márgara Millán,

> The process of decolonizing feminism(s) implies an involvement in and with the worlds of subalternized female subjects, a recognition of their cultural logics, and at least a willingness to think of a different relationship between human and nonhuman. It involves a predisposition to perform the *pachakuti*[6] as part of the feminist struggle. It is not an attempt to recover aesthetic and authentic roots in its purity, but to actualize different ways of being and being in the world to diminish the foundational force that capitalism inflicts on our everyday lives. (2011, 26)

Mignolo (2012), for example, argues that to think in terms of a geo-body-politics means to articulate some basic categories of a border epistemology as the first step toward decolonization. The colonial wound marks the location of such epistemology(ies)—as is reflected in the feminisms of Gloria Anzaldúa and the Afro-Brazilian feminist intellectual and anthropologist Lélia Gonzalez.

As a healer-writer-poet, Anzaldúa ([1990] 2009) works on the metaphors by which we apprehend the world, and in replacing them, she decolonizes our senses. Her project seeks to change the negative metaphors—which constructed the otherness of subaltern subjects in colonial contexts, often internalized by these subjects—by empowering counterimages. Decolonization of perception, feelings, and language itself is not possible without a healing process carried out through transformative images. It also necessitates a project of "translation as betrayal" of hegemonic knowledge/feeling/experiencing from the geo/body political location of the indigenous and/or mestizo women. From the perspective of this shaman poet, everything we do, say, or write affects both the human

---

[6] "Pachkuti, in the tradition of the Andean Aymara Indians, means to overthrow the world or to place it on its feet: it is a strong radical critique of capitalist modernity." (Millán, 2011, 26, my translation). In other words, it symbolizes a re-balancing of the world through a turn of events that could be a catastrophe or a renovation.

and the nonhuman worlds. Anzaldúa's decolonial cure presupposes, for Keating (2012), the articulation of a rather complex ontology that reflects, *avant la lettre*, the most recent debates by Western material feminists on onto-epistemologies, speculative realism, and criticisms of the limits of poststructuralism.[7]

Drawing a parallel with Anzaldúa's decolonial intervention situated on the North American–Mexican border, and going further south of the continent, I would like to emphasize the significant contributions of Gonzalez vis-à-vis hegemonic feminism. In the comprehensive analysis of Cardoso (2012), Gonzalez articulates key elements of a decolonial epistemology in *amefricanizing* feminism. For Cardoso,

> Gonzalez was a diasporic intellectual critically engaged in affective and cultural exchanges with intellectuals and friends along the so-called Black Atlantic, including activists from North America, the Caribbean, and Atlantic Africa. From this dialogue with several authors, she enacted a politics of translation of theories to develop transnational knowledges that aimed not only to explain how a racist matrix of domination was constituted in the Americas, but most importantly to intervene and transform such racialist worldviews. (2012, 115, my translation)

The concept of *Amefricanity*, articulated by Gonzalez from her location at another colonial wound (the experience of colonization/extermination of indigenous peoples, and the diasporic experience of blacks), recuperates these subaltern subjects' struggles against the coloniality of power. Like Anzaldúa's healing practices, Gonzalez draws on indigenous and African cultures from within to distance her cosmopolitical proposal from modern European epistemologies (Cardoso 2014). Elaborating concepts that provoke *pachakuti* as part of the struggle for decolonization of thought, Gonzalez, like Anzaldúa, plays with language, hybridizing it in what she will call *pretuguês*—a word play of black (*preto*) languages and Portuguese to highlight the African roots of the latter, often veiled by the canon.

Both Anzaldúa's and Gonzalez's translational mediations, coming from other geo-body-political locations than Western/hegemonic feminism, speak some of the roots of decolonial feminisms in Abya Yala. In the final section, I will return to the problem of cultural translation as a key element in the decolonization of feminist knowledges.

---

[7] For discussions on material feminism and onto-epistemology, see Alaimo and Hekman 2008; Barad 2007; and Coole and Frost 2010.

Feminism and Translation: Toward the Decolonization of Knowledge

A translocal feminist politics of translation, as Sonia Alvarez (2009) argues, is crucial to the decolonial turn and a key strategy in building partial connections to confront the equivocations or mistranslations that hinder feminist alliances, even among women who share the same language and culture, such as Latinas living in the United States and Latin American women. Translation—based not only on a linguistic paradigm, but more importantly, on an ontological one—therefore becomes a key element in forging political alliances and feminist epistemologies that are pro-social justice, antiracist, anti-imperialist, and decolonial. If women's movements in Latin America and other parts of the global South share various intersecting contexts of struggle, then "their conflicts with the 'scattered hegemonies' represented by the states, development industries, global markets, and religious fundamentalism create powerful; (even if only partially overlapping;) interests and identities. In this context, the project of translation among them becomes both newly possible and all the more pressing" (Thayer 2014, 404).

Moreover, in the interactions between Latina and Latin American feminisms, the travels of discourses and practices across geopolitical boundaries, disciplinary and others, encounter formidable roadblocks and checkpoints. For Norma Klahn (2014), to understand the coloniality of power, one needs to grasp the unequal travels and translations of feminist theories, texts, and practices, as well as their reception. In a lucid analysis of the place of women's writing at the time of *latinoamericanismo* and globalization, Klahn shows that testimonies (as well as autobiographical fictions, novels, essays, and poetry) written by women and linked to political struggles and social mobilization were instrumental in constructing a sui generis feminist practice. Klahn argues that through cultural translation, Latin American and Latina feminists readapted feminist liberation discourses from the West, resignifying them in relation to self-generated practices and theorizations of gender empowerment that have emerged from their lived experiences, particular histories, and contestatory politics.

Taking the example of the testimony, Klahn argues that this literary genre was mobilized by subaltern subjects, such as Rigoberta Menchú and Domitila Chungara, and their testimonial interventions, aiming, from the intersection between gender, ethnicity, and social class, to destabilize a Western feminism still centered on the notion of an essentialized woman. In deconstructing the dominant feminist discourse, Latin American testimonies not only constitute other places of enunciation, but also break with the Hispanic surrealist paradigm (magical realism) in favor of a realist aesthetics that brings the referent back to the center of symbolic and political struggles, documenting the violence and oppression of representation: life is not fiction. These texts, "translating/translocating theories and practices," imagine forms of decolonization of the coloniality of power.

Discussing the circulation of Anzaldúa's writings in the Bolivian plurinational context, Ana Rebeca Prada (2014) explains that any translation, without adequate mediation, runs the risk of becoming a double betrayal: first, that any translation already implies a betrayal of the original, and, second, a betrayal is also perpetrated to the extent that the translated text is appropriated as part of a sophisticated theoretical apparatus from the North. The work of mediation (i.e., placing the text in its historical and political context) is necessary so that the translation of these texts—coming from other latitudes in the North—can engage with local texts and practices, thus challenging the ways in which the South is consumed by, and conformed to, the North, thereby placing postcolonial critique not only in North/South conversations, but also South/South.

Prada develops a provocative analysis of how the Bolivian anarchist feminist group Mujeres Creando—who describe themselves as *cholas, chotas*, and *birlochas* (racist terms used in reference to indigenous migrant women in cities), and also adopt other designations of abject subjectivities (such as bitch, *rechazada, desclasada, extranjera*)—converse with Anzaldúa in transporting *Borderlands/La Frontera* to a context of feminist politics beyond the walls of the academy (where this author had originally been read), hence establishing affinities between the two political projects. Thus, the language of Anzaldúa, enunciated in the south of the North, was appropriated by the south of the South, and "incorporated de facto in a transnational feminism which (as *Mujeres Creando* since its beginnings stipulated) has no frontiers but the ones which patriarchy, racism, and homophobia insist on" (Prada 2014, 73). As she explains,

> Translating, then, becomes much more complex. It has to do with linguistic translation, yes, but also with making a work available (with all the consequences this might have, all the "betrayals" and "erasures" it might include) to other audiences and letting it travel. It also has to do with opening scenarios of conversation and proposing new horizons for dialogue. It also means opening your choices, your tastes, your affinities to others—which in politics (as in *Mujeres Creando*'s) can compromise (or strengthen) your principles. Translation in those terms becomes rigorously "strategic and selective." (73)

Boldly trafficking in feminist theories within contact zones (or translation zones), Latin American and Latina feminists are developing a politics of translation that uses knowledge produced by women of color in the North of the Americas to cannibalize[8] them, thereby shedding new light on theories, practices, politics, and cultures in the South and vice versa. In the Latin American context, other translation zones can be found in the works of subaltern/decolonial subjects such as the diaries of Afro-Brazilian *favelada* Carolina Maria de Jesus (1960), the writings of Afro-Brazilian feminist theorist Lélia Gonzalez (1988), the autobiographical novels of black Brazilian writer Conceição Evaristo, as well as the poetry, graffiti, and street performances of Mujeres Creando, to cite just a few examples. A preoccupation with not forgetting, with our "memory alleyways" (Evaristo 2006) and the telling of other stories, is undoubtedly a critical decolonial cultural practice. In the cautionary words of the Bolivian Aymara communitarian feminist Julieta Paredes,

> To refer to our own memory, to our ontogenetic and phylogenetic memory, connects us to our first real rebellion as *wawas* [girls], when we resisted and fought against the sexist and unfair rules of society, connects us to the rebellion of our great-grandmothers, who resisted colonial and pre-colonial patriarchy. (2010, 10)

Equivocal translations, invasions of the arena of politics by unusual earth beings, slowing down thinking, and rewriting memories and histories in the articulation of other knowledges are, therefore, ethical and political practices that decolonial feminists have initiated in many locations of our vast and dense Latin/a American terrain.

Resistance to the coloniality of gender implies, among other things, linguistic resistance, and I would also say, translational resistance. It means putting under erasure Eurocentric representation paradigms along with their anchorage in a dichotomous logic. Without giving up the (always equivocal) category of gender, but instead articulating it in ways that challenge the perverse binaries of modernity/coloniality, perhaps we can join forces with feminists—Latin American, Latina/o, black, and indigenous—in rethinking the colonial boundaries between human and nonhuman that have so far structured the coloniality of gender and power. In short, we certainly would be moving in the direction of a more robust notion of culture—and democracy—far more inclusive of other ontological communities.

---

[8] The metaphor of anthropophagy (also understood as cultural cannibalism), creatively explored by the Brazilian modernist writer Oswaldo de Andrade in his famous *Manifesto Antropófago* (Anthropophagy manifesto) (1928)—which became a reference in Latin American literary and cultural studies—refers to anticolonial strategy of cultural contact through which otherness (colonial modernity) is cannibalized in the process of cultural decolonization and the celebration of a new national identity. Among other resignifications, it has been appropriated as an example of Latin American translation theory by Haroldo de Campos (1975) and as a countercolonial proposal by Silviano Santiago (1989).

Acknowledgments

I am indebted to Agustín Lao-Montes (2014) for the term "connectant epistemologies," as well as for our personal exchanges on decolonial thought.

References

Alaimo, Stacy, and Susan Hekman, eds. 2008. *Material Feminisms*. Bloomington: Indiana University Press.

Alvarez, Sonia E. 2009. "Construindo uma política feminista translocal da tradução." *Revista Estudos Feministas* 17, no.3: 743–53.

Andrade, Oswald de. 1928. "Manifesto antropófago." *Revista de Antropofagiano* 1, no. 1 (May): 3, 7.

Anzaldúa, Gloria. 1987. *Borderlands/La Frontera: The New Mestiza*. San Francisco: Aunt Lute Books.

Anzaldúa, Gloria. [1990] 2009. "Metaphors in the Tradition of the Shaman." In *The Gloria Anzaldúa Reader*, edited by AnaLouise Keating, 121–23. Durham, NC: Duke University Press.

Barad, Karen. 2007. *Meeting the Universe Halfway: Quantum Physics and the Entanglement of Matter and Meaning*. Durham, NC: Duke University Press.

Campos, Haroldo de. 1975. *A arte no horizonte do provável*. São Paulo: Perspectiva.

Cardoso, Claudia Pons. 2012. "Outras falas: Feminismo na perspectiva das nulheres negras Brasileiras." PhD diss., Universidade Federal da Bahia.

Cardoso, Claudia Pons. 2014. "Amefricando o feminismo: O pensamento de Lélia Gonzalez." *Revista Estudos Feministas* 22, no. 3: 965–86.

Coole, Diana, and Samantha Frost. 2010. *New Materialisms: Ontology, Agency, and Politics*. Durham, NC: Duke University Press.

de la Cadena, Marisol. 2010. "Indigenous Cosmopolitics in the Andes: Conceptual Reflections beyond 'Politics.'" *Cultural Anthropology* 25, no. 2: 334–70.

de la Cadena, Marisol. 2015. *Earth Beings: Ecologies of Practices across Andean Worlds*. Durham, NC: Duke University Press.

Evaristo, Conceição. 2006. *Becos da memória*. Belo Horizonte: Mazza Edições.

Gonzalez, Lélia. 1988. "Por um feminismo Afrolatinoamericano." *Revista Isis Internacional* 9: 133–41.

Hall, Stuart. 1996. "When Was the Postcolonial? Thinking at the Limit." In *The Postcolonial Question: Common Skies, Divided Horizons*, edited by Ian Chambers and Lisa Curti, 241–60. New York: Routledge.

Jesus, Carolina Maria de. 1960. *Quarto de despejo: Diário de uma favelada*. Rio de Janeiro: Francisco Alves.

Keating, AnaLouise. 2012. "Speculative Realism, Visionary Pragmatism, and Poet-Shamanic Aesthetics in Gloria Anzaldúa—and Beyond." *WSQ: Women's Studies Quarterly* 40, nos. 3–4: 51–69.

Klahn, Norma. 2014. "Locating Women's Writing and Translation in the Americas in the Age of Latinoamericanismo and Globalization." In *Translocalities/Translocalidades: Feminist Politics of Translation in the Latin/a Américas*, edited by Sonia E. Alvarez, Claudia de Lima Costa, Verónica Feliu, Rebecca Hester, Norma Klahn, and Millie Thayer, 39–56. Durham, NC: Duke University Press.

Lao-Montes, Agustín and Mirangela Buggs. 2014. "Translocal Space of Afro-Latinidad: Critical Feminist Visions for Diasporic Bridge-Building." In *Translocalities/*

Translocalidades: Feminist Politics of Translation in the Latin/a Américas, edited by Sonia E. Alvarez, Claudia de Lima Costa, Verónica Feliu, Rebecca Hester, Norma Klahn, and Millie Thayer, 381–400. Durham: Duke University Press.

Lugones, María. 1987. "Playfulness, 'World'-Travelling, and Loving Perception." *Hypatia* 2, no. 1: 3–19.

Lugones, María. 2007. "Heterosexism and the Colonial/Modern Gender System." *Hypatia* 22, no. 1: 186–209.

Lugones, María. 2010. "Toward a Decolonial Feminism." *Hypatia* 25, no. 4: 742–59.

Mendoza, Breny. 2016. "Coloniality of Gender and Power: From Postcoloniality to Decoloniality." In *The Oxford Handbook of Feminist Theory*, edited by Lisa Disch and Mary Hawkesworth, 100–121. Oxford: Oxford University Press.

Mignolo, Walter D. 2000. *Local Histories / Global Designs: Coloniality, Subaltern Knowledges, and Border Thinking.* Princeton, NJ: Princeton University Press.

Mignolo, Walter D. 2003. *The Darker Side of the Renaissance: Literacy, Territoriality, and Colonization.* Ann Arbor: University of Michigan Press.

Mignolo, Walter D. 2013. "On Pluriversality." October 20. http://waltermignolo.com/on-pluriversality/.

Millán, Márgara M. 2011. "Feminismos, poscolonialidade, descolonización: ¿De centro a los márgenes?" *Andamios* 8, no. 17: 11–36.

Paredes, Julieta. 2010. *Hilando fino desde el feminismo comunitário.* La Paz, Bolivia: Deutscher Entwicklungsdienst / Comunidad Mujeres Creando Comunidad.

Prada, Ana Rebeca. 2014. "Is Anzaldúa Translatable in Bolivia?" In *Translocalities/ Translocalidades: Feminist Politics of Translation in the Latin/a Américas*, edited by Sonia E. Alvarez, Sonia E., Claudia de Lima Costa, Verónica Feliu, Rebecca Hester, Norma Klahn, and Millie Thayer, 57–77. Durham, NC: Duke University Press.

Pratt, Mary Louise. 1992. *Imperial Eyes: Travel Writing and Transculturation.* New York: Routledge.

Quijano, A. 2000. "Colonialidad del poder, eurocentrismo y América Latina." In *La colonialidad del saber: Eurocentrismo y ciencias sociales. Perspectivas latinoamericanas*, edited by Edgardo Lander, 201–46. Buenos Aires: CLACSO.

Santiago, Silviano. 1989. Nas malhas da letra. São Paulo: Companhia das Letras.

Segato, Rita L. 2003. "Género, política y hibridismo en la transnacionalización de la cultura Yorubá." *Estudos Afro-Asiáticos* 25, no. 2: 333–63.

Stengers, Isabelle. 2005. "The Cosmopolitical Proposal." In *Making Things Public: Atmospheres of Democracy*, edited by Bruno Latour and Peter Weibel, 994–1004. Cambridge, MA: MIT Press.

Thayer, Millie. 2014. "Translations and Refusals: Resignifying Meanings as Feminist Political Practice." In *Translocalities/Translocalidades: Feminist Politics of Translation in the Latin/a Américas*, edited by Sonia E. Alvarez, Claudia de Lima Costa, Verónica Feliu, Rebecca Hester, Norma Klahn, and Millie Thayer, 401–422. Durham, NC: Duke University Press.

Venn, Couze. 2006. *The Poscolonial Challenge: Towards Alternative Worlds.* New York: Sage.

Viveiros de Castro, Eduardo. 2004. "Perspectival Anthropology and the Method of Controlled Equivocation." *Tipití: Journal of the Society for Anthropology of the Lowland South America* 2, no. 1: 1–20.

CHAPTER 11 | Embodied Genealogies

Anzaldúa, Nietzsche, and Diverse Epistemic Practice

NATALIE CISNEROS

IN THIS CHAPTER, I LOOK to Gloria Anzaldúa's and Friedrich Nietzsche's work in order to develop a conception of what I call "embodied genealogies." I suggest that Nietzsche's work on genealogy can be read critically and strategically alongside Anzaldúa's thought in order to develop a conception of embodied genealogy as a mode of critical, historical, and transformative philosophical practice. On my reading, Anzaldúa's thought resonates with Nietzsche's conception of genealogy, a method of philosophical practice that sheds critical light on dominant ways of knowing by calling into question assumptions about historical necessity and rational progress. I show how considering Anzaldúa's work through this lens sheds light on her contributions to philosophical conversations about knowledge, identity, and community. At the same time, Anzaldúa's work can be read as a productive critique and necessary supplement to a Nietzschean conception of genealogical ways of knowing. I argue that considering Anzaldúa's thought and Nietzschean genealogy together yields a rich philosophical ground for thinking through questions about knowledge, embodiment, and identity in general, and the intellectual and political practice of Latina feminist philosophy in particular.

Nietzschean genealogy might at first seem a strange place to begin a conversation about liberatory theoretical practice, not to mention Latina feminist philosophy. Indeed, in the preface to her first monograph, Ofelia Schutte calls for scholars to confront Nietzsche's failings, including his classism, misogyny, and endorsement of slavery, rightly insisting that "as philosophers we have a responsibility not to cover up for him, especially when issues of justice and injustice are at stake" (1986, xi). But Schutte also suggests that Nietzsche's own mode of critique demands

Natalie Cisneros, *Embodied Genealogies* In: *Theories of the Flesh*, Edited by: Andrea J. Pitts, Mariana Ortega, and José Medina, Oxford University Press (2020). © Oxford University Press. DOI: 10.1093/oso/9780190062965.003.0012

that a Nietzschean reader engage critically with his imperialism and elitism: "if his critique is good . . . then it follows that the imperial taboos about European cultural superiority to which Nietzsche subscribed must tumble" (Schutte 1999, 70). Schutte's analysis demonstrates that this canonical philosopher's own work should be understood as necessitating philosophical pluralism, particularly with respect to "India, the South Pacific, all of Africa, the Near East, the Caribbean, Mexico, Central and South America" (70). Elena Ruíz also draws on Nietzsche's thought as a resource for Latina feminist theory, engaging in what she calls a "strategic reading" of Nietzsche's work in order to "unravel some of [the history of philosophy's] dominant assumptions of selfhood" (2016, 423). Ruíz's analysis illuminates how, despite his failings, Nietzsche's approach to language and identity harmonizes with that of Latina feminists, including Anzaldúa and Mariana Ortega, in developing antiessentialist accounts of selfhood. Both Schutte and Ruíz demonstrate how reading Nietzsche's work can be useful for anti-imperialist and decolonial projects in general, and Latina feminist theory in particular.

My critical and strategic reading of Nietzsche's *On the Genealogy of Morals* is inspired and informed by these projects. Following Schutte, I engage Nietzsche's text from the perspective of critique. That is, I hold that a Nietzschean perspective demands that we reject the myth of objectivity and embrace philosophical pluralism, even and especially with respect to Nietzsche's own thought. I follow Ruíz's practice of strategic reading by resisting the Eurocentric push to legitimate "the ideas of women of color by placing them neatly within preexisting framework designed and licensed by male philosophical privilege," while at the same time recognizing that "within the neocolonial world order, it can prove useful to wield traditional resources against that tradition" (2016, 423). Thus, though many of Nietzsche's views on marginalized groups, including women, are antithetical to a Latina feminist project, a critical strategic reading makes it possible—and fruitful—to consider how his work might be read productively for such a project. In this chapter, I read Nietzsche strategically in order to shed light on communal, embodied practices of philosophizing that are marginalized relative to the philosophical tradition, a tradition that has been formed in and through a "neocolonial world order" (423).

Rather than offer a systematic approach to Nietzsche's oeuvre, then, my project in this chapter engages in a critical and strategic reading of Nietzsche's methodology in his genealogical work, as well as his descriptions of the meaning, nature, and importance of genealogy as an embodied practice. Of course, many readers, including Michel Foucault (1980, 156) and Gilles Deleuze, have emphasized and explored the central role of the body in Nietzsche's work and in *On the Genealogy of Morals* in particular. Thus, Nietzsche's project is already understood as an embodied genealogy in this sense. But my reading of Nietzsche alongside Anzaldúa goes further to draw out the centrality of marginalized bodies as well as the important role of a community of bodies relative to this practice. Indeed, Nietzsche's "European cultural superiority" and misogyny underscore his devaluation of knowledge created from the perspectives of marginalized bodies and communities (Schutte 1999). And though Julian Young (2006) and others have argued that community plays a more important role in his thought than many readers have allowed, Nietzsche is most often read as an "extreme individualist" who is either "indifferent to society and the vast majority of those who constitute it or . . . regards society as valuable only insofar as it is a means for the production of exceptional individuals" (Clark and Wonderly 2015, 184).[1] Thus, at the same time that Nietzsche's account allows for—and indeed, at times seems to call for—the work of genealogy to be done in multiplicity, his development of the theme of epistemic diversity is incomplete at best (Young 2006; Clark and Wonderly 2015, 197–98; Schutte 1986, 129–30). This chapter, then, draws on Nietzschean genealogy, but, at the same time, it also transcends and transforms Nietzsche's thought. Indeed, Anzaldúa's thought is a necessary corrective to Nietzsche's conception of genealogy, and I show how reading these thinkers together offers a nuanced account of the multiplicity of embodied knowledges.

To this end, I first foreground my readings of Anzaldúa and Nietzsche with a brief discussion of the work that has already been done in Latina feminist philosophy on Nietzsche and Anzaldúa. Next, I offer a strategic and critical rereading of Nietzsche's work on genealogy in order to explain what I mean by embodied genealogical practice. I then turn to Anzaldúa's work to examine the central role of communities of bodies that have been marginalized in the production of embodied genealogies. Ultimately, I explore the practice of embodied genealogies in the context of academic spaces—and within the discipline and work of philosophy in particular. Though the work of Latina feminisms is, of course, done both outside and inside of academic spaces and institutions, I focus on academic philosophy as a case study in order to illuminate how the work of doing embodied genealogy is an always-already political project of survival and transformation.

Nietzsche, Anzaldúa, and Latina Feminism

In addition to making important contributions to Nietzsche studies and Latina feminism, Schutte was the first thinker to productively read

---

[1] See also Kaufmann 1975, 418; Nietzsche 2006, xxvii–xxviii.

these two traditions together, and my project here is deeply indebted to her work. Her (1986) book *Beyond Nihilism: Nietzsche without Masks* sheds light on the constructive and creative potential of Nietzsche's thought for a liberatory politics, and her later work on Nietzsche, gender, and politics expands this project to illuminate how Nietzschean thought is relevant in the context of political and antioppressive work of Latina feminism in particular. It is in part because of the deeply troubling aspects of Nietzsche's work that Schutte's turn to him as a philosophical resource for political projects—and for Latina feminism in particular—has sometimes been controversial. In a 2004 symposium on Schutte's thought in *Hypatia*, for example, while crediting and contextualizing her groundbreaking work in Nietzsche studies, feminism, and postcolonial thought, Linda Alcoff questions Schutte's reliance on Nietzschean thought: "Why isn't [Schutte's] valorization of Nietzsche more qualified, and why does she sometimes seem to separate form from content and emphasize the former?" (2004, 152). Alcoff's question is a deeply important one for any liberatory work that draws on Nietzsche, including my present project. For, even on Schutte's own terms, a serious and responsible engagement with Nietzsche's thought must take seriously his failings as well as his insights. In "Response to Alcoff, Ferguson, and Bergoffen," which appeared in the symposium, Schutte allows that she "could have been more specific," but she also rejects the form/matter distinction, and argues for the importance of Nietzsche's work for resisting "conceptual orthodoxies in the Western philosophical tradition" (Schutte 2004, 183). In "Nietzsche's Cultural Politics: A Critique," Schutte admits that "Nietzsche's obsession with the issue of cultural superiority and with the binary opposition superior/inferior represents a major flaw in his cultural politics," but also argues that Nietzsche's thought has generative and liberatory implications for "non-Eurocentric and feminist readers" in particular (1999, 69). Schutte's work argues that—and illustrates how—critical engagement with both the problematic and liberatory elements of Nietzsche's thought can be productive for Latina feminist philosophy. It is in this spirit that I read Nietzsche's genealogical work alongside Anzaldúa's thought.

Of course, an important—and diverse—body of work already exists within Latina feminist philosophy that explores the uniqueness and significance of Anzaldúa's work. For instance, in *Visible Identities: Race, Gender, and the Self*, Alcoff engages with Anzaldúa's work on mestizaje, or border crossing, in her discussion of Latina/o identities, describing as productive her strategy of "drawing out a positive identity through seeing how the mixed race person is engaged in the valuable though often exhausting role of border crosser, negotiator, and mediator between races"

(2005, 281). At the same time, Alcoff warns that border crossing is not "in and of itself a political good" (281) and worries about how conceptions of mestizaje have been used to reinforce dominant (and oppressive) power structures. Nevertheless, Alcoff's critical engagement with Anzaldúa in *Visible Identities* and throughout her work has pointed to its philosophical relevance and its usefulness for theorizing Latina/o identities in particular, pointing to the challenge and promise presented by her conception of mestizaje and of her "use of the personal voice for doing theory" (2006, 256). In *In Between: Latina Feminist Phenomenology, Multiplicity, and the Self*, Mariana Ortega shares similar worries about Anzaldúa's work. She admits that "it is not the case that Anzaldúa unproblematically confers epistemic praise on the new mestiza" (Ortega 2016, 34) and also illustrates the importance of Anzaldúa's work for developing a Latina feminist philosophy of identity. Indeed, she describes "Anzaldúa's complex vision of the self in the borderlands" (18) as an inspiration for Ortega's own view of multiplicitous selfhood.

My discussion of Anzaldúa and Nietzschean genealogy is not an attempt to critique or supplant these existing approaches to considering the significance of Anzaldúa's thought for Latina feminist philosophy. In fact, both the critical and productive elements of these projects are deeply influential to my current undertaking. In their work on Anzaldúa both Alcoff and Ortega also draw our attention to the resonances between Anzaldúa's and Nietzsche's thought. Ortega credits both thinkers with the insight that contradictions can be used productively (2016, 34). Alcoff goes even further, arguing that "Anzaldúa's epistemology comes closest to that of Nietzsche" (2006, 258), and describes how both thinkers conceive of the body and the personal as integral to the practice of theory. My discussion of Anzaldúa and Nietzschean genealogy in this chapter, then, is meant to expand upon and supplement existing ways of understanding Anzaldúa's work and what it means to engage in Latina feminist theory by exploring the productive resonances between these two thinkers.

Nietzsche and Embodied Genealogies

Describing her own projects as a Latina feminist philosopher, Schutte writes, "Nietzsche alone is clearly insufficient to take us where we want to go politically," but also insists that she "would not want to take the journey without Nietzsche" (2004, 183). What does it mean to, in Schutte's words, "take the journey" with Nietzsche when it comes to embodied genealogical practice? At numerous points throughout *On the Genealogy of Morals*, Nietzsche's description of the nature of his project as a genealogist is accompanied by a call for the work of comrades, beginning with the penultimate section of his premise: "Let it suffice that, after this prospect had opened up before me, I had reasons to look about me for scholarly, bold, and industrious comrades (I am still looking). The project is to traverse with quite novel questions, and as though with new eyes, the enormous, distant, and so well hidden land of morality" (1989b, 21). Nietzsche's project in this genealogy, then, is explicitly and self-awaredly incomplete. An effective answer to the prospect of a genealogy of morals must be made in multiplicity, by Nietzsche as well as worthy comrades. In imploring others to join him in the project of the genealogist, however, Nietzsche seems to be making an important statement about not only the great amount of work to be done by genealogists (although this is certainly an important consideration), but also the necessity of genealogical work that is done in greatly diverse variation, "as though with new eyes" (21). He echoes this call for a multiplicity of genealogical voices in a note to his first essay, where he makes another explicit call for genealogical work on morality: "The question: what is the value of this or that table of values and 'morals' should be viewed from divers perspectives; for the problem 'value for what?' cannot be examined too subtly" (55). It is clear, then, that with this repeated call for the production of genealogies, Nietzsche is also making a call for diversity of perspective in projects that ask questions about the value of values.

What does this call for diversity mean for Nietzsche? Who are these "comrades" to whom he calls, and how can and must their perspectives and ways of seeing through "new eyes" differ? Perhaps most urgently for this project: how do these differences manifest themselves in terms of the genealogical method and the possibility it might present for understanding marginalized ways of knowing in general and Latina feminisms in particular? Any answers to these questions must find their footing in an exploration of those elements that distinguish his genealogy from historical projects that assume linear, teleological development and pretend to make universal and objective truth claims. Nietzsche engages in an explanation of the differences between a historical project and a genealogical one, describing the possibility of the involvement of traditional philosophy in genealogical projects: "It may be left to academic philosophers to act as advocates and mediators in this matter too, after they have on the whole succeeded in the past in transforming the originally so reserved and mistrustful relations between philosophy, physiology, and medicine into the most amicable and fruitful exchange" (Nietzsche 1989b, 55). Here, as well as throughout this work, Nietzsche places much emphasis on the attention that should be paid by genealogy to physiology and the health of the body. Foucault usefully explicates the importance of physical life to genealogical projects in his essay "Nietzsche, Genealogy, History," affirming, "The body—and everything that touches it: diet, climate, and soil—is the domain of [genealogy]" (1980, 178). According to Foucault, this is because "the body manifests the stigmata of past experiences and also gives rise to desires, failings, and errors . . . the body is the inscribed surface of events" (148). For both Nietzsche and Foucault, the body is central to the genealogical project.

But the genealogist's return to the body, even on Nietzsche's—and Foucault's—own terms, cannot be merely a return in terms of "things studied." In following Nietzsche's description of genealogy as a "new way of seeing," attending to the body must also be an element of the genealogical project in terms of the perspectives of genealogists themselves. Nietzsche affirms that knowledge is perspectival, and acknowledges how epistemic work flows from specific locations in terms of time and space. In this way, Nietzsche demonstrates an awareness of and commitment to genealogical knowledge as embodied knowledge. If bodies are the "inscribed surfaces" of historical events, then the "new way of seeing" that Nietzsche understands as definitive of genealogical work must be a way of seeing that is fundamentally and unapologetically embodied. Genealogies are, therefore, perspectival in terms of the passions and imprintings of the bodies of genealogists themselves.

Though Nietzsche may not have intended or even imagined it, I argue that his call for "divers perspectives" and "new eyes" requires that the work of genealogy be done by a multitude and diversity of bodies. Further, my critical strategic reading departs from Nietzsche's expressed views by contending that unnecessary—or marginalized—bodies, as opposed to only those which have been historically deemed necessary, are particularly central to the genealogical project. This is an important starting point in beginning to answer questions about who can tell the stories of bodies, and in particular about the usefulness of a conception of embodied genealogy for Latina feminist projects. If the work of genealogy is to be transformative and effective in the ways that Nietzsche himself claims it should be, we must develop a pluralistic epistemic practice in light of embodied differences. Different bodies, who produce knowledge in different ways in accordance with different histories, locations, and life experiences, must be allowed to speak if the genealogical project is to be effective.

The status of physical life as central to the work of genealogists has implications, then, in terms of not just what is studied but is also definitive to the way that genealogists as embodied persons engage in genealogical work. Genealogies study bodies as the sites of descent, but genealogy itself is also a physical act that is composed of lineages that form and inscribe physical life. Indeed, Nietzsche describes this historical formation of the body as something that affects genealogists themselves: "Something of the terror that formerly attended all promises, pledges and vows on earth is still effective: the past, the longest, deepest and sternest past, breaths upon us and rises up in us" (1989b, 61). The physical lives of genealogists are not exempt from inscription by the forms of physical imprinting of lineages.

Thus, in setting up his genealogical project, Nietzsche rejects what Foucault describes as the mask that historical consciousness bears, where it is "neutral, devoid of passions, and committed solely to truth" (1980, 162). The myth of the disembodied gaze of the historian is uncovered by Nietzsche as an aspect of the will to power. In contradistinction to the historian's false claim of disembodied removal from physical life, genealogy is characterized by "historical sense." This way of thinking and seeing is fundamentally physical. It is oriented by bodies and their energies. As such, the genealogy, as distinguished from history in the traditional sense, "shortens its vision to those things nearest to it—the body, the nervous system, nutrition, digestion, and energies" (155). The epistemological work of genealogies is thus oriented by the physical lives closest to genealogists themselves. Put differently, genealogical knowledges emerge from physical life, not only in the secondary sense of studying bodies but also in terms of their very production as manifestations of instinct and sentiment. The physical lives of genealogists themselves remember particular histories, and their instincts and knowledges are not separate from the moral lineages they embody. Genealogies are always-already embodied.

What, then, does the status of physical perspective and knowledge—of genealogies as embodied—mean for Nietzsche's call for "divers perspectives" in the production of genealogical projects? Genealogical work is a manifestation of physical life in different ways for bodies which have been formed in different ways by different discourses and histories. For Nietzsche, philosophical knowledge is fundamentally personal: "In the philosopher . . . there is nothing whatsoever that is impersonal; and above all, his morality bears decided and decisive witness to who he is—that is, in what order of rank the innermost drives of his nature stand in relation to each other" (1989a, 14). Knowledges are both embodied and personal, and the drives of physical life, as constituted in different ways for different persons, manifest themselves in the production of knowledges in different ways. The strength of the genealogical perspective is in its acknowledgment and embrace of knowledge as embodied and perspectival. A critical strategic reading of Nietzschean genealogy thus reveals the importance of genealogies done by a diversity of bodies—including especially bodies that have been marginalized and whose embodied perspectives have been occluded from dominant histories and ways of knowing.

Anzaldúa and Embodied Genealogies

In the most straightforward sense, Anzaldúa's thought can be understood as genealogical because of how it introduces discontinuity into stories of historical necessity (1987, 119 and 238). Her embodied genealogical methodology can be seen perhaps most clearly in *Borderlands/La Frontera* (though her genealogical work is also, as I will argue in this chapter, further developed and deepened in her later writings). In this text, Anzaldúa gives a history of what she describes as the space of the Borderlands. Beginning with the "original peopling of the Americas," she traces the history of this region and its peoples through Cortés's invasion, Spanish colonization, and Anglo imperialism (5). In doing so, Anzaldúa provides a genealogy of the symbolic and literal borders between the United States and Mexico, describing how migrations, colonization, and imperialism shaped not only the land, but also identities, subjectivities, and languages. Her genealogy underscores that borders are, as she describes them, "unnatural boundaries," that originate in—and are maintained by—imperialism, theft, and colonizing violence rather than nature or historical necessity (3). In this way, her counterhistory of the physical, legal, linguistic, and psychic borders between the United States and Mexico disrupts narratives about these divisions that construct them as natural and/or justifiable. Understood in terms of Nietzschean embodied genealogy. Anzaldúa's text uproots our current ways of knowing and understanding by underscoring their contingency. *Borderlands* can thus be read as a genealogy of the emergence and transformation of particular ways of knowing, valuing, and being that resist of dominant knowledges, values, and structures of power.

The genealogical practice that Anzaldúa develops in *Borderlands* as well as her later work is embodied and perspectival in its focus on the way that histories, cultures, and relations of oppression and resistance constitute both physical life and ways of knowing. In *Borderlands*, Anzaldúa makes clear that her genealogy of the border is embodied not only in that it studies physical life, but also because her own body and experiences, which were formed on and by the border, animate her project. In her preface to the first edition, she characterizes herself as "a border woman," and *Borderlands* as a book that "speaks to [her] existence." She describes her work in this text as a result of an "almost instinctive urge to communicate, to speak, to write about life on the borders, life in the shadows" (preface). Her genealogy of the borderlands thus emerges from her own embodiment and life experiences as "a border woman."

In chapter 6 of *Borderlands* Anzaldúa describes in more vivid detail how writing is, for her, a "sensuous act," and describes her own theoretical practice as viscerally and painfully embodied: "escribe con la tinta de mi sangre. I write in red. Ink" (1987, 93). Anzaldúa's use of this imagery to describe the embodied practice of her work—of writing with "the ink of her blood"—resonates powerfully with her later characterization of writing in *Luz an lo Oscoro/Light in the Dark*, where she describes how "struggling with a 'story' (a concept or a theory) . . . is a *bodily* activity" (2015, 66):

> The body is the ground of thought. The body is a text. Writing is not about being in your head; it's about being in your body. The body responds physically, emotionally, and intellectually to external and internal stimuli, and writing records, orders, and theorizes about these responses. (5)

Like Nietzsche, Anzaldúa places the body at the center of philosophical practice, not in terms of what philosophy studies (although, as Anzaldúa makes clear in this passage, the body is indeed a "text"), but also as the place from which theoretical work emanates. Indeed, her account of how writing records the body's physical, emotional, and intellectual response resonates with Foucault's description of how genealogy "shortens its vision to those things nearest to it—the body, the nervous system, nutrition, digestion, and energies" (1980, 155). And, in the same way that, on my reading, Nietzsche's conception of genealogy as embodied entails an understanding of knowledge as perspectival, Anzaldúa's project should be understood as both embodied and perspectival. For both thinkers, genealogical knowledge emanates in different ways from different bodies who are situated differently relative to histories and power relations.

But a reading of Anzaldúa's work also extends and transforms the concept of embodied genealogies we get from even a strategic reading of Nietzsche. Indeed, Anzaldúa's conception of writing as a bodily activity sheds light on the central role played by knowledge that comes from bodies who have been in some way marginalized and/or deemed "unnecessary" to the dominant discourse. In this way, Anzaldúa makes a definitive—and transformative— contribution to a conception of embodied genealogy. Her political and philosophical practice answers Nietzsche's call for "scholarly, bold and industrious comrades" (1989b, 21) in a way that he could not have foretold. Thus, while Anzaldúa's work resonates with my strategic reading of Nietzsche, her work also contributes to a conception of embodied genealogies as a productive critique of Nietzschean genealogy. That is, in my reading Anzaldúa doesn't only engage in embodied genealogical practice, but also expands and transforms the meaning and significance of embodied genealogy itself.

Anzaldúa's work contributes to—and transforms—a conception of embodied genealogy by accounting for the central role of community relative to this epistemic practice in a way that Nietzsche's thought does not.[2]

---

[2] Although I emphasize Anzaldúa's work on community over her focus on the individual in this chapter, it is important to note that there exists a complex treatment and valuation of the solitary

Though Nietzsche occasionally calls for the work of other genealogists (besides himself) throughout his description of the genealogical project, he most frequently uses language of the self rather than the community, of the personal rather than the communal or dialogical (Kaufman 1975, 418; Nietzsche 2006, xxvii–xxxviii; Schutte 1986, 129–30). Even on my strategic reading, then, Nietzschean genealogy doesn't sufficiently account for how philosophical work—and the work of genealogy itself—is always already a dialogical and/or communal accomplishment. Nietzsche also fails to extend his account of embodied, perspectival knowledge to the embodied perspectives of marginalized genealogists. But while Nietzsche's call for comrades to join in his philosophical projects does not fully account for the vital role of diverse perspectives and communal dialogue in this achievement, Anzaldúa's thought is a rich resource for understanding the central role of community relative to the work of embodied genealogy. In her 1993 Essay "Border Arte," Anzaldúa describes the importance of community in enabling both survival of border artists and the production of their creative work. Writing to her fellow "border artists," she describes how "the political climate does not allow us to withdraw completely. In fact, border artists would wither in isolation. The community frees our spirits, and responses from our 'readers' inspire us to continue struggling with our art and aesthetic interventions that subvert cultural genocide" (2009, 182). For Anzaldúa, the project of surviving and flourishing—for border artists and also for "border" scholars and thinkers—is achieved with and through the existence of a community of "readers" in dialogue. And part of what it means to be marginalized, to be denied a voice, or to be forced to accept dominant ways of knowing and thinking, is to forsake one's community or communities. If, as I have argued, it is productive to understand Anzaldúa's work in terms of embodied genealogies, then the existence of a community of interlocutors should be understood as central to this kind of philosophical and political work. Indeed, Anzaldúa's account of the centrality of community to political, theoretical, and artistic work is a necessary supplement and corrective to a Nietzschean conception of genealogy.

---

self and the collective in her work. Exploring this productive tension, María Lugones writes that in *Borderlands/La Frontera* Anzaldúa "does not reveal the sociality of resistance" but also that she sees "enough evidence in her text to develop an account of the sociality of resistance" (1992, 36). Ortega also analyzes this complexity: "Despite her awareness of the relational aspect of identity . . . when discussing the question of transformation, Anzaldúa emphasizes the personal, inner journey" (2016, 36). Though the experiences and transformation of the individual are certainly a central concern for Anzaldúa in *Borderlands* and throughout her work, here I look at an essay from Anzaldúa's "middle writings" in order to highlight one side of this productive tension for the purposes of my critical project: Anzaldúa's awareness of the central nature of community relative to the work of transformation.

Anzaldúa shows us how, in the context of Latina feminism in the academy, community is a necessary condition for embodied genealogical practice, particularly the essential genealogical practice of bodies and communities that have been marginalized relative to dominant discourses and practices. In the case of Latina feminism in philosophy, the communal work of embodied genealogies is itself a mode of survival. As Linda Alcoff (2003), Kristie Dotson (2011), Kathryn Gines (2011), Mariana Ortega (2006), and others have convincingly argued, what it means to be a woman of color in philosophy is to exist amid—and despite—the constant threat of violent marginalization (see also Allen et al. 2008; Davidson, Gines, and Marcano 2010). Moreover, this threat isn't accidental or conditional, but is a foundational feature of dominant ways of thinking and knowing in this context. The very structures and norms that ground and contain our philosophical practice marginalize genealogies produced by bodies that have been made to suffer in various ways. Anzaldúa's analysis makes clear that this marginalization is inevitable when women of color are isolated. Women-of-color feminist philosophies—and women-of-color feminist philosophers—are thus marginalized when they are isolated from their communities. Just as survival, resistance, and embodied genealogical practice itself are made possible through the existence of what Anzaldúa calls a "border community," so is the project of Latina feminist philosophy realized through the existence of a community of interlocutors. Understanding Latina feminist practice in terms of embodied genealogy sheds light on the essential role that community plays in this kind of diverse philosophical project.

Anzaldúa also offers us a way of understanding what, precisely, constitutes the type of community that is productive for my conception of embodied genealogies, and for thinking about the work of Latina feminisms in particular as a practice of survival. This is a significant and complex contribution, for communal dialogue is not without its own dangers. In the same response to Alcoff, Ferguson, and Bergoffen that I discussed in the opening passages of this chapter, Schutte speaks to the way that "the notion of community can be oppressive insofar as it appears to dictate behaviors preferred by the majority or the collective, excluding other kinds of behavior as subversive or deviant" (Schutte 2004, 198). Indeed, Schutte finds Nietzsche's work particularly helpful in its critique of orthodoxies, which can constitute communities that are homogenous and oppressive (2004, 183). But, as I have argued, Nietzsche does not develop a robust positive account of an alternate vision of community (Young 2006; Kaufman 1975). Reading Anzaldúa and Nietzsche together, then, makes room for thinking about embodied genealogy as a communal practice of survival in a way that resists the homogenization and leveling down of difference that both thinkers critique.

But what does this "communal practice" entailed by embodied genealogy look like? First, following Anzaldúa, I argue that this communal practice is neither homogenous nor homogenizing. On the contrary, I have shown how understanding genealogical knowledge as always already embodied and perspectival underscores the importance of diversity in terms of the bodies of genealogists themselves. Anzaldúa's work explicitly affirms and offers an intersectional analysis of diversity in terms of race, ethnicity, culture, sexuality, gender, disability, and class. But her intersectional analysis—like my own conception of embodied genealogy as a communal practice—is not rooted in gender or racial essentialism. That is, while this communal practice does consist of differently embodied genealogists who produce different kinds of embodied genealogies, this is not because there are essential, ahistorical differences among differently gendered bodies, or "black," "brown," and "white" bodies, or because all women of color or all Latinas produce the same kinds of knowledge. My conception of embodied genealogy follows Anzaldúa's analysis by being attentive to the way that identities themselves are constructed, broken down, molded, and lived in a multiplicity of ways through distinct histories of power, oppression, and resistance.

Still, the kind of community that is envisaged and enacted throughout Anzaldúa's work is not practiced by either ignoring identity or by thinking only of the diversity of bodies in general, without regard to race, class, sex, or disability as categories or meaningful identities. Anzaldúa's insights bring to the fore how genealogical work is both more important and more fraught when it is engaged in by bodies who have in some way been marginalized or oppressed by dominant structures of power and ways of knowing. In *Borderlands*, she develops the concept of "la facultad," to describe "the capacity to see in surface phenomena the meaning of deeper realities, to see the deep structure below the surface" (Anzaldúa 1987, 38). *La facultad*, like the "historical sense" of the genealogist, "refuses the certainty of absolutes" and is "capable of liberating divergent and marginal elements" (Foucault 1980, 152–53). But Anzaldúa's analysis makes clear that both *la facultad* and the "historical sense" of the genealogist are most well developed in "those who are pounced on the most . . . the females, the homosexuals of all races, the darkskinned, the outcast, the persecuted, the marginalized, the foreigner" (Anzaldúa 1987, 38). Conceptualizing Anzaldúa's analysis as a genealogical project illuminates the particular importance of knowledge produced by bodies who have been marginalized or made to suffer, and explains that groups of people who share definitive locations within histories and structures of power and oppression can be marked by this differentiation in overlapping ways. The embodied perspectives of such people also both overlap and diverge. In this way, Anzaldua's work tells—and shows—us how communities and knowledges are formed through shared histories and experiences of both oppression and resistance. Thus, the kind of border community that Anzaldúa says is necessary for the work of the border artist—and the border thinker—is constituted by distinct histories, power relations, and identity categories at the same time that it is both diverse and fluid.

It is in this productive tension—between the historical and political specificity of community on the one hand and diversity and fluidity of community on the other—that we should understand the meaning of embodied genealogies as a communal practice and, in turn, the significance of understanding Latina feminism in terms of embodied genealogy. Indeed, the conception of communal genealogical practice that emerges from my reading of Anzaldúa and Nietzsche resonates with the community-building practices of Latina feminist philosophy itself. As this volume so vividly illustrates, capturing Latina feminist philosophy in its fullest multiplicity demands a recognition of not one, singular perspective or unified Latina feminist philosophy, but instead a rich diversity of Latina feminist philosophical perspectives, a dynamic conversation among multiple theoretical traditions. In this sense, though the term "Latina feminist philosophy" describes a set of discourses and practices that are not only incredibly diverse but also at times in tension with one another, this term must also be understood to signify a set of perspectives and ways of knowing that are rooted in community discussion and dialogue. The work of Latina feminist philosophy is thus a necessarily complex project, one that involves multiple perspectives and ways of knowing that are at the same time rooted in communal practice.

Thinking about embodied genealogy as a kind of communal practice also prompts reflection not only on philosophy as an abstract intellectual practice, but also on the challenges presented by philosophy as a discipline, profession, and set of institutions. Moreover, understanding Latina feminism as a communal, embodied, and genealogical practice of survival highlights the important philosophical work of developing community and coalition among and between Latinas in philosophy as well as with others across disciplinary and cultural boundaries. Conceptualizing Latina feminist practice in terms of embodied genealogy, then, reveals that the creation of spaces for communal dialogue among Latinas and other feminists in the context of the discipline of philosophy and the academy more broadly is an intrinsically political and philosophical practice—one that demands and enacts a transformation of institutions and structures of power and knowledge. Ultimately, making space for community, not forsaking it, means upsetting the boundaries and borders of disciplines, as well as those between theory and practice and between politics and philosophy.

In this way, the concept of embodied genealogies that I've developed through this strategic reading of Nietzsche and Anzaldúa adds to—and supplements—existing approaches to thinking about the significance of Latina feminism. Indeed, as we have seen, a conception of embodied genealogies can contribute to conversations about ways of knowing and Latina feminisms in a number of important ways. First, conceptualizing Latina feminisms in terms of embodied genealogies emphasizes how particular histories and structures of power make possible and give shape to bodies and the intellectual and political traditions they produce. That is, an understanding of embodied genealogies brings to the fore how ways of knowing emerge from within histories and structures of power and oppression, and how these histories have affected different bodies in different ways. Second, a conception of Latina feminism in terms of embodied genealogy offers us a new way of thinking about the dynamic interrelation between communal practices and the production of diverse knowledges about and through diverse bodies. This conceptual framework can help us understand how conversations among—and even tensions between—Latina feminisms not only can be illuminative and productive, but are indeed constitutive of this political and intellectual tradition. Third, thinking about the production of knowledge in terms of embodied genealogies lays bare the structures of power and oppression that make possible—and, conversely, hinder or foreclose the possibility of—the work of Latina feminisms. This project thus captures some of the many ways that Latina feminist theory enacts meaningful practices of survival, critique, and community-building, and also sheds light on the oppressive and violent structures of power that make this work challenging and sometimes painful.

References

Alcoff, Linda Martín. 2003. "Introduction." In *Singing in the Fire: Stories of Women in Philosophy*, edited by Linda Martín Alcoff, 1–14. Lanham, MD: Rowman & Littlefield Publishers.

Alcoff, Linda Martín. 2004. "Schutte's Nietzschean Postcolonial Politics." *Hypatia* 19, no. 3(August): 144–156. https://doi.org/10.1111/j.1527-2001.2004.tb01305.x.

Alcoff, Linda Martin. 2005. *Visible Identities: Race, Gender, and the Self.* New York: Oxford University Press.

Alcoff, Linda Martín. 2006. "The Unassimilated Theorist." *PMLA* 121, no. 1: 255–59.

Allen, Anita, Anika Maaza Mann, Donna-Dale L. Marcano, Michele Moody-Adams, and Jacqueline Scott. 2008. "Situated Black Women's Voices in/on the Profession of Philosophy." *Hypatia: A Journal of Feminist Philosophy* 23, no. 2 (April): 160–89. https://doi.org/10.2979/HYP.2008.23.2.160.

Anzaldúa, Gloria. 1987. *Borderlands/La Frontera: The New Mestiza.* Aunt Lute Books.

Anzaldúa, Gloria. 2009. *The Gloria Anzaldúa Reader.* Edited by AnaLouise Keating. Durham, NC: Duke University Press.

Anzaldúa, Gloria. 2015. *Light in the Dark/Luz en lo Oscuro: Rewriting Identity, Spirituality, Reality*. Edited by AnaLouise Keating. Durham, NC: Duke University Press.

Clark, Maudemarie, and Monique Wonderly. 2015. "The Good of Community." In *Nietzsche on Ethics and Politics*, edited by Maudemarie Clark, 184–202. New York: Oxford University Press.

Davidson, Maria del Guadalupe, Kathryn T. Gines, and Donna-Dale L. Marcano. 2010. *Convergences*. Albany: State University of New York Press. http://muse.jhu.edu/book/538.

Dotson, Kristie. 2011. "Concrete Flowers: Contemplating the Profession of Philosophy." *Hypatia* 26, no. 2 (May): 403–9. https://doi.org/10.1111/j.1527-2001.2011.01176.x.

Foucault, Michel. 1980. *Language, Counter-memory, Practice: Selected Essays and Interviews*. Ithaca, NY: Cornell University Press.

Gines, Kathryn T. 2011. "Being a Black Woman Philosopher: Reflections on Founding the Collegium of Black Women Philosophers." *Hypatia* 26, no. 2 (2011): 429–37. https://doi.org/10.1111/j.1527-2001.2011.01172.x.

Kaufmann, Walter A. 1975. *Nietzsche: Philosopher, Psychologist, Antichrist*. 4th ed. Princeton, NJ: Princeton University Press.

Lugones, María. 1992. "On Borderlands/La Frontera: An Interpretive Essay." *Hypatia* 7, no. 4: 31–37.

Nietzsche, Friedrich. 1989a. *Beyond Good & Evil: Prelude to a Philosophy of the Future*. Translated by Walter Kaufmann. New York: Vintage.

Nietzsche, Friedrich. 1989b. *On the Genealogy of Morals and Ecce Homo*. Edited by Walter Kaufmann. Reissue ed. New York: Vintage.

Nietzsche, Friedrich. 2006. *Nietzsche: "On the Genealogy of Morality" and Other Writings: Revised Student Edition*. Edited by Keith Ansell-Pearson. Translated by Carol Diethe. 2nd ed. New York: Cambridge University Press.

Ortega, Mariana. 2006. "Being Lovingly, Knowingly Ignorant: White Feminism and Women of Color." *Hypatia* 21, no. 3 (June): 56–74.

Ortega, Mariana. 2016. *In-Between: Latina Feminist Phenomenology, Multiplicity, and the Self*. Albany: State University of New York Press.

Ruíz, Elena Flores. 2016. "Linguistic Alterity and the Multiplicitous Self: Critical Phenomenologies in Latina Feminist Thought." *Hypatia* 31, no. 2: 421–36.

Schutte, Ofelia. 1986. *Beyond Nihilism: Nietzsche without Masks*. Rev. ed. Chicago: University of Chicago Press.

Schutte, Ofelia. 1999. "Nietzsche's Cultural Politics: A Critique." *Southern Journal of Philosophy* 37, no. S1 (March): 65–71. https://doi.org/10.1111/j.2041-6962.1999.tb01794.x.

Schutte, Ofelia. 2004. "Response to Alcoff, Ferguson, and Bergoffen." *Hypatia* 19, no. 3: 182–202.

Young, Julian. 2006. *Nietzsche's Philosophy of Religion*. New York: Cambridge University Press.

CHAPTER 12 | Between Hermeneutic Violence and Alphabets of Survival

ELENA FLORES RUÍZ

Te alejas de los nombres / que hilan el silencio de las cosas

—ALEJANDRA PIZARNIK

I know what will happen. You tell the story, and then it's retold as they wish, written in words you do not understand, in a language that is theirs, and not yours.

—EDWIDGE DANTICAT

IT IS DIFFICULT TO grasp the existential impact of living amid systems of interpretation that are legitimized by what they exclude, the limbic terror of maneuvering through life with discursive tools designed to deflect awareness of their own impoverishment and complicity in systems of domination. Every step betrays when bodying through terrains that exclude the synchronous appearance of women, melanoid bodies and unregulated sexualities outside the colonial ordering of everyday life. Every step caves in ways philosophical feminisms have yet to account for, steps women of color and Indigenous feminisms have long been taking to remedy the lived impact of having to take them in the first place. What tools, what hard-won strides and self-authoring skills have arisen to defy the colonial will toward epistemicides and the Western dialectic of erasure? What strategies have formed to name the silence colonized languages inhabit—this alien god gone astray in the flesh of those risen from the wretched of the earth? The answer, if the language of interpretive horizons is decolonized enough to hear it, is many.

Many grammars, vast and plural, have formed to protest the sense of loss that is knowing you speak ten languages yet only have words for one. Anzaldúa speaks. Paredes speaks. Menchú speaks. Yet this epistemic

Elena Flores Ruíz, *Between Hermeneutic Violence and Alphabets of Survival* In: *Theories of the Flesh*, Edited by: Andrea J. Pitts, Mariana Ortega, and José Medina, Oxford University Press (2020).
© Oxford University Press.
DOI: 10.1093/oso/9780190062965.003.0013

resilience comes at a cost, one that cannot be altogether forgone in an age of intensifying neocolonial violence, but which can be partly mitigated by laying bare some of the mechanisms operative in the continued resilience and systematicity of neocolonial oppression against women of color. Ours is a history of visible and hidden harms, of violence by another name that requires a different archaeology of knowledge than previously supposed by European political philosophies. Too often, the conceptions of injury and harm they espouse are based on a metaphysics of presence that excludes the bodies of the oppressed (so that both visible and invisible harms coexist in our lives to confound us, to shroud the normalized coexistence of democratic antislavery with institutional racism and sexism). Too often, the parameters for freedom they beget are based on colonial subjugation of alternative political formations and acquiescence to the forms of power that maintain the modern colonial gender system intact, so that deeper diachronic forms of violence against women remain sidelined, elided in our experience of our social worlds. Ours is a history of hidden harms taking place in open air, of histories buried by History. This demands an accounting.

This essay is one small step in that direction. I am interested in what keeps violence a productive phenomenon in the lives of women of color: what maintains and *sustains* the logical universe necessary to keep "resistance" a structural feature of our existence. We are undoubtedly resistant. Strong. We gather the slaughter and steward our pain towards survival: a beyond the beyond yet known. Yet this struggle is not an accidental feature of existence, but the outcome of deep, structural inequities and foundational fictions at the heart of modern liberalism and democratic civil society.

Disclosing these inequities and fictions alone will not yield their demise, as the rationalistic ideal behind such logical inference founders on the same epistemic foundationalisms that motivated European colonialism and imperialism. Tracing harms to their origins—even to unknown or undertheorized ontological levels of origins—dwells too much on the philosophical satisfaction reached by establishing more precise correspondences between self and world, or in grounding knowledge claims on yet more "primordial," transcendental conditions for human understanding. This alone is not the world. It's an explanatory framework for making sense of a world that will never be the world that most matters to those excluded by those frameworks: the lived-world(s) of marginalized beings often caught in the crags between disclosure and disappearance, between bones bent by pain that falls into medical metrics (and thus addressed as "real") and pain excluded by the unacknowledged sexist whiteness of those metrics. We acknowledge. And we're here to account. But this accounting, as a methodological pivot for our work, can never fully capture and remedy the harm itself. It can never be the thing that sutures closed the slaughter in the city square, that gives us back our missing loved ones, restores the water access route to our psyches, or frees our detained friends. It can never shake a tree limb with enough force to both dig up its roots and loosen the blood on its leaves. There is no blood on the ontological tree.

What philosophical investigations of structural oppressions in our lives *can* do, however, is in a very limited (but very important) way be theoretically responsive to the affective, phenomenological, and political consequences that emanate from the tacit continuity and unquestioned operationalization of structural oppressions in our daily lives.[1] It may even help catalyze our individual dismantling of the powerful asymmetries they produce—asymmetries once experienced as mystified factors in our interpretive lives. Revealing the productive violences sustaining the structural *systematicity* of oppressions can also help ground our voices in different kinds of self-confirming spaces that expand the possible modes of epistemic disobedience we can express. It is just one step, but one that can help us stand our ground when history, language, and philosophical systems gaslight us in the fight for our existence.

Looking at what keeps violence a productive phenomenon in the lives of women of color touches on a vision of liberation that I think is crucial for tackling the resiliency of colonial domination throughout its various historical iterations in neocolonialism, imperialism, and neoliberalism. It is a vision Graciela Hierro illustrated through her claim that, to date, strategies focused on empowerment and integrating women into existing hierarchies of social power have helped to "construct power to oppose power, but done little in the way of promoting a deeper, *ontological* vision of displacing the very centrality of gender subordination coursing through the many interlocking levels of culture" (Hierro 1994, 173).[2] Presently, the theoretical toolkit for thinking about such a move is very limited. Harms at the ontological level are almost unthinkable given that the analytic tools we have to grasp such a concept inflect (even to a minimal degree) predicative stability by virtue of their very use. In

---

[1] For influential sources and contemporary work that address the issue of epistemic violence in women-of-color feminist philosophy see Spivak 1988, 1998; Anzaldúa [1987] 2012; Schutte 1998; Ortega 2006; Dotson 2011, 2014; for work in feminist social epistemology that also engages epistemic violence with a more direct focus on the epistemic injustice literature see Pohlhaus 2011, 2012; Medina 2012, 2013; as well as Dotson 2012.

[2] Hierro herself did not propose a framework for an ontological foundation of feminist liberation in Latina America. As a thinker, Hierro rejected large-scale theorizing that moved ethics away from the embodied situation of women in Latin American (and Mexican women in particular). Her work did, however, pose important questions for developing what she saw as deeper, long-term structural solutions to women's persistent ideological domestication in education, to the "mala educación" used to perpetuate women's subservience to patriarchal domination, in part, by erasing powerful feminist genealogies from history. She sought to prepare the groundwork for the "conditions necessary for feminist revolutions," especially in sexuality and erotic life (1985, 113, my translation). It is this structural aspect of her work that has been influential in this project.

addition, the prevailing analytic paradigms in the social sciences and humanities have a difficult time identifying cultural formations prior to their appearance in social structures and socially legible interpretations of those structures. Our conceptions of *violence* are also hermeneutically compromised, leading to a situation where to talk about intersectional harms against women of color, and Indigenous women in particular, is to do so with frameworks that cannot acknowledge the fulsome complexity, depth, and systematicity of those harms. We are missing tools to talk readily and robustly about what's missing. One way to illustrate this is through what I call "hermeneutic violence."

Hermeneutic Violence

Defined as violence done to structures of meaning and intelligibility, hermeneutic violence has played an important role in the persistence of European colonialism through its various historical iterations in neocolonialism, imperialism, and neoliberalism. The idea of hermeneutic violence begins with a particular picture of how human beings understand and make sense of things that differs from the standard view in the social and natural sciences, where making sense of things is based on subject-dependent interpretations of a mind-independent reality. The understanding that arises from this naturalized framework is based on an objective knowledge that is reflective instead of prereflective, and is often reducible to cognitive procedures. This account does not foreclose social dimensions of knowledge, but it does bind them to doxastic attitudes and the epistemic effects they have on rational agents; at bottom, what does not drop out is a founding framework of an inner mind driven by neurophysiological processes and an outer world accessible through mental representations, even when talking about our shared intentions or "collective" forms of intentionality. On the hermeneutic view, the knowledge generated through this picture certainly counts as a kind of knowledge, but one that is limited to the history of social practices concerned with causal explanation and *explanatory understanding*, one that is very useful for distinguishing between things like knowledge attribution and possession. It is typically accompanied by a view of linguistic practice based on natural languages as tools or "mediums" of expression for the inner mental acts of knowing agents, thus making possible the manifestation of human understanding in propositional statements like "S knows that P." Under this framework the mind comes first, language second.

Hermeneutical understanding, by contrast, seeks to describe how human understanding is something we always already do prereflectively and cannot otherwise disengage ourselves from if we are to make basic sense of our world as we move about it.[3] The goal is not explanatory understanding but close, phenomenological description that gets at the contours of what it means to make sense of things, to hold them in a certain kind of intelligibility that is characteristic of human beings situated in particular historical contexts. This kind of basic, prereflective understanding serves to ground our various epistemic comportments (like self-reflexivity and intentionality) in a prior background of cultural interpretive familiarity that allows those comportments to emerge as meaningful possibilities for expression. Interpretive familiarity is in turn achieved by growing into a specific sociohistorical context that is held together by the shared reference points enacted in cultural acts and practices—a kind of referential background of meaning that prefigures ordinary language expression. Under this framework language (as an interpretive backdrop) comes first, the mind second.

The hermeneutic account of what makes intelligibility possible in the first place and the critique of representational language it upholds help frame hermeneutic violence as a unique kind of prereflective cultural violence that arose in the modern era in conjunction with the imperial and colonial projects of Western European powers. Bolstered by new linguistic strategies of subjugation in the Spanish war of unification and Reconquista of the Iberian Peninsula, European colonizers pursued a new kind of tactical occupation of Meso-America that differs from the standard historical account of colonialism as a war of cultural invasion driven by the state-building and religious projects of early modern European nation states. On the usual view, European colonizers "imposed" their worldview onto native Amerindians as either an intentional act of domination consistent with Western political paradigms of intercultural warfare (the most common view) or as an unintended byproduct of encountering a radically different culture, causing colonizers to revert to their default cultural understandings without critical self-awareness of their epistemic myopias. Because the benefit of keeping to the latter, uncritical perspective resulted in the self-serving accumulation or concentration of social power, the myopia that

---

[3] This view is typically traced back to post-Kantian philosophical traditions that critique the account of meaning and subjectivity generated by transcendental consciousness and the paradigm of pure reason (especially through the work of German thinkers like Wilhelm Dilthey, Martin Heidegger, and Hans-Georg Gadamer, but is also present in the works of Friedrich Nietzsche, Michel Foucault, Merleau-Ponty, Paul Ricoeur, Georgia Warnke, and Charles Taylor). While each thinker places a different emphasis on hermeneutical understanding (for example, on textual interpretation and translation, on the lived experience of the hermeneutical subject, the politics of the production of knowing subjects in hermeneutical contexts, or the ontological foundation for the interpretation of meaning), the account generated by Heidegger, Gadamer, and Taylor is unfortunately centered in contemporary philosophical discussions of hermeneutics (Ruíz 2018). While I strongly favor the accounts of meaning formation and interpretation found in Nietzsche's early works, Indigenous social theory, and in Gloria Anzaldúa's ([1987] 2012) *Borderlands/La Frontera*, I make critical, provisional, and strategic use of the traditional paradigm here.

yielded the cultural imposition is typically seen as quasi-intentional and therefore subject to ethical claims of unjust epistemic practices.

Hermeneutic violence can thus be understood as violence done to structures of meaning and intelligibility that allow for the meaning of everyday cultural acts and practices definitive of a cultural tradition to emerge, as in Nahua, Olmec, Ojibwe, and other Amerindian worldviews. Hermeneutic violence can't be done directly, like behavioral and inter-personal violence. *Nor can it take the shape of structural violence* since the structures of intelligibility are prereflective, and have not assumed readily visible (as in socially articulated) shape through patterned use in culture. They have not assumed the position of (material, social, cultural) objects within settings of interrelated practices that can then be linked up to one another in structural form. It is a more primordial, tacit violence that prevents oppressed peoples from achieving prereflective interpretive famil-iarity with one's world along the same lines as their historical oppressors. This does not relegate oppressed peoples to positions of muteness or agen-tial underdetermination; on the contrary, oppressed peoples who have suffered trauma to their interpretive resources and referential contexts of meaning are often hypervocal in their resistance and creative responses to their sense of displacement. There is certainly a worldly know-how and an experiential reality of significant epistemic standing: the long quillwork of communal alphabets of survival attest to this. The problem lies in the existing structures of power that permit the audibility of those resistant voices to rise in the official narratives of culture. Hermeneutic violence further suggests that one consequence of violence done to interpretive sys-tems *is a subordinated speaking position in culture.*[4]

As an analytic tool, hermeneutic violence can help us think through precursors to the cultural epistemicides that dominated the modern im-perial political projects of Western European powers (e.g., through strat-egies of religious, cultural, political, military, and especially racial and gendered violence). Its existence suggests that violence—deep violence, the kind that sustains and nurtures the limens of worlds where the savagery of power takes on cultural form, is not solely a destructive force. Quite the opposite. The disorders of socially visible oppressions are ordered ahead

---

[4] I am indebted to the work of Ofelia Schutte for the guiding contours of the ideas presented here. In particular, she has produced powerful accounts of the ways women of color and Indigenous women bear out the consequences of their hermeneutically subordinated speaking positions through culturally produced asymmetries and positions of what she calls "cultural alterity" (Schutte 1998). See also Schutte 2002. To be clear, the idea of hermeneutic violence was developed self-consciously outside the rising "epistemic injustice" literature in the early 2000s, turning instead to feminist interpretations of the *testimonio* and *cultural imperialism in interpretation* debate in Latin American literature (see Ruíz 2006). Fricker's (2007) work was available, but needed extensive decolonization to prove useful to my interests.

of their appearance in historical languages—what makes *that* mechanism hold, persist, sustain its own preservation throughout various permutations in culture is key to understanding the resilience of social oppressions throughout history. We can illustrate this by tracking the impact of hermeneutic violence on women in Latin America, particularly through the harms done to Native Amerindian discursive practices and the cultural structures erected to maintain them in the long term.

In Meso-America, the introduction of the Western alphabet and subject-predicate grammar (as well as the assumptions of exclusionary logic, interiorization, and narrative linearity that support it) have resulted in a unique kind of violence to the discursive practices of Native Meso-American communities that very often goes unacknowledged and *continues to harm* Indigenous women through their subordinated speaking position in culture. Colonization of pre-Columbian resources of expression with subject-object representational views of language covered over deep, metaphysical ambiguity laden in the interpretive backgrounds of Amerindian worldviews, and which could not be disclosed through the dominant conceptions of Western linguistics (where the mind comes first, language second). By weakening the relationship between Native Amerindians and the interpretive resources required to effectively participate in cultural processes, one powerful consequence of hermeneutic violence has been the degree of difficulty contemporary Indigenous women face in having claims of violence heard and recognized in their own language. Consider the double bind this creates: To cope with the fallout, contemporary *campesina* movements like El Movimiento de Mujeres de Cuscatlán constructed power to oppose power, identifying literacy as a primary community need and mobilizing *alfabetizadoras* (literacy teachers) throughout rural and Indigenous communities (Purcell-Gates 2000, 221). It would be difficult to critique this move as wrongheaded or ineffective since barring access to literacy has been a tool of gender-based violence since the start of colonial administrative bureaucracies. Foreign nongovernmental organizations operating in Latin America (often in conjunction with structural adjustment programs or Millennium Development Goals) have likewise focused on women's empowerment through alphabetic literacy, at times even recognizing the role Romanized alphabetic literacy played in colonial administration and domination of Indigenous communities. The structural oppressions created through colonial administrator's selective dissemination of cultural instruments of power have had palpable harms in the lives of modern Latin American women, especially racialized women in rural zones, yet the solutions are often bound to colonialism in such a way that they unwittingly help maintain the centrality of its organizing concepts in the negotiation of cultural processes. This speaks to Hierro's concern regarding the organizing fulcrum that sustains systems of subordination at the deepest, prepredicative levels of culture. But it also points to another double bind that goes unacknowledged as a kind of harm, whereby women are put in the impossible position, generation after generation, of defending a nonaccidental epistemic and interpretive scarcity in order to have claims of violence heard, recognized, or assert rights that were unnecessary to assert before rights-based discourses imposed the need to assert them as part of the social recognition of their agency. The liberal framework of women's empowerment is able to coexist almost seamlessly with the continued nonaccidental suppression of Native Amerindian languages and communities that create the need for access to literacy in the first place: when bill (PL) 5.954-C was introduced in in Brazil in 2013 to allow Indigenous communities to use their Native languages at school as well as develop processes of learning and assessment that best reflect the epistemic practices of Indigneous cultures, President Dilma Rousseff quickly vetoed it as "contrary to public interest" (Humanitarian News 2016). The long arc between 1513 and 2013 is shorter than it appears when we stop to consider the mechanisms behind the resilience of social oppressions.

Hermeneutic violence points to the ways the appearance of visible harms to marginalized communities is very often preceded by conditions of hermeneutic precarity and traumas to systems of interpretation. As a critical tool of analysis, hermeneutic violence can help us think through some of these deeply layered and complex predicaments as we move along the dual tracks of context-specific social justice work and collective reflection on our varied practices of liberation.[5] In the next section I turn to Latina feminist theory to highlight the creativity and epistemic resilience behind some of these varied practices, as they often take a significant physical and existential toll in women of color's lives. In particular, I point to the self-authoring skills and autohistorical practices Latina feminists have developed in response to the persistence of coloniality in women of color's lives. Drawing on Nelly Richard's work on cultural memory in postdictatorial Chile, I call these practices "alphabets of survival" and specifically turn to the work of Gloria Anzaldúa as illustrative of resistant practices to hermeneutic violence in a US-borderland context.

---

[5] The picture of hermeneutic violence would not be complete without a self-conscious nod to its own conceptual captivity in systems of domination. In fact, the idea is conceptually indebted to many of the interpretive dilemmas that arose in the Western philosophical tradition following German Romanticism and its rejection of the objective, naturalistic outlook of the so-called hard sciences (*naturwissenschaften*), limiting its normative reach in anticolonial thinking. This is why it is a strategic concept, meant to be deployed where useful and retired thereafter.

Alphabets of Survival

One of the lasting legacies of Latina feminist theory in the United States is the creation of a nonbinary "third critical space," as Norma Alarcón describes, that is generative of multiple points of subaltern resistance to the complex legacy of colonial domination on women of color's lives (2013, 205).

One way to think about such a space is as a relational epistemic resource hermeneutically marginalized communities produce in response to hegemonic interpretive spaces, one that illuminates alternative cartographies of reason for long enough to validate the sense, despite all evidence of reality to the contrary, of corporeally knowing *otherwise*. At times this can be a life-saving affirmation and an important praxis of self-healing from cultural trauma. At others it is an in-between state that facilitates critical transformations by expanding the limits of philosophical imagination to account for lives that are intricately affected by colonial domination, and which often do not have the ontological security afforded to those in settler epistemic communities. Generating descriptions, names, identities, art forms, narratives, and languages for lived experience (what together, I'm calling *alphabets of survival*) is therefore a critical aspect of this third space. Take, for example, Alarcón's account of the identic term *Chicana*:

> The name Chicana, in the present, is the name of *resistance* that enables cultural and political points of departure and thinking through the multiple migrations and dislocations of women of "Mexican" descent. The name Chicana is not a name that women (or men) are born to or with, as is often the case with "Mexican," but rather is consciously and critically assumed and serves as a point of redeparture for *dismantling historical conjunctures of crisis, confusion, political and ideological conflict and contradictions* of the simultaneous effects of having "no names," having "many names," "not know[ing] her names" and being someone else's dreamwork. (1990, 249–50)[6]

Drawing on Anzaldúa, Alarcón describes how identity and narrative practices are inherently creative in this context, since they rest on a prior rejection of the established hermeneutical power over discursive domains and *where no prior authorization for self-legitimation of such autoethnographic moments exists.*[7] On the philosophical hermeneutic view, self-authoring would be logically impossible, yet Latina feminists like Anzaldúa challenge the epistemic imperialism of that impossibility by drawing on the

---

[6] Emphasis added. She is referencing Anzaldúa.
[7] See especially Medina 2013 for an expansive account of epistemic resistance.

corporeal intuitions of subaltern knowledges—which *are* social and relational—in the multiple interpretive traditions she inhabits. In this vein, Anzaldúa builds theories that perform what she calls "interventions that subvert cultural genocide" by allowing for the possibility of self-making and self-mapping in the wake of hermeneutic violence (2015, 89).[8] One strategy she typically deploys is taking aspects of the devalued side of an Anglo-European binary (black/white, literal/nonliteral) and redeploying it in a way that subverts the stability of the binary, or in a way, "thirds" it. If "literal" is the dominant norm through which history is written, she takes the devalued side (nonliteral, fictive) and uses it to license personal and collective history that has been preemptively curated out of official (socially legible) history. *Autohistoria* is a prime example. "*Autohistoria,*" she writes, "is a term I use to describe the genre of writing about one's personal and collective history using *fictive* elements, a sort of fictionalized autobiography or memoir; and *auto-historia-teoría* is a personal essay that *theorizes*" (Anzaldúa 2013, 15 and 518, my emphasis). It is a relational theory that can produce alternative understandings (as *conocimiento*) of reality for marginalized peoples negotiating the imprint of cultural and personal trauma on their narrative lives: "You turn the established narrative on its head, seeing through, resisting, and subverting its assumptions. Again, it's not enough to denounce the culture's old account—you must provide new narratives embodying alternative potentials" (560). As Andrea Pitts explains, "Anzaldúa proposes *autohistoria-teoría* as a way to refer to the explicit task of developing theoretical resources out of descriptions of oneself and one's experiences. In this sense, speaking for oneself can extend toward others in ways that can be positive and conducive of further actions and forms of meaning-making" (Pitts 2016, 358).

One of the many things Anzaldúa's work teaches us is that memory-work is hard when meaning-making must also be fashioned to support it. Yes, it is hard when the social, cultural, and interpretive resources one relies on to confront the representation of the past in our daily lives are tacitly one's own, yet much harder when they're not. Indeed, it is much harder to contest social exclusions in our shared discourses—to address the social situation of Latinas in the United States and women of color in the global South, for instance—without recourse to the interpretive stability that comes with having a privileged subject-position in culture. Having privileged access to the cultural instruments for writing Official History— a voice that can be publicly heard, a pen with ink that can be published and read, a formal lexicon one is pre-predicatively at home with—certainly

---

[8] She is specifically referencing aesthetic interventions in this section, and Chicanx art in particular.

makes for a more facile contestation of History from within, but it is no easy task, for anyone.

I pause here, parsing and meting out ways to help us remember the general difficulty involved in bouldering history and language (to name a wound, redress a grievance, or heal a cultural harm) so as to not minimize the weight of human suffering on the scales of any life. Yet there are lives that bear weights that cannot be counted by the metrics given the most weight in public life; in the municipal hall, in the courtroom, in the day-to-day negotiations that hang precariously over marginal lives. The worry is that there are those who cannot combat social injustices and epistemic inequities without first having to see oneself *as another*—to do the epistemic equivalent of a double-shift workday of interpretive bridge-building and crossing-over so as to gain access to dominant cultural codes and established narrative modalities for *contesting* social roles in public life . . . to tools historically dispossessed from the very subjects most in need of cultural redress. On this view, K'iche women must learn Spanish or rely on translators, work with notions of narrative time discontinuous with their own, and so on, to get (for instance) legal redress on matters ranging from land title tenure and regularization to sexual assault and domestic abuse. One must often use another's voice to speak for oneself. And this is no small point. After all, herein lies the *pain* acts of attestation can bring when one is historically excluded from full and legitimate participation in the interpretive processes of culture: when to object, contest, or textualize dissent is to risk the experience of a fractured self, an enunciative standpoint that is torn between the twin crags of meaning/publicity and speechlessness/silence in the communal paradigms of history, politics, medicine, law . . . the places where our bodily experience of our "feminisms" is most often at stake.

Consider, for instance, Nelly Richard's poignant claim about the risk to our experience of selfhood when memory-work first requires a "*dis*remembering" (*una desmemoria*) of the imprint of cultural and social trauma on our lives, of the gendered politics of negotiating the imprint of violence and trauma with (often asymmetrical/inequitable access to) cultural tools and resources of expression that are themselves often conceptually impoverished and unaccommodating of the intersectionally complex experiential realities of Latin American women and women of color. The question is—to use her phrasing—how to acknowledge the epistemic vulnerability, the "rupture that grew out of the challenge of having to name fragments of experience that were no longer speakable in the language that survived the catastrophe of meaning" (2004, 4). Richard's response, in part, is through producing an aesthetic "alphabet of survival" that points to corporeal intuitions, to subaltern truths that dominant side of binaries suppress to maintain both the binary and the dominance it supports in culture;

they are "linguistic elements composing a new language based on, and necessitated by, *survival*" so that we don't, physically and metaphorically, *die of the truth*, to use Nietzsche's phrase (Richard 2004, 104).[9]

On this account, feminist anticolonial memory-work and autoethnography means more than the taxing psychic strain of—to use Otto Neurath's classic hermeneutic example—remaking a boat at sea. This is because it often requires a prior *undoing, uncoding, unbraiding, and dismantling of interpretive frameworks* that allow one to prereflectively handle, maneuver, and work with the materials the boat and the sea disclose *as available* to the oarswoman to survive and bridge-build while adrift—to remake culture with only the tools and language of her culture. It's a lot easier to rebuild when the things around you show up as things you can rebuild with, as tools ready to hand that can be used in the creative deployment of a new narrative. So the trick here is to appreciate the incredible difficulty one might face when one's position as a legitimate interpreter of culture is prematurely dismissed (at the interpretive level) when, owing to hermeneutic violence, one is not seen as having the right be out at sea in the first place—to appreciate the kinds of hurdles and double binds feminist anticolonial and decolonial work involves when one lacks access to privileged speaking positions at the same time that one is put in the material position to urgently communicate one's experiences as a matter of personal and communal survival.

Too often, whether reeling from state-sponsored lexicons of terror or traversing the epistemic land mines of sexist racism in daily life, we are forced to reconfigure survival. To coordinate our bodies across disjunctive times and opaque spaces in ways unsupported by the dominant cultural resources of meaning-making and interpretation. This is not an accidental harm. The relation between self and world, language and disclosure *is not symmetrically given to all in the postcolonial world*, so that our deepest social epistemologies are metaphilosophically compromised.

And yet. The thing about the lived body, the blood-soaked limen of our experience as gendered and raced beings bodying forth cloaked in the intricately woven language of culture, is that, existentially, the urgency is never without. We always begin where we are, in the grips of webbed circumstances and culturally proscribed meanings that lift our voices one way where we perhaps wanted to go another, even without knowing it. In that context, memory-work and making sense of experience is hard enough, for anyone. Much more for some, yes, and that is what motivates so much of this project—to give weight to the idea that hermeneutic happenings, disclosures, and disappearances *remain rooted*

---

[9] It should be noted that Richard points to art and aesthetic narratives of resistance.

in deeply value-laden colonialist frameworks that are based on deep violence, and that our conceptions of violence are tied to these hermeneutic limitations. Violence never emerges as a solitary phenomenon, but is held up by a wider system of interpretive disarmaments and armaments that prefigure its emergence in culture. The first step, one of many, is to then pierce cracks in the Western dialectic of erasure that now resides under the banner of philosophy and legitimate knowledge, which exercise control over what counts as harms and violence.

We are living in a time when the burden of proof for demonstrating the existence of complex and intersectional harms against women of color is laid upon our own ability to give an account of those harms in a language those in power can always already understand. Not only is this a harmful epistemic situation, it is structured by the fact that the interpretive resources required to do justice to that task are also hermeneutically compromised, I repeat, in a nonaccidental way. In turn, our experience must conform somehow to interpretive systems that pre-predicatively discount many features of our experiences, yielding a kind of existential self-harm by design. We sense that the ability to bear witness and testify to lived experience in a language capable of capturing this background violence is at the epicenter of claiming knowledge over our own lives: it's not me, you sense. This language thing is rigged. And yet, this is nothing new. *The struggle is real* because so much of it is not acknowledged *as being so*, because it's a hard-won self-authoring lexical skill to combat the pain that comes with living through experiences that are not acknowledgeable in official discourses. We develop alphabets of survival not only to look forward, but to reimagine a past that was not imaginable to begin with. Our lives survive on parallel tracks. This is because if we've tracked the concept correctly, hermeneutic violence makes sense of violence through the sense-making instituted by hermeneutic violence. Such realization can act as a paralytic to our liberation, hooking its epistemic dependencies on cultural recursion itself. It is, at day's end, the classical argumentative strategy of orthodox hermeneutists to trap one in a hermeneutic circle of interpretive production, a kind of performative contradiction that highlights the explanatory power of the human hermeneutic situation and the conditions for worldly meaning it discloses. It seems like an impossible bind to escape. That is, until you have to live it.

Making sense of our lives in more just ways requires interpretive frameworks that re-envision the relationship between self and culture through a different archaeology of know-how.

Women of color and Indigenous women face complex webs of intersectional harms and injuries that are difficult to pinpoint and remedy given the limitations of Western political theories of harm and injury. Often, women's experiences of violence are disaggregated to fit a disciplinary typology of violence that, while critical to the eradication of one (possibly mortal) harm, helps perpetuate the continuation of generations of gender-based violences as culturally acceptable phenomena. On the long view, the mortality is the same. We can do better. We must do better. And theory alone cannot get us there. While hermeneutic violence can help diagnose the existence of deep harms and traumas to our interpretive systems (and thus partly mitigate the effects of structural gaslighting in, for example, cross-cultural negotiations and human rights instruments), it can't help one actually *live,* breathe air that isn't toxic, or enact the daily creative continuance of oppressed peoples and communities. For this, we need an ontology that can be lived, articulated in the flesh without fear of slippage, breaks or contradiction, yet without promoting a metaphysics based on fixity and essences.[10] We need a third critical space, an in-between to violence and survival, and we cannot be dogmatic in our methodologies to achieve this. Between disclosure and disappearance, the struggle demands an open stance. As the Guatemalan poet Alenka Bermudez (2003) writes:

I reserve the right of the precisely exact
Spanish word
to name death and to name life
as long as the blood holds itself suspended
in our trees.

References

Alarcón, Norma. 1990. "Chicana Feminism: In the Tracks of 'the' Native Woman." *Cultural Studies* 4, no. 3: 248–57.

Alarcón, Norma. 2013. "Anzalduan Textualities: A Hermeneutic of the Self and the Coyolxauhqui Imperative." In *In El Mundo Zurdo 3*, edited by Antonia Castañeda, Larissa Mercado-López, and Sonia Saldívar-Hull, 189–206. San Francisco: Aunt Lute.

Anzaldúa, Gloria. [1987] 2012. *Borderlands/La Frontera: The New Mestiza*. 4th ed. San Francisco: Aunt Lute Books.

Anzaldúa, Gloria. 2013. "Now Let Us Shift . . . the Path of Conocimiento . . . Inner Work, Public Acts." In *This Bridge We Call Home: Radical Visions for Transformation,* edited by AnaLousie Keating, 540–76. New York: Routledge.

Anzaldúa, Gloria. 2015. *Light in the Dark/Luz En Lo Oscuro: Rewriting Identity, Spirituality, Reality*. Edited by AnaLouise Keaton. Durham, NC: Duke University Press.

Bermudez, Alenka. 2003. "Guatemala, Your Blood." In *Women on War: An International Anthology of Women's Writings from Antiquity to the Present,* edited by Daniela Gioseffi, 263. New York: Feminist Press at the City University of New York.

---

[10] See Ortega (2001), Lugones (2003).

Danticat, Edwidge. 2014. *The Farming of Bones*. New York: Soho Press.

Dotson, Kristie. 2011. "Tracking Epistemic Violence, Tracking Practices of Silencing." *Hypatia* 26, no. 2: 236–57.

Dotson, Kristie. 2012. "A Cautionary Tale: On Limiting Epistemic Oppression." *Frontiers: A Journal of Women Studies* 33, no. 1: 24–47.

Dotson, Kristie. 2014. "Conceptualizing Epistemic Oppression." *Social Epistemology* 28, no. 2: 115–38.

Fricker, Miranda. 2007. *Epistemic Injustice: Power and the Ethics of Knowing*. Oxford: Oxford University Press.

Hierro, Graciela. 1985. *Ética y feminismo, México*. Mexico City: Universidad Nacional Autónoma de México.

Hierro, Graciela. 1994. "Gender and Power." *Hypatia* 9, no. 1: 173–83.

Humanitarian News. 2016. "Brazil's Rousseff Vetoes Indigenous Education Project." February 17. http://humanitariannews.org/20160217/brazil-s-rousseff-vetoes-indigenous-education-project.

Lugones, María. 2003. *Pilgrimages/Peregrinajes: Theorizing Coalition against Multiple Oppressions*. Lanham, MD: Rowman & Littlefield.

Medina, José. 2012. "Hermeneutical Injustice and Polyphonic Contextualism: Social Silences and Shared Hermeneutical Responsibilities." *Social Epistemology* 26, no. 2: 201–20.

Medina, José. 2013. *The Epistemology of Resistance: Gender and Racial Oppression, Epistemic Injustice, and Resistant Imaginations*. New York: Oxford University Press.

Ortega, Mariana. 2001. "'New Mestizas,' '"World"-Travelers,' and 'Dasein': Phenomenology and the Multi-voiced, Multi-cultural Self." *Hypatia* 16, no. 3: 1–29.

Ortega, Mariana. 2006. "Being Lovingly, Knowingly Ignorant: White Feminism and Women of Color." *Hypatia* 21, no. 3: 56–74.

Pitts, Andrea J. 2016. "Gloria E. Anzaldúa's Autohistoria-teoría as an Epistemology of Self-Knowledge/Ignorance." *Hypatia* 31, no. 2: 352–69.

Pizarnik, Alejandra, and Orietta Lozano. 1990. *Alejandra Pizarnik, 1936–1972: Antología poética*. Cali, Colombia: Fundación para la Investigación y la Cultura.

Pohlhaus, Gaile. 2011. "Wrongful Requests and Strategic Refusals to Understand." In *Feminist Epistemology and Philosophy of Science: Power in Knowledge*, edited by Heidi Grasswick, 223–40. New York: Springer.

Pohlhaus, Gaile. 2012. "Relational Knowing and Epistemic Injustice: Toward a Theory of Willful Hermeneutical Ignorance." *Hypatia* 27, no. 4: 715–35.

Purcell-Gates, Victoria. 2000. *Now We Read, We See, We Speak: Portrait of Literacy Development in an Adult Freirean-Based Class*. New York: Routledge.

Richard, Nelly. 2004. *The Insubordination of Signs: Political Change, Cultural Transformation, and Poetics of the Crisis*. Durham. NC: Duke University Press.

Ruíz, Elena. 2018. "The Hermeneutics of Mexican-American Political Philosophy. *Inter-American Journal of Philosophy* 9, no. 2: 45057.

Ruíz, Elena. 2006. "How to Hear the Unspoken: Engaging Cross-Cultural Communication through the Latin American Testimonial Narrative." M.L.S. thesis, University of South Florida.

Schutte, Ofelia. 1998. "Cultural Alterity: Cross-Cultural Communication and Feminist Theory in North-South Contexts." *Hypatia* 13, no. 2: 53–72.

Schutte, Ofelia. 2002. "Indigenous Issues and the Ethics of Dialogue in LatCrit Theory." *Rutgers Law Review* 54 (Summer): 1021–29.

Spivak, Gayatri Chakravorty. 1988. "Can the Subaltern Speak?" In *Marxism and the Interpretation of Culture*, edited by Cary Nelson and Lawrence Grossberg, 271–313. Urbana: University of Illinois Press.

Spivak, Gayatri Chakravorty. 1998. "The Politics of Translation." In *Cultural Studies Reader: History, Theory, Practice,* edited by Gita Rajan and Jessica Munns, 95–118. London: Longman.

CHAPTER 13 | Hallucinating Knowing
(Extra)ordinary Consciousness, More-Than-Human Perception, and Other Decolonizing Remedios *within Latina and Xicana Feminist Theories*

THE PILGRIMS BECAME TRANSIENT citizens of the world in the 1600s when they *mistook* Wampanoag territory for empty lands waiting to be ravaged. The US Immigration and Customs Enforcement agency continues this set-tler colonialist and predatory project today. Unlike pilgrims, undocumented immigrants in the twenty-first century are cast as *illegal* and reside thereby at a place of fracture. They feel torn across boundaries of nation, race, class, gender, sexuality, and ability. Within this historical juncture, the shat-tering of subjectivity underlies the undocumented Latinx condition. Various archives of feminist, queer, and trans* of color praxis foreground feelings and knowledges about negotiating life as trespassers, as not quite fitting into the rule of legality. In so doing, they manifest extraordinary consciousness against a legacy of destitution and illegality.

This chapter examines the ways that Latinx subjectivities foster *more-than-human* and *more-than-ordinary* consciousness. Within Latina feminist theories in general, and Xicana feminist theories (XFT) in par-ticular, hallucinations denormalize and decolonize memories of mo-bility and transit. Between 2011 and 2014, I joined a network of radical Latinx and Xicanx performers, artists, and poets in the San Francisco Bay Area, where I encountered this hallucinating way of knowing.[1] Within

---

[1] I follow an *impure* understanding of Latinx and Xicanx subjectivity (Lugones 2003, 121–50). This network consists of cultural activists from diverse socioeconomic and geographical backgrounds, from cis and trans communities, including Chicanas, Mexicanas, Tejanas, Nuevomexicanas, Chapinas, Oaxaqueñas, Salvadoreans, Dominicans, Cubans, Puerto Ricans,

Pedro J. DiPietro, *Hallucinating Knowing* In: *Theories of the Flesh*, Edited by: Andrea J. Pitts, Mariana Ortega, and José Medina, Oxford University Press (2020). © Oxford University Press. DOI: 10.1093/oso/9780190062965.003.0014

an autoethnographic project documenting my awakening to antiracist transfemininity, I engaged this network for its potential to activate shared understandings of migration across space and across genders.[2] Their piercing work across Latinx generations informs this chapter's engagement with hallucinating perceptual repertoires.

My approach to Latina and Xicana feminist theories (LXFTs) pursues decolonial thinking at the intersection of anthropological theories of the mind and feminist philosophy. First, I place multisensory and hallucinatory ways of knowing at the center of LXFTs and their perceptual repertoire. Second, I demonstrate that this competence may thrive with Latinx and Xicanx subjectivities when they confront the psychic unrest inaugurated by heterosexualist colonial rules. Third, as it concerns hallucinations and their ties to non-Western and indigenous thinking, I focus on Latinas' and Xicanas' altered states of consciousness across spiritual, *more-than-human*, and healing practices of feminist agency such as *brujería* and *curanderismo*. Finally, I recognize the expansion of LXFT's hallucinating knowing within the spoken word of Yosimar Reyes, an undocumented activist and artist who is a member of a queer-of-color network in the bay area.

Coloniality and (Extra) Ordinary Consciousness

As experiential and phenomenological, perception presents the world to our situated and embodied senses. Typically, the sensual stimulus appears external to our perception. We often neglect the fact that our social and

---

and many more. They expand Chicana and Latina standpoints (Arredondo et al. 2003, 2–3). I join others who use "x" in Xicana to highlight both the Nahuatl spelling of the "ch" and the links among native peoples in the diaspora (Castillo 2014; Moraga 2011). I use Chicana and Chicano to signal that I am quoting the works of others or a different period.

[2] Transing (Stryker, Currah, and Moore 2008) and trans* point to practices that assemble bodily attributes and being into contingent structures and that, among other possibilities, may function within "gendered" territories. In 2008 at the National Women's Studies Association meeting in Cincinnati, I began to experiment with linguistic responses to coloniality's imposition of gender-centric metaphysics across women's, gender, and sexuality studies (Lugones 2006). Mainly, my concerns lie with *delinking* (capitalized) Gender from (lowercase) genders and (lowercase, between quotation marks) "genders." Linguistic responses point to intersubjective negotiations wherein those that the coloniality of gender places within the dark side of the colonial/modern gender system actively respond to the heterosexualizing of embodied differences. Gender allocutions mark Man *or* Woman as coloniality's primary bodily dichotomy within the domain of the human; genders allocutions mark the always already unattainable status of men *or* women and, finally, "genders" allocutions pertain to the always already unassimilable domain of embodied differences who remain neither men nor women, living betwixt and between not-quite-human animal and nonhuman animal (see also my dissertation, 2012). This chapter engages allocutions across Latinx feminist theorizing, such as *queer of color* or *lesbian of color*, as precisely embodiments whose materiality enacts transing betwixt and between not-quite-human and nonhuman animal. Thus, their transing lies beyond the realm of gender variability.

interpersonal histories are always already at play in our own perceptual field and situation. Ethnography and neuroscience tell us that cultures create specific framings of the relation between the mind and its interior/exterior boundaries. Members of some non-Western cultures emphasize interconnectivity, while westerners rely on clear-cut distinctions (Luhrmann 2011; Barrett 2004).

Sensory overrides induce altered states of consciousness, involving the experience of sensation in the absence of a source to be sensed (Luhrmann 2011, 72; Chiu 1989, 292–93). When your internet connection is slow over video calls, the image gets pixelated, and the voice loops and cracks. Sometimes, the connection speeds up, getting the parties caught up. In a synesthetic boost, we perceive internally what is not offered to the senses. Whether we trust them or not, cracks in our consciousness prompt *cultural invitations as a supply of both previous perceptual learning and sensual repertoires*. Did we hear that or did we just make it up? Are we hallucinating? The answer lies with history, it seems, much more than with psychobiology alone. Perceptual learning comprises the cultural conditioning that greatly shapes whether we experience hallucinations. Sensual repertoires relate to the way we are expected to experience hallucinations and to the role that culture plays in heightening one or more senses over the others (MacLean 2001, contra Noll 1983). Apparently, hallucinating consciousness is more widespread than stigmatizing psychology has it.

What about the consciousness of those who, under the rule of colonial legacies, don't have the privilege of staying out of the reach of Eurocentered sensual repertoires? What about not quite knowing whether our own condition entails a form of hallucinatory existence? Isn't our awareness, as offspring of colonial relations, as racialized exiles and immigrants, perplexingly more ambiguous, more fractured, and yet, as this chapter shows, not necessarily less reliable?

Colonizers suppressed indigenous practices, among them orality, animist spiritualities, pictographic knowledge, and sustainable farming, because they saw them as symptoms of degeneration or lack of humanity. Those living under coloniality experienced this extraordinary violence as ordinary (Fanon 2008; Maldonado Torres 2008; Mbembe 2003; Quijano 1991). Paradoxically, colonial rule also determined what counted as ordinary, and it marked anticolonial consciousness as nonhuman or evil-like and, in other words, as the very sign of insanity. Centuries later, the colonial imagination continues its contradictions. Whereas hallucinations become an everyday condition for the racialized, those untouched by colonial imposition keep their grip on baseline, ordinary, consciousness. Material life that was fulfilling for pre-Columbian communities remained in their perceptual field even throughout the process of colonial suppression. Mexica scribes and painters, who understood the continuity between the worldly and the nonworldly, heard, saw, read, and painted the stars and the divine wisdom that they communicated. Colonial rule has since made of sight the king of an impoverished sensual kingdom. As this chapter shows with respect to the practitioners of XFT and Yosimar Reyes's spoken word, an ancestral, hallucinogenic, domain underwrites their consciousness.

Deranged *Loquerías*

In "El Desorden," Laura Elisa Pérez fosters a perceptual disposition that hangs unhinged from a secularizing normative order (1999). Instead of avoiding what's deemed *pathological* by the condition of coloniality, she delves into XFT's disorderly ways of knowing. She examines non-institutional spiritualities in Chicana artists' literary, visual, and performance arts from the 1960s onward and focuses on their reappropriation of emblematic images of the Mexican American community and its religiosity. Pérez contends that, by disrupting the heterosexist, male-centered, and monotheist legacy of colonialism, nationalism, and Manifest Destiny, Chicana artists access altered consciousness not only as an imposition of coloniality but also as an oppositional response to its rule. They embrace what is *extraordinary*, such as nonconforming eroticism, what is *nonsensical*, such as virgin warriors, or also what is *aesthetically dubious*, such as what they call *domesticana rasquache*.[3] Reoccupying Aztlán, they respond to *cultural invitations* and hallucinate.[4] Becoming hallucinating subjects, they develop technologies of knowing not despite anxiety, fear, and confusion but rather because of them. Apparently, they thrive in *el desorden*, or what the West otherwise deems cognitive impairment.

Anticolonial feminist genealogies recognize XFT's cognitive plasticity around *sanity* and *insanity*. Mapping feminist methodologies of emancipation in the twentieth century, Chela Sandoval (2000) indicates that Frederic Jameson's manifesto against postmodernity fails to tell the truth of lesbians of color who, in the 1960s and 1970s, activated a "differential consciousness" kindred but also homeopathically resistant

---

[3] Amalia Mesa-Bains (1999) and Laura Pérez (2007) theorize aesthetic strategies of minoritized Chicana/o cultural production such as *rasquache* and *domesticana rasquache*. Although perceived as tacky, "insane," and ragged by the mainstream, *rasquache* affirms delegitimized Chicana/o culture. Imbued by a barrio or "underdog" sensibility, *rasquache* enacts an attitudinal disposition (Ybarra-Frausto 1991) that includes making beauty with what is available, such as strikingly disparate colors, waste, or cheap objects.

[4] Aztlán refers to both the US Southwest and the mythical place of origin of the Aztec people, ancestors of the Chicanx community.

to the mode of postmodern circulation. Gloria Anzaldúa summons this rebellious disposition with the term *loquería*, or "the crazies," also locating this psychological labor among lesbians of color who "choose" the path of queerness (1987, 41). Her theory of *conocimiento* offers a path of spiritual liminality (Delgadillo 2011), inspiring (r)evolutionary selves such as those she calls *los atravesados*, including "the perverse, . . . and those who cross over . . . the confines of the normal" (Anzaldúa 1987, 25).

The competence to navigate out-of-bound, disorienting, realities is a constant within LXFT. *Borderlands*/La Frontera equates leaping into the dark to the clash of cultures that "makes us crazy constantly" (Anzaldúa 1987, 80–81). María Lugones reflects on women of color in the United States who navigate ontological confusion in a state that feels like "schizophrenia" and who, thus, acquire epistemic flexibility as both outsiders and resistant inhabitants of multiple worlds (2003, 86; Ortega 2001, 2016). In several of Cherríe Moraga's plays, the theme of insanity figures in the daily struggles that Xicanas wage to reconcile a colonial past with ancestral decolonizing memories. LXFT counters a pervasive principle in Eurocentered Kantian thought whereby those who rely on the flesh as they seek a deeper understanding of cognition may experiment with regions of the mind that no one should trust (Kant 1964, 17). They risk derangement, or "artificial insanity." LXFT practitioners and other *atravesados* face the atrophy of their senses as they adapt to the condition of epistemic duplicity, of inhabiting hallucinations as both true to experience and confusing/(un)reliable.

That duplicity permeates hallucinating knowing among practitioners of LXFT implies that it stands at the crossroads of psychic bewilderment, between excitement and torture. Anzaldúa again reminds us that Cartesian dualism, and might we add Kantian somatophobia, operates as an injunction against indigenous and mestiza populations and their perceptual capabilities (1987, 59). They suppress from the sensual memory of colonial subjects "otherworldly events [and] . . . those fleeting images of the soul's presence and of the spirit's presence" (58).

For their attention to Xicanas' nondominant and migrant desires, Cherríe Moraga's theater plays map Xicana lesbian and gender-nonconforming subjectivity and embodiment. In the remainder of this section, I analyze in one of Moraga's plays, *The Hungry Woman* ([1995] 2001), the connection between (extra)ordinary consciousness, hallucinating knowing, and Xicana feminist agency against heterosexualism. From the essay "A Long Line of Vendidas" (1983) to her latest play, *The Mathematics of Love* (2015), Moraga envisions revolutionary sexual dissidence through the deconstruction of *La Malinxe* myth. Concerning Malintzin Tenepal, this myth accounts for her primordial role in mothering a new mestiza/o race after having had carnal relations with the conquistador Hernan Cortés. Both as bilingual translator and *mistress*, Malinxe's body becomes a heterosexist territory in dispute between mestizo (Chicano) cismen and invading (white) cismen.[5] Yarbro-Bejarano contends that Moraga's deconstructing the Chicana lesbian body, by reclaiming Malinxe, doesn't seek to make it whole (2001, 5). Rather, by "recognizing how it has been appropriated" and by having it hinge on its various parts—*labios* (lips), hands, face, legs, eye, and so on—Moraga represents Xicanas' nonconforming bodies in their contingent reconstruction, or "potential fatal perils of lesbian existence" (5). It is not surprising then that Moraga populates her plays with dystopic, sometimes otherworldly, and yet intimately real, gender-nonconforming, characters. They embody contradictions between the ordinary and extraordinary, between dutiful sister/mother and treacherous sellout, between conforming to colonizing patriarchy and being cast as an unimaginable homoerotic agent (Brady 2002; Moraga 2011).

Not unlike hallucinating subjects who *mistrust* their own senses, the leading lesbian characters in Moraga's plays painstakingly excavate self-delusion. In *The Hungry Woman*, the main character, Medea, breaks away from male-centered Chicano history because it conflates postapocalyptic Aztlán with heterosexist kinship. In a near future where today's ethnic minorities in the United States have split from white "Amerika" ("Gringolandia") and each has claimed its own territories, Medea, who is a midwife, and her lover, Luna, live as exiles in what remains of Phoenix. The lesbian lovers are raising Medea's son, Chac-Mool, with the help of her grandmother, the *curandera* (healer) Mama Sal. Set on a consciousness continuum including a facility described both as "insane asylum" and "mental hospital," Phoenix functions as the dumping site where outcasts and queers reside, where pollution and endemic poverty make its population feel lousy all the time.

Troubling a modernist and arrowlike timeline, the play relies on ancient Aztec wisdom represented by deities and other mythical figures, such as Coatlicue, Coyolxauhqui, and Huitzilopotchli. A Yaqui indigenous bloodline runs through Medea's family (Moraga [1995] 2001, 85), countering the notion that a Chicanx future or present requires the extinction of Native realities. The Cihuatateo, a chorus of four women warriors, performs Aztec rituals. When pressed to choose between joining his father by moving to Chicano "Aztlán," where cismale-centered nationalism rules landownership,

---

[5] Chicano speech sanctions colonizing violence by using the epithet *chingada* to describe activity that prompts ill-feelings. Its force derives from the notion that, by lying with Cortés (*chingar* in Nahuatl), Malintzin *consents* to be "fucked over" (Alarcón 1989, 61). *Malinche* or *malinchista* is anyone transgressing perceived group interests.

or staying in nonheterosexist Phoenix with Medea and Luna, Chac-Mool can't quite betray the paternal lineage. Reiterating the denigration of *female* powers among the Aztecs, Chac-Mool's failure to reject the males-first mandate speaks of the heterosexist ordeals, past and present, that prompt gender-nonconforming Xicanas to hallucinate a *queer Aztlán*.[6]

Despite feeling tormented, Medea poisons her own son to prevent ethnonationalist patriarchal rule from exhausting his existence. This act of both sacrifice and defiance throws Medea into a heightened state of unrest at the mental hospital:[7]

> If you [Chac-Mool] live, then why am I here? I've committed no crime. If you live, why then am I strapped into the bed at night? . . . Why are there locks and I haven't the key? Why? (Moraga [1995] 2001, 98)

This monologue enacts several of the features of hallucinations within LXFT. Before the presence of her son, whom she had supposedly poisoned, Medea posits that the true crime within the Xicanx community is the principle of putting cisgender masculinity at the center of life. Ancestral knowledge also reminds us that, under the watch of her own mother, Huitzilopotchli mutilated his sister Coyolxauhqui (Anzaldúa 1987). Governing Xicanx relations between and among women, men get loved, fed, cared for, and heard first. This hallucinating disposition arises precisely with the wounding of erotic agency, keeping Xicanas from putting their love for each other front and center of social relations.

Malinxe/Medea occupies a dilemmatic position *as racial traitor—if she conforms, she is sold; if she speaks, she sells out.* Her position *links two temporo-spatial domains where cultural invitations/injunctions to hallucinate arise for Xicanas.* Medea doesn't have the keys to unlock the coloniality-of-gender cage. Refusing identification with conforming and ordinary consciousness is not a matter of choice. Rather, it is a product of the colonial difference. Dwelling in this altered state as an opposition to coloniality is a way of weaving ethical relations such as Luna's and Medea's.

Curanderas and *Brujas* Activate a Feminist Third Eye

Practitioners of *loquería* draw attention to the sensual repertoire of Latinas' and Xicanas' (extra)ordinary consciousness. Non-Western cosmological

---

[6] On the denigration of the feminine among the Aztecs, see Anzaldúa (1987, 53). For an account of how trans* figures in the genealogy of Aztlán, see Galarte 2014.

[7] The geography of Phoenix conveys the spatiality of extraordinary consciousness that this chapter describes.

principles—Afro-diasporic, Nahua, Taino, Yaqui—underwrite the perceptual field of hallucinating subjects (Anzaldúa 1987; Moraga [1995] 2001; Lara 2006; Pérez 2007). Malinxes, *curanderas, tlacuilo/tlamatinime* artists, midwives, *brujas*, horses, and *hounsis* employ ancestral multisensory repertoires.[8] These repertoires (1) challenge Eurocentered ethnographic accounts of shamanistic perception, (2) foreground the ways that shamanic "flight" enhances cross-modal perception, and (3) underscore that LXFTs foster *bruja/curandera* positionalities and the contributions they make to feminist spiritual praxis.

Colonial chronicles and contemporary sources convey that women from indigenous and mestiza backgrounds typically occupy the role of healers.[9] Practitioners of same-sex eroticism also have ritual and healing roles in pre-Columbian and colonial records (Horswell 2005; Sigal 2003). Medicinal practices imbued in ancestral indigenous knowledge emerge from ecologies of interconnectivity among all that lives (Jones et al 2001). Ethnicity and racialization are both entrenched in the resilience of Latinx and Xicanx healing practices against the "frightening of spirit from one's body-mind" (Marcos 2006, 2; Pérez 2007, 27). Gloria Anzaldúa considers *nepantleras* the mediators who "facilitate passages between worlds" (2009, 248) while Moraga, Ana Castillo, and Anzaldúa herself are likened to *curanderas* who "pull out the subversive 'forgotten' . . . countervalues of women and Native peoples" (Pérez 2002, 59). The recurrence of spiritual praxis within LXFT speaks to the affinity between women's *curanderismo/brujería* and hallucinating knowing.[10]

Curanderismo shares both shamanistic and healing dimensions (Morrow 1997, 68; Noll 1983, 444). Practitioners of XFT devise feminist remedies to survive colonial legacies (Hartley 2010, 54). Patrisia Gonzales is a community health promoter-researcher who holds empirical knowledge about healing from the vantage point of belonging to indigenous communities (Kickapoo, Comanche, and Macehual). Countering ethnographic accounts, she doesn't differentiate between shamans and elders since such description downplays the feminist healing praxis of everyday *curanderas* and elders (2012, 12 and 217).

---

[8] *Hounsis* and horses are key roles that women practitioners play in voodoo and Santeria rites within the Afro-Latinx diaspora (Lara 2006; Sanchez Carretero 2005). *Tlacuilo/tlamatinime* were painters and wise-people who advanced philosophical/spiritual inquiry among the Aztecs (Pérez 2007, 13 and 22).

[9] In the 1980s, cisgender women represented 65 percent of Mexican healers (Marcos 2006). Healers self-identify as "shamans" in the Mexican states of Morelo and Chiapas (Marcos 2006, xviii).

[10] For a critique of the *bruja buena / bruja mala* schism and its secular underpinning, see Lara 2005, 22.

Medea as Malinxe follows a shamanistic path, and, as we'll see later, so does Yosimar Reyes with his spoken word artistry. Medea, being a midwife herself, looks after the community's regeneration. The Cihuatateo chorus punctuates the birthing of new beings with rhythmic chants, leading the characters and audience into a heightened state of consciousness, activating transient, shamanic subjectivities, and offering healing techniques against racializing heterosexism. When Luna visits Medea in the psychiatric ward, they acknowledge that they share dreams, each entering a common erotic encounter materialized through the explosion of a maguey (sentry plant) within a vagina (Moraga [1995] 2001, 94). From this twilight domain, they retrieve teachings about eroticism among lesbians of color. Carnal intimacy opens the door for a revolutionary pedagogy of shamanistic healing when Medea adds: "Is that how I died, Luna. Giving birth to myself?" Not putting cismen first is the condition, the cultural invitation, for Xicana hallucinating dispositions to arise.

Another sensual feature in *curanderas'* and brujas' visionary states is the preparation of perception to communicate with an otherworldly elsewhere (Marcos 2006). Rhythmic repetitions, burning copal resin, and praying, among other practices, extend sensual invitations into a flight where ritual specialists perform as messengers and attendants as witnesses (Gonzales 2012; Marcos 2006; Lara 2005). During travel, *curanderas/ brujas* translate visions into treatments, smells into remedies, sounds into colors, and words into touch. In the register of sensual cross-referencing, *flying* becomes visual, auricular, tactile, olfactory, and even orgasmic. Curanderas and brujas associate shamanic flight with translation of sensual modalities (MacLean 2001).

A spoil of fleshy desires, such as the maguey's explosion, LXFT's engagement with intimacy routes multisensory awareness toward shamanistic states. LXFTs offer curative perceptual dispositions to the colonizing suppression of other senses (Lloyd 1984; Jay 1988) and to "visuocentrism in perceptual theorizing" (O'Callaghan 2008).[11] Indeed, perceptual plasticity is greatly a matter of history, and of resistant histories.[12] Minoritizing perspectives tend to place these histories within the specific region of Latina

---

[11] Consider the encounter between the Inka Atahualpa and Fernando Pizarro in 1532 as an instantiation of colonial perceptual suppression. Atahualpa demanded, of Castilian emissaries, proof of the authority of their religious beliefs. At Cajamarca, Atahualpa dismissed the power of the Bible when the book didn't "speak to [him]" after "holding it close to his ears" (Poma de Ayala 1980, 2:357). Atahualpa operates in a world where he hears, sees, and perhaps even smells the nonworldly.

[12] Crucial is the neurocognitive research that makes room for the historical plasticity of perceptual experience and learning. Some tests show that the centrality of sight in Western modernity narrows the potential for cross-modal perception (O'Callaghan 2008, 325).

and Xicana lived experience without examining the key contributions that LXFTs make to the foundations of phenomenology and its epistemic roots beyond Eurocentrism.

Human animals have the capacity, on average, to both hallucinate and experience cross-modal perception. Neuropsychology shows that our perception cannot excise one sensual modality from another (O'Callaghan 2008, 328; Arabzadeh et al. 2008).[13] However, Western cultures deflate our disposition to make references, or transition references, across senses. As Medea does with the Cihuatateo, who connect drumming with the scents and visuals of birthing, hallucinating knowing encourages perceptual plasticity.

Socially legitimized in subaltern records of the colonial encounter, a competing sensual archive fought for its endurance against the taming of perceptual plasticity. Image-makers, image-readers, painters/scribes, and weavers shared the responsibility of recording and circulating authorized, otherworldly, knowledge (Gruzinski 1995; Mignolo 1995; Pérez 2007). Within XFT, this specific "queer mixture" between the tangible and intangible points to the spiritual and social function of glyphs in the Mexica tradition (Moraga 1993, 4). Glyphs incarnate prophetic realities that Chicana artists decipher with "the mystical third eye" (Pérez 2007, 34). Contemporary ethnographies, for instance, document these hallucinating and prophetic functions. Huichol arts offer sites for this type of reflection. Huichols are a Native people from Mexico's northwest who create colorful yarn painting and beadwork (MacLean 2001, 2012). According to one of their shamans, visionary colors enact a sacred language that can't be reduced to an arithmetic of symbols. The interpretation of these visions varies in response to the ways "the gods [and goddesses? (sic)] speak to [the shaman] by colors" (2012, 167). When artists, curanderas, and shamans employ a third eye, they engage colors as both word and song (MacLean 2001, 309) and transition spirit knowing into formal perceptual qualities.

Moraga's latest play, The Mathematics, undertakes a collective witnessing act with potential to heal relations across generations of Xicana, Mexican, and Nahua women. Tapping into time-traveling and Alzheimer's disease, the play deals with those fleshy entanglements that Kant likened to voluntary derangement. It makes tangible the fear that Xicanas, with

---

[13] Neurocognitive experiments supporting this premise follow simple models such as the tracking of perceptual responses to one or two sensual stimuli where the only modified variables are the number and sequence of stimuli. However, anthropological theories of the mind provide some support for the direction that I take with respect to "cross-modal perception." See also Serino et al. 2007 on multisensory peripersonal space.

their feminist third eyes, may experience before the power of spiritual solidarity, of becoming true intimate companions.

The Biltmore Hotel gathers the story's three geographies, present-day multicultural LA, the nightlife of big-band casinos in 1930s' Tijuana, and an eighteenth-century New Spain outpost. The main characters in this cross-generational dynamic are Peaches, living with Alzheimer's, her Daughter today, Malinxe, who apparently was her daughter in the past, and Nana, who is not only an eighteenth-century slave but also a hotel worker in the present. According to historical accounts, it might have been her own mother who gave Malinxe away to Cortés. Breathtaking for its shamanic juxtaposition, the play blends bickering and betrayal between mothers and daughters with their ongoing search for reciprocal love. Malinxe shows up as a dystopian, fashion-forward, divaesque traveler who is selfishly absorbed in online dating. Pretending to be checked-out, she knows why a treacherous reputation precedes her and why, within a heterosexualist social order, her claims to self-determination may grow into love between Xicana mothers and daughters.

Alzheimer's is not the only condition prompting contradictory timelines kindred to those at play in shamanic flight. In her dual role as hotel worker and eighteenth-century slave, Nana illustrates the working-class sensibility of *curanderas*, setting the stage for revelations that will come along with "sweat and purification" (Moraga 2015). We also learn of Malinxe punishing one of her servants with a thorny plant and of this excruciating pain opening doors into hallucinations.

Peaches's daughter, who has been mourning the passing of her lesbian lover, crosses into the hallucinogenic decentering of Xicano male subjectivity. While her whole family waits for *God*, "the" son, to begin the celebration of the fiftieth wedding anniversary of Peaches and her husband, Daughter keeps her cool because she has long figured out her brother's act. God is not showing up now, nor will he ever, and he hasn't for his family in a long time. By linking God, the son, to Cortés, whose arrival the Nahua mistook as god-like, *The Mathematics* allows Daughter, Malinxe, and Peaches to rehearse collective, hallucinating, and third-eye memory against the colonizing principle of putting cismen first.

Peaches, Malinxe, Nana, and Daughter reveal that the coloniality of gender is a condition—*a cultural invitation but also an injunction*—that casts suspicion upon the cognitive and affective capabilities of the colonized. In response, they concoct more-than-human, shamanic hallucinations. Next, the chapter's final section outlines connections between XFT's hallucinating resilience and Yosimar Reyes's undocuqueer tribute to his spiritual mentor.

"But Baby, You Are Not Deserted"

Reyes is an acclaimed poet that tours the country, blasting wisdom about the intersections of immigration, race, and sexuality.[14] With the termination of the Deferred Action for Childhood Arrivals (DACA) program, his current work authorization remains precarious. He is the cofounder of La Maricolectiva, a community-based performance group of queer undocumented poets. Self-defining as a brown boy "from the hood," he also grew up in a vibrant hip-hop black culture.[15] It matters to him that his words travel "in a way that is accessible; [so, that] any other little Yosimar . . . could pick it up." While I frame Reyes as a prime contemporary contributor to LXFT, this chapter covers limited connections between Reyes's milieu and these theories. Focusing on Reyes's video performance of his poem "TRE (My Revolutionary)," I analyze its main theme of nonnormative brown love and its decolonizing and hallucinating ritual.[16] I point out hallucinating affinities between his homoerotic, ritualistic performance of "My Revolutionary" and the tradition of *brujería/curanderismo* within XFT: (*a*) extraordinary, *loquería* consciousness; (*b*) hallucinating knowing; and (*c*) perceptual resilience and cross-referencing.

Set on the Caltrain commute, the performance cunningly connects contrasting geographies of conformity and destitution (Silicon Valley, San Francisco, East San Jose, and the East Bay). It begins with Reyes standing up, delivering the poem to commuters. He speaks to the camera but also to BART's passengers (Bay Area Rapid Transit). The ride illustrates the circulation of Reyes's spoken word performance, captured in video to honor Tre, his mentor and spiritual guide. It foregrounds the salience of spirituality for decolonizing activism and consciousness. According to research on shamanic prayer and incantation, their powers realize an all-encompassing sacred environment filled with rhythmic repetitions and other poetic techniques (Gill 1981). If *The Hungry Woman's* Cihuatateo invokes the birth of a new ethics of love between Xicanx mothers and sons, Reyes's love tribute to Tre declares the Caltrain commute a ritual setting for queer and transing encantations. By rendering passengers into witnesses, he invites them to his style of chanting and praying for gender-nonconforming brownness.

"For men like you I would ride a million BARTs. . . . And find your house beneath the brightest star," Reyes proclaims. In the vein of brujas who fly

---

[14] Among his literary influences, Reyes counts James Baldwin, John Updike, Henry Miller, Manuel Muñoz, and Cherríe Moraga (pers. comm., April 13, 2013).

[15] Unless otherwise noted, I use quotation marks in this section to signal fragments of my interviews with Reyes or quotes from "My Revolutionary" (2009)

[16] For the video performance, see Reyes 2011.

on brooms, or of *curanderas*' magic flights discussed earlier, Reyes takes on BART to subvert its meaning.[17] BART and Caltrain provide capital with the daily commutes of thousands of Latinx undocumented immigrants, but Reyes's spoken word delivers an atypical, anticapitalist expenditure, a loving tribute or *ride* to queer-of-color mentorship.

With the opening verse, Reyes forewarns against racializing geographies whose concrete "numbs the senses [and] cages the spirit." It excavates the emotions associated with (extra)ordinary consciousness for those facing the colonial aftermath. He values the teachings that Tre offers him about the effects of the city's buildings on brown bodies. Reyes takes a fierce phenomenological stance to underscore that Tre's spirit or freedom feels like "wind . . . sitting on top of the world," or "the tobacco you offered me to blow blessings." Rather than likening Tre's "freedom" to the sensual capacities of all minoritized bodies, "My Revolutionary" digs deeper into the anticolonial resilience of Xicanx perception. The line "You come from the desert but baby you are not deserted" contests the colonizing relation between capitalism and perceptual destitution. With Tre being originally from Ajó, Arizona, the poem links the trail of many undocumented immigrants who perish crossing the Sonora Desert to the danger of becoming "deserted," depleted by a Eurocentered project of destitution. For Reyes, as for LXFT, the horror of geographies numbing the spirit lies precisely with the erasure of multisensual capacities.

Reyes recognizes that by acting as healer on the stage, Tre pays tribute to the vital possessions of body and voice in their everyday sacredness, as "the only possessions we have in this world" to honor the spirits of "los antepasados" (ancestors). If Medea gives birth to herself by affirming the radical ancestral legacy of sensual cross-referencing, the poem honoring Tre equally cultivates the powers of bridging tangible and intangible domains. "Singing" materializes sacredness in the tangible form that healers give to remedies once they tether the elsewhere of consciousness to the emotional and bodily needs of those, such as the characters in Reyes's poetry, who face the condition of "illegality." In one segment Reyes assumes the positions that most commuters adopt, offering the visual of an undocuqueer as stowaway who, passing as another passenger, sits opposite to or with his back to other riders. The performance, however, reveals that "singing," as he puts it, makes tangible the more-than-human force of singing, of becoming *woke*, of invoking spirit "till this system crumbles, till this border breaks, till the earth shakes."

---

[17] Brooms underscore the availability of migrant women's labor, particularly Mexican American and Central American, for the domestic service sector in the United States. The feminist association between witches and brooms pulls this instrument away from the domestic domain of gender subordination.

Reyes's poem embraces sacred words ("sagradas") that, he claims, arrive "del más allá" (from elsewhere). "To get into the mood of the emotion," Reyes crafts worlds where undocumented immigrants find sites of nonconforming identification. The poetry slams organized by Youth Speaks, a nongovernmental organization that fosters poetry literacy in the Bay Area, gave Reyes the first platform to experiment with code-switching, his northern California Spanglish meshed with hip-hop vernacular. Mostly Berkeley and San Francisco youth dominated the slams of the mid-2000s, and Reyes felt that they had "a language that was so much more developed than where [he was] from." This marginal vantage point enables him to usher audiences into hallucinating rites rich in sounds and *loquería* that are not quite intelligible to all. Such as the Alzheimer's that haunts Peaches, Reyes's multilingual ceremonies strip their partakers of their (hetero)normative, monolingual status.

Perceptual resilience is part of the healing traditions that this chapter documents. *Curanderas* and brujas archive ancestral knowledge in their own flesh, transitioning one set of sensual clues into another. Reyes's ode to Tre also troubles any typical account of homoerotic sensuality. The attraction and desire binding Reyes and his mentor germinate within their identification as two-spirit beings. In the Native American and Meso-American cosmologies, "Two-spirited people are sexually mixed beings who enjoy a living relation with their Indigenous ways and spirituality" (Estrada 2003, 12). *Curanderismo* as the work of spirit healers, of specialists of the heart, remains the cornerstone of Tre and Reyes's two-spirit relation. The most carnal expression of their erotic and spiritual embrace unfolds with the stanza "You got me and together we are 4 spirits like the 4 directions." Permeability between two-spirited people, between nonbinary spirits becoming larger, and multiplying into four actualizes more than homoerotic mentorship since it challenges the notion that desire relies on binaries. It also foregrounds that the love between them borrows its true matter from sacred ancestors.

Might we call Medea, Peaches, and Tre kindred spirits? Might we consider Reyes's hallucinating rite a feature of broader epistemic and phenomenological histories that LXFTs have fostered for decades? Further research may provide more insight into these resilient responses to colonial injunctions. Coloniality entails for the colonized the experience of being perceived as *insane*, behaving as one—most of the time intentionally—and employing this competence to connect with other practitioners of *loquería*. As shown in this chapter, contributors to LXFT face one another at the edge of the (extra)ordinary. They heal *el susto* by doing intergenerational work, making of Latinx and Xicanx mothers and daughters a new *alien* race that doesn't put cismen first.

Against a Kantian legacy linking ordinary consciousness to reliable sight/knowledge, LXFTs generate hallucinating and richly sensual repertoires. Their practitioners employ tongue, skin, ears, eyes, nose, and "the mystical third eye" to carnally and spiritually decipher what they need for the enactment of healing rites. In the flight of altered consciousness, they gain new visions, totally unique, not quite nameable, half-seen, half-heard, half-tasted, and half-felt, a way of sensing that is as much compelling as it is frightening. Latinx and Xicanx curanderxs stand against the horror of sensual destitution, of the suppression of Indigenous perceptual repertoires. Under the sign of illegality, they present contemporary generations such as Reyes's with our more-than-human potential.

References

Alarcón, Norma. 1989. "Traddutora, Traditora: A Paradigmatic Figure of Chicana Feminism." *Cultural Critique* 13: 57–87.

Anzaldúa, Gloria. 1987. Borderlands/La Frontera: *The New Mestiza.* San Francisco: Aunt Lute.

Anzaldúa, Gloria. 2009. *The Gloria Anzaldúa Reader.* Edited by AnaLouise Keating. Durham, NC: Duke University Press.

Arabzadeh, Ehsan, et al. 2008. "Vision Merges with Touch in a Purely Tactile Discrimination." *Psychological Science* 19, no. 7: 635–41.

Arredondo, Gabriela F., Aída Hurtado, Norma Klahn, Olga Nájera-Ramírez, and Patricia Navella, eds. 2003. *Chicana Feminisms: A Critical Reader.* Durham, NC: Duke University Press.

Ayala, Felipe Guaman Poma de. 1980. *Nueva corónica y buen gobierno.* Vol. 2. Caracas, Venezuela: Fundación Biblioteca Ayacucho.

Barrett, Robert J. 2004. "Kurt Schneider in Borneo: Do First Rank Symptoms Apply to the Iban?" *Cambridge Studies in Medical Anthropology* 11: 87–109.

Brady, Mary Pat. 2002. *Extinct Lands, Temporal Geographies: Chicana Literature and the Urgency of Space.* Durham, NC: Duke University Press.

Castillo, Ana. 2014. *Massacre of the Dreamers: Essays on Xicanisma.* Albuquerque: University of New Mexico Press.

Chiu, Leo PW. 1989. "Differential Diagnosis and Management of Hallucinations." *Journal of the Hong Kong Medical Association* 41, no. 3: 292–97.

Delgadillo, Theresa. 2011. *Spiritual Mestizaje: Religion, Gender, Race, and Nation in Contemporary Chicana Narrative.* Durham, NC: Duke University Press.

DiPietro, Pedro José Javier. 2008. "Colonial Mappings, Decolonial Erotics: On the Production of Homoerotic Spaces in Northwestern Argentina." Paper presented at the Annual Meeting of the National Women's Studies Association, Cincinnati, OH, June.

DiPietro, Pedro José Javier. 2012. "Thirding as a Way of Arranging the Real: The Production of Decolonial Queer Spaces in the Southern Andes." PhD diss., Binghamton University.

Estrada, Gabriel S. 2003. "An Aztec Two-Spirit Cosmology: Re-sounding Nahuatl Masculinities, Elders, Femininities, and Youth." *Frontiers: A Journal of Women Studies* 24, no. 2: 10–14.

Fanon, Frantz. 2008. *Black Skin, White Masks.* New York: Grove Press.

Galarte, Francisco. 2014. "On Trans* Chican@ s: Amor, Justicia, y Dignidad." *Aztlán: A Journal of Chicano Studies* 39, no. 1: 229–36.

Gill, Sam D. 1981. *Sacred Words: A Study of Navajo Religion and Prayer*. Westport, CT: Greenwood Press.

Gonzales, Patrisia. 2012. *Red Medicine: Traditional Indigenous Rites of Birthing and Healing*. Tucson: University of Arizona Press.

Gruzinski, Serge. 1995. "Images and Cultural Mestizaje in Colonial Mexico." *Poetics Today* 16: 53–77.

Hartley, George. 2010. "'Matriz sin tumba': The Trash goddess and the Healing Matrix of Gloria Anzaldúa's Reclaimed Womb." *MELUS: Multi-Ethnic Literature of the US* 35, no. 3: 41–61.

Horswell, Michael J. 2005. *Decolonizing the Sodomite: Queer Tropes of Sexuality in Colonial Andean Culture*. Austin: University of Texas Press.

Jay, Martin. 1988. "Scopic Regimes of Modernity." In *Vision and Visuality*, edited by Hal Foster. New York: New Press.

Kant, Immanuel. 1964. *The Classification of Mental Disorders*. Doylestown, PA: Doylestown Foundation.

Jones, Michael Owen, Patrick A. Polk, Ysamur Flores-Peña, and Roberta J. Evanchuk. 2001. "Invisible Hospitals: Botánicas in Ethnic Health Care." In *Healing Logics: Culture and Medicine in Modern Health Belief Systems*, edited by Erika Brady, 39–87. Logan: Utah State University Press.

Lara, Ana-Maurine. 2006. *Erzulie's Skirt*. Washington, DC: RedBone Press.

Lara, Irene. 2005. "Bruja Positionalities: Toward a Chicana/Latina Spiritual Activism." *Chicana/Latina Studies* 4, no. 2: 10–45.

Lloyd, Genevieve. 1984. *The Man of Reason*. Minneapolis: University of Minnesota Press.

Lugones, María. 2003. Pilgrimages/Peregrinajes: *Theorizing Coalition against Multiple Oppressions*. Lanham, MD: Rowman & Littlefield.

Lugones, María. 2006. "Heterosexualism and the Colonial/Modern Gender System." *Hypatia* 22, no. 1: 189–219.

Luhrmann, Tanya M. 2011. "Hallucinations and Sensory Overrides." *Annual Review of Anthropology* 40: 71–85.

MacLean, Hope. 2001. "Sacred Colors and Shamanic Vision among the Huichol Indians of Mexico." *Journal of Anthropological Research* 57, no. 3: 305–23.

MacLean, Hope. 2012. *The Shaman's Mirror: Visionary Art of the Huichol*. Austin: University of Texas Press.

Maldonado-Torres, Nelson. 2008. *Against War: Views from the Underside of Modernity*. Durham, NC: Duke University Press.

Marcos, Sylvia. 2006. *Taken from the Lips*. Leiden: Brill.

Mbembe, Achille. 2003. "Necropolitics." *Public Culture* 15, no. 1: 11–40.

Mesa-Bains, Amalia. 1999. "'Domesticana': The Sensibility of Chicana Rasquache." *Aztlán: A Journal of Chicano Studies* 24, no. 2: 155–67.

Mignolo, Walter. 1995. *The Darker Side of the Renaissance: Territoriality and Literacy*. Ann Arbor: University of Michigan Press.

Moraga, Cherríe. 1983. *Loving in the War Years:* Lo que nunca pasó por sus labios. Boston: South End Press.

Moraga, Cherríe. 1993. *The Last Generation: Prose and Poetry*. Boston: South End Press.

Moraga, Cherríe. 2011. *A Xicana Codex of Changing Consciousness: Writings, 2000–2010*. Durham, NC: Duke University Press.

Moraga, Cherríe. 2015. *The Mathematics of Love*. Unpublished manuscript.

Moraga, Cherríe. [1995] 2001. *The Hungry Woman*. New York: West End Press.

Morrow, Colette. 1997. "Queering Chicano/a Narratives: Lesbian as Healer, Saint and Warrior in Ana Castillo's 'So Far from God.'" *Journal of the Midwest Modern Language Association* 30, nos. 1–2: 63–80.

Noll, Richard. 1983. "Shamanism and Schizophrenia: A State-Specific Approach to the 'Schizophrenia Metaphor' of Shamanic States." *American Ethnologist* 10, no. 3: 443–59.

O'Callaghan, Casey. 2008. "Seeing What You Hear: Cross-Modal Illusions and Perception." *Philosophical Issues* 18, no. 1: 316–38.

Ortega, Mariana. 2001. "'New Mestizas,' '"World" Travelers,' and 'Dasein': Phenomenology and the Multi-voiced, Multi-cultural Self." *Hypatia* 16, no. 3: 1–29.

Ortega, Mariana. 2016. *In-Between: Latina Feminist Phenomenology, Multiplicity, and the Self.* Albany: SUNY Press.

Pérez, Gail. 2002. "Ana Castillo as *Santera*: Reconstructing Popular Religion Praxis." In *A Reader in Latina Feminist Theology: Religion and Justice*, edited by María Pilar Aquino, Daisy L. Machado, and Jeanette Rodríguez, 53–79. Austin: University of Texas Press.

Pérez, Laura E. 1999. "El Desorden, Nationalism, and Chicana/o Aesthetics." In *Between Woman and Nation: Nationalisms, Transnational Feminisms, and the State,* edited by Caren Kaplan, Norma Alarcón, and Minoo Moallem, 19–46. Durham, NC: Duke University Press.

Pérez, Laura E. 2007. *Chicana Art: The Politics of Spiritual and Aesthetic Altarities.* Durham, NC: Duke University Press.

Quijano, Aníbal. 1991. "Colonialidad y racionalidad/modernidad." *Perú Indígena* 29: 11–29.

Reyes, Yosimar. 2009. *For Colored Boys Who Speak Softly.* Self-published chapbook.

Reyes, Yosimar. 2011. "My Revolutionary." YouTube video, May 17. https://www.youtube.com/watch?v=lq03sppYpGY

Sánchez-Carretero, Cristina. 2005. "Santos y Misterios as Channels of Communication in the Diaspora: Afro-Dominican Religious Practices Abroad." *Journal of American Folklore* 118, no. 469: 308–26.

Sandoval, Chela. 2000. *Methodology of the Oppressed.* Minneapolis: University of Minnesota Press.

Serino, Andrea, et al. 2007. "Extended Multisensory Space in Blind Cane Users." *Psychological Science* 18, no. 7: 642–48.

Sigal, Pete, ed. 2003. *Infamous Desire: Male Homosexuality in Colonial Latin America.* Chicago: University of Chicago Press.

Stryker, Susan, Paisley Currah, and Lisa Jean Moore. 2008. "Introduction: Trans-, Trans, or Transgender?" *Women's Studies Quarterly* 36, nos. 3–4: 11–22.

Yarbro-Bejarano, Yvonne. 2011. *The Wounded Heart: Writing on Cherríe Moraga.* Austin: University of Texas Press.

Ybarra-Frausto, Tomás. 1991. "Rasquachismo: A Chicano Sensibility." In *Chicano Art: Resistance and Affirmation, 1965–1985,* edited by Richard Griswold del Castillo, Teresa McKenna, and Yvonne Yarbro-Bejarano, 155–162. Los Angeles: Wight Art Gallery and University of California Press.

SECTION IV | Aesthetic Longings
Latina Styles, Bodily Vulnerability,
and Queer Desires

CHAPTER 14 | Stylized Resistance

Boomerang Perception and Latinas in the Twenty-First Century

STEPHANIE RIVERA BERRUZ

RACISM REMAINS A CONSTANT reality in the lives of women of color in the United States, a reality that manifests itself in varying capacities. María Lugones explores these experiences in her scholarship by examining the logic of sameness that cloaks racism and inhibits the preservation of difference. By analyzing the theoretical tensions produced between and among women of color and white women, Lugones develops an account of boomerang perception described as the racist and colonialist perception of people of color that denies their independence. On her account, people of color are constructed through a white imaginary lens, which collapses difference and implies that the construction of the nonwhite body is dependent on the vision or perception of the white body for its history, self-construction, and social perception.

This essay explores the complexity of the perceptual epistemological structures that comprise boomerang perception. I focus on the lived experiences of Latinas today and consider the ways in which boomerang perception plays out as part of social and cultural life by specifically looking at the way in which Latinas have become part of a commercialized homogenized identity. I argue that such constructions evoke a fake/real dichotomy that is rooted in the internalization of boomerang perception, which can be resisted through the insights offered by the work of Gloria Anzaldúa on *conocimiento*. The methodological framework of conocimiento elucidates a transformative embodied sense of knowing that can resist the impact of boomerang perception. In this capacity, I offer the case of resistance through chonga-style politics as one that exemplifies the possibilities of conocimiento.

Stephanie Rivera Berruz , *Stylized Resistance* In: *Theories of the Flesh*, Edited by: Andrea J. Pitts, Mariana Ortega, and José Medina, Oxford University Press (2020). © Oxford University Press. DOI: 10.1093/oso/9780190062965.003.0015

Thinking Through Boomerang Perception: Reflections on the Quotidian and Belonging

In "Boomerang Perception and the Colonizing Gaze: Ginger Reflections on Horizontal Hostility," the seventh chapter of *Pilgrimages/Peregrinajes*, María Lugones launches a theoretical exploration of boomerang perception, which she describes as an endemic dimension of racist racial perception in the United States. Broadly, boomerang perception is the way in which people of color are perceived through white eyes that see them only in relationship to white identity and construction. She describes the structure of perception in the following fashion: "The racist/colonialist perception is narcissistic, it denies independence to the seen, it constructs its objects imaginatively as a reflection of the seer" (Lugones 2003, 157).[1] The quotidian dimension of boomerang perception is found in the way in which it is folded into the education of young white children as they learn about their nonwhite peers through a framework of assimilation. The language that emerges takes the form of "Black people are just like us" or "Latinos are very similar to us." The consequence of this logic of perception is that white people are taught to think of racial difference nonreciprocally. People of color are understood only to the extent that they can accommodate white racial perceptual expectations. To this effect Lugones notes: "The white person is the original, the Black person just an image not independent from the seer" (157).

Following this schema, the nonwhite body is dependent on the vision or perception of the white body for its history, self-construction, and social perception. As a result, the racial other is constructed as imitative and robbed of any personal history or circumstance that is independent of whiteness.

As reflected in the title of the essay, Lugones opens her discussion on racist/colonist perception gingerly. She warns that her project should not collapse into an interrogation of the white-other binary, which she takes to be dangerous for people of color. Rather, she seeks to explore the implications of the internalization of boomerang perception for the construction of belonging in communities of color. One such consequence is the evoking of ethnic legitimacy tests within communities that construct some people as "real" participants in ethnic/racial communities and others as "fakes" (Lugones 2003, 159). The language of legitimacy finds expression through the real/fake dichotomy instantiated in phrases like: "You are not *really* Puerto Rican" or "You are not a *real* Latina."

---

[1] Lugones notes that this term originally comes from the work of Elizabeth Spelman.

The internalization of boomerang perception, or the seeing of other people of color through white eyes, impacts horizontal relationships, that is, the relationships between and among people of color. Lugones (2003, 156) insists on a horizontal focus because attention to the oppressor's construction of the subjectivities of people of color (hierarchical focus) can become paralytic. The audiential target of the essay is pointedly reflected in her opening dedicatory paragraph, in which she writes to "people of color; for women first and mainly, but also for men: green-eyed Blacks, never-been-taught-my culture Asian Americans and U.S. Latinos, emigres, immigrants and migrants, mixed-bloods and mixed cultures, solid core, community bred, folks of color" (151).

Central to Lugones's analysis of boomerang perception is not just the perceptual process itself, but also its intimate relationship to constructions of relatedness and belonging as these emerge through racialized intersubjective encounters. How I come to see myself as belonging to a community is to tell a racialized narrative of my encounters with others. However, racialized encounters are constructed in and through our racist environments from which none of us are immune. As a result, the formation of belonging is impacted by boomerang perception, which materializes in the form of legitimacy tests. To this effect she writes: "Thus, we administer legitimacy tests with white eyes on, and what moves us to administer the test is the same logic that invokes the distinction between original/real and the image/fake" (Lugones 2003, 162). Boomerang perception seeps into our quotidian encounters that construct our senses home, heritage, and descent whereby the impact of seeing with white eyes is harmful to the development of positive horizontal relationships.

Following her focus on the impact of boomerang perception on horizontal relationships, Lugones takes concern with the development of homeplace as a method of resistance. Building homeplace provides refuge and conditions survival because it forges the possibilities of an alternative vision and history of oneself that is independent of the oppressors' gaze (Lugones 2003, 159). However, the formation of belonging or the production of a seeing circle, as Lugones refers to it, can come to reinscribe the distortions of boomerang perception, detrimentally impacting horizontal relationships. The impact is most notably felt through fear, the intention of which is the possible loss of ones constructed community or homeplace. In her words: "One fears that one may become what one is in the racists perceiver's eye, and nothing else, all other subjectivity erased. And as I have argued, that is to become something insubstantial, dependent, a distorted image of white humanity. So one guards the seeing circle zealously" (160). Fear entrenched in the loss of subjectivity generates two decisive logics. On the one hand, one can be seen through the pangs of boomerang perception. On the other hand, one can resist the boomerang construction by creating and guarding ones seeing circle. But as Lugones notes, there is trouble in the oscillation between these logics because those outside of one's seeing circle are still being constructed through the white gaze (160). In the process, the real/fake dichotomy emerges and shapes relations of self to others as a method to guard homeplaces.

Lugones's analysis has two implications. On the one hand, people of color are constructed in the image of white people. Their senses of history, relatedness, and belonging are contingent on white history and identity with no perceptual reciprocity. One the other hand, people of color may be constructed as monstrously different as bad imitative copies of white identity (Lugones 2003, 158). Regardless of the construction of self, the internalization of boomerang perception entails damaged horizontal relationships because we come to see each other and ourselves through a white perceptual schema. In response we construct homeplaces or home seeing circles that are vigilantly guarded through ethnic/racial legitimacy tests.

A key feature of Lugones's analysis of boomerang perception is its quotidian entrenchment as it comes to shape the most intimate practices of the everyday lives of people of color. It participates in what Sharon Patricia Holland (2012) has termed the quotidian life of racism. Boomerang perception is not aberrational and comes to inform ordinary intersubjective experiences. It shapes how we understand our relative histories. Our world is one that requires history: a narrative of the past that explains our descent (Holland 2012, 20). One must have a history to be connected to other people, and this fact racializes history, while simultaneously placing deep importance on *relatedness* in the narratives we construct about ourselves, and others (21). The fact that we are racialized implies that we *belong* or are *related* to a certain social group. While clearly placing a deep importance on the problematic biological discourses that often congeal our senses of racial belonging, this observation also demonstrates the importance of how we perceptually ascertain belonging and relatedness to each other. Boomerang perception negatively impacts these types of social relationships. In what follows I explore the impact of boomerang perception with respect to Latinas in the United States, treading carefully to ensure a focus on intra-Latina relationships and not the white-other binary.

Latinas in a Commercialized Context: The Real/ Fake Dichotomy

The contemporary situation of Latinas is socially and politically complex. The world is permeated with and constructed through perceptions (e.g., boomerang perception) of people of color that leave senses of being self-disjointed (e.g., xenophobia), assimilated (e.g., passing), or violently objectified (e.g., hypersexualization). In this context, Latina identity is readily negotiated, challenged, or reinforced through the body (Mendible 2007, 4). It is a gendered, hybrid, and transactional site of ethnic identity articulated through embodiment (4). As a transactional site of ethnic identity, Latina identity has also become a signifier of commercialization and consumption in a world where boomerang perception overwhelmingly informs the narratives of cultural and racial authenticity. In our global economy, the Latina body has come to function as a type of negotiable currency that participates in the mythological national narrative of a multicultural United States (13). The trope of the exotic ethnic beauty has served as a commercialized spectacle of national incorporation using discourses of authenticity and realness, which belies the lived realities of Latinas today, who are overrepresented in high school dropout rates, teen pregnancy, and low-wage factory and domestic labor (14).

The "realness" of identity gains traction through cultural messages that register horizontal relations of identity through the possibilities sameness. For instance, a claim like "Real Puerto Ricans are only those born on the island of Puerto Rico" makes sense when cultural messages dictate that the only way to participate in the shared history of Puerto Rico is through a logic of homogeneity premised on a belonging that is built through birth and geography. Similarly, when we consider what it means to be a "real" Latina, cultural messages indicate that authenticity can be found in homogenous commercialized measurable scales. For instance, L'Oreal Group commercials for the "True Match" foundation centered Jennifer Lopez as (unlike any of the other models in the advertisement) 100 percent Puerto Rican. Carmen R. Lugo-Lugo (2015, 99) has subsequently argued that a claim to 100 percent Latina ethnicity is a marketable condition in a way that 100 percent whiteness or 100 percent blackness is not. Being "real" or "authentic," as opposed to fake or maybe only "50 percent," is given credence in a world where what it means to be Latina has been disjointed or objectified through a white perceptual process. Moreover, it is a process that now takes the object of identity as marketable and profitable.

Lugo-Lugo (2014, 126) argues that the pan-ethnic label of "Latina" is flattened through commercialization that homogenizes the term by lumping all Latinas into one category, and making it a desirable object of consumption through a narrative of pride. Having pride in ethnic, racial, or national heritage makes identification viable with the category. Unfortunately, the commercialized homogenization of Latina constructs the identity through a white imaginary lens that does not leave room for differences. The feeling of pride, Lugo-Lugo (2015, 136) argues, emerges from a sense of belonging, community, or accomplishment. However, it becomes very difficult to garner a sense of belonging when the category is manufactured in a manner that renders it vacuous due to the universalizing forces that are at play in its commercialization. To this effect, Lugo-Lugo (2014) writes: "In fact, we could describe Latina pride as the byproduct of a society that imagines Latinas in one way and that forces those who fall within the category (by label or identity) to create a fundamentally empty space from which to operate and in which to take refuge from their daily existence in that very society" (139). The narrative of authenticity marks the category of Latina as a commercialized, homogenized category that can only be real (authentic) or fake. If, as Lugo-Lugo suggests, the identity of Latina is produced through commercialization that universalizes and homogenizes, then it should be no surprise that the fake/real dichotomy is often deployed as a way of constructing a sense of belonging. However, the difficulties arise, much as Lugo-Lugo has noted, when we recognize that the category in the perceptual process has become empty in that it refers potentially to everyone and to no one. Hence, the identity of Latina in the US twenty-first century is often guarded zealously through the fake/real dichotomy because what it means to be "real" is so fragile in its construction. Commercialization has helped to make the category of Latina an empty, but desirable, object of identification.

The fake/real dichotomy gains epistemic traction when one has been objectified or rendered part of a narrative of sameness constructed through white perception that does not offer an independent narrative of history and self. Protecting the sense of belonging through narratives of "authenticity" and "realness" demonstrates just how impactful boomerang perception is in our constructions of quotidian belonging. In the case of Jennifer Lopez there is no construction of Latina identity that is not independent of a commercialized hyperfeminine and sexualized Latinidad that young Latinas aspire to participate in, thus constructing their relationships to each other through their abilities to approximate an embodiment of the "real" Latina. Moreover, the "realness" is sustained through the affirmation and protection of national and ethnic origins. After all, Jennifer Lopez is claiming 100 percent Puerto Ricanness, which subsequently implies 100 percent Latina. As Lugones has noted, one of the effects of boomerang perception on people of color is the protection of seeing circles that congeal around national or ethnic homeplaces. In this instance, Lopez's 100 percent status entails that there are certain criteria that qualify her as such and failure to meet those criteria will result in exclusion from the "seeing circle." The processes of producing states of inclusion and exclusion are sustained by rebuke of those that do not belong, but, given the state of commercialization, belonging seems in many capacities both desirable and unobtainable.

Resistant Logics

Lugones (2003) argues that resistance to boomerang perception cannot come from an attachment to nation and culture that mistrusts the perception of other people of color (161). Rather, resistance is found in the recognition that there are larger and more complex seeing circles that allow us to form collective subjectivities of resistance (160). The work for Lugones is in dismantling the effect of boomerang perception through the disavowal of dichotomous visions (real/fake) of other people of color that recognize the effects of boomerang perception. However, how do we go about constructing such a positive subjectivity? How can Latinas enact this collective labor of horizontal relationality? Although Lugones expounds on the conditions for resistance, the answers to these questions remain unanswered. As an offering in the direction of a resistant logic to boomerang perception I suggest we look to the work of Gloria Anzaldúa, who was deeply influential on the work of Lugones.

Resistance to boomerang perception on the part of Latinas (in their multiplicity) first and foremost requires acts of self-knowing that recognize the impact of internalized colonialist/racist perception that make the real/fake dichotomy viable in the first place. However, self-knowing is not an easy process. As Gloria Anzaldúa explains in *Borderlands/La Frontera* (1999) knowledge makes one more conscious and aware, but *knowing* (the action of knowledge internalization) is painful because after we are not the same person we were before (48). Knowing is transformative, but transformations are rarely easy. In "Now let us shift . . . the path of conocimiento . . . inner work, public acts" (2002, 540), Anzaldúa expands on the transformative action of self-knowing or conocimiento. She notes that conocimiento requires confronting what you have been programmed by your culture to avoid or unknow (*desconocer*). The path of conocimiento necessitates that we confront the traits and habits that have distorted how we see the world (541). In this context, the effect of boomerang perception yields desconocimiento through trauma on the subjectivities of people of color that preclude the possibilities of positive coalitional horizontal relationships. The vision of oneself in the throes of boomerang perception is one constructed through objectification, a line of self-perception that is not one's own. Seeing the world through white colonialist eyes and seeing fellow Latinas through these internalized perceptions is the result of the trauma caused by boomerang perception. Unsurprisingly, boomerangs in their nonreturning iterations are weapons intended to maim. The perception wielded through boomerang perception injures, breaks, objectifies, or disjoints its subject. Enacting self-knowing from conditions maimed through boomerang perception calls into question categories and artifices that we are conditioned to know ourselves through (e.g., race, gender, nationality) that then allow us to reformulate how we relate to ourselves and each other. It strikes me that resistance to boomerang perception will require that we recognize that the harm comes from the categories themselves, the boomerangs. As Anzaldúa (2002, 541) argues, the path of conocimiento requires questioning conventional systems of knowledge and their respective categories that have come to distort how we see ourselves and structure how we relate to others. So in guarding our seeing circles we must question how we have come to see fellow Latinas as objects that can be constructed as real/fake in order to render their participation in belonging appropriate. The path of conocimiento requires a skepticism of the binary categories that yield a sense of the self as "real," "fake," or "100 percent anything," as these become fragmenting categories. Fostering positive horizontal relationships among and between people of color must begin with the self; and Latinas are no different. The drive to understand others is, first and foremost, foregrounded by a drive to understand and love yourself (543).

Anzaldúa (2002) describes the process as "an opening up from all of the senses, consciously inhabiting the body, and all of its symptoms" (542). Conocimiento is multiple and challenges the conventional ways we look at the world (542). As a result, we must necessarily explore how our constructions of knowledge, identity, and subsequently reality violate other people's ways of being, knowing, and living (544). We must question boomerang perception; the process by which we come to construct other people through problematic categories that we ourselves internalize. To resist boomerang perception in our horizontal relationality the boomerang must be abandoned. In other words, the categories that construct impermeable seeing circles have to be interrogated, and one key method for doing so is through stylized resistance.

Latina Stylized Resistance: From Pachuca to Chonga

The process of critical interrogation foundational to conocimiento hinges on the development of a self-knowledge that does not rest on the use of ethnic legitimacy tests for the construction of positive self-identity. One method for ascertaining such knowledge can be found through stylized resistance, which deploys the use of embodied style as a way of resisting normative expectations of Latina identity. The use of embodied style requires a conscious inhabitance of the body as it is sculpted and molded to challenge gendered, sexual, ethnoracial norms. Furthermore, given that narratives of race, gender, and sexuality are crucial vehicles to the production of national identity, stylized resistance can interrupt expectations of multicultural assimilation often associated with appropriate Latina embodiment. Style is both self and other directed, and permeates one's sense of self as well as how others perceive our identity. As a result, it has political valence. The use of style can challenge the categories through which we construct the world and thus offers a path toward conocimiento.

The use of the body and its style to resist dominant systems of power is hardly new for Latinas in the United States. In *The Women in the Zoot Suit: Gender, Nationalism, and the Cultural Politics of Memory* (2009), Catherine S. Ramírez draws attention to the omission of Mexican American women in the 1930s–1940s from the history of the Chicano movement. Mexican American women who wore zoot suits were often termed *pachucas, chukas, cholitas, malinches* (xiii). Many were working-class and second-generation Americans whose families had emigrated to the United States, were bilingual, and were located in the urban centers of California and the Southwest (xiii). Ramírez demonstrates the way in which style for the women of the zoot suit era functioned as a form of resistance. By specifically focusing on *pachuca*-style politics, Ramírez centers the use of the body, gender performativity, and style as methods that interrupted the norms constructing femininity, sexuality, and nationhood. Women of the zoot suit era became a "sign of aberrant femininity, competing masculinity, or homosexuality during the early 1940s. As a nonwhite, working-class, and queer signifier, it was perceived as un-American" (Ramiréz 2009, 56).

Style politics, as Ramiréz refers to it, encompasses the use of clothing, hairstyles, and makeup to engage in subversive action (2009, 57). Generally, zoot suits were a sign of disposable income and socially underscored the instability of class and race (60). For some the zoot suit was viewed as a status symbol, a class accomplishment. However, for others, particularly those of the upper class, the zoot suit was read as excessive (61). The use of zoot suits interrupted the social norms of class ascribed to Mexican Americans of the time. It was further accompanied by a brazen attitude that deviated from the norms of femininity in the World War II era (2009, 61). Appropriate femininity was racialized (white) and characterized by the protection of domesticity whereby women were responsible for their homes, families, and appearance in efforts to preserve the nation (65). Furthermore, if women were recruited into the workforce, their femininity was always foregrounded in the process (67).

The *pachuca* emerged as a destabilizing figure whose use of style functioned as a method of subversion of the norms of her times both within her own community as well as within the broader US culture during World War II (Ramírez 2009, 81). The *pachuca* interrupted dominant narratives of femininity. The use of heavy makeup and at times short skirts ran against the image of the self-sacrificing mother (68). Although *pachucas* were feminine, their style was often read as excessively feminine. The feminine excess interrupted the norms of ladyhood that deemed them unpatriotic and pernicious to society (69). As a result, *pachuca* sexuality was rendered abnormal because the woman was apprehended as sexually available (70).

The Latinas that engaged in stylized resistance during in the World War II era provide an instructive historical framework for better understanding contemporary Latina stylized resistant politics. Ramírez's account calls attention to the way in which stylized politics is multidimensional. Style can interrupt discourse of class, race, femininity, sexuality, nationhood, and citizenship. For instance, the use of hyperfemininity and hypervisibility interrupts racialized gendered norms that teach appropriateness, particularly for young immigrant Latinas, through the deployment of respectable feminine bodily comportment that creates the possibilities of assimilation. Through the use of aesthetics, stylized resistance creates subversive action on and through the body that can interrupt oppressive vertical and horizontal relationships.

Recalling Anzaldúa's reflections in "now lets us shift" (2002), the path of conocimiento recognizes that the body is more than its marked categories (555). Identity is fluid, and we can share in an identity larger or wider than any social position or label (558). Identity has roots that extend. To this effect, Anzaldúa writes: "The roots del arból de la vida of all planetary beings are nature, soul, and body" (560). Anzaldúa's claim insists that the national boundaries that divide us from "others" (*nos/otras*) be porous. The cracks that make the fluidity of identity possible serve as gateways to *otras*/others (561). In this capacity, stylized resistance serves as a mechanism through which to participate in positive self-knowing that does not require the debasement of others and cracks at the artifice of zealously guarded seeing circles built on the language of authenticity and fakeness.

A more contemporary instantiation of Latina stylized resistance can be found through chonga stylized politics. Much like *pachucas*, chongas interrupt the discourse of the "proper" Latinas who are supposed to blend in, be quiet, respectable, and invisible. Chonga stylized politics interrupts the idea that real Latinas are those who can be appropriately folded into the narrative fiction of national multiculturalism. To this effect, the figure of the chonga operates as a critical intervention in the impacts of boomerang perception by gesturing toward a critical self-knowing that disrupts norms of gender, class, and sexuality. As such, chonga stylized politics resists the signification of Latinas as homogenized objects for consumption.

Embodying Resistance: Chonga Stylized Politics

Chonga stylized politics deploys the use of the body and its performative style to disrupt hegemonic norms coded in the language of authenticity that regulates Latina identity. Chongas are often described as young, low-class, slutty, tough, and hypervisible Latinas from south Florida (Hernandez 2009, 64). Their presence in visual culture reflects the way in which chonga bodies produce and reflect discourses about sexuality, ethnicity, and class (64). Most notably, the figure of the chonga sheds light on biases within Latina communities, as chongas have come to discursively represent what not to emulate, those against whom seeing circles are guarded. Yet at the same time chongas trouble the politics of authenticity by complicating the normative behavior imposed on Latina communities intended to produce the good/bad and real/fake dichotomy (64). Chongas are marked by what Jillian Hernandez has identified as a sexual aesthetic excess, which functions through the use of style often considered to be "too much": too sexy, too young, too cheap, too ethnic (66). However, rather than reading the sexual aesthetic excess as participating in the stereotyping of Latinas, we ought to understand it as potentially disruptive. The deployment of chonga style functions as a resistant measure to discourses of Latinas that attempt to empower by dissociating them from the sexual excess. By participating in sexual aesthetic excess, chonga identity renegotiates the relationship between agency and sexual identity, and in doing so calls into question what it means to be a good, real, and authentic Latina. Thus, chonga stylized resistance gestures toward a methodological resistance that reshapes self-knowing, as well as the relationships that Latinas have between each other that often read sexual excess as that which should be disciplined.

Anzaldúa (2002) articulates conocimiento as a form of spiritual inquiry that is achieved through creative acts where the body is a site of creativity (542). It is a process that she articulates in seven stages or stations through which relationships of the self are renegotiated and rearticulated. However, we are never only in one stage, but rather at the crossroads of many processes of conocomiento articulated through the mind/body/spirit. Informative for the role that stylized resistance plays in conocimiento is the fifth stage. The fifth station is one characterized by reconstruction whereby we recreate personal narratives that poke holes in the paradigms that construct our current reality. In so doing, we also aid in the cocreation of group cultural narratives (Anzaldúa 2002, 560). The fifth stage lays the possibility for alternative potentials that contribute to more expansive conocimiento (560).

In this context, the sexual aesthetic excess of chonga style can be read as not merely resisting the assimilative homogenized model of Latina identity, but also rearticulating a creative way of being that is resistant. Chongas grate against the politics of respectability that discipline Latinas into practices that fuel narratives of authenticity tied to appropriate femininity. Speaking to this point is the work of Prisca Dorcas Mojica

Rodriguez, a self-identified chonga *mujerista* blogger, whose writing thinks through the resistant dimensions of chonga stylized politics. In her "Chonga Manifesto" Prisca (2016a)[2] articulates a narrative of self that takes sexual aesthetic excess as a site from which to creatively embody resistance. She writes: "I wanted to speak in affirmatives about our boldness, power, and resilience. Because this is not a disembodied document; this document is reflexive of real women, real chingonas, who on a daily basis embody their praxis of resisting assimilation and white-washing. We put our brown bodies on display to disrupt narratives of respectability" (2016a). Prisca reflects a negotiation of subjectivity that actively and creatively uses the body to shift the understanding of the self toward new ways of knowing. Here the sexual aesthetic excess troubles narratives of what is read as too sexy, cheap, or ethnic. Hypervisibility resists the assemblage of what it means to be a respectable and good Latina through the excessive aesthetic embodiment of categories that negotiate inclusion and exclusion. A further quote from "Chonga Manifesto" speaks to the resistant dimensions of chonga feminine style: "I understand that growing up poor meant that people distrusted me because of my aesthetics, so I learned a particular kind femininity, which bubbles to the surface as my class mobility. So when I wing my eyeliner, outline my lips, put on my mini skirt and crop top, I am adorning myself with my war paint and armor. Because to you, I am not human—but it's okay because to me and to those who understand: I am a goddess." The use of makeup, which many readily refer to as a disciplining feminine practice, is rearticulated creatively, resisting the disciplining of the body by a shift in meaning. Further, part of the methodology of resistance through the sexual aesthetic excess involves a call to spiritual life that centers the figure of the goddess. Prisca's account demonstrates the way chonga stylized resistance through the use of the sexual aesthetic excess participates in a process that creatively expands the narrative of the self and others by picking apart the paradigms that construct reality, the crux of the fifth station of conocimiento. In this capacity, chonga stylized resistance offers a window into the many practices through which we can dismantle and recompose the self, thus forging a path of toward conocomiento with the self and with others.

Conclusion

I have argued boomerang perception functions as a way of unknowing that deeply impacts horizontal relational possibility as it problematically constructs bodies of color through a white racial lens that leaves them

---

[2] The author prefers to be referred to by her first name. I will subsequently refer to her as Prisca.

disjointed and objectified. The impact of this perceptual process on Latinas is violent and traumatic. It leaves in its wake a distinction between real/fake that serves on face to protect a location from which one can speak. Claiming the status of 100 percent Latina through whatever means necessary (gender, race, nation) ensures a connection to a homeplace that grounds identity. However, the construction of this seeing/speaking circle is problematic in that it reflects the internalization of boomerang perception, which thwarts positive horizontal relationality that recognizes difference. The construction of myself as 100 percent authentic anything necessitates that I potentially construct others violently as fakes and exile them. The solution is found in mending the wounds of white perception horizontally, questioning how even our deepest senses of identity might necessitate the wounding of others, even when those others are mirrors of myself. I invite chongas as a vision of what resistant healing to the wound of boomerangs might look like.

References

Anzaldúa, Gloria E. 1999. *Borderlands/La Frontera: The New Mestiza.* 2nd ed. San Francisco: Aunt Lute Books.

Anzaldúa, Gloria E. 2002. "Now Let Us Shift . . . the Path of Conocimiento . . . Inner Work, Public Acts." In *This Bridge We Call Home: Radical Visions for Transformation*, edited by Cherríe Moraga and Gloria Anzaldúa, 540–78. New York: Routledge.

Hernandez, Jillian. 2009. "'Miss, You Look Like a Bratz Doll': On Chonga Girls and Sexual Aesthetic Excess." *NWSA Journal 21*, no. 3: 63–90.

Holland, Sharon Patricia. 2012. *The Erotic Life of Racism.* Durham, NC: Duke University Press.

Lugo-Lugo, Carmen R. 2014. "Latinas and the Fractures That Unite Us: (Re)examining the Pan-Ethnic Marker." *Journal of the Latino Research Center* 8: 124–42.

Lugo-Lugo, Carmen R. 2015. "100% Puerto Rican: Jennifer Lopez, Latinidad, and the Marketing of Authenticity." *Centro Journal* 28, no. 2: 96–119.

Lugones, María. 2003. *Pilgrimages/Peregrinajes: Theorizing Coalition against Multiple Oppressions.* Lanham, MD: Rowman & Littlefield.

Mendible, Myra. 2007. "Embodying Latinidad: An Overview." In *Bananas to Buttocks: The Latina Body in Popular Film and Culture*, edited by Myra Mendible, 1–28. Austin: University of Texas Press.

Ramírez, Catherine S. 2009. *Women in the Zoot Suit: Gender, Nationalism, and the Cultural Politics of Memory.* Durham, NC: Duke University Press.

Reichard, Raquel. 2014. "Why Some Latinas Are Reclaiming the Term 'Chonga.'" *Latina*, February 24. http://www.latina.com/lifestyle/our-issues/why-latinas-reclaiming-term-chonga.

Rodriguez, Prisca. 2016a. "Growing Up as a Brown Girl: My Chonga Manifesto." *HuffPost Latino Voices*, January 7. http://www.huffingtonpost.com/prisca-dorcas-mojica-rodriguez/growing-up-as-a-brown-gir_b_8877898.html.

Rodriguez, Prisca. 2016b. "I Don't Need Anyone to Recolonize My Decolonized Body." *HuffPost Latino Voices*, April 15. http://www.huffingtonpost.com/prisca-dorcas-mojica-rodriguez/becoming-pretty_b_9677256.html.

CHAPTER 15 | Deracializing Representations
of Femininity and the Marketing
of Latinidad

*Zoe Saldana and L'Oréal's True Match
Campaign*

CARMEN R. LUGO-LUGO AND MARY K.
BLOODSWORTH-LUGO

[Living in the Dominican Republic] gave us such a beautiful
understanding of our ancestry, and the beauty of what it's like to
be Latina. That, at the end of the day, is the biggest essence of my
sisters and me—that whatever we have in our character, our fire,
our stubbornness, our love, it's all because of our roots. We're so
proud of it.

—ZOE SALDANA (Rogers 2013)

I did it all for love . . . who I am and my pride of being a Black
woman and a Latina woman and an American woman. That's
my truth.

—ZOE SALDANA (HipHollywood 2013)

LATINIDAD, WHICH IS TO say the cultural elements shared among Latinas/
os, has been articulated alternatively as a contested political, economic,
and social process (Beltrán 2010), a set of (orthodox) notions about
Latinas/os (Dávila 2008), and a site producing knowledge about a Latina/
o other (Aparicio 2003). Thus, Latinidad has been explained as a process,
a set of ideas, or a symbolic space, situating it between a mechanism and a
locale. Regardless of its exact articulation or constitution, a central feature
of Latinidad involves its standing as a social construct; that is, an idea born
from and developed by forces through social interaction. Accordingly, we

Carmen R. Lugo-Lugo and Mary K. Bloodsworth-Lugo, *Deracializing Representations of Femininity
and the Marketing of Latinidad* In: *Theories of the Flesh*, Edited by: Andrea J. Pitts, Mariana Ortega,
and José Medina, Oxford University Press (2020). © Oxford University Press.
DOI: 10.1093/oso/9780190062965.003.0016

follow Isabel Molina Guzmán's lead in maintaining that Latinidad "is shaped by external forces, such as marketing, advertising, popular culture, and the U.S. Census, and internally through the individual subjectivities and communal and cultural expressions of people who identify as Latina/o" (2010, 3). The notion of a plurality of subjectivities is key, here, for even single individuals can display different ways of articulating their positionality as a Latina/o and within Latinidad. As a case in point, we can consider the pronouncements of Zoe Saldana, recounted in the epigraphs, in which she describes herself as Latina, black, *and* an American with Dominican background.

In this chapter, we focus on Latinidad not only as an identity, but perhaps more importantly, as an embodied experience that is mediated or at times driven by external influences. We highlight Saldana, since within the world of Latina celebrities embedded within the US popular culture landscape, she embodies one of the more rare sets of circumstances and combinations of ethnicity, phenotype, and character portrayals to be found. Since Saldana's body does not conform to Hollywood's expectations concerning the "look" of a Latina, those with casting authority seem more eager to place her in roles portraying black or alien characters (sometimes in bright colors) than as a Latina.

Even though Saldana's articulation of her Latinidad is an inclusive one, always allowing space for blackness and Americanness, it becomes clear that she has long struggled with how she views herself ethnically or racially in relation to how others perceive and treat her. In fact, we can even note vacillation in Saldana's own pronouncements of her identity, which serve to underscore the difficulty of grappling with her reality as a woman of color in the United States. For instance, in an interview for *InStyle* magazine, Saldana states:

> I would come home from school and go, "Mami, What am I?" You know, cause I'm getting all kinds of things and people are mean. And Mami would look at me and go, "You are Zoe . . . You're my daughter, your grandma's granddaughter, you're Zoe. My mom wouldn't go, "tu eres una mujer de color [you are a woman of color] and always remember it, this world is going to be rough." My mom never f******* told us that, why would she? Why would she stop my flight before I even take off? (Ramos 2013)

It is not clear what Saldana means by "getting all kinds of things and people are being mean"; however, given what follows in her statement, we can assume that she is commenting on people's perceptions and judgments of her vis-à-vis her race and/or appearance. Saldana also vacillates when grappling with the concept of "ethnicity," as she remarks, "I literally run away from people that use words like ethnic. It's preposterous! To me there is no such thing as people of color 'cause in reality people aren't white. Paper is white" (Dionne 2013). Saldana's conflation of race and ethnicity in this last statement is telling, given her erratic yet simultaneous embrace and dismissal of racial and ethnic categories.

In a piece for *Ebony*, a couple of years prior to the *InStyle* interview, Saldana raises her African heritage, positioning it differently within the United States and Latin America:

> We have a Black president right now, so why the f—— would I sit down and talk about how hard it is for Black women in Hollywood when there's a Black president in my country? I am proud of my roots. Primarily when I eat, I want rice and beans . . . I don't identify as much with U.S. American history as I do with Latin American history. And so, I have bones to pick with Latin American people. There's a lot of growing that we still have to do that we aren't doing. We have to continue accepting our indigenous and our African heritage just as much as we embrace our European [blood]. (Gibbs 2011)

It is apparent that regardless of what racial markers she utilizes to describe herself, Saldana feels more comfortable engaging with and even contesting her ethnicity. We can also note Saldana's response to the question, "Why did you change the spelling of your name, from Zaldaña to Saldana?" in *Hispanic* magazine. Saldana replies, "I wanted to make it easier for everyone. Zaldaña was too complicated for everyone else" (Hernández 2004). By way of these comments, we can note struggles to operationalize ethnicity, ancestry, and race, as Saldana seeks to position herself (and her body) both within and against American mainstream ideas about ethnicity and race. Thus, at the same time that she does "not identify with U.S. American history," she makes it easier "for everyone else" in the United States to spell her last name. In this respect, we can note the interchange between external forces and individual subjectivities, discussed by Molina Guzmán, as shaping, in this case, an individual's articulation of Latinidad.

Returning to Molina Guzmán's point that Latinidad is constituted by a mixture of "external" and "internal" forces, we would like to explore in this chapter the role of external forces in the shaping of Latinidad, as these have the potential to become widely used and to shape agreed-upon understandings about Latinas/os. We can see the impact of these collective understandings of Latinidad on mainstream perceptions of Latinas (some of which become hardened stereotypes) and how Saldana's comments sometimes mirror and other times counter these perceptions. Keeping with this point, we can note a pattern prevalent in popular culture and marketing that creates a new aesthetics of ethnicity by both deracializing how women of color—and Latinas, in particular—are portrayed, while paradoxically racializing how they are treated. As this pattern becomes dominant, we can see why Saldana may sometimes appear to evade "race" (in the form of American blackness) and other times to incorporate it as a feature of her identity (in the form of Latin American blackness). In the case of our earlier point regarding casting decisions within Hollywood, the channeling of Saldana into black or alien characters works, on the one hand, to highlight race and evade ethnicity (black characters), and on the other hand, evade race and ethnicity altogether (alien characters of various colors). This practice can be better understood when examining constructions of Latinas/os within the United States. Thus, in the next section we briefly address the difficult predicament in which Latinas/os find themselves when engaging with race and ethnicity—the contradictory partners and antagonists of the idea(l) of Latinidad.

Latinas/os: On "Not Moving Away from Race"

In her book *Visible Identities*, Linda Martín Alcoff offers one of the more recognized and compelling discussions available concerning the complications involved with contemporary understandings of race (as phenotype) and ethnicity (as culture) when applied to Latinas/os in the United States (Lugo-Lugo 2015). Alcoff notes, "What better unites Latinas/os both across and even within our specific national cultures is not race or phenotype but . . . those features associated with culture" (2006, 34). Although Alcoff positions the label in *proximity to* (and never fully *within*) ethnicity, in her words, "Using only ethnicity belies the reality of most Latinos' everyday experiences, as well as obscures our own awareness about how ethnic identifications often do the work of race while seeming to be theoretically correct and politically advanced" (247). Alcoff also cautions that in the case of Latinas/os, "moving away from race to ethnicity is not necessarily moving away from race" (38). Or, as Silvio Torres-Saillant categorically states, "Latinos cannot escape the preponderance of race in the United States" (2003, 130). The paradox embedded within racial/ethnic categories as they have been developed and deployed in relation to Latinas/os has created an illusion that Latinas/os are both an ethnicity and a race.

Alcoff's application of David Theo Goldberg's concept of "ethnorace," here, is likewise illuminating. Alcoff remarks, "Ethnorace might have the advantage of bringing into play both the elements of human agency and subjectivity involved in ethnicity . . . at the same time that it acknowledges the uncontrolled racializing aspects associated with the physical body"

(2006, 246). Torres-Saillant relays a similar sentiment when he claims, "When it comes to oppressed minorities of color, we do not need to know the difference [between race and ethnicity] if they both translate into a common exclusion and disempowerment. . . . Both are fictitious. Both come from a similar effort to imagine a collective internally or externally" (2003, 147). The fabricated "nature" of race and ethnicity (or ethnorace), which in turn leads to the fiction of Latinidad, is all the more relevant when we consider Torres-Saillant's point about "common exclusion and disempowerment," along with Alcoff's concern about "the reality of most Latinos' everyday experiences." That is, regardless of their fictitious character, both race and ethnicity impact how Latinas/os are able to live their lives within the United States.

Accordingly, the complicated relationship between "invented" categories and "real" experiences must be considered when studying the collective effort of "Latinos to imagine themselves" racially. Of note, the data of the last two US censuses (2000 and 2010) have produced interesting results when it comes to Latinas/os, now the largest minority group in the United States, claiming a particular racial background. In the 2010 census, only 2 percent of Latinas/os identified as black, not much different from the 2000 census, in which 1.8 percent of Latinas/os identified as black. This can be juxtaposed to the fact that the majority of Latinas/os (53 percent) identified as white in 2010, compared to 47 percent in 2000. In agreement with the census data, Isabel Molina Guzman points out that "it is rare to find Spanish Caribbean people or celebrities who are willing to identify as Black" (2013, 214; see also Hernández 2003). As Molina Guzmán notes, of those Latinas/os identifying as black or mixed-raced within the United States (6.4 percent and 4.5 percent in 2000 and 2010, respectively), most tend to trace their heritage back to the Spanish Caribbean, including Cuba, Puerto Rico, and the Dominican Republic (2013, 214).

As we witness a shift in the numerical landscape and racial claims of Latinas/os, we can also observe a swing in popular culture, mass media, and marketing forces, as all appear eager to engage with Latinas/os by offering audiences and consumers interesting—if sometimes misguided—representations of Latinidad as ethnicity. Thus, as Latinas/os are being forced to select a "race" on US census forms, television producers, marketing executives, Hollywood, and popular culture more generally have begun to move beyond the now antiquated portrayal of Latinas/os as a one-dimensional racial group to constructing Latinas/os as a cultural group instead—which is to say, an ethnicity. This circumstance presents a fundamental change in the representation of Latinas/os as an exclusively phenotypical group (exemplified by "brownface" portrayals in films such as *West Side Story*). Although, to paraphrase Alcoff, moving away from phenotypical representations is not moving away from phenotypical representations, we do think it is important to consider and analyze new marketing efforts that attempt to do precisely this. Consequently, we offer Zoe Saldana's "True Match" commercials for the L'Oréal Group to highlight a marketing project seeking to privilege cultural heritage over racial identity, while ironically selling an array of cosmetics items precisely premised on phenotypical markers and differences. We examine Saldana's role in L'Oréal's True Match campaign to address the deracialization of a new aesthetics of Latinidad. We claim that while Hollywood simplifies or obscures Saldana's racial identity by rendering it black or alien, L'Oréal's campaign demonstrates the shift from racial to cultural representations of Latinas/os outlined in this section.

Zoe Saldana's True Match: The Marketing of a Latina

In 2012, the L'Oréal Group launched an unorthodox campaign for marketing their True Match foundation makeup. Referencing the notion of a "skin mosaic," the campaign included both print advertisements and television commercials and originally featured three specific celebrities: Beyoncé Knowles, Aimee Mullins, and Jennifer Lopez. Later, the campaign added other celebrities, including Zoe Saldana. In essence, "Going beyond the 'different hues' approach that these types of advertisements have historically utilized, L'Oréal presented to consumers the ethnic background of each celebrity . . . by placing the corresponding ethnicity or ethnicities of each celebrity in the bottom left corners of the television screen or print advertisement" (Lugo-Lugo 2015, 97). The first set of commercials and advertisements described Beyoncé Knowles as African American, Native American, and French; they characterized Aimee Mullins as Irish, Austrian, and Italian; and they pronounced Jennifer López 100 percent Puerto Rican. Once Zoe Saldana's advertisement was added, she was characterized as Dominican, Haitian, Puerto Rican, and Lebanese. We focus on Saldana's advertisement, here, since it marks a contrast to that of Jennifer Lopez's claims to be "100 percent Puerto Rican," which place Lopez squarely within the Latina label. In the case of Saldana, the combination of her phenotype and assertions of varied ethnicities complicate not only her individual positionality but also Latinidad, which is in effect deracialized and exclusively situated within the realm of ethnic heritage.

Each True Match commercial in the campaign begins with a short voice-over narration of the celebrity stating, "There is a story behind my skin: It's a mosaic of all the faces before it. My only makeup: True Match." The commercial then proceeds to discuss L'Oréal's thirty-three shades of True Match foundation going from "light" to "dark." Viewers are told that these shades include warm, cool, or neutral tones. Each commercial ends with the celebrity looking into the camera and delivering a special line. In the case of Saldana, that line is "My skin, my story, my true match." The labeling of Zoe Saldana through the four ethnicities we have mentioned, occurs approximately two seconds into the nineteen-second commercial through a very close close-up of Saldana's face. Her right lower cheek (and thus she) is branded with the ethnicities for a couple of seconds. The print advertisements show a photo of Saldana with the following caption running across the bottom: "The story behind my skin: Dominican, Haitian, Puerto Rican, and Lebanese. Zoe Saldana. 100% True Match N7 Classic Tan."

Since the beginning of her career, Saldana has claimed to be a black Latina, which is, in itself, a novel identity in popular culture given that Latinas/os have been historically portrayed as "brown." However, Saldana's L'Oréal advertisements convert the idea of a black Latina into a mixing of two nationalities or ethnic groups within the "Latina/o" label (Dominican and Puerto Rican) with two groups outside of it (Haitian and Lebanese). Saldana, who has stated that when acting she is "[c]reating the unknown, imagining the unimaginable," has also said that she does not see herself "in Jane Austen books" (Cutter 2014, 150). Of course, it is her racial background, and not her ethnicities, that likely prevent her from seeing herself as a Jane Austen character. And Saldana's way of creating "the unknown and imagining the unimaginable" has allowed her to play some of the most racially interesting characters of any Latina in Hollywood.

When answering the question, "How does heritage fit in with her roles?" Saldana replied, "I've played a Na'vi, and I've played an African-American, and I'm African-Latino," adding, "Artists, we have to be chameleons. If the shoe fits, by all means put it on" (Gibbs 2011). However, in the end, the L'Oréal advertisements, like the characters she has played, are not her creation. While we believe (or at least hope) that the ethnicities listed by Saldana (and the other celebrities) are identities with which she (and they each) identifies, given that the self-representation between the celebrities is so uniform (for instance, they all list ethnic and not racial backgrounds), we suspect that the L'Oréal marketing team intervened in the portrayals.

The representations of Lopez, Saldana, and Knowles, as dissimilar as they might appear, remind us of Ronald Sundstrom's engagement with the idea of "the browning of America" as an "unrequited American desire to escape the encompassing burden of race" (2008, 2). Sundstrom also discusses "browning" as "a form of color blindness" used to argue against certain "color-conscious" social programs and policies (2008, 54). Thus, escaping "the encompassing burden of race" is to avoid the responsibility of racism. US census numbers notwithstanding, Latinas/os have been the quintessential not-so-racial, racialized ethnicity. Hollywood and news/

marketing firms have taken advantage of this fact, and in the end, Latinas/ os can be—and can be represented as—many things, except for black. In fact, Latinas/os might provide the ultimate escape for the United States vis-à-vis the burden of race and racism while still permitting engagement with an "other." As Isabel Molina Guzmán conveys:

> Mainstream news and media industry journals such as *Variety* and *Ad Age* celebrate the "browning of America" by highlighting the increased vis- ibility of Spanish, Latin American, and US Latina/o actors; the growing demographic importance of Latina/o audiences; and the ability of Latina/o actors to draw in potentially more diverse and larger global audiences in the United States, Latin America, and Europe, among other sites. (2013, 211)

She adds, "In doing so, the entertainment industry press racially homogenizes Spanish, Latin American, and Latina/o actors as brown and racializes US Latina/o actors as culturally exotic foreigners, a cul- tural process" (2013, 211). Molina Guzmán (2010) defines this process as symbolic colonization and points out that in this representational schema, black Latina/o actors such as Saldana are left to carve out spaces for them- selves through nontraditional representations of Latinidad or through representations of US blackness. We move beyond Molina Guzmán's idea of symbolic colonization and the racialization of Latinas/os as brown by arguing that a new pattern is emerging in which Latina/o celebrities are systematically deracialized and re-ethnicized. The emphasis on ethnicity over race creates a new aesthetics that allows Latinas/os to inconsistently acknowledge race and treat it as a separate phenomenon from ethnic or cultural background, as depicted in interviews with Saldana at the start of this chapter.

The fact that the entertainment industry still racially homogenizes Latinas/os as brown does not contradict the fact that, as we have argued, popular culture appears to be moving beyond unidimensional racial representations of Latinas/os, for racial homogenization is a historical fact, and "moving beyond" is a recent trend. Both exist in our society today, and this coexistence allows Saldana to claim Haitian and Lebanese ancestry in a commercial, while still proclaiming to be Latina, all the while portraying black and alien characters alike.

Conclusion: Her Skin, Her Story, Her True Match

As we conclude, and given that we have developed an argument con- cerning aesthetics in this chapter, we should address one final point in relation to Saldana—the issue of Saldana and black aesthetics. While it is impossible to negate the fact that Saldana has found herself straddling a line between Latinidad and blackness, and while Latinidad vis-à-vis Saldana has never been called into question publicly or rendered controversial, the same cannot be said of her blackness. This issue recently came to the fore in relation to Saldana's selection to portray Nina Simone in the biopic *Nina* (Mort 2016). We refer to Paul C. Taylor's (2016) discussion of this topic in his book *Black Is Beautiful*, to briefly address this issue.

Taylor relays that Saldana's filmic portrayal of Simone was "unwelcome" by fans of the real-life Simone (2016, 35). He notes that the blogosphere reacted to the casting of Saldana by pointing to a perceived "erasure of Nina Simone's image" (35). Given the account developed by Taylor, "To be black in places like the United States has, for a very long time, involved having one's life chances indexed to the way one looks in quite particular and far-reaching ways" (64). In the case of Simone, Taylor maintains, "The personhood of Nina Simone, the ineluctably black personhood of a political activist and culture worker whose identity was bound up with black struggle and certain attendant modes of self-presentation has been effaced by the market imperatives that attach to Zoe Saldana" (67). Consequently, by "turning the Nina Simone story into a Zoe Saldana vehicle," "aspects of the story that make it interesting for a certain kind of black (or anti-whitely resistant) spectator" are "effectively set aside" (68).

Taylor develops the notion of "market imperatives" in this instance by indicating that the casting only appears "reasonable," if at all, "because Ms. Saldana is black *enough*, because any blackness would make her black enough" (68). The difficulty, as pointed out by Taylor, lies in the "different paths that light- and dark-skinned blacks sometimes take through the world," and that "the different meanings that attach to their bodies in properly racialized cultures are some settings worth taking seriously" (68). Differences between light- and dark-skinned blacks "might matter for casting" if the setting of Nina Simone's story is "shaped by the[se] imperatives" (68–69). As preparation for filming, Saldana's skin was darkened, and she was fitted for prosthetics to help her "match" Simone's likeness. This fact matters, for Taylor, and makes the portrayal different from other cases in which actors have changed their appearance to play a part.

Taylor's invocation of the "market imperatives" attached to Saldana is important, for in the case of her marketed Latinidad—or, that which makes her light-skinned—her blackness is clearly offset. And while we do not wish to engage in a comparative analysis between black and Latina/o aesthetics, it is also important to note Taylor's point that while Saldana might be "black enough" to portray Simone, from a Hollywood-ized perspective, she is not Nina Simone black. Thus, on the account provided by Taylor,

Saldana's Latinidad (and perhaps other ethnic elements or aspects) render her too light-skinned to portray the imperatives of Nina Simone's story. In the case of the L'Oréal True Match marketing campaign, phenotypical differences are run through ethnicity, so to speak, which clearly erases blackness in the production and promotion of the story lent to Saldana (and others). At the same time, insofar as Saldana's body is displayed in both the print and television ads themselves, her blackness is still visible and on display. This has been the predicament for Saldana—that in certain contexts, she is critiqued for not being "black enough," while in other settings, it is her very blackness that stands in the way of the project. We have maintained that in L'Oréal's marketing, Latinidad is deracialized in favor of an ethnicized aesthetic, rendering Saldana's blackness also marginal.

So, returning to Latinidad, if, as Beltrán states, Latinidad is both "a site of ongoing resignifiability—a political rather than a descriptive category" and "a moment when diverse and even disparate subjects claim identification with one another" (2010, 9 and 168), and if we heed Dávila's words that Latinidad can be "treated as an empty signifier within our ravenous global economy that shuns specificity, especially whenever profitable" (2014, 550), then the question becomes, what more can we make of Saldana's L'Oréal advertisements and their accompanying message? We should note that as a marketing strategy:

> The company chose to highlight the ethnic instead of the racial background of these celebrities, for it shows a certain level of understanding in regards to the distinction between the two, and perhaps more important, it signals that the L'Oréal Group felt more comfortable marketing ethnicity rather than race. . . . Think, for instance, that the idea of skin as a mosaic notwithstanding, Mullins had as much a claim to 100 percent whiteness as Lopez had to 100 percent Puerto Ricanness. We could also argue that, given the history of racial and ethnic constructions in this country, Knowles also had a claim to being 100 percent African American or Black (American). Instead, the L'Oréal Group [allows] Lopez to claim 100 percent Puerto Ricanness, while the whiteness of Mullins is disguised under several European ethnicities, and the blackness of Knowles is mediated by several ethnicities as well. (Lugo-Lugo 2015, 99)

In a sense, by accounting for both Latina/o and non-Latina/o ethnic backgrounds in Saldana, the set of advertisements simultaneously reifies Latinidad and reframes its scope. And although we would not question or attempt to measure Saldana's Latinidad (in relation to a Latino/a aesthetics), it is important to note that her body is being deployed to expand the notion of Latinidad itself. That is, considering the L'Oréal advertisements shows that Latinidad is both anchored in specificity and adrift in global capacity. The makeup company shows an investment in portraying the women in their campaign as ethnic hybrids (in fact, with the exception of Jennifer Lopez, and now Frida Pinto, who is described as 100 percent Indian, every featured celebrity claims no fewer than three ethnicities). Saldana is shown as a Latina who is a "new" Latina—as the ultimate hybrid capable of claiming both Latina/o and non-Latina/o ancestry. She is shown by L'Oréal to embody a new aesthetics wherein her Latinidad, blackness, and Americanness, though particular to her, are also universal in scope. Although it is "her skin, her, story, her true match," foundation bottles labeled "N7 Classic Tan" ultimately must have crossover appeal. And that is the perhaps the best lesson we can learn from the role of outside forces on current articulations of Latinidad.

References

Alcoff, Linda. 2006. *Visible Identities: Race, Gender, and the Self.* Oxford: Oxford University Press.

Aparicio, Frances. 2003. "Jennifer as Selena: Rethinking Latinidad in Media and Popular Culture." *Latino Studies* 1, no. 1: 90–105.

Beltrán, Cristina. 2010. *The Trouble with Unity: Latino Politics and the Creation of Identity.* Oxford: Oxford University Press.

Cutter, Kimberly. 2014. "All Eyes on Zoe." *Marie Claire* 21, no. 8: 144–50.

Dávila, Arlene. 2008. *Latino Spin: Public Image and the Whitewashing of Race.* New York: NYU Press.

Dávila, Arlene. 2014. "Locating Neoliberalism in Time, Space and 'Culture.'" *American Quarterly* 66, no. 3: 549–55.

Dionne, Evette. 2013. "Girl, Bye: Zoe Saldana Claims 'People of Color' Don't Exist." *Clutch*, May 17. http://www.clutchmagonline.com/2013/05/girl-bye-zoe-saldana-claims-people-of-color-dont-exist/#comment-1319756541.

Gibbs, Adrienne S. 2011. "Zoë in Wonderland." *Ebony* 66: 109.

Hernández, Ambar. 2004. "Zoe Saldana: From Dancer to Pirate to Office, This Actress Is Ready for More Roles." *Hispanic*, June, 72.

Hernández, Tanya K. 2003. "'Too Black to Be Latino/a': Blackness and Blacks as Foreigners in Latino Studies." *Latino Studies* 1, no. 1: 152–59.

HipHollywood. 2013. "Zoe Saldana Admits Being a Proud Black and Latina Woman." *HipHollywood*, February 27. https://www.youtube.com/watch?v=S4i6v5Xph3Q.

Lugo-Lugo, Carmen. 2015. "100% Puerto Rican: Jennifer Lopez, Latinidad, and the Marketing of Authenticity." *Centro Journal* 18, no. 2: 96–119.

Molina Guzmán, Isabel. 2010. *Dangerous Curves: Latina Bodies in the Media.* New York: New York University Press.

Molina Guzmán, Isabel. 2013. "Commodifying Black and Latinidad in US Film and Television." *Popular Communication* 11, no. 3: 211–26.

Mort, Cynthia, director. 2016. *Nina Simone.* Ealing Studios Entertainment.

Ramos, Zuania. 2013. "Zoe Saldana Talks Race, Beauty and Love on Revealing Interviews with InStyle and Latina." *Huff Post Latino Voice*, April 2. http://www.huffingtonpost.com/2013/04/02/zoe-saldana-latina-instyle-_n_3000938.html.

Rogers, Ray. 2013. "Zoe Saldana Talks Nina Simone Biopic." *Ocean Drive,* December 11. http://oceandrive.com/personalities/articles/zoe-saldana-on-playing-nina-simone.

Sundstrom, Ronald. 2008. *The Browning of America and the Evasion of Social Justice.* Albany: SUNY Press.

Taylor, Paul C. 2016. *Black Is Beautiful: A Philosophy of Black Aesthetics.* Malden, MA: Wiley Blackwell.

Torres-Saillant, Silvio. 2003. "Inventing the Race: Latinos and the Ethnoracial Pentagon." *Latino Studies* 1, no. 1: 123–51.

CHAPTER 16 | *Cámara* Queer
Longing, the Photograph, and Queer
Latinidad

MARIANA ORTEGA

> As an archival object the photograph's power derives as much
> from its affective magic as from its realist claims.
>
> —ANN CVETKOVICH (2014, 276)

THIS CHAPTER IS ABOUT visuality, ambivalence, and longing. And it is about
love, lust, and desire, my desire for women in all their ways of being women.[1]
As a Latina queer lesbian, I wonder about loss, not the loss of an official visual
archive or history of Latina women whose desire for women leads them to
loves of which many still dare not speak their names—but about a loss that
I feel in my day-to-day being in the world, a world in which women who
love and desire women experience violence, especially if they are women of
color; a world in which I need the company of a past that represents me; a
world in which an image written with light of those like me can bring com-
fort. Piercingly, it is about a loss of something that perhaps never was and is
in need of construction. The photograph both reveals and hides this loss.

In its language of light, the photograph has always called me, sometimes
more so than combinations of pigment and oil surrendered on a canvas. The
photograph touches me because, as Barthes reminds us, it shows a "that has

---

[1] Here I write about "love," "lust," and "desire." These terms point to complex practices and
ways of being that may or may not be intertwined in different contexts. I do not wish to conflate
them but I also do not wish to emphasize any of them as I examine how they are represented in
artistic production. Moreover, when I refer to "woman" I do not only mean women who have
been categorized as "women" at birth given biological features but include trans women as well as
genderqueer women. The phrase "women who love women" is not meant to indicate exclusionary,
essentialist lesbian identity.

Mariana Ortega, *Cámara Queer* In: *Theories of the Flesh*, Edited by: Andrea J. Pitts, Mariana Ortega,
and José Medina, Oxford University Press (2020). © Oxford University Press.
DOI: 10.1093/oso/9780190062965.003.0017

been," a portion of reality that has been placed before the lens (Barthes 1981, 77 and 115). But I know better. So did Barthes, as his punctum was a call to the affective dimension of the photograph despite its claim to indexicality (Brown and Phu 2014, 5).[2] What the photograph discloses may be not only a reality that has been trapped with light and hardened for the ages, the "that has been," but an open door to feeling and to the construction of a "has been that never was," chemical reactions fixed on metal and paper that represent desires and lusts, longings and yearnings.[3] So I think of David Deitcher looking at an old photograph of two young men sitting. Deitcher thinks that their pose is telling the viewer, "You know what we're about." He asks,

> Who are these two men, looking out across time from the other side of a sliver of glass? I am powerfully drawn to them, as I am to this old photograph and to others that share its most salient feature: the registration of physical affection between men from long ago. (Deitcher 1998, 23)

Deitcher wishes to know who these men are, as if knowing about love and desire could be fixed and stable.[4] But he is also afraid to find out that their friendly embrace is just that, a friendly embrace, and not the gesture of a love that dare not speak its name. He feels dismay in the face of the light that brings these men into being and, at the same time, causes them to fade away. Yet Deitcher chooses the "less grounded imaginary association" than empirical reality; he gives in to his longing that what he sees is two men in love (1998, 31). He is looking for a history of gay desire, gay love, gay presence, one that cannot be snuffed out, as he says the history of gay desire has been (23), or a history of sexuality that, as Laura Pérez says, has been "rendered spectral through discrimination" (Pérez 2007, 176).

Deitcher's wish to find, to construct, a visual history of gay desire/sexuality/love, prompts a certain uneasiness in me, because he is looking for photographic representations of the history of white gay men, and thus he continues

---

[2] See Brown and Phu 2014 for a collection of essays that disclose the different ways in which the photograph evokes feelings. Brown and Phu are thus in search of "affective archives" that allow us to reframe the history of photography given its emphasis on indexicality. They consider Barthes's notion of the punctum as key in queering photography and in disclosing its affective elements. As they state,

> Reading Barthes's moving reflections on photography attuned to the sensuous dimensions of his phenomenology helps disclose with jarring literalism the sexually loaded charge of the punctum, as a "prick" that arouses desire in photography . . . the punctum is a powerful concept because it, in fact, introduces a theory of feeling photography. This is a theory of feeling photography that, accordingly, amounts to a queering of photography. (5)

[3] I thank José Medina for this expression and for pushing me to think not just about the loss of something that was present and lost but also about the loss of something that was never there—"a that has been that never was."

[4] Desire is complex, changing through time and experiences—as we become attuned to signs of interest, arousal, attraction.

Anonymous, *Two Seated Men*, circa 1869. Collection of the International Center of Photography.

to center whiteness. As José Esteban Muñoz points out, there has been a "normativity of whiteness" in mainstream North American gay culture and in gay, lesbian, and queer studies of the late 1990s.[5] Yet, when looking at these two men and reading Deitcher's interpretation of the photograph, I also feel a deep longing—that of finding visual representations of Latinas who love and desire women. Immediately an image by Alma López comes to mind:

Why this image and not an old photograph of two Latina women touching as if to tell us, "Sabes lo que somos" or a well-known photograph depicting Latina lesbian desire and love? [6] As Pérez comments, this

[5] While there have been changes and the voices of those of color are more present, white queerness usually takes the center stage (Muñoz 1999, 9). For work on queers of color see Anzaldúa and Moraga 1981; Anzaldúa 1987, 1998; Chávez-Silverman and Hernández 2000; Cuevas 2018; Eng, Halberstam, and Muñoz 2005; Eng 2010; Ferguson 2004; Gaspar de Alba 2003; Gopinath 2005; Hames-García 2011; Johnson 2001; Johnson and Henderson 2005; La Fountain-Stokes 2009; Manalansan 2003; Massad 2007; Mitchell 2010; Muñoz 1999, 2009; Puar 2007; Rivera-Servera 2012; Rodriguez 2003, 2014; Vaid 2012; and Wat 2001.

[6] Latina artists have captured Latina lesbians in their lenses. Laura Aguilar's *Latina Lesbians* Series (1986–1989) is key in the history of Latina lesbians. See Yarbro-Bejarano 1998 for an important analysis of Aguilar's photography. See Gómez-Barris 2017a and 2017b for recent commentaries. See also Jones 1998. See Mitchell 2010 for an analysis of histories of Latina/o

Alma Lopez, *Lupe & Sirena in Love*, 1999. Sirena Series.

image is "symbolically claiming visibility for lesbian desire within traditional popular culture and religious culture" (Pérez 2007, 176). In this Chicana vision, sexuality, race, nationality, religion converge and remind us of the intersectional character of our existences. According to Pérez, Lopez's backdrop in this image "suggests that a history of intolerance of queer presence is also our legacy, interrogating the gender and sexual politics of Mexican and Chicana/o anti-imperialist discourses" (176). For me, as it does for Pérez, the image raises the question of Latina lesbian

sexualities. For well-known commentaries on Latina lesbians see Rueda Esquivel 2006; Torres and Pertusa 2003; Trujillo 1991; and Ramos 1987.

desire in connection to popular culture and a problematic history of intolerance within Chicana/o discourse. It also raises the possibility impossible desires and encounters in the context of the lives of Latinas who love and desire women.

I long to see Latina desire, lust, and love for women written with light, but I also wish to think more about this "queer presence" Pérez mentions. Here I thus examine photographic representations of queer Latinidad. First, I briefly discuss the terms "queer"[7] and "Latinidad" so as to suggest how these two terms problematize simple dichotomies and readings of what counts as Latinidad. Second, I appeal to Muñoz's notion of disidentification in order to analyze work by two contemporary Latino photographers, Manny Serratos and Ken Gonzales-Day. Finally, I connect the notion of disidentification and melancholia with the ambivalent, melancholic longing originally brought about by *Two Seated Men*. According to Muñoz, melancholy allows him (and other queers of color) "to take his dead with him." For me melancholic longing discloses the ever-complex terrain of the relationship between memory, belonging, and desire, a terrain of incessant mourning and loss that both pierces and tenderly embraces, and that is brought forth and hidden in writings with light.

Queer(ing) and Latinidad

Representations of two young men possibly loving each other in the nineteenth century and Lupe and Sirena loving are, as Muñoz would say, openings to new worlds. Yet they take me into a state of ambivalence, because they prompt both uneasiness and longing. They also portray the real and the imagined. While both *Two Seated Men* and *Lupe & Sirena in Love* may be read in light of simple binaries and uncontroversial histories, they need to be read through the lens of love, desire, and lust that is ever multilayered. Queer Latinidad is expansive—I thus need to go beyond the polarities of lesbian and gay, homosexuality and heterosexuality. We must turn to the queer in its queerness.

Here I use the term "queer" as an acknowledgment that sexuality is fluid and open-ended and that it may present itself in a plurality of ways.[8] While

---

[7] It is important to acknowledge the problematic status of the term "queer." "Queer" is a Euro-American signifier that has become the preferred term to describe those whose desire and sexuality is not confined to heteronormativity. Yet it is also connected to a liberal, humanist view that centers right-based claims that can be subject to cultural imperialist practices. See Massad 2002 for a discussion of the "Gay International." See Viteri 2014 for an account of the limits of the use of the term "queer" and other terms in the context of LGBT "Latinos" in Washington, DC, San Salvador, and Quito.

[8] According to Gloria Anzaldúa, by appealing to queerness, there is "more room for maneuver" (1998, 266). Ian Barnard explains that "queer is not a substitute for gay" (2004, 10). He points

I understand the complexity of debates that advocate for gay and lesbian identities, I wish to call for representations of Latinx[9] sexualities that go beyond traditional dichotomies despite my initial longing as "una de las otras" to find visual representations of Latina women who love women, a longing that may be read as only an appeal to lesbian identity.[10] However, I am interested in a visuality of queer Latinidad that acknowledges multiple desires and identifications. But first, let us remember Anzaldúa's warning about the term "queer:"

> Queer is used as a false unifying umbrella which all "queers" of all races, ethnicities, and classes are shoved under. At times we need this umbrella to solidify our ranks against outsiders. But even when we seek shelter under it we must not forget that it homogenizes, erases our difference. Yes, we may all love members of the same sex, but we are not the same. Our ethnic communities deal differently with us. (Anzaldúa 1998, 264)

Anzaldúa thus reminds us that race, ethnicity, class, nationality, religion, ability, and other social locations cannot be neatly separated from sexuality.

In addition to understanding the ways in which the term "queer" goes beyond an umbrella categorization of sexuality and beyond simple dichotomies such as gay/lesbian, it is important to understand how "Latinidad" goes beyond meaning "all things Latino" as it is commonly understood. "Latinidad" does not simply mean an organic understanding and appreciation of all things Latino or a valorizing of seemingly "authentic" cultural practices challenging colonialist and imperialist US ideology, as David Román and Alberto Sandoval claim (Aparicio and Chávez-Silverman 1997, 15). According to Aparicio and Chávez-Silverman, Latinidad describes "the set of images and attributes superimposed onto both Latin American and U.S. Latino subjects from the dominant sector" (15). Such images and attributes are the object of what they consider "hegemonic tropicalization."[11]

---

out that one of the strengths of the appeal to "queer" is that the term can be used to refer to gay and lesbian but also to disrupt that which is gay and lesbian. The term "queer" stands as a deconstructive position outside of the heterosexual/homosexual binary and points to practices that challenge heteronormativity.

[9] "Latinx" is a term that has recently become more popular to designate various sexualities and genders in the Latinx community that go beyond gay and straight and male and female. It has replaced "Latin@s," which was originally introduced to problematize the masculine ending in the Spanish plural.

[10] "Una de las otras" means "one of the others" and is Anzaldúa's preferred way to describe herself. She objected to the term "lesbian" because she considered it white and middle class and "representing an English only dominant culture" (1998, 265). She said that if she had to choose a term to describe herself, she would use "queer" or "dyke."

[11] Aparicio and Chávez-Silverman (1997) explain that to tropicalize means "to trope, to imbue a particular space, geography, group, or nation with a set of traits, images, and values" (8). Tropicalizing from a First World perspective is a hegemonic move. Aparicio and Chávez-Silverman

Against this trend of hegemonic tropicalization, Ana María Rodriguez queers the notion of Latinidad and understands the term as "the point in which discourses of history, geography, and language practices collide" rather than with national and cultural identities (Rodriguez 2003, 9). In this view, "Latinidad" allows for the possibility to question the systems of categorization that have defined Latinidad in the first place, just as "queer" allows for a questioning of heteronormativity and systems of categorization of sexuality. Thus, Latinidad encompasses not only designations of particular groups, and a general umbrella group for different "Latinos" but, like the term "queer," questions the very practices and systems that have attempted to define Latinidad—or as Aparicio and Chávez-Silverman would have it, the various tropicalizations underlying the definitions of Latinxs and Latin Americans. Keeping these important understandings of "queer" and "Latinidad," let us now return to the image of Lupe and Sirena in love.

Through a queer lens, *Lupe & Sirena in Love* is not only about lesbian desire and love. It is about recognizing the different possibilities of Chicanas and other Latinxs, whether lesbian identified or not, to desire or love other women; questioning the narrow religious construction that Guadalupe may represent; problematizing the geographies and borders that suppress immigrant Latinas; countering hegemonic instantiations about what it means to be a good Latina; recognizing the multiplicity of desires that have a place in our visual imaginary; and finding new desires, even in the face of erasure. *Lupe & Sirena in Love* discloses a longing of what exists, even if only in the imagination and through this longing—as a history of past visual representation of women-loving Latinas may or may not exist and I, like Deitcher, will have to construct it, as he wishes to construct a visual history of gay love. Like Deitcher, I also appeal to imagination and I let myself be haunted by queer spirits of a time past that will always accompany us now, even when they cannot be seen.[12] I also "look backwards" (Love 2009) not to redeem the past, or to forge an official constructive archive of photographic representations of Latinas who love women, to romanticize the past, or to be directed to

---

consider both the Anglo-American tropicalizations of Latin America (what produces a mythic idea of Latinidad) as well as tropicalizations arising from the so-called Third World that may have subversive potential and thus challenge Latinidad's own ideological constructions and problematize the monolingualism, ethnocentrism, and sexism in Anglo, Latino, and Latin American cultures. Rather than using the singular term "tropicalization" (as in "orientalism") they thus pluralize the term so as to show its bidirectionality.

[12] Here I refer to "haunting" in the sense that I wish capture that which is not present but lingers, something that is missing but that is in need of our attention. See Gordon 1997 for the fascinating and influential analysis of haunting in this sense. I think of *espíritus* in the context of work by Anzaldúa and other Latina feminists who appeal to the spirit world for guidance.

a positive future, but to acknowledge "the longing that characterizes the relationship between past and present" (31), as difficult as this past is.[13]

Disidentifications: Queering Light

In this queer spectral longing, I am moved by those representations that are not easily understood as assimilating or opposing structures of dominant ideologies but that in the words of the late José Esteban Muñoz, disidentify with such ideologies. Disidentification, according to Muñoz, is "descriptive of the survival strategies the minority subject practices in order to negotiate a phobic majoritarian public sphere that continually elides or punishes the existence of subjects who do not conform to the phantasm of normative citizenship" (Muñoz 1999, 4). "Disidentification for the minority subject is a mode of recycling or re-forming an object that has already been invested with powerful energy" (39). Disidentification happens at the level of artistic production or reception and is also a "making over," a "transfiguration," a "mode of recycling," that is attuned to the intersection of identities. One of his examples of disidentification include Marga Gomez's performance in which she portrays a truck-driving lesbian as sexy and glamorous rather than as an object of contempt and hate, as this identity is usually described in dominant culture. The point, then, is not simply identifying with a chosen object or symbol but to transform or transfigure it, thus making worlds anew (Muñoz 1999, xi). Another example provided by Muñoz is that of Isaac Julien's *Looking for Langston*, as well as instances of black men finding desire and pleasure in the photographs of black male bodies by Mapplethorpe, which have been interpreted as objectifying and demeaning of black male bodies. Yet, for Muñoz, this latter example illustrates a disidentificatory pleasure that both acknowledges what is disturbing in Mapplethorpe's work and that this pleasure cannot be easily dismissed.[14] Here the black body is "made

---

[13] Heather Love writes about "the negative affects—the need, the aversion, and the longing—that characterize the relation between past and present." She states that

this decision to look on the dark side comes out of my sense that contemporary critics tend to describe the encounter with the past in idealizing terms. In particular, the models that these critics have used to describe queer cross-historical relations—friendship, love, desire, and community—seem strangely free of the wounds, the switchbacks, and the false starts that give these structures their specific appeal, their binding power. (2009, 31)

For Love, the queer past is always bound up with loss (51).

[14] A deeply important feature of Muñoz's work is precisely this recognition of the complexity and multilayeredness of desire. Muñoz does not leave us with simplistic, dichotomous accounts of desire. He recognizes that is possible for a black man to find Mapplethorpe's photographs of black men both provocative and injurious. The power of the notion of disidentification rests in this rejection of purity and fragmented dichotomies, in the recognition and even affirmation of ambiguity and ambivalence as always already there within our desires.

over," transfigured, in the eye and the mind—"The object that is desired is reformatted so that dignity and grace are not eclipsed by racist exploitation" (72). Disidentification, then, works within dominant ideologies in order to disrupt them.[15] As we will see, disidentification is connected to melancholia, understood in Freudian contexts as a mourning that does not end. The longing within me initially prompted by *Two Seated Men* is an ambivalent, melancholic longing in that it is prompted by both loss and the desire to make new worlds. But let us turn to other representations of queer Latinidad written with light and see what disidentifications we may find.

Sinners to Saints by Manny Serratos

 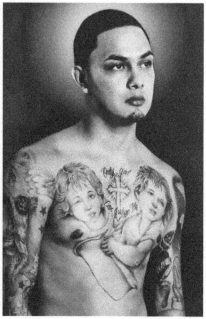

In the series Sinners to Saints Manny Serratos presents tattooed Latino male bodies as strong, desirable, and sensuous, unlikely in dominant white

---

[15] It is interesting to note that disidentification does not just disrupt dominant ideologies. It disrupts the photograph itself. In *Camera Obscura* Barthes claims that a photograph is never a memory; rather, it is a countermemory, one that is "violent," not because it portrays a violent act but because it "fills the sight by force" (1981, 91). According to Barthes, given this violence, nothing can be refused or transformed in the photograph. Muñoz's account of disidentification is very much an example of the very possibility of transformation that happens when we view photographs. In this sense, Muñoz's discussion of disidentification as connected to the photographic image goes beyond Barthes.

culture in which such bodies are feared and suspect. In the second photograph the fullness of the lips, lips touched by amaranth red invoking the feminine, serve as a punctum that leads the viewer to wonder about this body's sensuousness and sexuality. An image that is used to "exploit and deny" identity becomes pleasurable, erotic, and self-affirming (Muñoz 1999, 74). Not only that, these bodies are not on their path to hell, as the dominant religious and cultural paradigms may attest, but are protected, as the auras of light around their heads place them above the human and closer to heaven—and as is tattooed on one of the bodies, "only god can judge" them.

There is a "transfiguration" at work here of what Daniel Enrique Pérez calls the "queer macho," a figure that Pérez thinks has been prevalent in Chicano/Latino cultural production for decades and that destabilizes the straight/gay and macho/maricón binary and that he finds in the works of Latino artists Alex Donis and Hector Silva (Pérez 2009, 12). For Pérez, the "queer macho" figure removes both the "queer" and the "macho" from their historically abject state so that their stereotypes can be dismantled. It also accepts contradictory elements and gives them new light. Queering the macho frees this figure from the misogyny and violence that he is usually associated with. As he notes, "The queer macho permits Chicano/Latino men to be portrayed as courageous and heroic, masculine and feminine, (homo)erotic and beautiful. The queer macho challenges both heteronormative and gay paradigms" (Pérez 2009, 10). Serratos's photographs thus open up new possibilities for queerly understanding the "homeboy" figure, and for disrupting hegemonic tropicalizations of Latinos. Disidentification is at work at various levels in these photographs: the "gangbanger" as sensual, the Latino as desirable, the "derelict" as saintly. Serratos is working from within the dominant culture, neither completely assimilating his subjects to dominant views of a violent Latino culture nor completely rejecting them.[16]

While Serratos's photographs in *Sinners to Saints* point to disidentification as a way to destabilize the macho/maricón binary and can be understood as part of a visual history of queer Latinidad, photographs by Ken Gonzales-Day from his series *Profiled* present us with another

---

[16] While the title of the series, *Sinners to Saints*, points to a dichotomy of the bad sinner and good saint and a possible linear narrative, these men do not fit neatly into such dichotomy and cannot be simply understood as having changed their ways from sinners to saints such that now they remain in a special place worthy of admiration. Dominant norms and practices may change through time. Disidentification does not rest on a linear vision of time and transfiguration; it can be understood as connected to the perils of change and fluctuations of power. Muñoz admits that while disidentification has tremendous transformative potential and great possibility for empowering queers of color, he admits that it is not always an adequate strategy of resistance or survival for all minority subjects, as sometimes resistance needs to be direct (Muñoz 1999, 5).

possibility of disidentification by juxtaposing unlikely figures so that an opening is made for a new world of desire and interaction that cut across races and racism.

Consider *Untitled II* from the series:

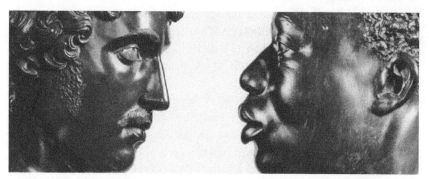

Untitled II (Antico [Pier Jacopo Alari-Bonacolsi], *Bust of a Young Man* and Francis Harwood, *Bust of a Man*, The J. Paul Getty Museum, Los Angeles), 2010, Lighjet on aluminum.

In *Untitled II* we find an unlikely pair facing each other: the bust of a classical figure representative of the Western ideal of whiteness, and an eighteenth-century bust of a black figure, representative of the non-Western, what is usually relegated to anthropological musings. An initial reading of this work suggests Gonzales-Day's purposeful use of the history of profiling both in Western aesthetics and law enforcement in order to counter the ideals of Western beauty, ideals that become pieces of marble, bronze, or wood forgotten in the storerooms of famous museums such as the ones in which Gonzales-Day found the objects for the photographs of this series.[17] No longer are these objects so far away temporally and spatially. Indeed, the gap in time of these cultural productions could be considered as symbolic of the space between the practices connected to the admiration of Western ideals and those practices relegated to typing, classifying non-Western undesirable bodies. Here they are together, facing each other, ready to have a conversation . . . or are they?

---

[17] A fascinating aspect of this series is that Gonzales-Day traveled extensively to various famous museums such as the J. Paul Getty Museum, the Museum of National History in Chicago, as well as well-known museums in Europe to find the busts and sculptures for his series, but he did not pick famous works in the galleries. Instead he sought out pieces from the storerooms of these museums, pieces that were destined to be forgotten.

As opposed to interpretations of the series that highlight the element of cross-cultural communication,[18] a queer reading of this photograph points to the intertwining of race, class, and sexuality. In my reading, Gonzales-Day is offering a possibility for a new world in which these two figures symbolic of radically different and dichotomous worlds of taste, class, race, power can desire each other. Consider a variation of the work:

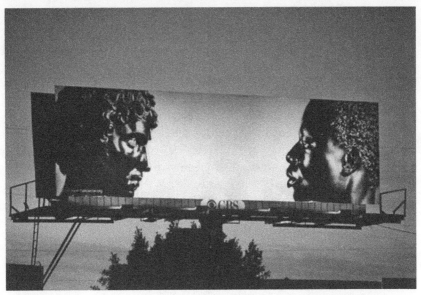

Untitled (Antico [Pier Jacopo Alari-Bonacolsi], *Bust of a Young Man* and Francis Harwood, *Bust of a Man*, The J. Paul Getty Museum, Los Angeles), in *How Many Billboards* http://howmanybillboards.org/, MAK Center for Art and Architecture.

Against the backdrop of the Los Angeles sky at dusk, a queer reading emerges. I see these two figures and find possibilities of sensuous bodily communication. Western and non-Western, white and black are not necessarily condemned to a "face off" or to remain in separate times and spaces, without possibility of sexual contact that is not forced, colonial, imperial. I thus find a kind of disidentificatory pleasure in this work by interpreting the symbolic body of color not in its abject position in dominant society but as full of sensuous and sexual possibilities.[19] I "make

---

[18] The critic Mark Feeney writes that this series is about cross-cultural communication and witnessing "a cross-cultural dialogue all the more eloquent for its silence." He also states that "idealized, marmoreal beauty seems to contemporary taste more banal than beautiful, a kind of glorified embalming" (Feeney 2011).

[19] It is important to note that within the range of sensuous and sexual possibilities there remains the possibility of oppression and denigration. My aim here is not to romanticize all possible queer sensuous and sexual encounters but to point to their very possibility.

over" these figures in the dominant context as well as in the context of this series.[20]

While I recognize the problematic symbolic function of these figures, a queer seeing opens different possibilities.[21] Such an opening of possibilities is not intended to negate the history of brutal colonialism, racism, and denigration associated with sexual and other encounters across races. We cannot forget this history. In response to Barthes's question, "Who will write the history of tears?" I reply that this history is being written, in ink, in light, in tears, by the very people who have cried and those who inherit that history. Bodies of color have shed so many tears and continue to do so given persistent economic, cultural, and ideological violence against them (us). As I write this, with anxiety—with sadness, with love—the Orlando tragedy is still "a flor de piel."[22] No. A queer disidentificatory reading that opens sensuous possibilities cannot and will not allow us to forget or to ignore such violence. Ultimately, I find disidentificatory pleasure in the work of these contemporary Latino photographers in order to fulfill my longing for visual representations of queer Latinidad so as to make sense of my own queerness, not so that I can think of a positive queer future but so that I can endure my present, so that I can *be*.[23]

---

[20] I have a disidentificatory pleasure in the dominant context given what these busts represent in dominant culture. I also have a disidentificatory pleasure within the context of this series because as far as I am aware Gonzales-Day has not explicitly described the work in terms of sexuality and not all the works lend themselves to this type of reading. Yet I opt for a reading of these particular photographs that does not separate race from sexuality.

[21] It is precisely future possibilities that queerness enacts. Unlike theorists such as Bersani and Edelman, Muñoz thinks that the future is the domain of queerness. As Muñoz puts it,

Queerness is a structuring and educated mode of desiring that allows us to see and feel beyond the quagmire of the present. The here and now is a prison house. We must strive, in the face of the here and now's totalizing rendering of reality, to think and feel a then and there . . . we must dream and enact new and better pleasures, other ways of being in the world, and ultimately new worlds. (2009, 1)

[22] See http://www.cnn.com/2016/06/12/us/orlando-nightclub-shooting/ for information on this brutal event. *A flor de piel* is a difficult idiom to translate. It makes a connection between flowers and skin in order to denote overwhelming emotion that is deeply connected to our bodies. It means that our feelings are present and can be exposed at any moment.

[23] My view here is thus similar to Heather Love's in the sense that my aim is not the affirmation of a queer present and future. I agree with her that it is necessary to recognize loss and abjection and to be mindful of that hurtful part of queer history (Love 2009, 30). Love states,

Rather than attempt to "overcome" identity, I want to suggest a mode of historiography that recognizes the inevitability of a "play of recognitions," but that also sees these recognitions not as consoling but as shattering. What has been most problematic about gay and lesbian historiography to date is not, I want to argue, its attachment to identity but rather its consistently affirmative bias. (45)

Conclusion: A Note on Melancholic Longing

I wish to conclude with a note on melancholic longing that, as Muñoz would say, is "riddled with queer possibilities" (1999, 63) and suffused with ambivalence, with the queering disidentificatory pleasures learned from both Serratos's and Gonzales-Day's photographs and that was prompted by Deitcher's analysis of the photograph of the two seated men. For Muñoz, disidentification is, like melancholia, an ambivalent structure of feeling that retains the problematic object and taps into the energy that is generated by the contradictions and ambivalences that arise at the loss of an object (71).[24] As he states,

> I am proposing that melancholia, for blacks, queers, or any queers of color, is not a pathology but an integral part of everyday lives . . . it is this melancholia that is part of our process of dealing with all the catastrophes that occur in the lives of people of color, lesbians, and gay men. I have proposed a different understanding of melancholia that does not see it as a pathology or as a self-absorbed mood that inhibits activism. Rather, it is a mechanism that helps us (re)construct identity and take our dead with us to the various battles we must wage in their names—and in our names. (74)

My longing is one that is melancholic in the sense of Muñoz's account as it connected to loss, to the loss of so many LGBTQ bodies and the loss of something that, like Deitcher, I do not know if it ever existed—a visual testament to my existence and to the existence of those like me.

For Muñoz, melancholia is a mourning that takes a different turn—it is one in which one mourns for oneself, one's community, "for one's very history" (Muñoz 1999, 73). Such mourning does not end, as if it were directed in a linear manner, with a final letting go of the lost object. As Muñoz says, "Whereas lives that are either/or/and black and queer remain on the line, there is no 'normal' teleological end in sight for mourning" (74); mourning becomes life affirming or a resistant melancholia as it allows for a (re)construction of identities that were not meant to be. For me, melancholic longing is one that opens possibilities of new worlds of visuality after so much loss of LGBTQ lives, a sense of loss that moves us to long for a past *and* a present, and to attempt to make new worlds, worlds in which there will still be loss and shame and in which we will carry our dead with us but in which we can also *be* who we want to be—worlds

---

[24] Muñoz disagrees with the Freudian view that melancholy, which amounts to a mourning that cannot let go of the lost object, is pathological. For an important analysis of melancholy and race see Cheng 2001.

in which we do not only *imagine* and *hope* that the two seated men are lovers.[25] I, we, are haunted by this sense of loss (Gordon 1997).[26]

While Muñoz mentions lesbians in his discussion of this newly configured melancholia, his examples center on the artistic production of gay men, on gay men's lives and mourning of their loss. Thus my initial longing turns into yet more mourning, the lost object being Latina desire, lust, and love for women and the visual representation of such desire, lust and love. I feel the loss; I feel the void. It is one that returns. It is based on multiple erasures. Latina desire for women has been erased from dominant culture and dominant culture's artistic production; it has also been minimized from gay/lesbian culture but also from queer culture/history/ art as the latter centers the experience of the queer white male and sometimes the queer male of color. Where do we find Latina desire, lust, and love? With what light has it been written? My question is not intended to lead us back to inadequate and simplistic dichotomies—gay/lesbian heterosexual/homosexual—but points to a more encompassing vision of queer Latinidad . . . one that does not forget Lupe and Sirena in love.

Acknowledgments

I would like to thank Andrea Pitts, José Medina, Kelly Oliver, and Ellen Armour for their helpful comments on earlier drafts of this paper.

References

Anzaldúa, Gloria. 1987. *Borderlands/La Frontera: The New Mestiza*. San Francisco: Aunt Lute Books.

Anzaldúa, Gloria. 1998. "To(o) Queer the Writer." In *Living Chicana Theory*, edited by Carla Trujillo, 263–76. Berkeley, CA: Third Woman Press.

Anzaldúa, Gloria, and Cherríe Moraga, eds. 1981. *This Bridge Called My Back: Writings by Radical Women of Color*. Watertown, MA: Persephone Press.

Aparicio, Frances and Susana Chávez-Silverman, eds. 1997. *Tropicalizations: Transcultural Representations of Latinidad*. Hanover, NH: University Press of New England for Dartmouth College.

Barnard, Ian. 2004. *Queer Race, Cultural Interventions in the Racial Politics of Queer Theory*. New York: Peter Lang.

---

[25] The status of queer futurity is a highly contested one given Leo Bersani's publication of *Homos*, in which he connects gayness to asociality (Bersani 1995). Major queer critics have responded to Bersani. For commentaries on the ten-year anniversary of *Homos* see Caserio et al. 2006.

[26] This loss is one that cannot be overcome by the various achievements of queers of color in the past, present or future—or by the homonormativity that has become pervasive given the equal rights campaign's success in achieving gay marriage.

Barthes, Roland. 1981. *Camera Lucida*. Translated by Richard Howard. New York: Farrar, Straus and Giroux.

Brown, Elspeth H., and Thy Phu, eds. 2014. *Feeling Photography*. Durham, NC: Duke University Press.

Bersani, Leo. 1995. *Homos*. Cambridge, MA: Harvard University Press.

Caserio, Robert L., Tim Dean, Lee Edelman, Judith Halberstam, José Esteban Muñoz, Vitaly Chernetsky, Nancy Condee, Harsha Ram, and Gayatri Chakravorty Spivak. 2006. "Conference Debates: The Antisocial Thesis in Queer Theory." *PMLA* 121, no. 3: 819–28.

Chávez-Silverman, Susana, and Librada Hernández. 2000. *Reading and Writing the Ambiente: Queer Sexualities in Latino, Latin American, and Spanish Culture*. Madison: University of Wisconsin Press.

Cheng, Anlin. 2001. *The Melancholy of Race: Psychoanalysis, Assimilation, and Hidden Grief*. New York: Oxford University Press.

Cuevas, T. Jackie. 2018. *Post-Borderlandia: Chicana Literature and Gender Variant Critique*. New Brunswick: Rutgers University Press.

Cvetkovich, Ann. 2014. "Photographing Objects as Queer Archival Practice." In *Feeling Photography*, edited by Elspeth H. Brown and Thy Phu, 273–296. Durham, NC: Duke University Press.

Deitcher, David. 1998. "Looking at a Photograph, Looking for a History." In *The Passionate Camera: Photography and Bodies of Desires*, edited by Deborah Bright, 23–36. London: Routledge.

Eng, David L. 2010. *The Feeling of Kinship: Queer Liberalism and the Racialization of Intimacy*, Durham, NC: Duke University Press.

Eng, David L., Judith Halberstam, and José Muñoz. 2005. "What's Queer about Queer Studies Now?" *Social Text 23*, nos. 3–4: 1–17.

Feeney, Mark. 2011. "Cross-Cultural Dialogue in Photographs of 'Ken Gonzales-Day: Profiled.'" https://www.bostonglobe.com/arts/theater-art/2011/10/06/cross-cultural-dialogue-photographs-ken-gonzales-day-profiled/Evk9gozoQt5DhNRfLCpKhM/story.html.

Ferguson, Roderick. 2004. *Aberrations in Black: Toward a Queer of Color Critique*. Minneapolis: University of Minnesota Press.

Gaspar de Alba, Alicia, ed. 2003. *Velvet Barrios: Popular Culture and Chicana/o Sexualities*. New York: Palgrave Macmillan.

Gómez-Barris, Macarena. 2017a. "The Plush View: Makeshift Sexualities and Laura Aguilar's Forbidden Archives. In *Axis Mundo: Queer Networks in Chicano L.A*, edited by C. Ondine Chavoya, David Evans Frantz, and Macarena Gómez-Barris. New York: Prestel.

Gómez-Barris, Macarena. 2017b. "Mestiza Cultural Memory, The Self-Ecologies of Laura Aguilar." In *Laura Aguilar: Show and Tell*, edited by Rebecca Epstein. Los Angeles: UCLA Chicano Studies Research Center.

Gopinath, Gayatri. 2005. *Impossible Desires, Queer Diasporas and South Asian Public Cultures*. Durham, N.C: Duke University Press.

Gordon, Avery F. 1997. *Ghostly Matters: Haunting and the Sociological Imagination*. Minneapolis: University of Minnesota Press.

Hames-García, Michael. 2011. "Queer Theory Revisited." In *Gay Latino Studies: A Critical Reader*, edited by Michael Hames-García and Ernesto J. Martínez, 19–45. Durham, NC: Duke University Press.

Johnson, E. Patrick. 2001. "'Quare' Studies, or (Almost) Everything I Know about Queer Studies I Learned from My Grandmother." *Text and Performance Quarterly* 21, no. 1: 1–25.

Johnson, E. Patrick, and Mae G. Henderson. 2005. *Black Queer Studies: A Critical Anthology*. Durham, NC: Duke University Press.

Jones, Amelia. 1998. "Bodies and Subjects in the Technologized Self-Portrait: The Work of Laura Aguilar. *Aztlan: A Journal of Chicano Studies* 23: 203–19.

La Fountain-Stokes. Lawrence. 2009. *Queer Ricans, Culture and Sexualities in the Diaspora*. Minneapolis: University of Minnesota Press.

Love, Heather. 2009. *Feeling Backward, Loss an the Politics of Queer History*. Cambridge: Harvard University Press.

Manalansan, Martin F. 2003. *Global Divas: Filipino Gay Men in the Diaspora*. Durham, NC: Duke University Press.

Massad, Joseph. 2002. "Re-orienting Desire: The Gay International and the Arab World." *Public Culture* 14: 361–85.

Massad, Joseph. 2007. *Desiring Arabs*. Chicago: University of Chicago Press.

Mitchell, Pablo. 2010. "Making Sex Matter: Histories of Latina/o Sexualities, 1898 to 1965." In *Latina/o Sexualities: Probing Powers, Passions, Practices, and Policies*, edited by Marysol Asencio, 38–47. New Brunswick, NJ: Rutgers University Press.

Muñoz, José Esteban. 1999. *Disidentification: Queers of Color and the Performance of Politics*. Minneapolis: University of Minnesota Press.

Muñoz, José Esteban. 2009. *Cruising Utopia: The Then and There of Queer Futurity*. New York: New York University Press.

Pérez, Daniel Enrique. 2009. *Rethinking Chicana/o and Latina/o Popular Culture*. New York: Palgrave Macmillan.

Pérez, Laura. 2007. *Chicana Art: The Politics of Spiritual and Aesthetics Altarities*. Durham, NC: Duke University Press.

Puar, Jasbir. 2007. *Terrorist Assemblages: Homonationalism in Queer Times*. Durham, NC: Duke University Press.

Ramos, Juanita, ed. 1987. *Compañeras: Latina Lesbians, an Anthology*. New York: Latina Lesbian Historic Project.

Rivera-Servera, Ramón H. 2012. *Performing Queer Latinidad: Dance, Sexuality, Politics*. Ann Arbor: University of Michigan Press.

Rodriguez, Juana María. 2003. *Queer Latinidad: Identity Practices, Discursive Spaces*. New York: New York University Press.

Rodriguez, Juana María. 2014. *Sexual Futures, Queer Gestures, and Other Latina Longings*. New York: New York University Press.

Rueda Esquivel, Catriona. 2006. *With Her Machete in Her Hand: Reading Chicana Lesbians*. Austin: University of Texas Press.

Torres, Lourdes, and Inmaculada Pertusa, eds. 2003. *Tortilleras: Hispanic and U.S. Latina Lesbian Expression*. Philadelphia: Temple University Press.

Trujillo, Carla. 1991. *Latina Lesbians: The Girls Our Mothers Warned Us About*. Berkeley, CA: Third Woman Press.

Vaid, Urvashi. 2012. *Irresistible Revolution: Confronting Race, Class and the Assumptions of LGBT Politics*. New York: Magnus Books.

Viteri, María Amelia. 2014. *Desbordes: Translating Racial, Ethnic, Sexual, and Gender Identities across the Americas*. Albany: SUNY Press.

Wat, Eric C. 2001. *The Making of a Gay Asian Community: An Oral History of Pre-AIDS Los Angeles*. Lanham, MD: Rowman & Littlefield.

Yarbro-Bejarano, Yvonne. 1998. "Laying It Bare: The Queer/Colored Body in the Photography of Laura Aguilar." In Living Chicana Theory, edited by Carla Trujillo, 277–305. Berkeley: Third Woman Press.

CHAPTER 17 | # Vulnerable Bodies

Juana Alicia's Latina Feminism and
Transcorporeal Environmentalism

JULIE AVRIL MINICH

THROUGHOUT SUMMER 2014, US news reported ceaselessly on unauthor-
ized border crossings by children from Central America seeking reuni-
fication with parents in the United States.[1] After escaping violence in
Guatemala, El Salvador, and Honduras, these children faced new trauma
in the United States: housed in overcrowded detention facilities, sent to
court without representation, and targeted by anti-immigration groups. In
July, protestors in Murrieta, California, blocked buses bringing children to
a local detention facility, carrying signs that circulated widely, including
"Murrieta Is Not a Dumping Ground" and "Send Them Back with Birth
Control." Depicting the children as toxic waste and surplus population,
these signs corroborate Sarah Jaquette Ray's (2013) observation of a "troubling contradiction within environmental thought—that in producing en-
vironmentalist bodies, it must produce ecological others" (10). Ecological
others are those whose *"physical,* material bodies often bear the costs of
environmental exploitation," even as "their bodies are *discursively* perceived as threats to national, racial, or corporeal purity" (19).[2] Yet this use
of environmentalism to scapegoat vulnerable bodies is not inevitable; an

---

[1] This essay was written in spring 2015 and revised the following year, well before reports of
the Trump administration's brutal treatment of Central American migrants, particularly children,
surfaced in 2018 and 2019. Academic publishing procedures prohibited me from revising this
essay again to address this escalation of violence toward Central American migrants on the U.S.-
Mexico border, but I also believe that leaving the essay unrevised has another effect: helping to
make visible how the later crisis did not simply arise out of nowhere but resulted from years of
physical, political and rhetorical violence that slowly intensified over time.

[2] For historical accounts that specifically show how Mexican immigrants and their descendants
have been represented as ecological others—or as contaminants threatening the US body politic—
see Molina 2006 and McKiernan-González 2012.

Julie Avril Minich, *Vulnerable Bodies* In: *Theories of the Flesh*, Edited by: Andrea J. Pitts, Mariana
Ortega, and José Medina, Oxford University Press (2020). © Oxford University Press.
DOI: 10.1093/oso/9780190062965.003.0018

environmental justice paradigm posits a markedly different account of the links between migration, poverty, and the environment.

This essay examines how the Bay Area–based Chicana feminist muralist Juana Alicia fosters environmental justice activism that values vulnerable lives in her two most famous murals: *Las Lechugueras* (1983), painted at Twenty-Fourth and York Streets in San Francisco's Mission District, and *La Llorona's Sacred Waters* (2004), with which the artist replaced *Las Lechugueras* after its wall was damaged.[3] Writing against the mainstream environmentalism that produces environmental others, literary critic Priscilla Solis Ybarra (2009) argues that "in a Mexican American context, humans and the natural environment are inextricably linked and there-fore responsible and responsive to one another," with writers like Jovita González and Gloria Anzaldúa modeling "an active engagement with the environment, a form of environmental literature that . . . concerns living in and with nature, in an active, mutually transformative, but also mutu-ally sustaining way" (185). This essay extends Ybarra's argument to Juana Alicia's visual art and elaborates how her Chicana feminist aesthetics align with environmental justice work.

Juana Alicia, who uses no surname professionally, was born in Newark to Mexican-Jewish parents and grew up in Detroit; she discovered polit-ical art and murals through Diego Rivera's *Detroit Industry* frescoes at the Detroit Institute of Arts. Two defining features of her work are its ra-cial diversity (featuring images of Black bodies alongside the indigenous bodies that often populate Chicana/o art) and its depiction of bodies that are disabled, in danger, wounded, or healing. In addition to appearing in the murals discussed here, these elements are also visible in the following Juana Alicia mural projects and collaborations: *SanArte: Diversity's Pathway* (completed in 2005 at the University of California, San Francisco medical building, which engages themes of art and health), *Maestrapeace* (completed in 1994 at the San Francisco Women's Building, a collabora-tion with the Maestrapeace Art Works Collective[4] that features corporeally diverse women), and *El lenguaje mudo del alma / The Silent Language of the Soul* (completed in 1990, at César Chávez Elementary School, a col-laboration with Susan Kelk Cervantes that honors the multiple languages, including American Sign Language, used at the school). Guisela Latorre describes Juana Alicia as placing "women at the center of the activism seeking to demand social and environmental justice" (2008, 207–8); the artist herself writes in a statement on her website that "it is my respon-sibility as an artist to be an activist for social justice, human rights and

---

[3] Both murals can be viewed on the artist's website: www.juanaalicia.com.

[4] The Maestrapeace Art Works collective includes Juana Alicia, Miranda Bergman, Edythe Boone, Susan Kelk Cervantes, Meera Desai, Yvonne Littleton, and Irene Pérez.

environmental health" (Juana Alicia, n.d.). Although her work has not received significant attention from disability scholars, the corporeal diversity that pervades it is crucial to her activist impact. In both *Las Lechugueras* and *La Llorona's Sacred Waters*, Juana Alicia depicts human bodies interacting with, depending upon, and permeated by their environments.

This essay explores how Juana Alicia gives visual form to an environmental ethics that prompts a politics of inclusion, equitable resource distribution, and bodily diversity. I align Juana Alicia's work with a concept that Stacy Alaimo terms *transcorporeality*, "the movement across bodies" that "reveals the interchanges and interconnections between various bodily natures" (2010, 2). Alaimo argues that "emphasizing the material interconnections of human corporeality with the more-than-human world . . . allows us to forge ethical and political positions that can contend with numerous late twentieth- and early twenty-first-century realities in which 'human' and 'environment' can by no means be considered as separate" (2); Juana Alicia is particularly concerned with the interconnections between the more-than-human world and the corporeality of our planet's most vulnerable humans. Her murals demonstrate what antiracist, feminist, disability, environmental, and other social justice movements share: an investment in radical interdependence between different kinds of bodies and beings.[5] They depict disabilities created by environmental hazards (including pollution, pesticide poisoning, and the privatization of water) without reducing disability to tragedy, prompting viewers to envision a world in which working-class communities of color are not forced to bear the brunt of environmental risk.

Las Lechugueras

Las Lechugueras is Juana Alicia's most famous mural, widely recognized as the cover image for two iconic books in Chicana/o studies: José David Saldívar's *Border Matters* and Eva Sperling Cockcroft and Holly Barnet-Sanchez's *Signs from the Heart*. *Las Lechugueras* was painted on the side of La Taquería San Francisco (which remains in business) in the Mission District, a historically working-class Latina/o neighborhood in San Francisco. As its name suggests,[6] the mural depicts a lettuce harvest, with a man driving a tractor to the left and an immigration control car to the bottom right. At the center are several muscular women whose labor provides the focal point; overhead, a crop duster sprays them with green

---

[5] Examples of this interdependence in her work include the use of prosthetics, coexistence with service animals, and attention to built and natural environments.

[6] *Lechugueras* means "lettuce workers."

rain. The most prominent worker is a pregnant woman who carries a machete in one arm and a head of lettuce in the other; her translucent belly exposes her baby.[7] Side by side near the center of the mural, the pregnant belly and the lettuce present a contrast: similar in size and shape, the lettuce is impenetrable and firm, the belly exposed and vulnerable. These two images exemplify the mural's condemnation of labor systems that protect produce while leaving defenseless the workers who tend it; the disparity between the hearty lettuce and the fragile bodies around it also prompts an eco-critique of agribusiness preferences for plants that are attractive and easy to ship but less nourishing.

The transcorporeality of *Las Lechugueras* extends to the relationship between the mural itself and the community in which it exists: While it is common for murals to appear on the walls of Mexican restaurants and grocery stores, the themes of environmental health, food production, and labor make the placement of *Las Lechugueras* at a taquería particularly significant. Because the mural was painted before gentrification began displacing Mission residents and because of San Francisco's proximity to California's Central Valley (called the "breadbasket" of the United States), those purchasing food at the taquería in the 1980s were likely to be connected to agricultural labor, whether as current/former farmworkers or as relatives of farmworkers. (Juana Alicia herself moved to the Mission in the early 1980s after organizing farmworkers in Salinas, California, in the 1970s.) At the time of its creation, the mural made a dual intervention: reminding customers of the conditions faced by farm laborers and reminding workers of their rights.[8] This address to workers is important because, as Sarah Wald (2011) points out, many advocates for sustainable agriculture tend to focus on consumer citizenship, missing "an opportunity to recognize and empower producers" (580). In other words, the

---

[7] Given the emphasis within mainstream feminism on reproductive choice, the word *fetus* might seem more appropriate here than *baby*. I use the word *baby* to align my work not with reproductive choice but with what Dorothy Roberts terms *reproductive liberty*: "Reproductive liberty must encompass more than the protection of an individual woman's choice to end her pregnancy. It must encompass the full range of procreative activities, including the ability to bear a child, and it must acknowledge that we make reproductive decisions within a social context, including inequalities of wealth and power" (1998, 6). In other words, I use the word *baby* here not to make a blanket argument for fetal personhood but to emphasize that this particular fetus is depicted as a baby valued in spite of the inequalities of wealth and power (which take material form through pesticides) that endanger this *lechuguera*'s reproductive liberty.

[8] Although it is beyond the scope of this essay to discuss the rapid gentrification of the Mission District in the 2000s, it is worth noting that one consequence is that those living in proximity to the neighborhood's historic murals are no longer those depicted in them. As an illustration of how the clientele of this particular taquería has changed, a quick scan of its Yelp! page reveals diners seeking to satisfy "inner-LA girl-late-night-taco-truck cravings" (user Breanne T., February 4, 2015) or lamenting its need for "a little sprucing up" (Rose H., January 22, 2015; one only hopes that this hypothetical "sprucing" would leave the mural intact). On the day I accessed the taquería's Yelp! page, none of the front-page reviews noted the mural at the taquería.

mural depicted an experience that those who lived in its presence knew intimately, empowering a local working-class population to protest the agricultural industry, rather than simply urging wealthy consumers to buy organic.

Alongside local concerns, the mural also addresses transnational politics. Cary Cordova notes that beginning in the 1970s, the arrival into the Mission of Central American activists prompted more Central American images in local murals; she cites as an example Juana Alicia's 1988 mural *Alto al Fuego / Ceasefire* (located a few blocks southwest on Mission Street and painted five years after *Las Lechugueras*, just after Juana Alicia returned to the United States from painting a mural for the National Teacher's Union in Nicaragua, while its revolutionary government was at war with US-funded counterrevolutionaries).[9] The references to Central America in *Las Lechugueras* are more subtle, given that the mural was painted before the artist traveled to Nicaragua but after the Mission and its artistic community had seen extensive organizing against US interventions in Central America.[10] In *Las Lechugueras*, the crop duster's menacing presence calls to mind US-funded warplanes flying over Guatemala, El Salvador, and (via bases in Honduras) Nicaragua.[11] The connection between the crop duster and these warplanes is emphasized by the fact that the plane shares the same color as the immigration control vehicle and the pesticide rain; the green connecting these three images suggests a link between the agricultural practices that destroy workers' bodies, the immigration control apparatus that threatens their security, and the US-funded instruments of political unrest prompting people to migrate north. In positing this link, the mural also predicts the political conditions that led to the 2014 child migrant crisis, in which many children sought asylum from violence in Central America following the US interventions.

Crucial to Juana Alicia's articulation of environment, labor, and transnational politics is her depiction of the workers' bodies. Mexican and Chicana/o murals are well known for celebrating male laboring bodies, depicting the dignity of undervalued work. However, the gendering of the bodies differentiates *Las Lechugueras* from this tradition. As the feminine pronoun in the mural's title emphasizes, its workers are women, and

---

[9] For more information about *Alto al Fuego* and images of the mural, see Juana Alicia 2007.

[10] Cordova documents transnational Latina/o organizing in the Mission throughout the 1970s and 1980s, as "artists and activists used the ideals of revolution in Nicaragua to express the political needs of Latinos in San Francisco and the Americas" (Cordova 2010, 213–14) and "helped popularize a pan-Latino, or Raza, identity in politics and subsequently encouraged activism across national borders" (215).

[11] Cherríe Moraga's (1994) play *Heroes and Saints*, which also deals with the pesticide poisoning of agricultural workers, similarly uses the sound of crop dusters to call to mind war planes. Written in the late 1980s, the play premiered at the Brava Theater Center, located across from the mural at the same intersection.

the muscularity of their bodies demonstrates that the stamina associated with agricultural labor is not the sole property of men.[12] The femininity of the mural's subjects is further emphasized by their bright makeup and earrings, reflecting self-fashioning practices by which working-class women use makeup and jewelry to claim their bodies as worthy of adornment and care.[13]

This assertion of bodily dignity also undergirds the mural's disability politics. *Las Lechugueras* shows that "the human body is never a rigidly enclosed, protected entity, but is vulnerable to the substances and flows of its environments, which may include industrial environments and their social/economic forces" (Alaimo 2010, 28). As novelist Victor Martínez observes in an essay (Martínez n.d.) originally distributed as a pamphlet by La Galería de la Raza[14] and now available on Juana Alicia's website, the women's clothing is "tissue thin," offering "little protection" from sun or pesticides. Furthermore, the belly of the pregnant *lechuguera*—rendered translucent to expose her baby—provides the mural's focal point, locating its political claims in two bodies: one female, one potentially disabled. The mural thus protests the poisoning of the baby without invoking her life as a tragedy. Instead, just as the child's mother is represented as simultaneously strong and vulnerable, the baby's placement at the center of the mural constructs her as a desired and valued member of her community and its future.

Disability scholar Alison Kafer, who critiques representations reinforcing the idea of disability "as a terrible unending tragedy" and implying that "any future that includes disability can only be a future to avoid" (2013, 2), argues that disability activists must also protest the endangerment of workers. She insists upon "a difference between denying necessary health care, condoning dangerous working conditions, or ignoring public health concerns (thereby causing illness and impairment) and recognizing illness and disability as part of what makes us human" (4). Simultaneously protesting the pesticide poisoning of workers and asserting the value of the baby's life (whether that baby is ultimately disabled or not), *Las Lechugueras* offers an environmental justice vision that aligns with Kafer's disability critique. In a similar vein, Wald critiques food movements that

---

[12] It is worth noting that the creation of a mural also requires strength and physical stamina, qualities women are often socialized not to display; this may be one reason why, as Cordova observes, there is a "long-standing stereotype that mural painting, especially Chicano mural painting, [is] a practice best performed by men" (2006, 364).

[13] Drawing from the work of Jennifer Craik, Marci R. McMahon writes: "The term *self-fashioning* highlights the intersections of dress with bodily performance and the possibility of these sites in the negotiation of gendered and racialized ideologies" (2011, 25).

[14] La Galeria de la Raza is a cultural center located one block east of the mural at the corner of Twenty-Fourth and Bryant Streets.

construct farmworkers "as a byproduct of an industrial food system," and "inadvertently imply that immigrant workers will disappear when the food system shifts to a more sustainable local model" (580). Kafer and Wald ask how to protest environmental injustice without treating the bodies of those affected as tragedies to be eradicated. For Juana Alicia, the answer lies in recognizing the transcorporeal relationship between the body—in its racial, gender, class and sexual specificity—and its environment.

The trans-corporeality of *Las Lechugueras* registers on three levels: that of body, through porosity of clothing and skin; that of community, through porosity of boundaries between the subjects of the mural and its viewers; and finally that of nation, through porosity of borders, evoked by the Border Patrol / warplane images. The mural depicts transcorporeality as radical practice, by positioning the exposed baby at the center of the mural, but also as danger. As Alaimo reminds us, there is a "sinister" (2010, 45) element to the transit of chemicals and toxins through bodies and their environments. Yet even in revealing the perils of transcorporeality, the mural resists treating bodily or national purity as the answer; as mentioned, the impermeable lettuce is rendered as an object of critique. *Las Lechugueras* rejects an environmentalism of conservation and preservation in favor of one of inclusion, one that relies not on the expulsion of ecological others but on valuing vulnerable lives. Since the mural was painted, its intervention has grown more urgent, as the rhetoric around the 2014 child migrant crisis shows. Juana Alicia's environmentalism rejects the construction of the ecological other, drawing instead from movements for the protection of workers and the movement of people across borders.

La Llorona's Sacred Waters

In 2004, when damage to the *Las Lechugueras* wall required its demolition, Juana Alicia replaced *Las Lechugueras* with *La Llorona's Sacred Waters*. She calls this new mural "the daughter of the first" (Juana Alicia 2007) since both highlight themes of gendered labor and environmental justice. *La Llorona's Sacred Waters* depicts protests against feminicide in Ciudad Juárez, Mexico; the privatization of water in Cochabamba, Bolivia; and the construction of dams that flooded farmlands in India's Narmada Valley. As Latorre observes, this mural underscores "the negative effects of globalization on marginalized communities around the globe" while acknowledging that globalization "has ushered in the realization among many Chicana feminist artists that the struggles of the Third World and of women of color around the world bear striking similarities" (2008, 210). Whereas *Las Lechugueras* was painted in a community connected to agricultural labor, *La Llorona's Sacred Waters* was painted in a community incorporated unevenly into transnational capital, as the Mission District was by 2004 a much more gentrified space in which capitalism's beneficiaries and victims lived uneasily together. *La Llorona's Sacred Waters* reminds viewers of the interconnection between struggles for social and environmental justice taking place across the globe; its transcorporeality emerges through its representation of geographically disparate bodies connected through anticapitalist and environmental justice struggle. As Juana Alicia asserts, traveling to Nicaragua in the mid-1980s taught her that "we live in a war zone in the Mission, connected by gangs, police violence, immigration, the AIDS epidemic and economic injustice to the millions of our southern cousins in Mexico and Central America" (Juana Alicia 2007). In *La Llorona's Sacred Waters*, she expands that connection beyond Mexico and Central America to the entire planet.

Where Juana Alicia's memoir essay depicts marginalized communities united by the effects of transnational violence, her art depicts them united by transnational resistance. In *La Llorona's Sacred Waters*, this resistance is represented by the two indigenous Mexican women who occupy the most space in the mural: Mexica/Aztec water deity Chalchiuhtlicue and La Llorona, the mythical weeping woman who kills her children and eternally cries for them. Chalchiuhtlicue stands over the mural, her face at the center top, bringing together each of the struggles depicted in the mural. The goddess is traditionally shown with a stream of water flowing from her skirt that includes babies of both genders; Juana Alicia replaces the babies with La Llorona, who appears (her arm around a male child) at the bottom right. Above La Llorona is the US-Mexico border, represented by barbed wire and helicopters; to her left are images from the Narmada Valley and Cochabamba. The mural is a feminist retelling of the Llorona myth; instead of killing her children, this Llorona holds a child she has rescued from a flood and reaches out to save another. Like *Las Lechugueras*, then, this mural predicates its ethical claim on the bodily vulnerability of children deemed disposable in the larger social imaginary; also like *Las Lechugueras*, it insists upon the value of these children to their communities. Given the mural's critique of the capitalist appropriation of natural resources (farmland along the Narmada River, water in Cochabamba, desert land on the US-Mexico border), it is worth asking why the artist represents the story of corporate capitalism and environmental devastation as a Llorona story. As Domino Renee Perez notes, the Llorona myth is about cultural exchanges—sometimes friendly, sometimes brutal—that emerged with the conquest of Mexico, and most versions of it depict her as an indigenous woman who kills, then mourns, the children she bears to a Spaniard (in some versions her lover and in others her rapist). As a result, the Llorona story from its inception has been about competing claims to land and resources, struggles visible in the maquiladoras of Ciudad Juárez and in Cochabamba and the Narmada Valley.

The conquering Spaniards of the traditional Llorona myth are replaced in the mural by the helicopters and barbed wire of the US-Mexico border and a man whose shoes hover over the women of Cochabamba, representing the Bechtel Corporation (which sought to purchase water rights in Cochabamba). Both entities are positioned on either side of Chalchiuhtlicue but smaller in size than the goddess, presenting them as competing (but ultimately less powerful) forces. Geographer Laura Pulido defines environmental racism as a mechanism through which "corporations consciously choose to jeopardize and kill thousands," particularly those deemed "racially expendable," through their disregard for the environment (814); by placing the image representing the Bechtel Corporation alongside the indigenous goddess, Juana Alicia builds on this insight to align the multinational corporation (and its participation in environmental racism) with the earlier forces of the conquest of the Americas. Similarly, the helicopters and barbed wire that block the free movement of people are also put in the role of Spanish conquerors. By including these forces in the mural but rendering them smaller than La Llorona and Chalchiuhtlicue, the mural balances the imperative to "identify culprits and name names, so that the global community will understand who the guilty parties are and how we should respond to them" (Pulido 2015, 815) with a commitment to centering the lives and experiences of women of color.

La Llorona's Sacred Waters invites its viewers to reinterpret not only the events it depicts but also other events unfolding since its creation. Like *Las Lechugueras*—which acquires new interpretations in the context of current debates about children crossing the US-Mexico border—*La Llorona's Sacred Waters* seems to read now as a response to Hurricane Katrina, which caused disastrous flooding in the city of New Orleans and throughout the Gulf Coast of Louisiana the year after the mural was painted. With its striking image of a young Black child being rescued from rising flood waters, the mural seems to offer a direct counter to the devastating posthurricane images of poor and working-class New Orleans residents, mostly African American, awaiting rescue from the floods that destroyed their homes and livelihoods. In fact, the connection between the mural and Hurricane Katrina goes deeper than mere proximity of dates. In response to ecological disasters in the Gulf Coast region, Stephanie LeMenager notes that "repeated invocation of Gulf Coast residents' threatened 'way of life,' . . . indicates that Gulf Coast people have fallen out of (or were never included within) the concept of modernity, where life practices are not clearly tied to place" (2011, 29). Like the people of the Gulf Coast, the residents of Cochabamba, the Narmada Valley, and Ciudad Juárez are excluded from modernity, those LeMenager describes as "humanity defined as ecological, in the sense of those whose 'way of life' is conditioned by a regional ecosystem" and who "may as well be recognized as humanity unprotected by rights or status—the human animal whose primary community is nonhuman" (29). What *La Llorona's Sacred Waters* proposes, however, is that those excluded from modernity (and those, as Pulido notes, most vulnerable to environmental racism) form a community of their own, a latent solidarity in the face of ecological disaster and the capitalist expropriation and destruction of their resources.

This solidarity is represented in the mural's transformation of La Llorona from a woman who kills her children to one who saves children. Perez notes that "Chican@s who revise La Llorona lore frequently interrogate the misogyny, classism, or colonialism at the center of some versions" (2008, 5); in feminist retellings in particular, "La Llorona acts against and on sources of oppression or empowers women to do the same" (6). Juana Alicia further revises the myth by altering its racial dynamics. Where the traditional version involves an indigenous Llorona and indigenous-European children, Juana Alicia depicts La Llorona as indigenous or mestiza and the child as Black. This opens the mural to multiple interpretations: perhaps the child depicted in the mural is hers, and La Llorona's relationship to her lover represents the enslavement of Black and indigenous people during the conquest, or perhaps La Llorona has no biological connection to the child she saves, only the affective bond of shared struggle. Either way, Juana Alicia tells the traditional Llorona story, in which white dominance is central, by emphasizing Black-brown solidarity in the face of that dominance. Recalling the attention that Juana Alicia gives in *Las Lechugueras* to bodily diversity among Latinas/os, the racial difference between La Llorona and the child in this mural also emphasizes the bodily diversity of Latinidad and reminds viewers that political allies do not always have bodies that are shaped in predictable ways or appear as expected. The Chicana feminism of this mural is not only transnational but also multiracial.

The relevance of *La Llorona's Sacred Waters* to events (like Hurricane Katrina) taking place after its completion underscores the prescience of Juana Alicia's Latina feminist environmental critique. The mural emphasizes the interconnectedness and interdependence (or transcorporeality) of human beings with each other through the economic flows of capitalism and the literal flowing of water. Just as an economic system that benefits only some at the expense of many is unsustainable, so too are environmental practices that limit access to natural resources to only a few at the expense of many. In addition, the mural reminds us of the bodily vulnerability we all share in the face of our planet's changing climate and diminishing resources, advocating a relationship to the planet that is attentive to both its ecological fragility and the need for more equitable resource distribution.

To conclude, I return to the story that opened this essay: the 2014 humanitarian crisis on the US-Mexico border in which undocumented Central American children were characterized as an environmental disaster. This story demonstrates that social movements predicated on conservation often characterize the vulnerable as a threat. The work of artists like Juana Alicia makes visible theoretical ties that can unite multiple movements for justice, including feminism, antiracism, and disability activism, and that the interventions of such work need to be theorized in and through a framework that recognizes all of these sites of struggle. In Juana Alicia's art, disability and bodily vulnerability emerge not as signs of tragedy or crisis but as common features of shared humanity that bind people together in a political community. As a result, her murals force us to confront difficult questions about how we construct communities, whom we imagine as insiders and outsiders, how we inadvertently exclude people even as we advocate for a more just society, and which bodies we believe are politically viable and which we do not.

References

Alaimo, Stacy. 2010. *Bodily Natures: Science, Environment, and the Material Self.* Bloomington: Indiana University Press.

Chavez, Leo R. 2008. *The Latino Threat: Constructing Immigrants, Citizens, and the Nation.* Stanford, CA: Stanford University Press.

Cockcroft, Eva Sperling, and Holly Barnet-Sanchez, eds. 1993. *Signs from the Heart: California Chicano Murals.* Albuquerque: University of New Mexico Press.

Cordova, Cary. 2006. "Hombres y Mujeres Muralistas on a Mission: Painting Latino Identities in 1970s San Francisco." *Latino Studies* 4, no. 4 (Winter): 356–80.

Cordova, Cary. 2010. "The Mission in Nicaragua: San Francisco Poets Go to War." In *Beyond El Barrio: Everyday Life in Latina/o America*, edited by Adrian Burgos, Frank Guridy, and Gina M. Pérez, 211–31. New York: New York University Press.

Juana Alicia. n.d. "About/Biografía." Accessed March 20, 2015. www.juanaalicia.com.

Juana Alicia. 2007. "Remembering the Mission: A Reflection." September 20. www.juanaalicia.com.

Kafer, Alison. 2013. *Feminist, Queer, Crip.* Bloomington: Indiana University Press.

LaTorre, Guisela. 2008. *Walls of Empowerment: Chicana/o Indigenist Murals of California.* Austin: University of Texas Press.

LeMenager, Stephanie. 2011. "Petro-Melancholia: The BP Blowout and the Arts of Grief." *Qui Parle* 19, no. 2 (Spring–Summer): 25–55.

Martínez, Victor. n.d. "Harvesting Hope: A View of Juana Alicia's Mural 'Las Lechugueras.'" Accessed March 20, 2015. www.juanaalicia.com.

McKiernan-González, John. 2012. *Fevered Measures: Public Health and Race at the Texas Mexico Border, 1848–1942.* Durham, NC: Duke University Press.

McMahon, Marci R. 2011. "Self-Fashioning through Glamour and Punk in East Los Angeles: Patssi Valdez in Asco's *Instant Mural* and *A La Mode*." *Aztlán* 36, no. 2 (Fall): 21–49.

Molina, Natalia. 2006. *Fit to Be Citizens? Public Health and Race in Los Angeles, 1879–1939*. Berkeley: University of California Press.

Moraga, Cherríe. 1994. *Heroes and Saints and Other Plays*. Albuquerque: West End Press.

Perez, Domino Renee. 2008. *There Was a Woman: La Llorona from Folklore to Popular Culture*. Austin: University of Texas Press.

Pulido, Laura. 2015. "Geographies of Race and Ethnicity I: White Supremacy vs White Privilege in Environmental Racism Research." *Progress in Human Geography* 39, no. 6: 809–17.

Ray, Sarah Jaquette. 2013. *The Ecological Other: Environmental Exclusion in American Culture*. Tucson: University of Arizona Press.

Roberts, Dorothy. 1998. *Killing the Black Body: Race, Reproduction, and the Meaning of Liberty*. New York: Vintage.

Saldívar, José David. 1997. *Border Matters: Remapping American Cultural Studies*. Berkeley: University of California Press.

Wald, Sarah. 2011. "Visible Farmers / Invisible Workers: Locating Immigrant Labor in Food Studies." *Food, Culture & Society* 14, no. 4 (December): 567–86.

Ybarra, Priscilla Solis. 2009. "Borderlands as Bioregion: Jovita González, Gloria Anzaldúa, and the Twentieth-Century Ecological Revolution in the Rio Grande Valley." *MELUS* 34, no. 2 (Summer): 175–89.

INDEX

For the benefit of digital users, indexed terms that span two pages (e.g., 52–53) may, on occasion, appear on only one of those pages.

coloniality of gender, the, 3, 4, 6, 14, 37, 44, 204–5, 230. *See also* Lugones, María Cristina
    dark side of, 78–79, 80–81, 82, 83, 85
    light side of, 78–80, 81, 83, 84–85, 87, 89
    violence of, 79–81, 82–83, 84–85, 89
coloniality of knowledge, the, x, 40–41. *See also* Palermo, Zulma; Mignolo, Walter D.
coloniality of language, the, 31, 34, 179–80. *See also* Lugones, María Cristina; Mignolo, Walter D.
coloniality of power, the, 6, 14, 39–40, 48–49, 57. *See also* Quijano, Aníbal
colonization, 24–25, 40, 48–49, 79, 118, 144–45, 196
    and dehumanization, 174, 179
    and indigenous populations, 29, 46, 136–38, 182
    and language, 209n4, 210–11
    logic of, 54–55
    and modernity, 39
    neocolonization, 100–1
    symbolic, 259
    and women, 45, 174
color blindness, 258–59
Combahee River Collective, 57
communication, 6, 31, 136–37, 178–79, 180–81
    bodily, 275–76
    cross-cultural, 18–19, 24, 275, 275n18
    cross-racial, 25–26
Conner, Randy P., 57–58
consciousness-raising, 47, 100, 101, 102–3
Cordova, Cary, 285
Cornejo Polar, Antonio, 41–42
cotidiano, lo. *See* quotidian, the
counteridentification, 75, 75n2, 85, 86–87. *See also* disidentification
Crenshaw, Kimberlé, 157–58. *See also* intersectionality
criminalization, 57–58, 75, 79, 99, 141. *See also* illegality
critical theory, 19–20

Cuban socialist revolution, 57–58
cult of domesticity, 78–79
cultural alienation, 18–19
cultural invitations, 221–23, 226, 227, 230
cultural translation, 55–56, 175–76, 179–80, 182, 183
curanderismo, 220–21, 230–34

da Silva e Orta, Teresa Margarida, 97
Dagara tribe, 57n5
Daly, Mary, 13–14
Dávila, Arlene, 261
Davis, Angela, 57
de Beauvoir, Simone, 66–67, 106, 107–8
de Jesus, Carolina María, 184–85
de la Cruz, Sor Juana Inés, x, 97–98
    Carta Atenagórica, 99–100
    and development of feminism in Latin America, 97–100
    and lesbianism, 98
    and Nahuatl (language), 98
    Primer Sueño, 99
    on racial and gender equality, 98–100
de Lima Costa, Claudia, 6
de Vieryra, Antonio, 99–100
decolonial feminism, 11, 13, 40–43, 76–78
    development of, 18–19, 22
    and gender, 29, 76, 90
    and hegemony, 174, 175–76, 182
    and national difference, 12–13
    and philosophy, 16
decolonial feminist *movidas*, 84, 86–88
decolonial possibilities, 29–31, 35–36
decolonial theory, 2–3, 5, 11–12, 13, 14, 16–17, 23–24, 54
    and Caribbean thinkers, 76
    as hegemonic, 48–49
    key features of, 138–39
decoloniality of gender, 34–35
decolonization, 2–3, 12, 56, 137–38
    of education, 64
    of epistemology, 60–61
    of feminism, 24, 26, 35–36
    and literature, 139
    as practice, 55–56

faithful witnessing, 145–47

Fanon, Frantz, 39, 61–62
  Black Skin, White Masks,
    136–37, 150–51
  and complexity, 148–49
  and decolonization, 137–38
  and embodiment, 136–37

Femen, 11–12

Femenías, María Luisa, 3, 114–15

feminicide, 48, 174, 287–88

feminist liberation theology, 66–67

Feminist Majority Foundation, the, 11

Fernández de Santa Cruz, Manuel (bishop of Puebla), 99

Flores Ruíz, Elena, 6, 188–89

Foucault, Michel, 43n1, 189–90, 193–94, 197, 200–1
  and Enrique Dussel, 62–63

fragmentation, 129–30, 139–40

Fraser, Nancy, 20–21

freedom, 81–82, 83, 84–85, 90, 97, 111–12, 127–28, 136n2, 204–5, 231–32

Freud, Sigmund, 20–21, 271–72, 277–78

Fricker, Miranda, 46

Gandhi, Mahatma (Mohandas K.), 68

Gaos, José, 97–98, 104–5

García, Alma M., 57n4

García Márquez, Gabriel
  One Hundred Years of Solitude,
    150–51, 151n36

Gargallo, Francesca, 4–5

gay sexuality, 265–66, 268–69, 268–69n8, 269n9, 270–71, 273, 276n23, 278n25, 278

gaze, the, 40, 45, 241
  colonial, 85
  feminist, 108
  male, 97, 101, 173–74
  white, 241

gender
  as category, 2–3, 83–84
  as hybrid, 18
  identity, 13, 16, 20–21, 24, 25, 26
  liberation, 13, 24, 25
  and race, 33, 35, 76

gender binary, 3, 11–17, 29, 34–35

gender complementarity, 15, 29, 42

gender eliminativism, 24–25

Gianella, Alicia, 46

Gilroy, Paul, 20–21

Gines, Kathryn. *See* Belle, Kathryn Sophia

Glazer, Nathan, 20–21

global hegemony, 62–63, 287–88

Goldberg, David Theo, 255–56

Gómez, Marga, 271–72

Gómez-Peña, Guillermo, 62n6

González, Jovita, 282

González, Lélia, 181–82, 184–85

González, Michelle A., 167–68

González-Day, Ken, 7–8, 268
  Untitled II, 273–76

Gossett, Hattie, 1–2

Gramsci, Antonio, 19–20

Grosz, Elizabeth, 164–65, 167

Gruzinski, Serge, 39

Habermas, Jürgen, 19

Hall, Stuart, 61–62, 175

Hames-García, Michael, 138–39, 143–44

Haslanger, Sally, 16

Haudenosaunee, 15

hegemonic feminism, 6, 11–12, 34, 63–64, 102, 182

hegemonic tropicalization, 269–70, 269–70n11

Heidegger, Martin, 42, 43n1, 208n3

hermeneutical understanding, 207–8

hermeneutical violence, 6, 206–11
  definition of, 207, 209
  and linguistic practice, 207

hermeneutics of suspicion, 18

Hernández, Jilian, 248

Hernández, Tanya, 256

heteronormativity, 54–55, 59–60, 63–64, 66–67, 71, 74n1, 81–82, 270

heterosexuality, 55–56, 57–58, 66, 71, 78–79, 80–84, 86–87, 119–20, 123, 125, 137n5, 220–21, 221n2, 224, 229–30, 268–69, 278

on feminist philosophy in Argentine academy, 109–10, 113–14
and philosophy as feminist praxis, 110–12
magical realism, 183–84
Maldonado-Torres, Nelson, 43n1, 138–39
La Malinche, 98, 224, 226, 227, 229–30
Manet, Édouard, 173–74. *See also* Olympia
Manso, Juana, 97
Mapplethorpe, Robert, 271–72
La Maricolectiva, 230
Martín Alcoff, Linda, x, 3
  on Gloria Anzaldúa, 191–92
  on Nietzsche and Anzaldúa, 192
  on Ofelia Schutte, 190–91
  on race and ethnicity, 255–57
  Visible Identities, 191–92, 255
  on women of color in philosophy, 199
Martínez, Elizabeth "Betita," 57
Martínez, Jacqueline, 127–28
Martínez, Victor, 286
Martínez López, Enrique, 98–99
Marx, Karl, 62–63, 65–66
Matory, Lorand J., 161–62
Max-Neef, Manfred, 20
Maya concept of *In'Laketch*, 55–56
Medina, José, 148–49
melancholia, 271–72, 277–78
Mellino, Miguel, 42–43
memoir, 5, 157–58
memory, 31–33, 36
memory-work, 212–16
Menchú, Rigoberta, 65
  and *testimonio*, 183–84
Méndez, Xhercis, 4
Méndez Plancarte, Alfonso, 98–99
mestizaje, 41, 118–19, 127, 131, 191–92
  and national identity, 59
  as product of intentional interpretive choices, 23
  spiritual, 164
metaphysics of presence, 204–5
Mexica culture, 222, 229
Mexico, 188–89, 229, 287–88
  Ciudad Juárez, 287–88

imperialist annexation by US, 60–61
in Latin American literary scholarship, 58–59
Mexican Revolution, 59–60
Spanish conquest, 150–51
Mignolo, Walter D., 39
  and border epistemology, 181
  on border gnoseology, 62n6
  and poly/plurilanguaging, 179–80
  and thinking otherwise, 151–52
migration, 141
Millán, Mágara M., 181
Miller, Francesca, 66–67
Minich, Julie Avril, 8
Mohanty, Chandra Talpade, 12–13
Mojica Rodriguez, Prisca Dorcas, 249
Molina-Guzmán, Isabel, 252–53
  on the browning of America, 258–59
  on Latinidad, 254–55
monolingualism, 25–26, 232
Moraga, Cherríe, x, 1–2, 70
  as *curandera*, 226–27
  The Hungry Woman, 224–26, 231
  and insanity, 223–24
  The Mathematics, 229
  and theory in the flesh, 136–37
Moreno Vega, Marta, 5
  on African heritage, 159–62
  on composing memoir, 157–58
  and Orisha and Christian practices, 164, 166, 167–68
  and spirituality, 164–66
  When the Spirits Dance Mambo, 158–59
more-than-human, 220–21, 232, 233, 283
Movimiento de Mujeres de Cuscatlán, El, 210–11
Moya, Paula M. L., 5, 147–48
Moynihan, Daniel Patrick, 87
Mujeres Activas en Letras y Cambio Social (MALCS), 1–2
mujerista theology, 21–22, 23, 24. *See also* Isasi-Díaz, Ada María
mulataje, 59
Mullins, Aimee, 257